Consumer Reports

HOME COMPUTER BUYING GUIDE

The Home Computer Buying Guide covers, in a convenient format, the latest buying tips and product Ratings from CONSUMER REPORTS. Published by the nonprofit Consumers Union, CONSUMER REPORTS is a comprehensive source of unbiased advice about products and services, personal finance, health and nutrition, and other consumer concerns. Since 1936, the mission of Consumers Union has been to test products, inform the public, and protect consumers. Our income is derived solely from the sale of CONSUMER REPORTS magazine and our other publications and services, and from nonrestrictive, noncommercial contributions, grants, and fees. We buy all the products we test. We accept no ads from companies, nor do we let any outside entity use our reports or Ratings for commercial purposes.

OTHER BUYING GUIDES FROM CONSUMER REPORTS

- ◆ Best Buys for Your Home
- ◆ New Car Buying Guide
- ◆ Used Car Buying Guide
- ◆ Consumer Reports Buying Guide

OTHER PUBLICATIONS FROM CONSUMER REPORTS

- ◆ Sport-Utility Special
- ◆ New Car Preview
- ◆ Used Car Yearbook
- ◆ Travel Well for Less
- ◆ Consumer Drug Reference
- ◆ Guide to Baby Products

Consumer Reports

HOME COMPUTER BUYING GUIDE 2002

THE EDITORS OF CONSUMER REPORTS

Published by Consumer Reports ◆ A division of Consumers Union ◆ Yonkers, New York

First printing, September 2001
Copyright © 2001 by Consumers Union of United States, Inc., Yonkers, New York 10703.
Published by Consumers Union of United States, Inc., Yonkers, New York 10703.
All rights reserved, including the right of reproduction in whole or in part in any form.
ISSN: 1530-3713
ISBN: 0-89043-959-1
Manufactured in the United States of America.

TABLE OF CONTENTS

Start Me Up

For home users, the personal computer has morphed into an incredible array of tools and toys. Yes, it's still a useful piece of office equipment with practical word-processing, accounting, and presentation functions. Yes, it's an ever-more essential method for doing homework. But that's just scratching the surface. New systems let you capture video from a camcorder and use your computer to edit home movies—or even create a video DVD that you can play in your living room. The computer has become the ultimate jukebox, affording access to voluminous audio libraries that enable users to download online recordings in minutes. Wondering if the latest Hollywood blockbuster is worth seeing? Watching a video preview can help you decide.

The home computer can be a video arcade, with graphics sophisticated enough to please the most easily bored game enthusiast. It's an online mall with inventory that would impress any shopaholic. Publishing software enables you to create a newsletter like a pro. Photo-imaging software lets you compile a digital family photo album. Financial-management programs help you pay bills, save for retirement, and calculate the cost of buying a home. Want to invest in stocks? The home computer is the way to tap into an online brokerage. It's also a dating service, a travel agency, a news wire, a betting parlor, an encyclopedia, a meeting hall, an auction block.

USING THIS BOOK

This book is designed to help you make the most out of your computer equipment—from homework to home office. It's divided into three parts. The first, "Turned On," focuses on how you can use a computer to its maximum advantage and includes CONSUMER REPORTS' expert advice on shopping for key services. The chapter on navigating the web explains how high-speed broadband options such as a digital subscriber line (DSL) or cable modem not only show you a web home page almost instantaneously but also give you entrée to many web sites and services that a standard modem can't accommodate conveniently. You'll also find sections on using a computer to edit photos taken with a digital or film camera, turning video shot on a camcorder into an appealing production with many professional touches, and creating compact-disc compilations of music downloaded from the Internet or copied from other CDs. There are also chapters that give an overview of web sites and software of interest to grownups and children, plus advice on what to look for when shopping or booking travel online. Plus there are CONSUMER REPORTS' e-Ratings of online shopping sites.

The second part, "Plugged In," helps you sort through the myriad choices you'll face when shopping. You'll see buying advice on desktop computers, laptops, and PDAs, as well as important accompaniments such as monitors, printers, fax machines, and copy machines. There are also sections on those pieces of home-entertainment equipment that have recently entered the PC's orbit: camcorders, CD player/recorders, digital cameras, and MP3 players. Other chapters give you essential information on telephones and setting up a comfortable and functional home office.

In the back of the book, you'll find a reference section, with the latest CONSUMER REPORTS Ratings, plus a comprehensive glossary and profiles of the major home-computer and home-office brands.

TRENDS FOR 2002

Technology evolves at an amazing rate. Change seems to be a constant. At the same time, there are concerns about how the technology is used in people's daily lives. Here are key trends affecting the marketplace and the way computer users work and play.

Microsoft still rules the software realm

Microsoft remains the overwhelming leader of the PC software field. Virtually all non-Mac computers purchased for home use run on a version of Microsoft's Windows operating system. The newest version for home users, called Windows XP Home Edition, is expected to be quite different from its predecessor, Windows Me. Windows XP is based on Windows 2000 and Windows NT. Windows XP takes a function-oriented approach, making it easy to manipulate output from cameras and camcorders and input for MP3 players. (The downside of Windows XP is that the overhauled interface of the new operating system may require users familiar with Windows to learn a few new tricks.) Windows XP Home Edition and the version for business use, Windows XP Professional, are expected to be available commercially in the fall of 2001.

Included in the Windows operating system is the Internet Explorer browser, for surfing the web. The competing Netscape Navigator browser can also be installed and used. It was Microsoft's aggressive moves against Netscape that led to the antitrust suit filed against Microsoft by the Justice Department and 19 state governments, litigation that has proved to be a significant distraction for the software giant. In 2000, a federal judge ruled that Microsoft's operating system constituted an illegal monopoly and ordered that the software giant be broken up into two companies: one for the operating system and the other for the Internet and applications. But in 2001, a federal appeals court disqualified the federal judge and ordered that another federal judge reconsider whether the software giant should indeed be broken up. The federal appeals court did agree that Microsoft had maintained an illegal monopoly.

Although Microsoft makes application programs for the Macintosh, Macs have an operating system all their own made by Apple. An overhaul, called OS X (the "X" is the Roman numeral 10), was released in the spring of 2001. The biggest thing Mac OS X and Windows XP have in common aside from the curiously fashionable "X" in their names is their commercial roots. While Windows XP was derived from personal versions of Windows, Mac OS builds on Unix, an operating system designed for large networked computer systems. Among other things, Mac OS X promises improved multitasking, which means better performance when multiple applications are running. For more on Windows XP and Mac OS X, see page 102.

Machines get cheaper and faster (so what else is new?)

As has become the rule, the prices of computers and other pieces of home-office equipment keep going down while speed keeps going up and products become easier to use. Today's computers range in price from under $1,000 to well over $3,000. Weak demand for new computers in 2001 meant that excellent values were easier to find than ever.

A prospective buyer can now take advantage of the many amazing industry advances. The processors, or "brains," of today's high-end machines have a clock speed of 1.7 gigahertz (1.7 GHz), or 1,700 megahertz (1,700 MHz), which means that they operate at an amazing 1.7 billion cycles per second. Intel, the dominant processor maker, was expected to begin selling a 2-GHz chip in the second half of 2001. It was Intel's rival, Advanced Micro Devices (AMD), that first broke the 1-GHz barrier, in 2000. Added speed will be most noticed by those who play computer games or tap into the Internet's burgeoning video and audio capabilities.

Apple Computer, which revolutionized computer design with the translucent, colorful, easy-to-set-up iMac, has gone a step further by adding dual processors to some of its G4 Power Macs for extra oomph. The simple design and intuitive operating system of Macintoshes make setup and day-to-day computing easy. And they have earned high marks from CONSUMER REPORTS for service and reliability. (See "The Apple Alternative," on page 106.)

The evolving web

The Internet, once a curiosity, has become, for many, a necessity. A lot of people are beginning to embrace various products and services that enhance its use.

INSTANT INTERNET. The age of high-speed Internet access, commonly known as broadband, has dawned. In 2001, some 9 million households subscribed to a broadband service, millions more than in 2000. The rest of the households with Internet access continued to rely on much slower dial-up connections using their computers' modems.

Cable TV services provide the majority of broadband connections, with phone companies accounting for most of the rest, typically through DSL. Satellite companies such as DirecTV are a distant third, though growing.

The broadband market has changed in several ways over the past year. Two major companies in the DSL market, Flashcom and Northpoint, went out of business, temporarily stranding thousands of broadband subscribers. Some observers worry that other broadband suppliers may fail, given the continued turbulence of the market. Meanwhile, broadband has gotten more expensive.

Satisfaction with broadband services is high. According to a CONSUMER REPORTS survey, more than 70 percent of broadband users said they were highly satisfied with their providers, compared with 56 percent of dial-up users. But the survey found that broadband users were twice as likely as dial-up users to have trouble establishing an account.

MUSIC INDUSTRY ALL SHOOK UP. An audio-compression technology called MP3 has revolutionized the way people listen to music. Over the past two years, millions have downloaded MP3-encoded songs—many of them of copyrighted—from sites that let people swap music files and listen to them on their PCs. Not surprisingly, the recording industry has responded with litigation. In 1999, the major record labels sued Napster, a company whose web site facilitated the downloading of music for free. A series of court rulings have forced Napster to restrict access to music by major performing artists. Programs such as MusicCity Morpheus (which can be downloaded from *www.musiccity.com*) are picking up where Napster left off. The programs let you connect directly to other people's computers to share files. Lack of a central server means that it would be extremely difficult for the recording industry to stop file swapping under such an approach. Meanwhile, sites such as MTV.com are starting to charge a fee for copyrighted songs.

To address copyright and security concerns, the recording industry has developed the Secure Digital Music Initiative. It relies on digital watermarks embedded in music tracks that restrict copying when read on special playback devices. In the summer of 2001, a Princeton professor claimed that such an encryption system could be cracked.

Record companies aren't the only ones worrying. The major Hollywood studios are trying to block the use of computers to copy DVD movies. And book publishers are watching the growth of e-books—books downloadable from the Internet onto computers and special handheld book readers.

GROWING PAINS ONLINE. The months since the March 2000 peak of the Nasdaq market have been less than kind to the web-based "new economy." Hundreds of publicly traded Internet companies have shut down since Wall Street began applying the same brutish skepticism to them that it applies to others. Still, the Internet remains a potent force, with seemingly countless sites catering to interests including personal finance, real estate, parenting, health, and hobbies. Online retail continues to gain momentum, with bricks-and-mortar and catalog retailers strengthening and refining their web operations. Travelers can book airline and hotel reservations on travel sites such as Expedia.com and Travelocity.com. Buyers and sellers of used merchandise no longer have to content themselves with flea markets, garage sales, and thrift shops. Online auction sites such as eBay.com bring together fans of antiques, collectibles, and other goods. (For the pluses and minuses of buying and selling online as well as CONSUMER REPORTS' e-Ratings of online retail sites, see "The Virtual Mall," Chapter 5.)

DVD developments

DVDs (digital versatile discs) look like CDs, but do a lot more. A DVD-ROM drive, now common in most high-end and middle-range computer systems, allows you to play software (for games, say) or use your home computer as a personal movie theater. Such a drive holds 4.7 gigabytes (GB) of data on a single-side, single-layer disc, enough for a full-length film. DVDs offer content that you won't find on standard videos, including sound tracks in other languages, subtitles, and actors' biographies. DVD-ROM discs can only be played on a computer;

video DVD discs can be played on a computer or a DVD player. "Rewritable" DVD drives hold out incredible potential for people who want to store backup files on disc, make music or multimedia compilations, or create movies. DVD is mired in a battle over formats, with DVD+RW, backed by Hewlett-Packard and others, vying with DVD-RW/DVD-RAM, backed by a group of manufacturers known as the DVD Forum. For now, most computer users with high storage needs will probably want to use a CD-RW drive, which is included with many desktop computers.

HOW CONSUMER REPORTS TESTS EQUIPMENT

Equipment rated in this book is tested at CONSUMER REPORTS' labs in Yonkers, N.Y. The products are bought at retail just as a consumer would acquire them. We send shoppers to buy specific models based on which are top sellers or innovative designs.

Our tests are scientific, and we are constantly refining our procedures. Right now, for example, our technical staff is working on setting up a "private web" to make tests involving the Internet—which is inherently unstable and always changing—more consistent.

For home computers, benchmarks are used to assess how quickly machines can simultaneously run a number of applications, including a word processor, a spreadsheet, and a web browser. Much of the work we do in the computer labs mimics how a piece of equipment

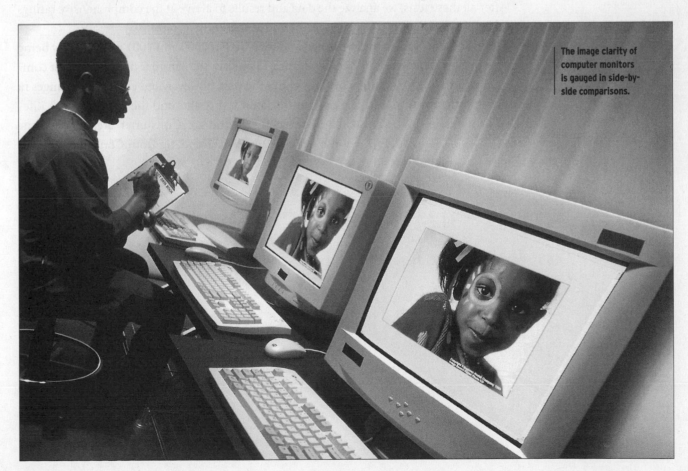

The image clarity of computer monitors is gauged in side-by-side comparisons.

KEY TO THE SYMBOLS

Throughout Home Computer Buying Guide, you'll find quick tips, advice, and other helpful information.

TECH TIP. These at-a-glance tips can help make your computer more efficient.

SHOP SMART. Look here for strategies to get the most for your money when you're shopping for equipment.

would be used in the home. Testers read the owner's manual, try out all the switches, and experiment with the features. We try to answer likely consumer questions: How easy is the system to set up? Can components be replaced with industry-standard parts? Are the manuals comprehensive and easy to read? If the PC is marketed for games, how smooth is its 3-D graphics capability?

For printers, testers compare text, graphics, and photos printed at several quality modes for various models. We also gauge the printers' speed. To assess the image clarity of monitors, testers do side-by-side comparisons. The quality of digital cameras, scanners, and other imaging equipment is assessed by comparing images created using the products. For instance, engineers inspect glossy 5x7 prints created by each digital camera tested, using its best-photo mode. We use the model's supplied software and output all prints to the same photo printer. For every piece of equipment, we carefully assess features—do they add to usability or just make an item more complicated? We check ergonomic functions—how does the camera feel in the hand?—and assess battery life, if there's a battery.

After all these tests, we analyze the data and results to arrive at the comprehensive ratings we publish in CONSUMER REPORTS magazine and in this book.

Some of the products that we tested and reviewed in 2000 and 2001 were already being replaced by new models as this book was going to press in the summer of 2001. We test computers and home-office equipment throughout the year, however, and cover how changes in technology affect your daily life. Look for the latest test results and the column "Tech Life" in monthly issues of CONSUMER REPORTS magazine or Consumer Reports Online (*www.ConsumerReports.org*). You also get access to e-mail updates from Consumer Reports Online when you buy this book.

PART 1

Turned On

Navigating the Web

Few creations have so rapidly and profoundly changed our way of life as the popular, user-friendly version of the Internet—the World Wide Web. Since it gained widespread use about five years ago, the web has changed the way people buy things, from a Regency romance novel to a Regency armchair to a Buick Regency. It has altered the nature of democratic government. City, state, and federal agencies all have web sites. Important information about product safety, legislation, court decisions, and most government programs are just a few mouse-clicks away. Most candidates for elective office maintain a web site, the better to speak directly to the voters about their platform. The web has transformed entertainment, making it possible to quickly acquire music and share it with others (once free, now often for a fee). Popular authors from Stephen King to Tom Wolfe use the web page as well as the printed page, offering books on the Internet (nowadays the terms "web" and "Internet" are used interchangeably). It's possible to listen to a radio station from the opposite side of the country or halfway around the world by connecting with the station's web site. The web has given new meaning to "keep in touch." By far the most popular online activity is sending electronic mail, or e-mail, often with attached electronic snapshots—photos taken with a digital camera and converted to a small computer file.

You can find vehicle-safety data from recalls to crash-test results on the National Highway Traffic Safety Administration's web site.

Chances are, the web is already familiar territory. You probably have e-mail at work. Your employer may have its own web site. And if you bought a new computer in the past two years, you were almost certainly offered a substantial rebate if you signed up for service with a particular Internet provider.

15

The two standard browsers are Internet Explorer and Netscape Navigator. They let you find a web site and keep track of sites that you visit frequently.

This chapter answers these questions: What are the best choices now for Internet service? How can you use the web to its best advantage? Do you use the Internet so much that you could benefit from a high-speed connection? What do you need to know to protect yourself from cyber-intrusions—companies loading you up with unwanted e-mail (the online equivalent of junk mail, called spam), companies tracking your online activities without your knowledge, hackers debilitating your computer with a virus? What do you need to know to be sure your children are protected when they go online?

CHOOSING AN INTERNET PROVIDER

Should you sign up with a big gun (such as America Online with its millions of subscribers) or a local provider? Either approach has its advantages.

By one estimate, nearly 10,000 companies provide Internet service. Some give you little more than the telephone number you need to get connected via a computer's standard modem. Most also offer a web browser—Microsoft's Internet Explorer and AOL Time Warner's Netscape Navigator are the standard ones. Some providers use their own. In addition, you usually get e-mail service, access to subscribers' online discussion groups, space to create your own web page, and, often, some how-to advice on crafting an attractive page.

The largest Internet providers also come with a wealth of unique content and services: One-click access to selected online shopping sites, for example, or news, instant messaging, special chat rooms, online stock trading, elaborate controls to protect children, and so on. The largest service, America Online, offers the most content. AOL dominates the field because it recognized early on people's aversion to getting their hands dirty with technology and their need to communicate with many others.

Most families use one of the largest national or regional Internet providers. America Online has more than 23 million U.S. subscribers. Close behind are CompuServe (owned by AOL Time Warner), MSN (owned by the software behemoth Microsoft), AT&T Worldnet, EarthLink, Prodigy, and BellSouth. Monthly fees range from about $20 to $25 for unlimited access. Many providers have less expensive plans available if you go online only a few hours per month.

To find out how these big Internet providers compare, in March 2001 CONSUMER REPORTS surveyed a national sample of people who use them, asking how well the services performed in such important areas as speed, connection availability, and technical support.

Monthly cost and reputation matter most in the selection of an Internet provider, according to the survey. When we asked why respondents chose their present Internet provider, these reasons came up most often: 32 percent said the monthly fee was lower than others; 26 percent said friends recommended it; and 22 percent said it was easy to check e-mail at home.

ARE 'FREE' ISPs WORTH A TRY?

Some Internet services charge you nothing to go online. Instead, they make their money by selling advertising that's a constant onscreen presence. How do free services compare with fee-based ones?

The two biggest free services, Juno and NetZero, are scheduled to merge. But even before they joined forces, both were backing away from free, unlimited web access and e-mail. NetZero has imposed a $9.95 monthly fee for use above 40 hours, while Juno has said it will limit use.

Neither Juno nor NetZero provides some standard services such as free live phone support, free web hosting, or compatibility with Macintosh computers. But if you can live with those limitations, you may want to consider a free Internet service as a backup or as an extra path onto the Internet when you travel.

INTERNET PROVIDERS

Overall Ratings — In performance order

Better ◀——▶ Worse

	OVERALL SATISFACTION	CONNECTION			SUPPORT	E-MAIL	DOWNLOADS
		AVAILABILITY	SPEED	INTERRUPTIONS			
AT&T WorldNet	78	●	●	◒	○	◒	◒
BellSouth	76	○	○	○	◒	○	◒
EarthLink	76	○	○	◒	○	○	◒
Prodigy	73	○	◒	○	○	○	○
Qwest	70	○	○	○	○	○	◒
America Online	68	○	◒	●	○	◒	◒
CompuServe	67	○	○	◒	◒	○	○
MSN	67	●	○	○	◒	●	○

Based on findings of a March 2001 survey, which were first published in the September 2001 issue of CONSUMER REPORTS magazine. Overall Satisfaction differences of 5-points or more are meaningful.

The survey behind the Ratings

The Ratings are based on 1,640 responses to a nationally representative sample of individuals who have Internet access through a dial-up connection, typically with a 56k modem. **Overall satisfaction** reflects the respondents' overall experience with their Internet provider. A score of 100 would mean that all respondents were completely satisfied; 80 means very satisfied, on average; 60 means fairly well satisfied, on average. **Connection availability** is based on the percentage of respondents who experienced no difficulty with the availability of their connection in the previous month. **Speed** reflects the percentage who said their connection had been too slow during the previous month. **Interruptions** measures the percentage who said the connection had ever been interrupted during the previous month. **Support** measures satisfaction with the Internet provider's technical support services. **E-mail** measures satisfaction with the provider's e-mail service. **Downloads** measures problems related to downloading articles or data for personal use. (Full disclosure: At press time, CONSUMER REPORTS was negotiating a content-sharing agreement with America Online.)

When users switch services, it's most often because of a troublesome phone connection. The main reasons users gave for switching Internet providers were these: 35 percent said the phone connection was often interrupted; 31 percent said the connection was too slow; and 29 percent said they had trouble connecting because the phone was busy too long.

In addition to the big national or regional Internet providers, there are thousands of smaller, local ones. You can get a list of the ones that serve your area at *www.thelist.com,* which claims to include 9,700 providers.

In less populated areas, speedy access to a local access number may be more desirable than a large Internet provider's well-developed content, for example. But a smaller provider may not offer access numbers in other parts of the country, which you may need when traveling, and it may not be as financially stable as the major providers are. If you do decide to go with a small local provider, ask other users in your area about the service's dependability and customer support.

Switching Internet providers can be like moving to a new home. To change an e-mail

DISCOVERING THE INTERNET

The Internet can initially be overwhelming. But it's yours to discover once you start off on the right foot. When you log on, you'll always start at the home page of your online service or Internet provider (or whatever page you set up as your home page). Most of these sites have a basic search function and other functions that may be enough to let you do a thorough web search.

Other sites, known as portals and search engines, can do a much better job of pointing you in the right direction. A portal is a multifaceted site that combines search capabilities with a host of other enticements, such as shopping, weather, news, chat, and so on. One of the biggest benefits of portals is the ability to start at a portal's home page, which you can customize to your liking. A search engine is typically a no-frills site that's dedicated to rummaging through the tens of millions of web pages and culling those that fit your search request. There's no charge for using either a portal or a search engine. Information on specific portals and search engines can be found on pages 28 and 30, respectively, in Chapter 2.

Once you call up a search engine on your computer screen, you then enter a few keywords or navigate through a series of indexes to find links to web sites on the topic you've chosen.

Most search engines examine a different mix of web sites, using a slightly different search method. Results can yield both highly relevant and laughably off-topic results for any search engine.

Some search engines summarize the contents of the web sites or newsgroups they find that contain your search terms. That means you're left at the mercy of the spotting and indexing methods of the engine's administrators. You may get more results from a search engine that simply provides snippets of text from each site it finds, but some snippets may be confusing.

It's not worth spending a lot of time selecting the ideal engine for a search. The engines are so accessible and the searches themselves so fast that it's best to try several. After regular use, you'll find one or two that consistently deliver the type of results that work for you.

address with minimal interruption, keep your old account open for an extra month or two after you start using the new one. If you have an e-mail address book, send a message to everyone in the book informing them of the change. Use automatic forwarding, if your older provider offers it, to avoid having to access the old account directly. If you'd rather pay someone to forward your e-mail for you, *www.reroute.com* will do it for $10 per month or $25 for three months. Make sure you've complied with your old provider's rules for closing an account, to avoid problems with bills.

FASTER WEB ACCESS

Perhaps tired of the "World Wide Wait," many have abandoned the standard dial-up connection in favor of one of the high-speed Internet access options.

Most people who surf the web still connect to their Internet provider the old-fashioned way—through the modem built into their computers. That approach works well enough, though it can often entail some tapping of fingers as a web page is called up. The standard dial-up modem, V.90, delivers the fastest possible access at a nominal 56 kbps (56k), but actually only 50 kbps even in the best conditions.

But a growing number (9 million in a recent count) have adopted high-speed Internet access, commonly known as broadband. Such a connection—transmitted by cable modem, digital subscriber line (DSL), or satellite—is two to 10 times faster than a conventional dial-up connection. Little wonder, then, that people who have broadband love it. In a recent CONSUMER REPORTS survey of Internet users, 71 percent of those with a broadband connection said they were highly satisfied with it, compared with only 56 percent of those with a dial-up connection.

The most commonly used bandwidths in the consumer market are expressed in kilobits, or thousands of bits per second (kbps). The standard 56k modem can move data at a maximum rate of 56 kbps. Broadband, which refers to a bandwidth of at least 128 kbps, is on whenever your computer is turned on, so you don't need to dial a number every time you want access. Broadband gives you entrée to many new web sites and services that a 56k dial-up connection simply can't accommodate conveniently—sharing home videos with far-flung friends or family, say, or accessing complex multimedia sites rapidly.

Cable modem

Cable modem, which uses the same cable that delivers TV programming, is available where the local cable-TV provider has upgraded its equipment. A special modem, separate from the TV converter box, handles the Internet traffic. Cable modem now accounts for about 70 percent of broadband connections.

Cable systems are designed like small networks, sharing the data-carrying capacity (bandwidth, as it's known) among a group of subscribers. Cable has the capacity to deliver speeds as high as 10 megabits per second (Mbps), equal to 10,240 kbps, for each channel the cable company devotes to data. But the more people online, the less bandwidth available for each home. Depending on a neighborhood's usage pattern and its cable provider's ability to manage it, cable-modem users can experience noticeable slowdowns in web access, though they are likely to be less noticeable than with a dial-up connection.

Digital subscriber line

Telephone access, commonly known as DSL (digital subscriber line), uses a digital signal to transmit large amounts of information over an existing phone line, without interfering with voice calls. Voice and data move at different frequencies and so do not interfere with each other. DSL does, however, use a special modem.

DSL doesn't have the maximum bandwidth capacity of cable—its typically 128 kbps to 1.5 Mbps, depending on the service you buy. But because DSL works on a private line, its

---

BROADBAND TIPS

To enjoy the full benefit of broadband:

◆ Be sure the equipment is compatible if you plan to install your own modem.

◆ Obtain a printed version of any contract or terms of service; online versions can change.

◆ If you can, get a contract with a guarantee of minimum bandwidth. Also look for a contract that offers rebates in the event of outages.

◆ Avoid services that levy nonrefundable charges, early cancellation fees, or charges for customers who miss appointments.

◆ Watch out for contracts that come with limits on usage, the number of home computers you can connect to the Internet, or the size of e-mail messages you can send.

◆ Ask the provider if it's set up to assign you a dynamic Internet identifier, one that changes regularly so that others online can't permanently pin down your location. A connection with a fixed address can compromise privacy by branding your computer.

◆ Keep written records of service interruptions and calls to the provider's technical support service. The records may prove crucial to getting any refunds.

◆ Check the actual speed of your connection as soon as service begins and periodically thereafter. Two web sites that measure speed coming into your house at no charge are *www.computingcentral.com* (click on "speed test") and *www.2wire.com*. A speed-measuring program called DU Meter can be downloaded free from *www.hageltech.com*. If the speed seems consistently slow, contact your Internet provider. If your computer runs on Windows, you may be able to improve speed by fine-tuning the operating system. For more information, go to *www.speedguide.net*.

THE DSL HEADACHE: INSTALLATION

Cable installations are straightforward mainly because one company handles everything. Digital Subscriber Line (DSL) hookups can be more complicated.

Deregulation of local phone service has opened the DSL market to independent companies known as competitive local exchange carriers, or CLECs. The CLECs, in turn, contract with Internet providers, which retail the service and provide technical support. Since the local phone company is always involved because it owns the phone lines, installing DSL can mean coordinating the work of multiple companies.

Stories of installers failing to show up for scheduled appointments are legion. However, two developments promise to make it easier to get DSL.

◆ Local phone companies are now required to allow competing providers access to existing phone lines carrying voice signals. That should reduce the need for phone-company installers to visit consumers' homes.

◆ Do-it-yourself kits for DSL as well as cable should become more commonplace.

---

bandwidth isn't shared with neighbors and so doesn't slow down as usage increases.

However, a DSL signal can't be used over distances more than two to three miles from the telephone company's central switching office. Homes too far from that office can't receive DSL service at all. Technological improvements now being developed may expand the current range.

There are actually several types of DSL available. If you mostly surf the web and are more likely to receive than send large amounts of data, look first to the type called ADSL, for asymmetric digital subscriber line. It supplies more bandwidth into the home than out from it: 384 kbps in but only 128 kbps out, for example. Speeds up to 1.5 Mbps or greater are available for a higher monthly fee.

Satellite-based services

Satellite-based services, such as Hughes' DirecPC, use a special dish and receiver. Until recently, getting the Internet via satellite meant a connection only for data streaming into your house; you still needed a dial-up connection for two-way communication. Now, however, one of the major satellite providers, StarBand, offers a high-speed, two-way connection. DirecWay, another major provider, was expected to follow suit by the end of 2001.

Satellite service is the most costly alternative. As of mid-2001, unlimited access from StarBand cost $70 per month plus $500 for equipment and $200 for installation. The company says professional installation is required. Prices for DirecWay are expected to be comparable.

Even if you already have satellite TV service, you'll need a second small dish antenna if you want satellite-based broadband. The data are routed through a different satellite from the one handling TV broadcasts, and a single antenna can't point to two satellites.

In some parts of the country, however, satellite service may be the only practical way to get any broadband service at all.

You can expect to pay $50 per month or more for broadband service, whichever type you choose. That's a little more than what many families now spend for an Internet provider such as AOL plus a separate phone line for the Internet connection. Cable-modem service tends to be cheapest if you're already a cable-TV subscriber.

Installation can be expensive. Charges for installation and hardware reportedly go as high as $300. Fortunately, not everyone pays retail to get broadband service. Many providers offer free or discounted installation and equipment in return for a year's contract. In addition to the modem, you may also need a network card for your computer (about $40).

Do you need a privacy firewall?

Having a connection that's always on makes your computer an easier target for online hackers and other mischief makers. That's because you usually have what's known as a fixed Internet address with a broadband connection, making it easier for a miscreant to find you. With a dial-up connection, you have an Internet address that varies; each time you dial up to connect, you follow a slightly different path online and so have a different tag to let others online know how to find you. You're most vulnerable if your Windows network file- and printer-sharing feature has been activated, or if you run a web server on your computer.

You can reduce your exposure by turning the computer off when no one is using it. To test your system's vulnerability, try ShieldsUP, a free service at *www.grc.com*. ZoneAlarm, a software firewall for Windows users is available free to individuals and nonprofit organizations at *www.zonelabs.com*. Macintosh users should investigate a product called Who's There? Firewall Advisor. It can be downloaded from *www.opendoor.com*. After a 10-day trial, you pay $39 if you want to keep it.

Cable modem vs. DSL vs. satellite service

Cable modems and DSL connections perform comparably; neither technology can claim an advantage in speed or reliability. However, cable-modem service has a slight edge in cost and in being less troublesome to set up and maintain. Satellite service is by far the most expensive to install and carries the highest monthly charges, but it may be the only option if you don't have access to cable or DSL service.

The first step in shopping is to find out which providers can serve your home. One call to the local cable-TV company should tell you whether you can get cable-modem service. Finding out about DSL can be a bit more involved. If you're satisfied with your current Internet provider, give that company a call first. Staying with your provider also lets you keep existing e-mail addresses. To locate DSL providers in your area, go to *www.dslreports.com* or *www.getspeed.com*. For information on the two major satellite-based services, go to *www.starband.com* or *www.direcway.com*.

PRIVACY AND YOUR PC

The potential for invasion of privacy has become one of the most troubling aspects of many people's growing reliance on the web. But there are things you can do to control privacy invaders.

Every time you buy online, or even just request information from a web site, you leave behind a digital trail of valuable information about yourself that companies are eager to acquire. According to a study by the Federal Trade Commission, more than 90 percent of the online retail web sites it sampled collected personal data from consumers who visited. Yet the FTC found that only 2 percent of all commercial web sites had a comprehensive privacy policy.

As more and more people go online regularly, protecting consumer privacy is becoming a front-burner concern. Cybermerchants routinely gather names, addresses, and credit-card numbers as they process orders. Many also ask shoppers for their e-mail address and phone number so they can send a confirmation of the transaction or contact them if there's a problem with the order. That's legitimate, but too many companies go far beyond those reasonable boundaries to solicit other information—your age, occupation, hobbies, even household income—that has nothing to do with your purchase. The potential problem, of course, is that companies can misuse it by deluging you with solicitations to buy other products or by selling the information to other businesses.

Here are some of the practices and issues you should be aware of before you double-click and send personal data across the Internet.

The cookie monster

Cookies—digital "crumbs" that are dropped onto your hard drive when you visit a web site—are the way online marketers learn about you. They contain the electronic equivalent of a Social Security number, which is used to track your movements on the web and identify you when you visit other sites; the cookie alerts the marketer that you're there so it can look up its file of your interests. Then companies deploy banner ads—or those annoying pop-up ad boxes—that are supposed to match your interests as you view sites.

A big player in the realm of cookies is DoubleClick. As soon as you visit a site affiliated with the company's network, DoubleClick enters into its private database whatever information it can get about you—your ZIP code, your area code, the organization you work for, or the type of computer you use. (DoubleClick says it doesn't collect your name and e-mail address.) At the same time, DoubleClick can also start collecting information about the actions you take online. You can "opt out" of DoubleClick's system by going to *www.doubleclick.net* and following directions to its privacy settings.

Here are some other ways to protect yourself from cookies:

DELETING YOUR COOKIES FILE. If your web browser is Netscape Navigator 3.0 or higher, you can delete your cookies file. Search your hard drive for the file "cookies.txt" and delete it. In doing so, you may lose some settings, such as web-site passwords. With Internet Explorer 3.0 or higher, cookies are not labeled as such, but you'll find them (in multiple files) in the "cookies" subfolder within the Windows operating system's "Windows" folder or, after launching Explorer, in the Preferences of Mac's Edit menu.

BLOCKING COOKIES. To prevent DoubleClick or anyone else from re-creating cookie entries, choose the menu option in your browser that asks your permission every time someone tries to modify your cookie file or files. But because a cookie file identifies you as a previous visitor to that site, you'll have to retype a password and possibly reselect preferences each time you revisit a site. You need to weigh cookies' potential convenience against your own privacy concerns. A web site can't use cookies to obtain your e-mail address directly, but a cookie can associate you with an e-mail address you've volunteered.

TAKE OFFENSIVE ACTION. Install software that protects your cookie files. Users of the Windows operating system can check out *www.mcafee.com*, *www.cookiecentral. com/files.htm*, or *www.junkbusters.com/ht/en/cookies.html*. Macintosh operating system users can download Cookie Cutter at *www.shareware.com*. In addition, AdSubtract CE "Cookie Edition" ($14.95 online, from *www.intermute.com*) lets you block ads and enable cookies site by site.

SURF ANONYMOUSLY. A piece of software known as an anonymous remailer is a free program that alters the return address of an e-mail or discussion-group message so that your name and address are never seen. You can find such a program at *www.anonymizer.com*.

You've got spam

Millions of unsuspecting Americans have been spammed—sent unsolicited and unwanted e-mail, sometimes dozens of pieces a week. How does spam work? Renegade entrepreneurs spew spam to the far reaches of the Internet, millions of pieces at a time. Some get addresses by harvesting them right off chat rooms and message boards. Others pirate names from membership directories of Internet providers or get lists from companies that do business online. Spammers also use software that generates e-mail addresses at random.

Spammers hawk get-rich-quick schemes, fraudulent deals, and pornography, among other things. It's so cheap to send spam that it's profitable even if relatively few consumers bite.

Increasingly, Internet providers and others are successfully fighting back. The providers are working to perfect filters that eliminate spam before it hits your in box. Spam is a big deal to them because it's a financial threat. According to one estimate, 15 to 20 percent of America Online's monthly fee goes toward controlling spam. A huge volume of e-mail can overload servers, preventing desired customers from signing on. It can even crash servers, putting an Internet provider out of business temporarily. And it can turn off customers, resulting in a loss of membership.

The FTC, which gets thousands of complaints about unsolicited e-mail, has notified senders they were possibly violating federal computer-fraud and postal statutes, and has taken action against companies such as pyramid schemers. A private nonprofit group, the Mail Abuse Prevention System (its initials spell spam backward), maintains a "real-time blacklist" of spammers and tries to persuade Internet providers not to accept mail from those on the list. For information, visit these web sites: *http://mailabuse.org/* or *www.spamfree.org/*.

> ### KEEPING THE SPAM OUT
>
> **Avoidance is the best means of controlling spam. Here are some tips:**
>
> ◆ Before you buy online, be sure the company has a policy against selling your e-mail address. If it doesn't, consider buying elsewhere.
>
> ◆ If your Internet provider allows multiple screen names, use a "public" name for chat rooms and for buying online, and a "private" name for other e-mail.
>
> ◆ You can buy spam-filtering programs or use the free ones offered by Internet providers such as America Online and CompuServe. They block e-mail from certain addresses or allow e-mail only from the addresses you specify.
>
> ◆ Complain to your Internet provider about spam you receive and forward the entire spam message, including the long "header."

DIGITAL CHAPERONES FOR KIDS

Can online filtering software keep young web surfers from visiting sites inappropriate for them? The answer is a qualified yes, sometimes.

Are you concerned that your kids will encounter sexually explicit material online? Recent studies show that such content appears on just 2 percent of web sites. Even so, it's easy to reach a site with X-rated content, via a major search engine, using terms such as "Bambi" or "adult." Pornography isn't the only troublesome area. According to the Simon Wiesenthal Center, there are now some 3,000 hate-promoting web sites. Countless other sites accessible to children promote drug use, fraud, or bomb making.

The federal government hasn't been effective at restricting children's access to sexually oriented content online. The Supreme Court struck down one law, the Communications Decency Act, on First Amendment grounds. Congress then passed the Children's Internet Protection Act, which requires schools and libraries that want federal funding to filter objectionable Internet content. This law, too, is facing a court challenge.

The only federal law offering explicit protection to young web surfers at home is the Children's Online Privacy Protection Act, which prohibits any web site from collecting a child's personal information without parental consent.

Who has the primary responsibility for protecting children when they go online at home? The parents of the 26 million U.S. youngsters who surf the web, that's who. According to a survey by Jupiter Research, seven out of 10 parents handle the issue by being present when their kids go online. Only 6 percent use stand-alone filtering software, products that promise to steer kids clear of undesirable material.

The basics of filtering

Each of the products that CONSUMER REPORTS recently tested filters web content by interposing itself between your computer's web browser and Internet connection, then preventing objectionable content from getting through. Some filters let you decide in advance whether to filter different types of content, such as profanity or sex information. Depending on the product and how a user configures it, a child trying to access an off-limits site may receive a warning message, a browser error message, or a partial view of the blocked site. Sometimes, the browser itself will shut down. Filtering-software designers use one of three approaches to determine whether a site merits blocking:

SOFTWARE ANALYSIS. A site's content can be rapidly analyzed by software. The filter may render a judgment at the time a child tries to access the site, or check a list of sites to block. The presence of certain phrases or images may render the site objectionable. While efficient, software analysis has its drawbacks. The software may decide to block a web site that's completely beyond reproach only because it contains a prohibited word. It may partially block a site, preventing text from appearing but letting through photos or on-screen images with embedded text. Or it may block images but not text. Most software we tested blocked both words and images.

HUMAN ANALYSIS. Some companies have their staff review sites individually, then place them on a list to be blocked or designated as suitable for children. This time-consuming process limits the number of sites that can be reviewed. Given the web's volatility, numerous objectionable sites can very easily remain perpetually outside the reviewer's scrutiny.

SITE LABELING. Several of the products we tested incorporate a popular ratings system run by the nonprofit Internet Content Ratings Association, or ICRA. This program, in which web-site owners voluntarily label their content, has been around for several years. The ICRA system recently expanded its labeling to include drugs, alcohol, tobacco, and weapons, plus the context in which words appear.

Netscape's browser doesn't have the feature, but Internet Explorer can filter sites using these labels, including the expanded ICRA labeling (you'll find it listed as "content advisor" under Internet Options in the Explorer menu).

CONSUMER REPORTS has found this feature in Explorer ineffective as the sole filtering technique, mainly because the many sexually explicit sites that aren't rated won't be blocked. You can set the feature to block all unrated sites, but that will block so many unrated sites as to make browsing pointless. Among the conventional sites that aren't rated are those of the White House, the U.S. Senate, the House of Representatives, and the Supreme Court.

Site labeling also depends on the honesty with which sites rate themselves. We found one site containing profanity that slipped past Explorer's filter because the site owner chose a label that didn't accurately reflect the site's content. Until far more sites suitable for children are properly labeled, labeling must be considered a complement to other filtering techniques, rather like motion-picture ratings.

How well do filters block bad stuff?

CONSUMER REPORTS' main test determined how well the filters blocked objectionable content. We configured all six products for a 13- to 15-year-old; we also tested AOL's Young Teen (ages 13 to 15) and Mature Teen (ages 16 to 17) parental controls. We pitted them all against a list of 86 easily located web sites that contain sexually explicit content or violently graphic images, or that promote drugs, tobacco use, crime, or bigotry.

We sampled web sites that appear high on lists turned up by popular search engines, thereby identifying sites that a consumer could readily encounter. The number of sites we used was sufficient to allow us to differentiate within the wide range of effectiveness we found. We are confident that the relative differences in performance that we found would hold up if we conducted additional sampling of sites.

AOL's Young Teen control, the best by far, allowed only one site through in its entirety, along with portions of about 20 other sites. All the other filters allowed at least 20 percent of the sites through in their entirety. Net Nanny displayed parts of more than a dozen sites, often with forbidden words expunged but graphic images intact.

Only a few filters were able to block certain inappropriate sites. In some cases, that probably reflected differences in filtering techniques more than differences in judgment. Faulty though it may be, for example, filtering based on objectionable words apparently helped Net Nanny and Internet Guard Dog intercept a site with instructions on bomb making that eluded most others.

However, differences in judgment seem the most likely explanation for why only Cyber Patrol and both AOL controls blocked the Operation Rescue anti-abortion web site, which contains photos of aborted fetuses. Such differences raise questions about how people decide what gets blocked.

According to AOL, the Young Teen control performed so well because it lets kids see only the sites on its approved list. Mature Teen blocks access to a list of prohibited sites. Kids could view an inappropriate site just because it wasn't on the Mature Teen list. (AOL considers the lists proprietary and does not disclose the number of sites on them.)

Do filters block good stuff?

In some cases, filters block harmless sites merely because their software does not consider the context in which a word or phrase is used. Far more troubling is when a filter appears to block legitimate sites based on moral or political value judgments.

To see whether the filters interfere with legitimate content, we pitted them against a list of 53 web sites that featured serious content on controversial subjects. Results varied widely. While most filters blocked only a few sites, Cybersitter 2000 and Internet Guard Dog blocked nearly one in five. AOL's Young Teen control blocked 63 percent of the sites. According to AOL, its

E-MAIL HOAXES

As the number of people using e-mail has skyrocketed, so have the number of hoaxes, rumors, and urban legends—some benign, some not so.

These organizations keep tabs on e-mail hoaxes:

◆ Department of Energy Computer Incident Advisory Capability *(http://hoax busters.ciac.org)*

◆ Urban Legends and Folklore *(www.urbanlegends.about.com)*

◆ Urban Legends Reference Pages *(www.snopes.com)*

◆ Vmyths.com *(www.Vmyths.com)*

staff and subscriber parents choose the sites kids are allowed to see using this control, with an emphasis on educational and entertainment sites. Our test sites may have been blocked because they didn't meet AOL's criteria, not because they were controversial.

Perhaps the most extreme example of conflicting judgments: AOL, Cyber Patrol, and Cybersitter 2000, which keep their blocked-site lists secret, blocked Peacefire, an antifiltering site that provides instructions on how to bypass filtering products. Net Nanny, which makes its list public, didn't block it.

What parents can do

Nearly all the filters offer some control over the disclosure of personal information, such as name and address. But we found such privacy protection too weak to rely on. Most of the products we tested failed to block one objectionable site in five. AOL's Young Teen (or Kids Only) setting provides the best protection, though it will likely curb access to web sites addressing political and social issues.

Filtering software is no substitute for parental supervision. People who visit sites they don't want their kids to see can delete the browser's offline files, where it saves copies of recently visited web pages. Check your child's online activities by reviewing the browser's history list and bookmarks. To check for adult images your child may have downloaded, search your hard drive for images or compressed files–those with names ending in .gif, .jpg, .tif, or, .zip. Two sites providing information on how to protect children are *www.getnetwise.org* and *www.safekids.com*.

COMBATING VIRUSES

Computer viruses can wreak havoc with your computer and even destroy some or all of the data on your hard drive. Fortunately, it's relatively easy to prevent a virus from invading your PC.

Basically, a virus is the electronic equivalent of the common cold, created by a group of electronic pranksters and spread through files downloaded from the web, from shared floppy disks, or even from infected software. Most viruses are relatively harmless; they may display a silly message or some other minor annoyance. Others can delete files, cause system crashes, spread the virus to every e-mail address on your address list, and worse.

If you take a few precautions, there's no reason to fear being infected by a virus.

USE ANTIVIRUS SOFTWARE. This is your best defense. There are several reliable programs designed to recognize and destroy any virus that finds its way into your system. Popular programs include McAfee VirusScan *(www.mcafee.com)* and Norton AntiVirus *(www.symantec.com)*. They're included in the software bundles of many new computers. You'll also find them in the "utilities" aisle of many software departments.

SCAN DISKS. Don't use programs on floppy disks that you get from another person before first checking them with an antivirus program. And don't leave floppy disks in the computer drive. Rebooting the computer with a floppy in place is a common way that viruses spread.

DOWNLOAD CAREFULLY. Take precautions when downloading software, especially freeware or shareware. In fact, never download a file whose name ends in .doc or .exe unless your antivirus software is up-to-date. Most commercial software is safe, but viruses have been known to show up just about anywhere.

2

Life Online

The Internet took a beating during the recent market downturn. Many sites came and went; others were gulped up by larger sites and disappeared. But there are still an overwhelming number of sites to explore, for reference, fun, and profit.

This chapter starts with portals—sites that present themselves as launching points for exploration. You can make a portal your home page, and you can customize that page with your choice of news, weather, shopping opportunities, and more.

One of the most common uses of the web is research. To get your investigation off on the right foot, you'll probably want to try a search engine. Plug in the right combination of words and phrases, and a good search engine will return a wealth of information. We cover the most popular ones.

This chapter also tours many of the sites that have made the web a daily companion to millions. Financial sites can help you get your financial affairs in order with tools for personal finance planning, investment research, and portfolio tracking. Health sites let you research nutrition as well as treatment of illnesses and injuries. News sites operated by newspapers, magazines, broadcasters, and others let you stay informed with a few clicks of the mouse. Entertainment sites provide music, movies, and reports from Hollywood.

There are web sites and services that let you set up a virtual office, complete with e-mail, fax capabilities, and data storage. Real-estate sites provide useful resources for home buyers and sellers alike. Homework and reference sites help students and their parents too with tough homework assignments. Parenting sites offer information on raising a family. Special-interest sites are visited by gardeners, bird watchers, cooks, genealogists, stamp collectors, book lovers, and pet owners.

Every web tour starts with a URL—that's a Uniform Resource Locator, a fancy term for a web address.

PORTALS

You may want to set up your computer so your web experience always starts with a portal. The ability to customize a home page on these doorways to the web is a benefit.

A portal is a multifaceted site that combines search compatabilities with other enticements. Operators of portals want you to visit their pages repeatedly and click on their services—that's what pays their bills. Ads are one source of revenue. When users click on them, portal owners prove their usefulness to advertisers. Shopping sponsors are another. If you buy something from a portal's "store," odds are the portal will receive a fee. Portals do offer some useful benefits, such as free e-mail, instant messaging, and chat services. On the other hand, because portals offer so much information, they can sometimes be confusing to navigate.

One of the biggest benefits portals offer is the ability to customize your own pages. You can choose the news you want to view whenever you log on, the weather for your neck of the woods, local sports scores, horoscopes, and more. If you choose to make a portal your home page, your browser will automatically open to it whenever you log on.

In addition to customizing content, you can decide, at least to some extent, what your home portal page will look like. Some sites let you lay out the news in two- or three-column formats. Others let you select designed themes and colors. They're preformatted by the portal, so you don't ultimately have as much choice as you have when you customize your Windows desktop, for example. But you can easily try them out and revert back to the original look if the colors are too bright or the page is confusing.

Here are some of the major portals.

AOL *(http://my.aol.com).* You don't have to be an America Online member to use the AOL portal. Just select My AOL, and you can customize the site to your liking. Although the layout options aren't that exciting, there are plenty of content choices, such as traffic reports, guides to your local government, and travel information including a Fare Watcher that alerts you to air-travel bargains.

EXCITE *(www.excite.com).* Choose a photo to display at the top of your page from categories such as nature, travel, and art. Content choices let you customize the site. You'll also find a quote of the day, as well as moon, tide, sunrise/sunset, and weather data. Excite gets its news from a variety of services.

LYCOS *(www.lycos.com).* Lycos calls itself a launch point instead of a portal, but perhaps that's just its marketing department's way to differentiate the site. Lycos is somewhat customizable. For example, you can choose how many headlines are displayed for each of the news services you select, and you can get links to local newspapers. Some things, such as mention of promotional contests, can't be removed when you

customize the page. You can add a second page and change the color of the display. Lycos offers sports scores, lacking on some portals.

MSN *(www.msn.com)*. MSN is many sites in one. Even with a 19-inch monitor, there's a full screen of Microsoft-chosen content to get through before you get to your personalized stuff. Among the free services offered are HotMail, MSN Messenger Service, and live chat. You're not given a lot of layout options. For example, you can't choose the number of columns you see or which items go in which column.

NETSCAPE *(www.netscape.com)*. Owned by AOL/Time Warner, Netscape provides services such as e-mail, an events calendar, and Instant Messenger. Areas of interest include autos, computing, and entertainment. You can also choose MyNetscape and customize your portal with local weather, horoscopes, local sports, news (from AP, Reuters, and ZDNet), stock quotes and local events listings. A recent redesign makes it easier to lay out the content of your page as you wish.

YAHOO! *(www.yahoo.com)*. Yahoo!, like MSN, is many sites in one. It's rich in content developed by itself or obtained through partnerships. Yahoo! Finance, for example, gets you stock quotes, business news (from news services and press releases), a variety of stock charts, chat rooms (also by company), and frequently updated market summaries explaining the state of the market each day. Yahoo! also runs auction sites, provides bill-paying services, and lets you build an online store. You can choose top news stories from Reuters, National Public Radio (for audio news), ABC News, the Associated Press, and more. And you can get customized lottery results, comics, and local TV and movie listings. A selection of themes (such as summer, seashells, or spring) lets you tweak the look of your page.

ONLINE PLUG-INS: A TROUBLESHOOTING GUIDE

Plug-ins are small add-on programs that expand the capability of a web browser. Such software makes it possible for a user to tune in to an Internet radio station, listen to archived online music, play an online video game, view a multimedia online site, or read documents stored in PDF or PKZIP format.

To use a plug-in, you first have to download it from the Internet, a CD-ROM or DVD-ROM, or another computer. To download from the Internet, usually all you have to do is click a hyperlink or button that says "Download."

Most plug-ins have free versions that you can download, and these are just fine for regular users.

If you decide you need to, you can download an enhanced version for a small fee. Enhanced versions of plug-ins come with extra features needed by creators of web-site content and others.

After you have clicked "Download," an installer icon will sometimes appear on your desktop. Click the installer icon and follow the instructions. The plug-in should be ready for use, though some plug-ins require the computer to be rebooted.

Sometimes instructions to setting up plug-ins are ambiguous. If you have difficulty downloading a plug-in, consider these solutions to common problems:

◆ To decompress downloadable files, you need a decompression utility. If you don't have one, try WinZip for Windows PCs or Stuffit Expander for Mac.

◆ Many sites limit the number of users who can access files at any given time. If you receive a message saying that the site's capacity has been reached, try downloading at a less busy time.

◆ If your Mac is set at "Mute," you won't be able to hear audio content even if you have properly downloaded the appropriate plug-in. Click into "Control Panels," then "Monitors and Sound," then "Sound." You can then turn off the "Mute" button. For Windows PCs, just click the speaker icon on the lower right-hand corner of your screen, and uncheck "Mute."

SEARCH ENGINES

These help you get to web content quickly. Learn to use several to get the best results, since search engines choose the links they display in different ways.

Search engines and their relatives are useful tools that rummage through tens of millions of web pages to find what you want. Search engines vary widely in the way they look for information, the way they present results, and even the way they let you perform a search. There are varying degrees of advanced searches offered, different ways to set up your preferences for a search, and interesting variations on the search engine theme. Google, for instance, provides links based on the number, quality, and context of pages that it thinks you want. A site called Direct Hit ranks sites by volume of use (but that doesn't mean they're useful sites—people often look for joke pages, for example). When choosing the search engine that will work best for you, it helps to understand how it works. Take a look at the "About Us," "How It Works," or "Technology" links you'll find on the search engine's home page.

It helps to know how to do a search. If you're looking for a phrase, place quote marks around it. Otherwise, you might end up with a site that uses all the words you asked for, but not as one citation. For example, a search of "German chocolate cake" might turn up several sites or pages about the German language, others about chocolate, and still others on baking.

Boolean phrasing can often help. If you're looking for a site that includes information on both mutual funds and stocks, type this into the search window: "mutual funds" AND stocks. The quote marks around "mutual funds" will get you the entire phrase, while the all-capital-letters "AND" will tell the engine to include only sites or pages that cover both mutual funds and stocks. If the search engine offers an advanced option, click on that for more tips.

Like portals and most other web sites, search engines often make money from banner ads on their home and results pages. Search engines also accept money from advertisers for "sponsored links." Not all search engines make it clear which of the links they give are paid links. For reviews of how search engines operate, visit SearchEngineShowdown.com.

ABOUT *(www.about.com)*. About puts a human face on its searches of its directory of web pages, but the results can be a little cluttered and confusing. It helps to understand how the results work before you get started. For example, when you do a search for "ornithology," you get the following: suggestions for searches of related topics; links to About guides, articles, chats and discussions; links to Web sites outside the About pages; and links to About's partner sites (usually shopping sites). But if you don't know that About has a special guide for "Birding," you'll miss a lot of the best customized information. One approach is to find the special guides in the category links before doing a traditional search.

ASK JEEVES *(www.askjeeves.com)*. No need to formulate complicated Boolean phrases on the Ask Jeeves site. Instead, ask your question in natural-language form—for example: "Where can I learn more about ornithology?" Once you submit your question, Ask Jeeves provides you with plenty of links, along with options to refine your search further, such as "find information about the hobby birding," or "find encyclopedic resources."

DOGPILE *(www.dogpile.com)*. Dogpile is a metasearch engine, which means it culls other engines in its searches. A search for "ornithology," for instance, turned up 10 sites (for starters) from GoTo.com, one site from LookSmart (a shopping site selling a Charlie Parker jazz album titled "Ornithology"), and so on.

GOOGLE (*www.google.com*). Unlike Yahoo! and other portals that include search components, Google is a search engine and nothing more. It also provides text from the page that includes your terms so you can preview the content before you link to it. Google currently searches a base of 1.3 billion pages. The engine bases a page's relevance to your search on the number, quality, and context of other pages that link to it—a strategy that gets good results but potentially leaves out a great new page no one knows about. Unlike other search engines, Google automatically assumes the Boolean "AND" between terms. You don't have to type it.

One interesting feature of Google is its specialized searches. You can peruse government sites only or sites within a specific university. Google's advanced search lets you, for example, search for exact phrases or restrict a search to a foreign language. Google also offers a version that can be accessed by cell phones, personal digital assistants (PDAs), and pagers.

If you don't want to go through a complete search, Google tells you to trust it to find the one best page you need. Do that by clicking the "I'm Feeling Lucky" button. If you're a fan of category listings, you can get them on Google. You click on the "Google Web Directory" on the home page of Google to get there. Google clearly identifies "sponsored links."

NORTHERN LIGHT (*www.northernlight.com*). Don't let its somewhat cluttered home page throw you off—Northern Light is full of tools for various types of searching. But you can also perform a simple search just by typing your words or phrase into the standard search box.

A search on "ornithology" returned more than 78,000 results, with highly relevant sites listed at the top. But you get a bonus—Northern Light also organizes its findings into what it calls custom search folders. In the "ornithology" search, Northern Light provided folders for Birds, Birding, Manuscript Collections, Bird Migration, Natural History Museums, and more. Each of those categories was further organized into still narrower categories.

Like Google, Northern Light has a number of specialized searches. Business Search lets you fine-tune your research by industry, date range, and even publication. Special Editions are limited-topic groupings of searches compiled by real people at Northern Light. They include subjects such as genetically modified foods, wireless technology, and electronic commerce. And GeoSearch lets you find hospitals, insurance rates and other location-sensitive information by address, state, and ZIP code.

MAMMA (*www.mamma.com*). Mamma is another metasearch engine. You can also restrict your searches to MP3 files, video, or images. The results garnered in a search of "ornithology" weren't all that commendable. Three of the top 10 returns were actually shopping sites.

OINGO (*www.oingo.com*). Oingo takes meaning to heart when you do a search. For example, enter "mind" and it lets you refine your search by the various meanings of mind—judgment, recollection, intellect, idea, cared. Oingo's home page offers a simple category listing that won't overwhelm you with an overly exhaustive catalog of topics. And you can choose two sets of results—from Oingo or another search engine, AltaVista.

VIVISIMO (*www.vivisimo.com*). Vivisimo is more a clustering engine than a traditional search engine. Not only does it go out and search results from a number of other search engines (such as Alta Vista, All the Web, Open Directory, and more), it also clusters those listings into directories that look a lot like the directory listings you find on Windows Explorer, giving the listings a hierarchical view.

YAHOO! (*www.yahoo.com*). Drill down is the name of the game when you do a search at Yahoo! The search engine of its directory of web listings organizes results into what it calls

WIRELESS WEB

If you're looking for wireless content for cell phones, PDAs, and pagers, try these special search engines. WAP (wireless application protocol) is a standard for displaying information on small devices.

◆ Calaba
(www.calaba.com)

◆ Fast WAP Search
(http://wap.fast.no/)

◆ 2ThumbsWAP
(www.2thumbswap.com)

category matches. "Ornithology" turns up groupings such as "Science> Biology> Zoology>Animals, Insects and Pets>Birds." Click "Birds" and you'll find handy subcategories—Aviaries, Birding, Journals, and more. This technique helps you narrow your search quickly. And if you want to go straight to links, Yahoo! provides a top layer of broader links with each set of results. If you don't want to formulate your own search, start with the category listings on the Yahoo! home page. Under Government, for example, you'll find Military, then Law, Ethics, Chats and Forums, and other choices. Other sites use this approach as well.

FINANCE

You'll find an array of powerful money-management tools on the Internet in the areas of personal planning, investment research, and portfolio tracking.

The Internet has been nothing short of revolutionary when it comes to managing your money. You can bank, shop for financial services, buy and sell stocks, track your portfolio, and pay your bills online.

But it's crucial that you shop carefully before using any of these services. Keep in mind how a site makes its money—if it's selling a service, even the most helpful feature may have an underlying propositional aspect. Because you have to give information to do business with a bank, pay close attention to privacy policies. Beware of false tips and phony news stories in chat rooms. Don't trust spam solicitations inviting you to invest in various financial schemes. Make sure a site is secure by looking at its URL. A site using Secure Socket Layer (SSL) technology will have an address preceded by "https," and you'll see a closed lock icon at the bottom of your screen.

There are three broad kinds of financial help online: personal planning, investment research, and portfolio tracking.

Personal planning

Many sites, including those of various brokerages, mutual funds, and insurance companies, offer planning help. Examples: Charles Schwab (*www.schwab.com*), Fidelity (*www.fidelity.com*), Merrill Lynch (*www.merrilllynch.com*), Prudential (*www.prudential.com*), T. Rowe Price (*www.troweprice.com*), and Vanguard (*www.vanguard.com*).

The Securities and Exchange Commission may be the government's overseer when it comes to stocks and other investments, but it's also there to help the average consumer. Click on its interactive tools section (*www.sec.gov/investor/tools.shtml*) for a Mutual Fund Investment Calculator, which helps you estimate and compare the costs of mutual funds. The SEC also provides links to a retirement fund calculator, Social Security planner, and quizzes.

Bloomberg's web site (*www.bloomberg.com*) tracks current market activity and business news. Bloomberg's Tools icon helps you tend your own business. You can track your portfolio, get stock quotes, and crunch numbers with one of the eight calculators—mortgage, total return, currency, emergency fund, education cost, 401(k), lease/buy, and savings.

The editors of SmartMoney (*www.smartmoney.com*) offer a variety of money-management options. Among the plethora of tools are an asset allocator, a broker meter that measures the speed of your broker's Web site, and a mutual fund finder and analyzer. An online bill-paying center lets you receive, review, and pay all your bills online. The cost is $8.95 per month; you can get a free three-month trial.

Investment research

Fund managers are profiled in detail at Brill's Mutual Funds Interactive *(www.funds interactive.com),* a site run by the financial journalist Marla Brill. FundLink connects you to the home pages of more than 100 mutual funds, while Funds101 takes novices through a lesson plan on mutual funds. The Toolshed includes stock charts, prospectuses, corporate earnings, and SEC filings. Hit the Research & Tools button at CBSMarketWatch *(www.cbsmarket watch.com),* and you're taken to a page stuffed with trackers, indexers, and analyzers. You can look up the best and worst performers, get information on IPOs, and check out a variety of stock screeners. CBS runs this site in conjunction with Data Broadcasting Corp.

The web site of Morningstar *(www.morningstar.com)* lets you set your own criteria and choose stocks and mutual funds based on those parameters. The site gives information on company performance, valuation, and stock performance to aid in your decision making. The Fund Selector on Consumer Reports Online *(www.ConsumerReports.org)* is run in conjunction with Morningstar. Standard and Poor's Select Fund *(www.standardandpoors.com/on-funds)* lists mutual funds that meet its criteria. You can download a copy of the list in Adobe Acrobat PDF format. The Mutual Fund Investors' Center *(www.mfea.com),* a site sponsored by the Mutual Fund Education Alliance, a group of no-load mutual-fund companies, lists 12,000 funds in its database. A chart can help you select funds by identifying your basic objectives (maximum capital growth, high current income, and so on).

An "off-center view" of the mutual fund industry is what the editors of FundAlarm *(www.fundalarm.com)* say you'll get at their site. FundAlarm's mission is to help its readers decide when to sell, rather than buy, a fund. To that end, FundAlarm identifies 3-Alarm Funds—those that have "consistently underperformed."

Portfolio tracking

Most portal sites offer portfolio tracking. Yahoo! Finance *(http://finance.yahoo.com),* for example, lets you track up to six stocks, by name or ticker symbol. You can view daily, weekly, monthly, or yearly charts summarizing the Dow, Nasdaq, Standard and Poor's index, and more. The Motley Fool *(www.fool.com)* tracks portfolios with a touch of humor. There's Fool's 13 Steps to Investing Foolishly, Investing Basics, Choosing a Broker, and Mutual Fund Basics. You don't have to own Quicken software to track your portfolio on the Quicken web site *(www.quicken.com).* The site lets you add or remove dozens of criteria from your portfolio, including Morningstar Overall Grade, Category P/E, Industry ROE, and more.

HEALTH
Wresting the facts you need from the mass of medical information—and misinformation—on the World Wide Web can be difficult. Start with the right search engine.

The web is a bountiful source of information on health. Experts offer insight and advice, tools help you track bad allergies, and calculators set weight-loss and exercise goals. You can also test the protection afforded by your health plan and keep an eye out for products recalled because of safety issues.

Health-oriented sites aren't perfect. Many have a financial stake in selling particular products or therapies, which may taint their objectivity and expose you to intrusive commercial messages. For example, when CONSUMER REPORTS researchers typed "sleep disorders" into the search box of CBS HealthWatch, an ad for zalephon (Sonata), a sleeping pill, appeared on the top of the screen, complete with information provided by the pill's manufacturer on insomnia. Meanwhile, sites aimed at health-care professionals are often too technical and too abundant for consumers.

Because the quality of medical information on the Internet is uneven, a focused—rather than random—search is the best way to begin. A general search engine can pose problems. For example, when we typed "Lyme disease vaccine" into the Yahoo! search engine, the first 10 references included links to "Cheryl's Lyme Disease Site," "Dawnie's Lyme Site," and "Jean's Lyme Page." Those sites contained individuals' personal experiences with the disease. While such accounts may provide some useful insights, they're hardly authoritative sources.

Instead of using a general search engine, the best place to start is usually Medlineplus *(www.medlineplus.gov)*, the National Library of Medicine's consumer-health site. It connects you to the 11 million medical citations listed in Medline, the world's largest database of medical literature. Medlineplus also points you to helpful tools such as a medical encyclopedia and several dictionaries; a drug reference guide; general background and detailed reports on treatment of various medical conditions; and links to hundreds of health organizations. Because Medlineplus is so comprehensive, it can also be overwhelming. But you can restrict your searches by selecting one of three content areas: health topics and news, drug information, and medical encyclopedia.

Other sites of note include the site of the National Center for Complementary and Alternative Medicine *(nccam.nih.gov/nccam)* and Quackwatch *(www.quackwatch.com)*, which concentrate on identifying dubious alternative health-care claims, and Medwatch *(www.fda.gov/medwatch/safety.htm)*, which contains the latest information on new drugs and recently identified risks.

It's been said often, but it's worth repeating. If you go to web sites for medical information, be sure to follow up with a doctor before undergoing any treatments. There are many factors to consider with any illness or injury.

Here is a sampling of health web sites.

CBS HEALTHWATCH *(www.cbshealthwatch.com)*. CBS HealthWatch has plenty of health news, but you get more than news on this rich site. Look up an over-the-counter or prescription medication, and you'll get information on side effects, precautions, and interactions. Allergy sufferers can enter their ZIP codes for a daily, localized allergy report, while a weight calculator lets you determine your optimal size.

If you're wondering how good your health plan is, a tool provided by the National Committee for Quality Assurance offers report cards for plans by geographic area. (But not every health plan is covered here.) The report cards grade access and service, quality of providers, staying healthy, and living with illness. Topic centers cover 48 topics related to the broader categories of family health, healthy living, and diseases and conditions.

CBS HealthWatch is operated by Medscape, which got its start in 1985 getting paper-based patient records stored electronically; the company now runs several medical-information web sites, including Medscape.com, a resource for medical professionals.

INTELIHEALTH *(www.intelihealth.com)*. Among the sources for InteliHealth's information are the Harvard Medical School and the University of Pennsylvania School of Dental Medicine. InteliHealth articles emphasize the "how-to" aspects of health care, with tips on preventing injuries, maintaining nutritional excellence, and controlling diseases such as asthma. There's a Drug Resource Center and an Ask the Pharmacist column, as well as a Poison Resource Center with a prevention fact sheet. A physician locator from the American Medical Association lets you find a doctor by name or specialty.

You can learn and play on this site, too, with interactive tools such as "Perfect Pitch," a mini-movie that teaches about human body movement using a virtual pitcher's skeleton tossing a baseball. The Symptom Scout, an interactive version of the "Harvard Medical School Family Health Guide," asks progressive questions about your symptoms, coming up with a preliminary diagnosis and, of course, usually recommending a visit to a doctor. Manage My Health lets you track immunizations, determine health risks, monitor disease conditions, and more.

KEEP KIDS HEALTHY *(www.keepkidshealthy.com)*. Founded by a Texas pediatrician, this site helps parents deal with health issues of every kind. A detailed asthma section, for example, offers a peak flow calendar, a tool for tracking peak flow zones, treatment options, and lots more. The breastfeeding center doles out advice on nutrition, weaning, frequency, and milk production. The main site can also be browsed by age, from newborn to adolescent. Growth charts, a vaccine schedule, and product recalls keep your kids' health on track. And a baby-naming guide helps you decide whether he's a Noah or a Christopher or whether she's a Jennifer or a Marlena.

MYWEBMD *(www.mywebmd.com)*. One of the neatest features on MyWebMD is the Diet and Fitness Journal. Put in your weight goal, add the foods you eat daily (calories are automatically calculated) and the exercise you did (calories burned are also calculated). Add foods you eat often to a list for faster access. You get a tally of the calories you need to lose your target weight and the number to maintain your current weight, along with calories burned from the exercise you entered, calories consumed, and the different food groups and number of servings in your daily diet.

SAFECHILD *(www.safechild.net)*. Among other things, it has an archive of recalled products, news, and a setup for e-mail notification of recalls. It's a project of the Consumer Federation of America Foundation.

NEWS AND ENTERTAINMENT
**Track a breaking story, check the weather, listen to a new music release—
the web gives you a huge range of news and entertainment online choices.**

Online news options include sites sponsored by major news organizations such as CNN and The Washington Post. All the major TV networks have a web site, as do many local TV stations. National Public Radio's site lets you listen to or read news and features, plus it links you to sites of member public radio stations.

While litigation has forced music-swapping sites such as Napster.com to change the way they do business, there is still plenty of music on the Internet. A new version of Napster.com is trying

THE END

Most web addresses have one of these suffixes:

◆ com–commercial
◆ org–organization
◆ edu–education
◆ net–network
◆ gov–government
◆ mil–military

to comply with recent court rulings. Sites such as MTV.com offer copyrighted music for a fee and some samples for free. Meanwhile, programs such as MusicCity Morpheus (downloadable from *www.musiccity.com*) are letting people connect to others' computers to share files and download music for free. Under this approach, there's no central server that can be shut down.

Here is a sampling of news and entertainment sites.

ATOM FILMS *(www.atomfilms.com)*. Fans of short films, animations, and oddball video will easily get their fill at Atom Films. Dramas, comedies, Euro (imports from the Continent), and extreme are among the categories. Caution: They aren't kidding; the "extreme" category may be offensive to you. Most of the films are no more than 15 to 20 minutes.

You can watch some films without joining, but get access to more when you sign up. (All the site asks for is screen name, e-mail address, password, gender, age, and ZIP code.) You don't have to download anything if you have a media player. (Choices include Windows Media, Real Player, and Quick Time.) You should be able to view most films (though not with the quality you might hope for) with a 56k modem, but a broadband connection will produce better results. You can also download many of the films to a handheld computer.

BROADCAST.COM *(www.broadcast.com)*. Tune in to radio broadcasts from across the country and around the world. Broadcast is now a part of Yahoo!'s network of sites. Be prepared to do quite a bit of configuring as Yahoo! tries to figure out which media players you have installed, and which you want to use.

Once you get past all the configuring and downloads, you can choose a radio station by musical genre or location. But there's another glitch here: Broadcasts of many of the listed stations have been suspended—temporarily, Yahoo! says—because of copyright issues.

There's more than radio on Broadcast. You can check out newscasts live (when available) from network affiliates throughout the U.S. There are audio books, movies, and TV shows as well. But be warned—configuring this site and getting your media player or players running with it can be a challenge.

CNN.COM *(www.cnn.com)*. Up-to-the-minute news, informative graphics, audio, video, columnists, and plenty of opportunities for live chat fill the pages of CNN.com. Send chat messages to favorite shows like "The Spin Room," "Burden of Proof" and "Talk Back Live." This is the ultimate site for news junkies. There are even movie trailers, performances, and celebrity interviews. Category coverage includes sports, entertainment, weather, science and technology, law, and health. Free e-mail newsletters give you updates on top news, CNN shows, legal news, live chats, and more. CNN is owned by AOL Time Warner, so you'll have to put up with the Netscape "toolbar" that sits on top of the site. (Netscape is an AOL property.)

E!ONLINE *(www.eonline.com)*. Gossip mavens, celebrity hounds, and just-plain fans can bone up on the latest Hollywood chitchat. The hearsay and rumors are augmented by interviews, Ted Casablanca's Awful Truth, music clips, and movie trailers. Movie, music, and TV reviews try to ensure you see the best of what's coming up. When you're all caught up on the news, take a few quizzes (such as the "Survivor" trivia quiz) or kick back with a few games of Couple Concentration, where you match the stars with their significant others.

ESPN.COM *(www.espn.com)*. Name a sport, and you're likely to find it on ESPN.com. Stories about the latest games, columnists, audio, and lots of video footage keep you abreast of what's happening with your favorite teams and athletes. Live chats put you in touch with players, coaches, and commentators.

The hottest feature on this site, though, is ESPN GameCast for Major League Baseball. Watching a GameCast of a ball game, you'll see a simple graphic of a baseball diamond, batter and pitcher photos when available, text that tells who's at bat and who's pitching, and play-by-play action. Click on a batter or playing position, and you'll get up-to-the-minute stats about that player. A variety of fantasy sports lets you be part of the action; you can even receive wireless updates about your team.

SALON (*www.salon.com*). The writing at the online magazine Salon is subtle, concise, and sharp. Beefy political stories; irreverent social commentary; and book, TV, music and movie reviews are all entertaining reads. You'll find lots of literary material as well, particularly in the Salon Audio section. One recent link had a recording of J.R.R. Tolkien reading from the second book of his "Lord of the Rings" trilogy, "The Two Towers." You can also search for your favorite poets reading their latest works.

You don't need to be a member to read the non-premium issues of Salon, and the advertisements are not much more obtrusive than those in most print publications. The site did recently run a promotion of the premium edition on the home page, vaguely masked as a story. Salon owns The Well, an Internet community, but its promotion of the site is low-key.

SLATE (*www.slate.com*). Owned by Microsoft, Slate is filled with links to various MSN content. But this cultural magazine also offers up a variety of stories on politics and culture. One interesting regular section covers what other recent magazines covered, with short synopses of the main stories. Every article offers readers the opportunity to gripe, praise, or participate in discussions about the story. Use the My Slate option to save, print, e-mail, or listen to the articles you select.

SONICNET (*www.sonicnet.com*). You don't have to register or sign in to listen to SonicNet's radio station, which lets you choose from Pop, Rock, R&B, Broadway, World, Folk, Woodstock (both the '69 and '99 varieties), and more. Of course, there's a Buy Music button so you can immediately purchase what you're listening to. You don't have to buy anything, but you do have to listen to SonicNet ads every few songs. To get the radio, you only need a Microsoft codec (compressor/decompressor program), which takes less than 10 seconds to download with the modem that comes with your computer.

If you want a more targeted listening experience, register for MyStation. Registration requires a screen name and password, ZIP code, and birthday (gender is optional). You also need to let the site know at least one type of music you like (this sets you up for the kind of music you'll hear).

The site, which is run by MTVi Group (in turn owned by MTV/Viacom), presents music news and reviews that include samples from albums. You'll also find feature stories, top music listings, guest DJs, and MP3 downloads. The guest DJs section is a fun concept, but disappointing in its execution. You don't hear from the DJs; you just get to listen to their music selections. The site also includes some videos. There's a good selection, as you might expect. But you'll need a high-speed broadband connection.

The bottom line on this site: music, music, and more music. There are samples all over, even in the ads, reviews, and feature stories. That makes sense, since the main goal of this site is to sell—what else?—music.

SPINNER (*www.spinner.com*). Who needs a radio? Grab the Spinner download and start listening to some of the more unusual musical genres you're likely to encounter anywhere. In fact, you get seemingly endless choices for genre and subgenre from the Spinner's playlist. You can choose Neo Japan or Nature Sounds, Summer Daze, or Klezmer. Or you can go for more traditional sounds such as Swing, Classical 101, and Super '70s. When you're tired of rocking out, take a listening break with AudioBooks.

The interface of the Spinner player is a little confusing—it doesn't resemble your stereo receiver much at all. Click around a bit to familiarize yourself, then customize your channels. You get a lot of information about the music you're listening to: The length of the song being played is provided, and the Spinner interface tells you what's currently playing (artist, song, album). Additional information is available about each artist and song with a single click. You also get a sneak peek of what's coming up next. Rate the songs you hear, or add them to your Song Pad for future reference. Click open the categories on your channels to find out who's currently playing, or open up the My Channels page to view all the currently spinning tracks in one place (don't forget to hit your Refresh button to update). Best of all, you'll never have to listen to ads.

THE WEATHER CHANNEL *(www.weather.com)*. Enter your ZIP code, then customize your weather page with a meteorologist's fantasy toolbox: maps that show Doppler radar, severe weather watches, wind and water temperature, earthquakes, snowfall forecasts, and more.

HOME OFFICE
**Professional-services and tech-support sites give home-office workers
some of the amenities that workers in "real" offices take for granted.**

If you've got a home office, you may be interested in services such as fax, professional e-mail, computer storage space, and lots of other aids. Many of these services are offered free on the web, with no obligation but signing up and having some data shared in aggregate form. Tech-support sites on the web tune up your computer, help you troubleshoot, and provide assistance when you want to better understand the inner workings of your equipment. Employment sites give you an electronic help-wanted section.

Fax services
J2 Global Communications *(www.j2.com)* lets you receive faxes in your e-mail inbox. You configure this handy, free tool with your choice of e-mail address, and J2 provides the fax number. You can also have voice messages sent to your e-mail. If you want to send faxes with J2, however, you'll have to pay for the Lite ($4.95 per month) or Premier ($12.50 per month) service. There's also a per-minute rate for usage. The Lite service lets you run conference calls with up to seven participants, send and receive faxes, access your e-mail by phone, and more. The Premier service lets you establish a local or toll-free number to unify all your communications and create a virtual office.

Free e-mail
Most portals offer free e-mail, but there are also other e-mail-only services including HotMail and NetAddress. Although it provides a substantial number of options for customizing your service, HotMail (*www.hotmail.com*) is plagued by junk mailers. A Bulk Mail option automatically forwards blanket messages to its own folder. But even with the Bulk Mail option turned

on, far too many spam e-mail messages reach the inboxes of HotMail users. Still, HotMail is fast, reliable, and easy to use. You can even set it up to page you when you get a new e-mail message. NetAddress *(www.netaddress.com)* is much better than HotMail at keeping out the spam. Although it can sometimes be a little slow to access, it does have some handy features, such as the ability to send out an automatic vacation message. Both HotMail and NetAddress let you set up folders for organizing your mail.

Tech support

Home workers and small-business owners probably don't have their own tech-support departments, but several web sites may help you solve hardware and software troubles, as well as prevent future woes.

With its documents on subjects such as error beep codes and BIOS settings, you might think PC Mechanic *(www.pcmech.com)* is for the hard-core tinkerer. But the site generally explains things quite clearly and, as the troubleshooter introduction says: "A computer isn't that complicated. It's just a collection of parts." New articles are posted often, so the data are up to date. Best of all, you don't have to register to get at this useful information. You can even read the community posts, although if you want to post a message yourself, you'll need to sign up. Tom's Hardware Guide *(tomshardware.com)* provides a similar service, along with news and product reviews.

There are also sites built just to help you avoid trouble and keep your PC tuned in tip-top condition. PC Pitstop *(www.pcpitstop.com)* runs free, safe diagnostic tests on your computer, letting you know about the health of your system's memory, hard drive, and more. The site works by installing a few small utility files on your hard drive. When the online tests are finished running, you can check your results against similar systems and read tips on how to remedy problems. PC Pitstop offers its services free, but uses that information in aggregate, anonymous form for its database.

You can also keep your browser healthy by clicking over to BrowserTune *(www.browser-tune.com/bt2kfast)*. Developed by the PC guru Fred Langa, Browsertune tests the integrity of your browser—by homing in on more than 300 browser features—without installing or downloading any files. Like PC Pitstop, the Browsertune tests are free.

Storage space

For computer users strapped for space on their hard drives, FreeDrive *(www.freedrive.com)* can provide some relief. With the free service, you can get 5 megabytes (MB) of storage space online, so you can access your data from anywhere. You can share files in your storage space with colleagues (access is password-protected), and you can even burn CDs from the site. If you need room to grow, opt for 65 MB of space for $4.95 per month, or 150 MB for $9.95.

Employment

If you're looking for a career change, or want to attract new employees, try a few of the online job boards. As its name suggests, Monster *(www.monster.com)* is one of the biggest. Among its myriad services, there are special pages for senior executives, recent college graduates, and freelancers. In case you're thinking of relocating, check out Monster Moving for mover quotes, planning tools, change-of-address, and more. Tools at CareerBuilder *(www.careerbuilder.com)*

include a layoff survival kit and salary wizard. You can also check out sites specific to your career. For example, StarChefs (*www.starchefs.com*) offers listings for culinary jobs, while Mediabistro (*www.mediabistro.com*) tracks opportunities for editors and writers.

PARENTING

With these sites, you can connect with other moms and dads, find activities to keep the kids busy, and get answers to age-old parenting questions.

Many of these sites are the web versions of the various parenting magazines on the newsstand; others, like Clubmom.com, are exclusively online. All of them help you pick names for your baby and identify kid-appropriate movies and include tools such as immunization checklists and pediatrician finders.

AMERICAN BABY (*www.americanbaby.com*). Everybody loves a quiz. You can start your perusal of American Baby with any number of quizzes, on what type of TV mom you are, to measure your baby-feeding IQ or to figure out your baby's personality type. Features cover basic baby care, baby of the week, nutrition, and fun and games.

CHILD FUN (*www.childfun.com*). Although it's hard to dig through the ads and partnerships on Child Fun's opening page, you'll be rewarded when you browse the activities list. Pick a holiday, and get a batch of arts-and-crafts suggestions along with a bit of holiday background information. Or try the edible play-dough recipes. The site is a bit amateurish at times, but that also gives it a homey feeling. Skip the Freebies section, unless you're interested in the likes of free "Survivor" T-shirts and Visa charge-card applications.

CLUB MOM (*www.clubmom.com*). The topics at Club Mom are divided into three main categories: cooking, driving, and parenting. The cooking section covers not only recipes but also food allergies. The driving section is sponsored by General Motors, and you'll see links and the manufacturer's name prominently displayed all over these pages. But the site covers all auto manufacturers—the day we visited, there was a review of a Lexus. Message boards address subjects such as car maintenance, insurance, and "minivan moms." The parenting section includes information on topics such as child care and education. Club Mom, as you might expect from its name, has the feel of a community to it, with many quotes on the main pages from message boards and other member postings. There is one navigational faux pas: You have to keep clicking back to the main page to get from one main topic to another.

When you join Club Mom, offers for magazines such as *Reader's Digest* appear at the bottom of the registration page. The first issues are free, but bills will follow for subsequent issues, which you can mark "cancel."

FAMILY EDUCATION (*www.familyeducation.com*). Family Education is part of the Learning Network's group of web sites. It offers a variety of tools for parents. For example, TV and movie reviews help parents navigate the world of mass media, protecting their kids from things they don't want them to watch. There are tips on how to keep kids away from TV, and quizzes on topics like TV moms and dads. Book clubs, arts and crafts projects, articles on family outings, and child-rearing advice round out the site. Activities and advice are divided up by kids' age and grade, while special sections such as the Learning Pod help kids improve their test scores.

PARENTING *(www.parenting.com).* The site of *Parenting* magazine offers a toolbox of compelling gear for mothers and fathers. The Baby Namer lists the top five boys' and girls' names. It also includes Celebrity Baby Naming quizzes and histories of African-American names. The toolbox also contains a due-date calculator; checklists for immunizations, babyproofing your home, and choosing a pediatrician; and frequently asked questions on issues such as breast-feeding, toilet training, and fertility. A complete set of financial-planning tools is also included.

PARENTS *(www.parents.com).* This site, affiliated with *Parents* magazine, divides its articles by your child's age, with stories for children up to 12 months, 1 year old, 2 years old, or 3 or 4 years old. Each section is subdivided into topics such as sleeping, discipline, milestones, and play. There are also topic areas that cover pregnancy, values, and safety. Chats with physicians and family therapists let you connect with experts.

HOMEWORK AND REFERENCE

These sites can help you help your children get their homework done and their term papers written and maybe even have some fun while learning.

The many homework and reference sites you'll find on the web make the kids work at it while helping them learn. You'll find math help sites, online encyclopedias, and all manner of reference books free for the perusing.

ASK DR. MATH *(www.mathforum.com/dr.math).* It's not the most attractive site, but Ask Dr. Math can be useful. From the home page, you can search the archives for a specific math topic, look through the FAQ, or cull the archives by class level (elementary, high school, etc.). If you can't find the answer to your question in the archives, you can write Dr. Math directly.

BRITANNICA.COM *(www.britannica.com).* Considering that *Encyclopedia Britannica* in book form consists of 32 volumes, it's no surprise that the web site is rich and multifaceted. Click on a topic such as History and Humanities, and you're taken to a page that offers original articles on the subject, outtakes from "vintage" versions of the encyclopedia (such as a 1771 article on mummies), a batch of web sites handpicked and rated by Britannica experts, and entries from the encyclopedia itself. You pay $5 per month or $50 per year for access to the full text of any article. The opening paragraphs of the articles can be read for free.

FEDERAL REGISTER *(www.access.gpo.gov/su_docs/aces/aces140.html).* Access government documents both executive and legislative at the official Federal Register site. You can search by type of document (such as presidential papers), for laws, and bills, by year (back to 1994) and by specific date. You can also look for federal regulations, laws and other documents at the National Archives and Records Administration *(www.nara.gov).*

HOW STUFF WORKS *(www.howstuffworks.com).* "Stuff" can be just about anything at this site, founded by the author Marshall Brain (his real name). You'll learn how animal camouflage works, how to pick a lock, how your kidneys operate, and more. Once you've viewed the detailed, illustrated articles, you can join in the forums to post a question or continue the discussion.

INFO PLEASE *(www.infoplease.com).* Dream up an almanac and you'll probably find it here—world, U.S., biography, sports, weather. You can search through any or all of the almanacs; links take you to related sections or move you to the prior or next entry in each book.

MERRIAM-WEBSTER *(www.m-w.com)*. Free thesaurus and dictionary lookups are available at Merriam-Webster's site, where you can also play word games, get a word-of-the-day sent to your inbox, and use the Barnhart Dictionary Companion's quarterly update of new words.

NATIONAL GEOGRAPHIC *(www.nationalgeographic.com)*. Video features, multimedia maps, and of course National Geographic's reporting characterize this site. Archives of magazines back to 1996 are available. Reader forums, live lectures, and games round out the site.

REFDESK *(www.refdesk.com)*. There's so much information on the home page of RefDesk, you almost don't know where to begin. But if you're looking for answers, you've come to the right place. You'll link with one click to reference tools such as Ask the Experts, Fast Facts 2001, and Homework Helper. Flip through the Old Farmers Almanac, find out who's leading which country with ChiefsofState.com, and do some spying with the CIA's World Factbook 2000.

REAL ESTATE

Real-estate sites help you in several ways, with mortgage calculators, school rankings, and just about anything else you need to know.

There's more to buying a home than deciding you want a center-hall colonial. You need to research the attractiveness of the neighborhood and the quality of civic amenities. And then there's that mortgage. Various sites can help take some of the guesswork out of buying a home, though they won't be able to tell you if that dog next door always barks at dawn.

HOMEADVISOR *(www.homeadvisor.com)*. This site from MSN has a portal feel to it—user-friendly, colorful, easy to navigate. If you click on the Selling Your Home section, you'll be taken step-by-step through the process with a variety of wizards, starting with making the choice and finishing with getting preapproved for a loan. A slew of tools will also get you through the buying process. Start by finding an agent in the area you've targeted and figuring out a budget. Then use the Find a Neighborhood wizard to learn more about the places you'd like to live. Add homes you like to the My Homes list. Or just get yourself salivating with the Virtual Tours of Expensive Homes.

REALTOR.COM *(www.realtor.com)*. This is the official site of the National Association of Realtors. Realtor.com goes beyond the sale and purchase of a home by partnering with Homestore, a site for home-decorating, gardening, and moving information. Realtor.com's home page displays current interest rates, and real-estate news stories that cover topics such as trends affecting interest rates. There's a guide describing various architectural styles, and a glossary that explains real-estate terms. You can search for properties by category, such as home, new home, condo, multifamily, or farm.

A salary calculator (part of the Homestore network) figures out what you'd need to make in your new city to have the same living standard after you move. You'll also find school and crime reports and financial calculators ranging from home affordability calculators to rent-vs.-buy tools. There are plenty of tools for sellers, too, including a listing of prices nearby homes sold for. The Relocation Wizard provides a detailed—but daunting—timeline of close to 90 tasks you'll need to accomplish to move, from estimating how much you can spend on a new home to throwing a housewarming party. The house listings let you get down to specifics—central air, pool, age of house, and more.

REALTY.COM *(www.realty.com)*. When you provide Realty.com with your e-mail address, you can get updates on listings based on parameters you set. Neighborhood stats come from Monster Data.com and include average household income, median age, average rainfall, cost-of-living data, high-school achievement, and more.

There's a mortgage calculator, as well as calculators for determining whether fixed or adjustable mortgages are better, how-to advice on reducing mortgage payments, and information on paying points and making down payments. A link with Handyman Online gets you free estimates for home-improvement jobs.

HOBBIES AND PASTIMES

Philatelist? Horticulture expert? Amateur ornithologist? There's a site out there for you and others of like interests that's designed to make pursuing your hobbies more fulfilling.

Whatever your interest, there is likely a web site for you. A good place to start is with any association related to what you're interested in. Gardeners, for example, can check out the American Horticultural Society's home page or the National Gardening Association. Tennis players can find out about local leagues and tournaments through the U.S. Tennis Association's site. Or you can start with a portal and see what other member hobbyists are up to. MSN, for example, has a community called Birds and Blooms, for those interested in birding and gardening. At About.com, you'll find channels for hobbies from soap making to stamp collecting, model railroading to woodworking.

Here is a sampling of special-interest sites.

CARE FOR PETS *(www.avma.org/care4pets)*. The American Veterinary Medical Association has put together a page for pet owners in need of advice for their feline, canine, equine, and other friends. The vets cover animal safety (traveling with your pet, safety tips for kids and safety at home), pet loss, health issues and buying a pet. There's a place to send your pet stories for consideration as story of the month, and a Kids' Korner with activities to teach children about animals.

GENEALOGY.COM *(www.genealogy.com)*. This is one of the largest of many genealogy sites. Other big ones include FamilySearch.org and Ancestry.com. For $9.99 per month or $79.99 per year, a subscription to Genealogy.com buys you access to a slew of records for building a comprehensive family history. If you're just getting started, there's plenty to do free on the site. Search the Social Security Death Index, take a few lessons on how to trace your immigrant origins, or browse the Genealogy Research Directory. The latter is full of national, state, international, ethnic, and religious resources. If you decide to ante up the subscription fee, you can search marriage records, land records, military records, society journals, and more.

iVILLAGE BOOK CLUB *(www.ivillage.com/books/bookclubs/welcome/)*. The web is replete with book discussion groups. The one at iVillage covers a lot more than fiction. You can also read and discuss history books, science fiction and fantasy, African-American authors, and more. You can even start your own book club. Authors frequently join iVillage for live chats, and features in the book club offer advice on what to read, trivia quizzes, and sneak previews of upcoming books.

NATIONAL GARDENING ASSOCIATION *(www.garden.org)*. This association's home page takes you to several gardening subcategories, including flowers and bulbs; fruits, vegetable and herbs; home and hearth; lawns and landscaping; and garden care and pests. Each section includes several feature articles, news, how-to projects, an events calendar, message boards, and shopping links. The fruits-and-vegetables page features the fruit of the month, and includes information on trees, nuts, and herbs as well. A section called Gardens for All will get your kids started with spade and hoe.

STARCHEFS *(www.starchefs.com)*. Chefs today have nearly the cachet of movie stars. Cooking fans can click on the head shot of a favorite culinary artist and be taken to a page of recipes (with wine suggestions), interviews, the restaurant where they can find the chef live at work, and cookbooks he or she authored. A culinary job finder is offered to help serious cooks put their skills to practice, and Ask the Sommelier and Ask the Cheesemonger get you tips on wine and cheese.

THE VIRTUAL BIRDER *(www.virtualbirder.com)*. Attention birdwatchers and amateur ornithologists: Do midwinter storms have you trapped inside with your binoculars hanging uselessly in a closet? Are you unable to get to your favorite birding environment, say, South Florida? Click your browser to the Virtual Birder, and you can birdwatch year-round, night and day. Take a trip to the Auburn Cemetery in Cambridge, Mass., a popular spot during spring migration. Photos of the cemetery include highlighted birds. Click on the bird, make your ID, and score points with correct answers. There's a song matcher to help you brush up on your audio birding skills, and a warbler guide for the northeastern United States to help sort out those confusing spring warblers.

3

Sights and Sounds

Today's cameras, camcorders, CD player/recorders, MP3 players, and scanners let you assume an amazing degree of creative control over your photos, home videos, or the music you listen to. Here is a look at how the gear can put you in command of digital content. For more information on the hardware, see Chapter 7.

Video-editing packages let you use your computer to transform raw video into fairly sophisticated productions, with fades and other transitions, a voice-over, a title and credits, and music. The computer has also become a photo-editing tool. Images shot on a digital or even a film camera can be manipulated for size, shape, and appearance.

Until recently, listening to music using digital technology almost invariably meant listening to a prerecorded compact disk. If you wanted to make your own recordings, you had to use cassette tape or niche formats such as MiniDisc. Now you can download music for a fee or free from the Internet. You can make your own music CDs by using a CD player/recorder or a computer with a CD drive that "burns" CDs. And there's digital music to go, in the form of portable MP3 players. The capability of making your own DVDs on a computer has shown up in expensive desktop models from brands such as Apple and Compaq but hasn't become mainstream yet.

LIGHTS! CAMCORDERS! ACTION!

Camcorders and newer computers with a generous amount of hard-drive space make it possible for an amateur to create video productions that aren't decidedly amateurish.

With the right hardware and software, it's relatively easy to connect a digital camcorder to a computer for video editing. Your computer will need lots of hard-drive space and speed—one second of video from a digital camcorder occupies 3 to 4 megabytes—but even computers costing less than $1,000 are capacious and fast these days. You'll also need a matching input at the computer end—known as a FireWire, an IEEE-1394, or an iLink port—and 4-pin-to-6-pin FireWire cable. If your computer lacks such a port, you need to buy an adapter card and FireWire cable.

Editing video shot on an analog camcorder may be slightly more cumbersome. Instead of using a FireWire port, you'll need to have a video-capture card installed in the computer. The card will have an analog video input. Or you can use an outboard video capture device, which typically uses a USB connection to the PC.

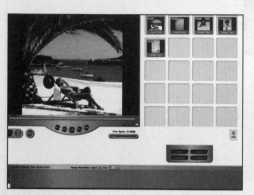

Until recently, video editing meant either a substantial outlay for hardware and computer software or tedious dubbing of scenes. The first alternative cost too much for amateurs. The second screamed "amateur video."

New software has changed that. Apple was the first to include a pro-style editing program on some of its computers. Dell and Sony also make editing software available, and there are stand-alone programs.

Many packages work this way: You connect the camcorder to the computer and patiently transfer clips to the hard drive. All have some sort of onscreen staging area for the clips. Editing means using the mouse to drag a clip to a time line, trimming the length of each clip as needed. You can then add fades, dissolves, and other transitions; a voice-over; a title and credits; and music. Then you can transfer the edited version back onto tape.

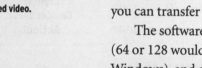

Apple's iMovie screen has a place to preview footage and assemble the edited video.

The software requires a newish, fairly powerful computer—at least 32 megabytes of RAM (64 or 128 would be better), a processor running at 233 megahertz (faster would be better for Windows), and a hard drive with several gigabytes free. CONSUMER REPORTS recently looked at these packages: Pinnacle Systems' Studio DV, Ulead's Video Studio, and the iMovie program built into Macs. Here's what we found:

For Windows

THE TAKE ON STUDIO DV. Of the two Windows programs CONSUMER REPORTS tested, this one scored higher. It takes time to figure out but includes a good tutorial and instruction manual. Onscreen controls make capturing video and segmenting footage into scenes pretty easy. Studio DV also has an automatic scene-capture mode that creates clips by splitting footage according to the camcorder's time stamp or by gross changes in lighting.

Studio DV comes with a big selection of effects and more than 100 scene transitions, 150 canned-sound clips, and 25 music clips. Videos can be exported in AVI, MPEG, and RealVideo formats (different methods of compressing a file to conserve hard-drive space and downloading time).

THE TAKE ON VIDEO STUDIO. This program makes scene capture tedious. Unlike the other two programs, Video Studio lacks onscreen controls for the camcorder. The package also has a less intuitive user interface, with hard-to-read labels and lots of unneeded jargon. There's no manual. A straightforward "wizard" guides you in making simple videos, but anything more advanced takes far more effort. Video Studio can handle a few more file formats than Studio DV. But CONSUMER REPORTS found it to be less convenient and appealing.

For Macintosh

THE TAKE ON IMOVIE. The program is now standard on most new Macintosh desktop and laptop computers; it's also available from Apple as a download. iMovie offers automatic scene capture, much like Studio DV, and similar drag-and-drop editing. Included is a small but sophisticated selection of transitions, sound clips, and title graphics–including music-video styles, cross-dissolves, and such. Other transitions can be downloaded from Apple's web site. The iMovie program gives you all the editing tools you'll need–crop, split, paste-over, and more–to make a nice-looking video. You can preview movies before they're finished. You can convert full-color footage to sepia or black and white, or add motion effects such as reverse, slow-motion, and speed-up. And you can adjust the brightness and contrast of a clip by moving an onscreen slider–handy if you want to partially compensate for a poorly exposed original.

Thanks to a good online tutorial, Apple's software was the easiest of the tested programs to figure out. It includes all the tools needed to create competent home videos.

IN THE DIGITAL DARKROOM

Computer technology and an array of commercial services give you 21st-century alternatives to compiling your snapshots in a photo album.

Digital images seem to be everywhere. Family and friends swap them across the world. Every kind of web page has them. Legions of devoted home photographers use their computers to alter images captured by their digital cameras, digital camcorders, or scanners—cropping, adjusting color and contrast, adding textures and other special effects, and so on. (For more on the hardware, see Chapter 7.) Many enjoy making prints, greeting cards, and T-shirt transfers on their inkjet printers, or sharing the images via the Internet. Others turn to the growing network of stores and web sites that handle digital as well as film images.

Software that manipulates images

Digital cameras usually come with image-processing software, such as Adobe PhotoDeluxe, MGI PhotoSuite, Microsoft Picture It, and Ulead PhotoImpact. Adobe PhotoDeluxe, a home version of a powerful professional program, Adobe PhotoShop, is the most common. With them, you can touch up photos. There's often an instant-fix option to improve brightness and contrast or adjust tint. Another common tool lets you fix red-eye in flash pictures. You can crop photos, put them in ovals or other distinctive shapes, and straighten tilted images. You can create a mirror image or turn a photo upside-down. And you can reduce a photo's resolution, making the file small enough for an e-mail attachment to be viewed on screen.

Most software packages also give you a palette of creative tools. You can, for example, turn a color photo into a black-and-white print or into something resembling a painting–brush

BEFORE

AFTER

BEFORE

AFTER

Image-editing software, bundled with digital cameras or available separately, lets you make a variety of enhancements and alterations. In the photo at top right, some skiers have been "erased" to achieve an effect. The portrait on the bottom right has been improved in brightness and contrast, and some wrinkles have been removed from the face.

strokes and all. With a steady hand, you can outline a section of one image, then put it into another photo. You can eliminate distracting details and remove skin blemishes and other imperfections. There are ways to remove scratches and other flaws from old photos you've scanned, darken or lighten specific areas for emphasis, or throw a background into soft focus.

Most image-handling software makes it easy to print images various ways—putting multiple copies on the same sheet, printing on a T-shirt transfer, or sending the photo to a web site. If you dislike the software supplied with your digital camera, you can buy one of the other packages for about $50.

Making images digital

Whether you do it yourself with a scanner, or take your photos to a local drug store to have them digitized, scanning lets you transform film prints into digital files that you can either manipulate and store on your computer or upload to one of many online services or to your own web page. You can also scan an image directly into a running application, such as greeting-card software, or an e-mail or fax program, or you can save it for future use.

SCANNING IT. A relatively inexpensive way of digitizing photographs is using your own flatbed scanner.

While available software can compensate for some less-than-perfect originals, when scanning, try to avoid photos or drawings with noticeable flaws; a scanner may reproduce those flaws just as a copier would.

A higher-resolution scan produces an image that is more suitable for printing or photo enlargement, but the scanning time will be longer—two to five times longer than scanning at lower resolution—and the file produced can become quite large. Scanner manufacturers recommend, and CONSUMER REPORTS' tests confirm, that a resolution of 150 to 300 dots per inch (dpi) is sufficient for most tasks, including copying photographs. For copying line art with fine details or text, or if you plan to double the size of a photo later, use 600 dpi. For an image to be e-mailed, posted on a web site, or viewed on a monitor, 75 to 100 dpi is sufficient.

To get the best results, preview an image using the scanner's driver software. Use a preview scan to adjust brightness, contrast, or color, or to focus on the primary subject by cropping unwanted material.

If you want to save an image, use the hard drive in the format and resolution appropriate for the way it will be used. Photos can be saved in JPEG format to reduce file size. For images to be e-mailed, use greater levels of JPEG compression to further reduce file size. For images to be put on the web, adjust the file's resolution to alter the image's size on the screen. Uncompressed formats such as TIFF can be used if you plan to store the images on inexpensive, high-capacity media such as CDs or Zip disks, but JPEG compression is fine for most photos. (See Guide to Picture File Formats, page 133.) When saving successive revisions to disk, be careful not to overwrite the original file. Image-editing software provided with the scanner lets you make more extensive edits and prepare an image for other uses.

A scanned color photo printed as is may be perfectly acceptable to look at, but don't expect it to match the original's colors exactly. To get a closer match, you'll need to tweak the image with image-editing software, described in the section above.

USING COMMERCIAL SERVICES. Drug and discount chains offer scanning services. More and more, these photofinishers don't care whether your snapshots exist as files from a digital camera or as files you create by scanning conventional film negatives or prints. Depending on the service, you can have your film images scanned and stored on a floppy diskette, Picture CD, or the higher-quality Photo CD, or uploaded to a web site. Picture CDs are $5 to $10 per roll, while Photo CDs, which can be used for superb, richly detailed enlargements, run $20 to $30.

Making prints at home or at a kiosk

With an inkjet printer, you can print photos comparable in quality to photographic prints. You can also print banners, stickers, transparencies, T-shirt transfers, or greeting cards. In CONSUMER REPORTS' tests, most inkjets experienced very slight fading or color shifts that probably wouldn't be noticeable in everyday use. But with some models, the magenta or yellow ink faded noticeably. For more, see Printers in Chapter 8.

An alternative is using one of the thousands of freestanding photo-handling kiosks operated by Kodak, Fuji, and others in pharmacies, one-hour photo labs, and other stores. They're a handy way for you to make custom prints on the spot, without using your own computer.

Kodak's Picture Maker kiosks typify the hardware. They have a TV-style screen that displays the photo and changes you make to it, along with controls that let you choose the picture size and layout. The kiosks can read the memory card from a digital camera, a Picture CD or Photo CD, or a diskette; they also have a built-in scanner, so you can make reprints from an existing picture, a print from a diskette, or a slide. You can crop and enlarge the image or enhance it by changing the brightness or color balance, or by correcting red-eye.

A built-in thermal dye-sublimation printer delivers prints quickly. Such prints are more permanent than those output by most inkjet printers. Prints made at a kiosk range in price from $6 to $12 per sheet.

Posting photos online

A growing roster of image-handling services and web sites will post your work on the Internet for you, let you share snapshots in online albums or through e-mail, and make traditional color prints. Some services let your e-mail recipients also order reprints printed from your original files.

With images shot on a film camera, you mail the roll to the image-handling service, which digitizes the images and, if desired, makes prints. You are notified by e-mail when the process is completed. You use the image-handling service's web site to attach the images to e-mail or include them in online photo albums. With images shot on a digital camera, you upload them to the image-handling service's web site from your computer. Kodak and PhotoWorks are among the biggest services, along with more recent start-ups such as Ememories.com, Ofoto.com, and Shutterfly.com. Some old-line photofinishers, including Mystic Color Lab, Signature, and York, also have a presence on the web. America Online offers its "You've Got Pictures" service with Kodak. The CVS pharmacy chain, among others, also partners with Kodak for its online service. Photofinishing sites offer a wide range of services. They may also imprint mugs, tote bags, and such with your images; store your images on their servers; or create digital versions of film snapshots when they process the original rolls.

Online companies price reprints and enlargements to be competitive with walk-in stores. Expect to pay 25 to 50 cents for a 4x6; $1 to $2 for a 5x7. (We've found that a do-it-yourself

IMAGE HANDLING
These web sites process digital and traditional film images.

Ememories:
www.ememories.com

EzPrints: *www.ezprints.com*

Fuji: *www.fujifilm.net*

Kodak: *www.kodak.com*

Mystic Color Lab:
www.mysticcolorlab.com

Ofoto: *www.ofoto.com*

PhotoWorks:
www.photoworks.com

Shutterfly:
www.shutterfly.com

Snapfish: *www.snapfish.com*

PHOTO-SHARING SITES

These sites allow you to post photos so others can enjoy them.

HP's Cartogra:
www.cartogra.com

Intel's GatherRound:
www.gatherround.com

Photo Point:
www.photopoint.com

8x10 inkjet print costs about $1.) The processors use regular silver halide paper and chemicals, as when printing from negatives, so reprints should last a long time.

If you upload images from a digital camera or a scanner, some processors may reduce the resolution in the original if your file does not fit their procedures. In that case, your prints might not look as crisp as you expect. Be sure the processor will use the resolution you provide.

If you upload an image that doesn't fit standard frame sizes—a long, skinny panorama, say, or a square shot—be sure to indicate how you want it printed. Some sites let you check a box to say that you want the whole image (no cropping), even if it means large, uneven margins; others may automatically crop an image's sides to force it into the frame, eliminating picture areas.

Online sharing

Some online photo sites are happy to store your images digitally and let you caption shots, arrange them into albums, send e-mail "postcards," and so on. Online storage can be a good backup even if you store the images on your own computer. Sellers on eBay and other online auction sites use digital images to advertise their wares.

But there are limits to the amount of storage offered, on how long shots stay up (perhaps just 30 days or until you stop being an active customer), or on the image resolution (to reduce storage needs).

Some sites exist largely for sharing, or as some say, building a photo "community." GatherRound.com, from Intel, HP's Cartogra.com, and PhotoPoint.com are examples. HP's site, for instance, gives members 15 megabytes (MB) of online image storage. The site also lets you buy T-shirts, mugs, and other items imprinted with your photos. And it includes how-to advice and useful links. Many Internet service providers also supply subscribers with online storage.

If you use a photo-processing company to store photos online, be aware that you may not be able to get at the files. Ofoto.com, for instance, will make reprints, but users cannot access image files; you will, however, receive only your film negatives when the company processes your film, not the digital images you also paid for.

If you avail yourself of online storage, be clear on the privacy policy. Some sites use passwords for album access, and you can share the password with family and friends. Others have open areas, where strangers can see your snapshots; you may not want that.

DO-IT-YOURSELF CDs

A computer with a CD-burner disc drive and appropriate software or a CD player/recorder allows you to make your own kind of music on compact disks.

Finally, after years when the only way to make your own recordings was to use cassette tapes or niche formats such as MiniDisc, there are now affordable ways to record your own CDs. The computer-based method uses a CD-burner disc drive and software, which now come standard with all but the least-expensive desktop computers. (You can buy a drive and software for an older PC for $200 and up.) You can also record CDs using a new type of audio component—a CD player/recorder. It has one to three trays holding CDs for listening or copying, along with a drive that holds a blank CD for recording. (For more on the hardware, see Chapter 7.)

Both methods allow you to copy entire discs or to dub selected tracks from multiple discs to create your own CD compilations. Both will record to CD-Rs (discs you can record on only once) or CD-RWs (rewritable discs that can be reused repeatedly). CD-Rs play on almost any CD player, while CD-RWs generally play only on new disc players configured to accept them.

Computers vs. CD player/recorders

Here's how burning CDs with a computer compares with making them with a CD player/recorder:

RECORDING QUALITY. Both methods copy music digitally, with little or none of the degradation that occurs when making recordings on tape. In CONSUMER REPORTS' tests, the recordings from the computer and component CD player/recorders were audibly (and even electronically) indistinguishable from the original CD. That's true even when we recorded at speeds higher than "real time," unlike high-speed dubbing on a tape deck, which yields worse recordings than real-time taping.

SOURCES FOR MUSIC. In addition to copying from CDs, both computer-based drives and component systems let you record from LPs, cassettes, or even TV or radio sound. Some models even have a microphone input, offering a low-cost way for home musicians to make digital recordings of their performances. With a computer, you can connect almost any music source (except maybe a turntable) directly to the sound card. The computer also lets you burn CDs of MP3 files downloaded from the web.

COPYING ENTIRE CDS. To copy a CD on your computer, you load it and follow the onscreen menus. With two drives, you insert the source CD and simply copy it to a blank disc in the other drive. If your computer has only one drive, you first copy the CD onto the hard disk, then remove it, load the blank disc into the tray, and follow the menu directions to burn the CD onto the blank disc. CD recorders have separate trays for the blank and recorded CDs; you use the remote control or console to quickly complete copying.

MAKING COMPILATION CDS FROM CDS. A computer provides maximum flexibility for assembling a CD from several prerecorded discs. When you insert a CD into the drive, the track list is displayed on your screen, letting you drag the desired tracks into another panel. As you insert successive CDs, you can see the playlist for your CD-to-be and change the order of the tracks. With a CD recorder, you program selections from up to three discs in the changer, a process familiar to anyone who's programmed a multidisc CD player. If there are only two trays (one for record, one for play), you must swap discs in and out. Most units show a running total of the time as you program tracks.

RECORDING FROM ANALOG SOURCES. Using a CD player/recorder to record a CD from a vinyl LP or cassette tape is much like making an audiotape with a cassette deck. You select an analog external recording mode, pause the recorder, and set the recording levels (a task the recorder does automatically when recording from a digital source). Once recording is under way, you generally insert track numbers between selections, using the remote—another step the recorder does automatically when recording from CDs. A few tested models inserted track breaks between songs recorded from cassettes, but most in analog mode ran songs together into one long track.

To record from cassettes using a computer drive, you simply connect the cassette deck to the computer's sound card. To record from LPs, you need to connect the turntable to a pre-amplifier (found in most receivers) to boost its signal strength to a level the computer can read; the preamp is then connected to the computer. While CD player/recorders usually capture every flaw in an analog recording, the computer's burning software often includes sound processing that will reduce defects such as the snap and crackle of a vinyl LP.

Most recorders also come with the optical digital inputs that allow another digital audio component—say, a digital audiotape player—to be connected to the unit directly. Some also have the coaxial inputs that some older digital devices use.

COST OF BLANK DISCS. Computers and components use different type of discs. The CD-Rs for a computer are about $1, and computer CD-RWs are about $2—compared with $2 to $5 for music CD-R or CD-RW discs configured for use in a CD player/recorder. The higher price for music discs is due mostly to a surcharge imposed to reimburse copyright holders such as

Portable MP3 players, which come in various shapes and sizes, play digital files created on your computer.

musicians, who feared a loss of revenue from unauthorized home recording. To tell if you're buying a music disc, look (carefully—the box designs are frustratingly alike) for the words "For Digital Audio Recordings" or "Recordable CD for Music Use."

Blank discs also differ in their recording capacity, which ranges from 74 minutes to 80 minutes. Also, some cannot accept certain recording speeds (look for words such as "All Speed Recordable" on the box). Unlike some tape recording (videocassette recording, for example), the speed at which you record a CD doesn't affect capacity or quality, only how long you have to wait for the recording process to be completed.

THE ABCS OF MP3

The still-evolving technology that lets you take your digital music compilations anywhere still requires some technical savvy.

If you'd like to stash an hour of your favorite songs, sonatas, or symphonies in a pocket-sized package, the words "MP3 player" might be music to your ears.

Like the now-ubiquitous portable compact disc (CD) and tape players, MP3 players are battery-operated, handheld devices with headphones that let you listen to music on the move. For more on the hardware, see Chapter 7. But instead of using CDs or tape cassettes, these devices, priced at $175 to $400, store digital music in their internal memories or on removable cards, discs, or other storage media. And unlike portable CD players, most MP3 players are solid-state devices with no moving parts, which eliminates skipping, even on a bumpy road. The amount of music you can store varies. A player with 64 megabytes (MB) of memory will hold about an hour's worth of CD-quality MP3 files. Cards, discs, and other storage media typically come in 32- or 64-MB configurations. If you want, you can delete old tracks and add new ones.

There's another major distinction: You don't buy prerecorded tapes or discs, but instead create your own digital MP3 files. Using software that comes with the

DIGITAL DILEMMAS: WHAT'S LEGAL, WHAT'S NEXT

With digital recording evolving rapidly, there are several developments that complicate decisions on buying and using equipment:

Is it legal? The controversy swirling around Napster and MP3.com centers on the legality of downloading copyrighted music from the Internet. Some artists and record companies contend this is stealing. Similarly, the software for "burning" CDs warns that users "may be violating copyright law."

Many legal experts believe copying music only for use on your own MP3 or CD player is covered under the "fair use" provision of copyright law and under the federal Audio Home Recording Act, which legalizes such home-taping activities as taping CDs to play in the car. And while the legality of sharing MP3 files online without permission from the copyright holder is before the courts, it is legal to download music from web sites that offer files with the full permission of copyright holders, sometimes at no charge.

Buy now or wait? Copyright concerns could lead to some changes in technology. Alarmed by the likes of Napster, record companies are working with computer and electronics companies to make it more difficult to copy digital music and distribute it over the Internet without paying for it. Forthcoming encryption technology could make some MP3 players sold today unable to accept new music in the future—as early as next year—if their firmware can't be upgraded to comply with new standards. The Secure Digital Music Initiative, known as SDMI, is among those promulgating such standards to protect copyrighted music from unauthorized distribution.

Another change in the offing: Several new music formats said to work better with encryption technologies—including Windows Media Audio and Advanced Audio Codec—have emerged as alternatives to MP3, and others are likely to follow. Current MP3 players may not support all new emerging formats.

While the debate rages, Consumers Union has urged caution about the adoption of encryption technology that might unduly restrict the free flow of public information. Libraries, for instance, can use MP3 files to make audio materials available over the Internet, just as they now lend CDs, cassettes, and videotapes.

Clearly, digital music technology is not yet mature, so it's likely we'll see a stream of less expensive, more capable equipment. Today's players may not be state-of-the-art for long, but prices are low enough and, our testing shows, performance good enough that some folks may want to invest now.

player, you can download music files from the Internet or convert audio CDs to MP3 files on your computer—a process known as "ripping." Then you transfer the MP3 files from the computer to the portable player.

If you don't care about having music-to-go, you don't need to buy a player. You can go on the Internet to download free software for playing MP3 files, then leave the music on your home computer for listening at home or work. (Another at-home option: new jukebox recorders. Costing about $600 to $900, these audio components allow you to rip CDs and transfer MP3 files to a hard drive. You then play the files over your sound system.)

Clearly, listening to MP3 music is more involved than, say, popping a CD or tape into a player and pushing a button. Good documentation would help, but unfortunately, the instructions that came with the models we tested were somewhat incomplete. If you don't know your way around a computer, you may need help from someone who's more technically savvy.

Tuning up

To use an MP3 player, you start by installing the software that comes with the player onto your computer. Almost all players are compatible with computers that run Windows 98 and later versions of Windows, and many also work with Windows 95. There are many Mac-compatible models on the market, and some vendors allow you to download Mac drivers from their web sites.

There are two software components: The PC-to-player interface and the jukebox software. While the player and jukebox functions are separate on a few players, most models integrate them into one application. The player function lets the computer communicate with the player and includes a browserlike application that allows you to drag and drop files from the computer's hard drive to the player's memory. The jukebox software records tracks from a CD in your CR-ROM drive onto your computer as MP3 files. It also keeps track of MP3 files and lets you organize music into categories and customize your own playlists. Most players come with third-party jukeboxes. RealJukebox and MusicMatch are among the most common. If you don't like the jukebox that comes with the player, you can download different software, including MusicMatch and Windows Media Player 7, from the Internet at no charge.

Once the software is installed, you can record tracks from audio CDs by inserting them in your computer's CD-ROM drive. You start the jukebox, hit Record, and the tracks are converted to MP3 format and stored on your computer's hard drive. You get the cleanest recordings when the jukebox software transfers the CD tracks directly to the computer's hard drive in their original digital format, rather than converting them to analog and then back to digital. If your computer and the jukebox software don't handle this well, you can try analog extraction instead. Some software will give you a choice of analog or digital extraction.

You then transfer the MP3 files to the player, which connects to the computer via a USB or parallel port. High-speed USB connections permit faster file transfers, are generally easier to use than parallel ports, and can be shared among different peripherals. For instance, you could have a keyboard, a printer, and an MP3 player plugged in at the same time. With a parallel port, you can plug in only one device at a time unless a pass-through connector is used. If it isn't, you have to connect and disconnect devices or use a switchbox. Most computers more than a few years old don't have USB ports and require a player with a parallel connection or in some cases installation of a USB port board.

4

Software for Fun and Profit

Once you've got your computer set up and turned on, it's time to start thinking about loading it up with software. But before you spend a penny on new programs, check your system to see what's already on there.

For starters, there's the operating system—the software that controls the basic operation of the computer. Windows and Macintosh aficionados continue their longstanding debate over which operating system is better. Proponents of Windows cite the wide range of compatible software and the flexibility of Windows machines, while Mac fans like to point to intuitive ease of use, plus the excellent graphics and video capabilities of Apple machines.

The newest version of the Windows operating system—which most PCs use—is Windows XP. The latest update of the Macintosh operating system, which drives Apple machines, is OS X now in version 10.1. Both sport a new look with a familiar feel, have new features and capabilities, and make further inroads into multimedia applications and Internet use than their predecessors did.

Windows XP is based on Windows 2000, which was, in turn, based on Windows NT, a system predating Windows 95. Available in both home and business versions, Windows XP has much of the same look and feel as earlier Windows systems, including a taskbar and application windows. But there are important new features some of which have been hallmarks of Macs for years. You can, for example, apply different "skins," changing the way XP looks drastically, not just in color and background, but even the shape of bars, buttons, and boxes. You can have more than one family member "logged" on the computer at once, switching quickly between each user's settings, Internet bookmarks, and even open documents. Windows XP also has a more stable core than previous versions of Windows and promises fewer application crashes and very few system "halts," which require rebooting.

Microsoft has tried to make as many older applications work under Windows XP as

A customizable Start menu helps you find your way around Windows XP.

possible, but it has acknowledged that some will have to be upgraded. Microsoft is enforcing tight control on each copy of Windows XP, requiring online registration of a specific PC. You won't be able to install the copy on a second PC. If you change to a new PC, or even upgrade one extensively, Microsoft will require you to reregister Windows XP again for the new PC. Whether that process becomes a nuisance remains to be seen. Microsoft has raised the bar in terms of the level of PC that will work with Windows XP, so existing PCs may have to be upgraded. During an upgrade, a survey of your computer's capabilities lets you know which hardware or software will or won't work.

Mac OS X builds on a version of UNIX, an operating system designed for large networked computer systems. OS X is a true multitasking operating system that provides better performance when multiple applications are running and faster switching between them than earlier versions did. It can also get the most out of the dual-processor Power Mac desktops, which have been available for some months. To realize the benefits of OS X in terms of performance and the new streamlined, taskbar-equipped interface, you have to buy new versions of applications that were written for OS X. Because it's such a drastic change, instead of trying to make OS X work with earlier software, Apple has built in a version of Mac OS 9. You can quickly switch to it to run older applications.

In addition to providing basic functionality to your PC, operating systems include a range of applets, or mini-applications, such as a calculator, a simple text processor, an address book, and a paint or drawing program. You also get games such as Solitaire and Minesweeper, sound recorders for creating your own system sounds, and media players for viewing multimedia clips. To access them, click on the Start button on Windows, then Programs, then Accessories. On the Mac, you'll find them on the Apple drop-down menu on the left side of your screen.

PRODUCTIVITY SOFTWARE. "Works" programs, suites of programs that run together, are bundled free with many systems. For Windows machines, you can choose Microsoft Works Suite. It bundles a spreadsheet, database, an address book, and more with the Word 2000 word processor, Money 2001, a personal finance application, Streets & Trips 2001, a mapping program, PictureIt! publishing software for organizing, storing, and publishing photos, and the Encarta encyclopedia. Apple's basic productivity software is called AppleWorks, which gives you a word processor, presentation package, drawing software, a painting application, a database, and a spreadsheet.

Office offerings from Microsoft for both Windows and Macintosh are full-blown versions of productivity software. For Windows, Microsoft is already selling the Windows XP version of Office. It includes Word (a word processor), Excel (a spreadsheet), PowerPoint (for presentations), Access (a database), and Outlook (an e-mail/personal information application). Office for Macintosh OS X serves up Word, Excel, PowerPoint, and Entourage (e-mail and personal information manager).

Microsoft isn't the only company that offers suites of productivity applications. Corel, for example, offers WordPerfect Office 2002, which includes WordPerfect 10, QuattroPro 10 (a database), CorelCentral 10 (an e-mail program), and Corel Presentations 10 (for presentations). Lotus sells SmartSuite, a package that includes WordPro (a word processor), 1-2-3 (spreadsheet), Approach (database), Freelance (creating graphics), Organizer (a personal-information manger), and Fast Site (web publisher).

OTHER SOFTWARE. Your computer might also include a video-editing program (Apple's iMacs come bundled with iMovie for editing your own videos; Windows includes Movie Maker) or a CD-creating program (iTunes for burning your own CDs is also on iMacs). The web browser Internet Explorer is installed on Windows machines and Macs. Virtual PC is a program that allows Macs to run Windows applications, and may be useful if a piece of software you want only comes in a Windows version.

What's on the shelves?

Entire catalogs and dozens of Web sites are devoted solely to the sale of computer software, not to mention those endless aisles in computer superstores where literally thousands of software titles by hundreds of companies are stacked for your inspection. Each is packaged in an appealing, brightly colored box designed to grab your attention. With prices ranging from under $20 to $300, they can run up your credit-card bill. So how do you decide which programs are worthwhile and will best suit your family's needs? Your first step should be to familiarize yourself thoroughly with what's available. A look at various categories of software begins on page 58. You'll find a broad selection at computer stores, through mail-order and e-commerce companies, or from manufacturer's web sites.

Upgrading software

Manufacturers are constantly upgrading programs, so there are always new versions of software arriving on the market. Many software programs use the decimal system to identify the version, so a program numbered 6.0 means it's the sixth major version, and a version number such as 5.1 tells you that version 5 of a program has been modified somewhat. A number such as 5.01 is an indication of slight tweaks. Other programs, including many Microsoft products, simply use the year to identify an upgrade: Money 2001 and Encarta 2001, for example.

Often, if you already have a software program installed in your computer, you don't have to buy an entirely new program; you may be able to purchase a less-expensive upgrade kit. But be careful not to pick up an upgrade kit when you really need the entire program. With games, for example, you might see a number of "expansion packs." But you'll need the original game in order to run these programs. Check with the software manufacturer to see if the version you have is indeed upgradeable.

SPEECH-RECOGNITION SOFTWARE

Tired of typing? Want your thoughts to go directly from your lips to your computer screen? Now they can—almost.

Speech-recognition software lets you speak into a microphone attached to the computer and have your words appear in a word-processing document just as if you had typed them. Speech-recognition software can be a godsend for people with physical disabilities that hinder typing, anyone whose job requires input while the hands are occupied, and for people who just can't type.

Some complaints about voice-recognition software have included the amount of hard-drive space these programs eat up, and the inaccuracy of the translation from your voice to your computer. Manufacturers are addressing those problems and the situation is getting better. Dragon Naturally Speaking Preferred 5.0 (Lernout & Hauspie, $180, Windows or Mac), for example, takes up 150 MB of disk space. You need at least 64 MB of RAM to run it, and a 266-MHz processor. But it learns as you teach it, improving its accuracy after you run a 30-minute "training program."

IBM's contribution to speech-recognition is ViaVoice Standard Edition, $57. With versions for Windows, Macintosh, and Linux operating systems, there are also personal and professional editions available. Using ViaVoice for Windows, Personal Edition, for example, you can navigate the Web (using Internet Explorer) with voice commands.

Software for free

Some software is available free online. For example, you can make and send greeting cards from a large number of web sites (such as *www.americangreetings.com and www.bluemountain.com*). If you need encyclopedic knowledge, both Britannica *(www.britannica.com)* and Encarta *(http://encarta.msn.com)* let you look up an almost infinite amount of data. (Brittanica, which once made its information available for free, is now charging for full articles.) If your personal finances are relatively simple, you might even find you can meet those needs on the web. Try Quicken's site *(www.quicken.com),* or another of the financial sites noted in Chapter 2. ZDNet *(www.zdnet.com;* free membership is required) offers downloads of all manner of free software, from utilities to web-site building programs.

Shareware is another option. You buy shareware using the honor system—download and try out the software free, then pay the developer if the program meets your needs, and remove it from your hard drive if it doesn't. CNet's download area at *http://downloads.cnet.com* includes downloads for both Windows and Mac machines. Other shareware sites include PassTheShareware.com and SharewarePlace.com.

CREATIVITY PROGRAMS

Programs that "paint" can help bring out the inner Picasso in you. You'll also see software that helps you design greeting cards, publish newsletters, touch up digital photos, and more.

Children and adults alike can exercise their creativity with painting programs, greeting-card designers, tools that let you touch up photographs, and more. While there are many professional-level programs available, such as Adobe Illustrator and PageMaker, there are also plenty of options for the nonprofessional.

For starters, your operating system likely includes a simple paint program that lets you draw with "colored pencils," paint with a spray can, and even use an eraser to get rid of mistakes. But you can go beyond these elementary programs with creativity and drawing programs, many of which also incorporate features for photo manipulation.

Paint Shop Pro 7 (Jasc, Windows only, less than $100), for example, includes tools for touching up photos, creating Web animations, experimenting with special effects, and more. Adobe Photo Deluxe Home Edition 4.0 (Adobe, Windows only, $49) and Photo Deluxe 2.0 Mac (Adobe, Mac only, $49) help you import photos into a desktop machine, organize them into photo albums, and touch them up. If you've been hearing about Adobe PhotoShop but fear it is beyond your capabilities, try PhotoShop Elements (Adobe, Windows and Mac, $99). Designed specifically with the novice artist in mind, you can work with both digital and traditional photos, cropping pictures, removing red-eye, repairing overexposures, and more. With Microsoft's PictureIt! Publishing Gold (Microsoft, Windows only, $44.95), you can create your own greeting cards and newsletters, and touch up your photos before adding them to your creations.

Greeting-card packages allow you to create impressive greeting cards using personalized greetings and your own or prepackaged art. Some programs also include video and audio clips, which you can incorporate into the card and send via e-mail. Others give you the tools to set up web pages to post a baby or wedding announcement or share other special moments

Paint Shop Pro 7 has tools that let you touch up photos.

with faraway family members. Greetings 2001 (Microsoft, Windows only, $29.95) gives you plenty of design choices, with more than 4,000 templates, 12,000 images, and 500 animations to get you started.

For a do-just-about-everything package, there are PrintMaster Platinum 11 (Learning Co., Windows only, $39.99) or PrintMaster Gold Publishing Suite 4.0 (Learning Co., Mac only, $9.99). With the Party Creator Wizard, you can create invitations, banners, place cards, and even party hats. The Photo Workshop provides special effects and image-enhancing features for your picture collection. Sound and video capabilities let you produce multimedia masterpieces. More than 200,000 images give you plenty of material to work with.

GAMES

Computer users looking for alternatives to games depicting violent gunplay have a broad selection to choose from.

Action, strategy, driving, pinball, role-playing, cards, sports, board games, puzzles, simulations —and you thought you didn't like computer games because the only thing out there is shoot-'em-ups. On the contrary. You can work your brain, relive your childhood, and invent new worlds with computer games. Prices have dropped significantly over the past few years. Here's a look at some of the popular games available.

AGE OF EMPIRES GOLD EDITION (Microsoft, Windows only, $19.95). Start by building tribes in the Stone Age and work your way up to controlling the Roman Empire (by purchasing expansion packs) in this Microsoft game. Although the game is set in a historical context, you can also create your own scenarios. And you can play with others, challenging up to eight additional tribes in your quest to conquer the world.

EVERQUEST (Sony, Windows only, $9.99 for classic version). A hybrid computer/online game, EverQuest lets you enter its world as a member of one of 12 races and 14 classes. You get skills and inborn abilities to help you make your way across three continents, where you'll learn spells and collect magical artifacts.

FLIGHT SIMULATOR 2000 PROFESSIONAL EDITION (Microsoft, Windows only, $79.95). Aviation enthusiasts and flying freaks can hit the wild blue yonder with various Microsoft Flight Simulators. There's the Classic version, the Combat version for would-be World War II aces, and the Professional Edition. The latter includes rich color, true elevation data, seasonal effects, real-world weather, four new aircraft (including the grounded-in-real-life Concorde), 20,000 airports worldwide, and new cities in 3-D detail.

HIGH HEAT MAJOR LEAGUE BASEBALL 2002 (3DO, Windows only, $39.95). Argue with the umps, set up your own league, schedule play from exhibition through playoffs, listen to the play-by-play coming from the two-man TV booth. High Heat includes real-life player rosters and stats.

HOYLE BOARD GAMES (Hoyle, Windows and Mac, $29.95). Backgammon, Chinese checkers, dominoes, and Snakes & Ladders are all bundled into one package. You can play against one of 10 included characters, or create your own opponent. Hoyle also neatly packages a variety of card games such as crazy 8s, go fish, pinochle, war, and a dozen other favorites in its Hoyle Card Games offering.

MYST III: EXILE (Ubi-Soft, Windows and Mac, $44.99). Puzzle- and mystery-solving in a world made up of eye-catching graphics and mystical music characterized Myst and Riven, the first two games in the series. Now Myst III continues the legend with five new ages (or worlds) to explore, a new storyline, and a new central character.

NASCAR RACING 4 (Sierra, Windows only, $49.95). Zoom along 21 different race tracks, compete with up to 43 drivers online, and let your animated pit crew service your authentic NASCAR race car.

PINBALL ARCADE (Microsoft, Windows only, $19.95). Travel through time and pinball history with Microsoft's Pinball Arcade. With seven different pinball machines—one from each decade, starting with the '30s—you'll gain new appreciation for the silver ball and turn yourself into a time-traveling pinball wizard.

SIM CITY 3000 UNLIMITED (Electronic Arts, Windows, $39.95; Mac, $49.95). What started out as a city-building simulation game has grown to include simulation of families and roller coasters as well. With the latest version of the original, Sim City 3000 Unlimited, you build your city, then see how it holds up in the face of natural disasters, overcrowding, crime, pollution, and other impediments.

TROPHY BASS 4 (Sierra, Windows only, $19.95). Take a trip to a "tournament lake"—you get a choice of 25, including Lake Champlain, Lake Mead, and Lake Winnebago. Your objective is to land a trophy fish using GPS navigation, compass skills, and depth sounding. Choose just the right tackle from real-life products. Once you've succeeded in your mission, mount your catch in a virtual photo album so you can tell that fish tale over and over.

Trophy Bass 4 lets you "fish" without every having to leave your home.

FINANCE AND TAXES

The broad selection of financial products includes software for balancing your checking account, filing taxes, and checking credit-card transactions.

Financial programs are designed to give you a clear snapshot of your spending, savings, tax situation, and investments. There are several different categories, some focused on specific areas (such as online banking or saving for retirement) and others offering comprehensive planning tools. The personal versions cost about $50. The professional accounting applications, useful if you're managing a small business, start at about $150 and can cost as much as $300. Some programs are available at no cost from banks (you've probably received promotional materials from your bank with your monthly statement) in conjunction with other bank services. Most financial software now has direct links to the Internet, allowing you to access your investment portfolio, check current interest rates, download your credit-card transactions, and pay monthly bills online.

You could track such financial information in a spreadsheet program such as Microsoft Excel, but specialized financial programs do a lot of the setup work for you.

Personal finance

Intuit and Microsoft dominate the personal finance space with Quicken 2001 Deluxe (Intuit, Windows and Mac, $45) and Money 2001 Deluxe (Microsoft, Windows only, $45). These programs help you manage your money from planning a budget to saving for college to paying bills electronically. You can balance bank accounts, calculate loan costs, and bank online.

Among Quicken's features: 30 performance indicators for your investments; missed bill reminders; capital gains estimator; and improvements in its statement reconciliation functions. Money includes an asset allocation wizard that helps you distribute investments among various options. It takes you through a detailed setup process, and the Account Register provides real-time feedback as it monitors your financial condition. Less expensive Standard versions of Quicken and Money are also available.

Intuit and Microsoft also offer packages tailored to small businesses. Quicken 2001 Home and Business (Intuit, Windows only, $79.95) and Money 2001 Deluxe and Business (Microsoft, Windows only, $84.95), for example, let you manage home and business finances in the same program. QuickBooks 2001 (Intuit, Windows only, $150) and QuickBooks Pro (Intuit, Mac only, $200), meanwhile, are more traditional accounting programs. An alternative to it is MYOB Accounting Plus Version 10 (MYOB, Windows only, $210) and AccountEdge for the Mac (MYOB, Mac only, $250). You can import data directly from Quicken into MYOB, and the program starts you up with 100 charts. It performs inventory transfers, volume customer discounts, and payroll functions.

Tax packages

You can import data from your financial software into your tax software if you buy compatible packages. Microsoft's Money integrates with Kiplinger's TaxCut (H&R Block, Windows and Mac, $29.95), while Intuit's Quicken works with its own TurboTax (Intuit, Windows and Mac, $29.95). A preinterview in TaxCut gets users started, while a tax-planning function helps you figure out how to save on next year's taxes, plan stock purchases or sales, increase deductions, and more. When you buy TurboTax Deluxe, you also get one free state download. Access is provided not only to official IRS publications for help, but to live tax experts. If your employer and financial institutions are signed up with TurboTax's program, the software will automatically retrieve W2 and investment data for you.

SOFTWARE FOR CHILDREN

In addition to being entertaining and educational, good children's software has engaging characters and activities that children will want to return to repeatedly.

The packages all make similar promises: they're fun and entertaining, they will keep your child occupied for endless hours, and they're educator-approved. But how do you know which software title will actually provide a rewarding, enriching, and enjoyable experience for your child? Well-designed software is easy for a child to use with some adult help. It also affords lots of opportunities for users to get involved and control what's on the screen, without passive staring at the monitor (as kids do with TV). It's relatively easy to install and runs well on your home computer.

Of course, software is no substitute for good teachers and textbooks, or stories read aloud at bedtime. But it can engage fleeting young attention spans and boost skills such as reading, math, and computer literacy—while turning off the TV set. Edutainment titles, which generally cost $10 to $30, are available in the categories below. Most are available for both the Mac and Windows.

'Edutainment'

Many parents of grade-school children share a common frustration: finding "educational" software that keeps kids amused and coming back for more as they get older. The category that best fits the bill is known as "edutainment" software—educational and engaging software that endeavors to teach young minds critical thinking skills while keeping them entertained. In other words, it's fun for kids and good for them, too. There are several categories of software that fall under the "edutainment" umbrella.

BUYING THE RIGHT SOFTWARE FOR YOUR CHILD

Here are tips on choosing children's software.

Know your child's interests. Is your 9-year-old fascinated with geography? Is your 5-year-old fed up with Teletubbies? Many programs are strongly thematic, which could be appealing—or a turn-off. Still, don't let a preschooler, or even an early grade-schooler, dictate your decisions. At younger ages, children tend to go for glitzy packaging, which can be deceptive.

Know the program's computer requirements. Almost all children's software these days requires a CD-ROM drive, and some cutting-edge 3D games are on DVD. Most can be used with either the Windows or Macintosh operating system. But look carefully at the box; many of the newer multimedia titles require significantly more power (at least a 133-MHz Pentium processor) and a good deal of available hard disk space to run efficiently. Most of the fairly new computers on the market plus those that are less than three years old will run most children's software without problems.

Buy software your child can grow into, not out of. Your child's age should be in the lower half of the suggested age range. Also, you can reduce the suggested age range at both the top and bottom end for most titles. For example, a program that says it's appropriate for 6- to 12-year-olds is probably more appropriate for children 5 to 11. Suggested grade levels may be a better guide.

Don't judge software based on flashy packaging. The same goes for signature cartoon or storybook characters. Rather, try to find a program with activities that will interest your child.

Consult friends, teachers, librarians, and magazine reviews for tips on programs. People with firsthand experience using a program can tell you whether it engages young players—and how long it keeps them coming back for more before they get bored.

Shop around for bargains. Software is often on sale. The manufacturer's suggested retail price may be $39.99 for a certain title, but you may find it for $19.99.

Try before buying. If possible, test the software in the store. Some retailers have in-store setups allowing customers to sample software.

Recycle. As your kids make room for new software, ask them to consider giving titles they have outgrown to younger friends, a school, or the local library. But to keep from violating the software's license, you'll first need to uninstall it from your hard drive.

CREATIVITY. These programs use storytelling, writing, and drawing to help children gather information, form ideas, and set goals. They don't focus on syntax, grammar, or the other mechanics of writing. Instead, they try to motivate kids to write stories by providing clever, enjoyable tools, which include everything from 3D effects to animation clips. Kid Pix Deluxe 3 (Learning Co., Windows and Mac, $29.99) includes an Electric Mixer that lets kids have fun with photographs and special effects. They can also create slide shows and paint images using the sound of their voice. JumpStart Artist (Knowledge Adventure, Windows and Mac, $19.99) lets kids make animated movies, and introduces them to famous artists' styles.

INTERACTIVE STORYBOOKS. These generally don't teach children to read, but electronic storybooks may motivate them to read, give a sense of what a word is, and show how text should be read. Children often find these multimedia programs entertaining. They are probably best for kids just beginning to read. The Reader Rabbit series (LearningCo.com, Windows and Mac, $19.99), and Clifford the Big Red Dog Thinking Adventures (Scholastic, Windows and Mac, $19.99) are some popular titles.

LANGUAGE ARTS. The "drill" approach is central to these programs, which are designed to give children practice in basic skills such as matching words with pictures, alphabetizing, vocabulary, and phonics. But if children lack such skills, these programs won't teach them; it's a good idea for parents to monitor activities. With Reading Blaster (Knowledge Adventure, Windows and Mac, $19.99), kids dive undersea to learn phonics, spelling, vocabulary, and more. There are three versions: for children 4 to 6, 6 to 7, and 7 to 8.

MATH. Like the language arts programs, these titles are also drill-oriented. Drilling doesn't teach anything new; it gets kids to practice what they've already learned. Still, the best programs can help increase the "thrill of the drill," making it more fun. They also automatically increase in difficulty as kids progress. Math Blaster (Knowledge Adventure, Windows and Mac, $19.99) has kids zapping numbers to learn to add and subtract. There are three versions: for children 6 to 7, 7 to 8, and 8 to 9. Less fun-oriented and more of a serious study aid for older kids is Math Advantage 2002 (Encore Software, Windows and Mac, $39.99).

Games for kids

There are multimedia versions of all the classic games you played as a child, such as Monopoly and Scrabble, along with versions of popular TV game shows such as "Jeopardy" and "Wheel of Fortune." But the kinds of games most kids today will choose are space-age multimedia titles, some of which contain a surprising amount of sexual content and graphic violence. One ratings organization that screens software is the Entertainment Software Rating Board, a nonprofit that issues ratings symbols for software boxes and also rates Internet sites.

The good news is that there are many exciting and entertaining games that are appropriate for children from toddlers to teens. Look for suggested age ranges on the packaging. And if you're in doubt about whether a title is appropriate for your child, ask other parents for suggestions. Here's an overview of the categories you'll find:

ACTION. Childhood games from dodge ball to hide-and-seek have always centered on action. Children's software games are no different. Kids, with their hands glued to the mouse or joystick, are in the center of the action, maneuvering alien creatures, steering fighter jets, and battling mysterious forces of evil. A great number of games fit the "action" genre, more commonly referred to as "shoot-'em-ups." Some of these titles are alarmingly violent, designed to

AGE-APPROPRIATE CHILDREN'S SOFTWARE

Looking for software suitable for a child of a certain age? Here's a look at some offerings:

For young children

Freddi Fish 4 The Case of the Hogfish Rustlers of Briny Gulch (Humongous Entertainment, ages 3 to 8, Windows and Mac, $19.99). Known as the "Nancy Drew of the under-sea world," Freddi sets out to solve another mystery in this CD-based game, taking kids on an adventure designed to help them learn problem-solving skills. For example, to help Freddi use a disguise to capture the rustlers, children must barter with other characters to wind up with the hat, belt buckle, and bandana Freddi needs. Kids under five may have trouble finding and solving all the clues.

Happy Birthday, Maisy! (Simon & Schuster Interactive, ages 3 to 6, Windows and Mac, $19.95). Kids interact with Maisy and her friends at Maisy's birthday party. Six activities take place within a TV-style cartoon as kids participate in the celebration.

Reader Rabbit Kindergarten (LearningCo.com, ages 4 to 6, Windows and Mac, $19.95). A summer-camp setting, cute characters and animation, and a system to chart progress make this CD good for practicing kindergarten skills. Drills include putting food containers in size order and playing matching games. The program tracks right answers and can adjust the difficulty level. It also provides help in needed areas and prints custom workbooks for added practice.

For elementary-school-age children

ClueFinders 4th Grade Adventures, (LearningCo.com, ages 7 to 9, Windows and Mac, $24.95). There's a sinister plot afoot that aims to unleash evil energy from the past on an unsuspecting world. As budding archaeologists, kids travel to Egypt to stop the evil-doers. Along the way, they learn geography, science, math, and language arts.

Jump Start Adventures 4th Grade (Knowledge Adventure, ages 7 to 9, Windows and Macs, $29.95). The adventures on this CD have a different ending each time your child plays. The games teach math, geography, history, and reading as kids rescue stolen maps and retrieve hidden treasure. The second CD includes a trip to Adventure World, where kids skate, rock-climb, snowboard, and mountain bike.

Magic School Bus Discovers Flight Activity (Microsoft/Scholastic, ages 6 to 10, Windows and sometimes Macs, $19.95). Ms. Frizzle and her class literally take off in this latest installment of the Magic School Bus series. Kids learn about flight, aircraft, and flying animals as they play games and fly a hot air balloon.

Star Wars Yoda's Challenge Activity Center (Lucas Learning, age 6 and up, Windows and Macs, $19.95). Kids join Yoda in the Jedi Council Chamber, where they are challenged with six missions of varying degrees of difficulty. When Yoda is satisfied with their newly learned math and reading skills, he presents them with a certificate.

For older children

Myst Masterpiece Edition (Ubi-Soft, age 10 and up, Windows, $29.99; Macs, $39.99). Players explore a mysterious island, seek clues that will send them to different worlds, and return to the original island of Myst with the book pages they find in the worlds. Those book pages and other clues slowly help them unravel a mystery and right a wrong. Riven and Myst III are the follow-ups to this graphically beautiful, engaging game.

Star Wars Pit Droids (Lucas Learning, age 9 and up, Windows and Macs, $19.95.) When kids are finished solving the 300-plus mazes and puzzles in Star Wars Pit Droids, they can create puzzles of their own.

Sim City 3000 Unlimited (Maxis, age 10 and up, Windows, $39.95; Macs, $49.95). This update of Sim City contains hundreds of new buildings to help populate the city players create. Try to keep control of your metropolis as it takes on a life of its own!

Where in the World Is Carmen Sandiego? (LearningCo.com, age 9 and up, Windows and Mac, $9.99). In this program, players collect information about the characteristics and destinations of Carmen's henchmen, get arrest warrants, and follow them until they're captured. Along the way, players learn about geography and different countries, although there's not a lot of problem solving involved.

appeal to adolescent boys. Of course, there are innocuous action titles, too. Note: Most action games require the purchase of either a joystick (a large control knob) or a flight yoke (a small steering wheel).

LOGIC AND DEDUCTION. Computer games are excellent at helping to teach deductive reasoning. By spinning an interactive story and placing the player in the middle of an enticing mystery, the game draws children in like a good mystery novel. By clicking on the screen and following a series of clues, the player moves the game along. Some of the most popular children's titles in this category are in the Myst series (Ubi Soft, Windows and Mac, $29.99 to $44.99), for older children, and Where in the World Is Carmen Sandiego? (LearningCo.com, Windows and Mac, $9.99), for grade-schoolers. There's also a new Nancy Drew CD-ROM series (Her Interactive, Windows only, $19.99) for budding detectives who've outgrown Carmen Sandiego.

SKILL. Descendants of the earliest computer games such as Pong and Pac Man, some of these titles challenge players to use hand-eye coordination to compete against the computer in a series of games, races, or puzzles. Others, such as the Sim series (Maxis, Windows and Mac, $19.95 to $39.95), require you to design a building, a park, or an entire city. There are also computer versions of old standbys such as Monopoly, Scrabble, and Solitaire by various manufacturers.

SPORTS. Any young sports fanatic will probably get a kick out of the dozens of sports CD-ROMs on the market, such as Backyard Soccer 2001 (Humongous Entertainment, Windows and Mac, $19.99) and Barbie Super Sports (Mattel, Windows only, $19.99). Most major sports such as basketball, football, baseball, hockey, golf, and soccer, along with Motocross and NASCAR, are available. Most titles aim to recreate the on-the-field experience and place the players in the center of action—often pitting them against realistically rendered images of favorite sports stars. And you don't have to be a kid to love these programs; a substantial percentage of sales are to players age 18 and above.

WHIMSY. Certain toys—dolls, stuffed animals, animated figures—have always captivated the imaginations of younger children. The computer software industry has tapped into this loyalty with a variety of software featuring kids' favorite fictional pals. These range from storybook games featuring characters from Disney such as Mulan Animated Storybook (Disney, Windows or Mac, $14.99) to television cartoons such as Blue's 123 Time Activities (Humongous Entertainment, Windows and Mac, $9.99) to creativity programs such as Barbie Cool Looks Fashion Designer (Mattel, Windows and Mac, $19.95), which lets girls design and make outfits for Barbie, complete with a 3D onscreen runway show, and The American Girls Premiere 2nd Edition,(LearningCo.com, Windows and Mac, $36.99), which lets them stage a variety of plays featuring six doll heroines.

REFERENCE

Need information pronto? Looking to while away a rainy afternoon with an encyclopedia? Planning a trip? These tools may be useful.

While the web is fast becoming the "reference library" of choice for many, some people may prefer to have reference material at hand without running up phone charges or waiting for information to download. Disc-based (whether CD-ROM or DVD-ROM) reference materials such as encyclopedias, map software, genealogy programs and other educational software may make sense. These programs will dazzle you with their video and audio capabilities, not to mention the sheer volume of information available. Here's what you will find.

Encyclopedias

Things are changing in the digital encyclopedia industry, with some of the less-popular titles seemingly on their way out. But Britannica, Encarta, and Grolier are still selling software.

One change for the better involves the delivery medium. Time was, you had to keep switching CDs when you used a digital encyclopedia, but with Encarta and Britannica going onto DVD-ROM, all the data fits on one disc.

Encarta is available in a wide variety of forms. There are standard, deluxe, and Africana versions (the latter features an interactive exploration of African culture), as well as an interactive world atlas. The Encarta Reference Suite (Microsoft, Windows only, $75), meanwhile, bundles the deluxe encyclopedia, the Africana encyclopedia, the atlas and the World English Dictionary. (If you're looking to expand your language horizons, there's also the Encarta Language Learning series for French and Spanish.) The 2001 Grolier Encyclopedia (Grolier, Windows and Mac, $50) has nearly 60,000 articles, a 200,000-word dictionary, a thesaurus, 137 timelines, 1,200 maps, and more on two CDs. With the Britannica 2001 DVD Edition (Britannica, Windows only, $60), you can create customized charts and graphs, look at the world from a 360-degree angle, and learn about 191 countries from both a global and local point of view. A CD version, which also sells for $60, has fewer visual and audio features than the DVD version.

Genealogy

Family tree software is growing in importance and becoming an ever-more vital component in today's home software libraries. For $99, you can get started growing your tree with Family Tree Maker 8.0 Collector's Edition(Genealogy.com, Windows only). If you've already done piles of research and don't know where to turn next, Family Tree Maker will review your work and suggest new sources. Thanks to its relationship with Genealogy.com, Family Tree Maker is filled with advice on getting your tree posted on the Web.

Now on DVD, Generations Deluxe 2001(Sierra, Windows only, $50) includes access to a professional genealogist. You also get comprehensive charting capabilities and a set of Internet research tools. For genealogy web sites, see page 43.

Maps

Don't get lost, get connected! If you're planning a trip or just like to daydream, pick up a mapping program. TripMaker Deluxe 2001 (Rand McNally, Windows only, $29.95) sends you in the right direction with printable maps detailing the route from one destination to another. It includes preplanned trips, detailed information on national parks and other attractions, and roadside restaurant recommendations. AAA Map'n'Go 7 (DeLorme, Windows only, $30) lays out your travel plans by the fastest or the most scenic route, or by one you choose. You won't go hungry or sleepless, thanks to its AAA restaurant and lodging guides. These packages cost about $30.

Streets & Trips 2001 (Microsoft, Windows only, $44.95) works with your handheld GPS.

Plug the receiver into a laptop running the program, and you can pinpoint your exact location. Besides the traditional road maps, you can use a product such as Topo U.S.A. (DeLorme, Windows only, $30)—with interactive topographical maps—to take a hike or climb a mountain.

UTILITIES
Like many other valuable appliances, a computer may work better with maintenance. These products will provide a little TLC for your Windows or Mac PC.

Utilities keep your computer running smoothly and cleanly, performing functions like security, virus-fighting and clean-up. Tools for basic maintenance are included in all operating systems, but add-on software products such as antivirus software, uninstallers, backup tools, and utilities suites can make the day-to-day operation of your computer easier. Before purchasing these products, make sure they're compatible with your operating system's version. (Note: Most suites come with many of the other types of utilities built in such as a hard-disk space optimizer, a file-saver program, and repair utilities to diagnose and fix disk problems.)

Antivirus

Computers may be made of silicon chips, wires, and plastic, but they can get sick—sometimes fatally so. One of the most common ailments is the virus, a maliciously written piece of program code that can get buried in a legitimate program or floppy disk. There are actually thousands of viruses that can be transmitted via shared software and, most commonly, via files downloaded from the Internet. Although many viruses are relatively benign, others can fill your hard drive with useless data, destroy everything on your hard drive, or replicate by sending themselves out to every e-mail address in your contact book. Antivirus programs scan your e-mails, downloads and other files to detect and destroy viruses before they damage your system. Antivirus programs cost about $30 to $70; some offer free updates while others charge for that service.

One of your biggest worries where computer viruses are concerned is making sure your antivirus program can find all the latest infections. Norton Anti-Virus 2001 (Norton, Windows only, $39.95) solves that problem with automatic updates that work in the background while you're doing other tasks on your PC. There's also Norton Anti-Virus for Macintosh 7.0 for Macintosh computers running OS 8.0 and higher, $69.95, and Symantec Anti-Virus 2001 for Palm OS, $39.95.

VirusScan 5.21 (McAfee, Windows only, $29.95), for example, detects dangerous ActiveX or Java applets, and catches viruses in your e-mail before you even open a message.

Uninstallers

Uninstallers clean the junk out of your computer, and help you uninstall programs in an intelligent manner that cleans out not only the main program files but registry changes and other related files scattered across your hard drive. These products retail between $30 and $50.

The new Fast & Safe Cleanup feature in Norton CleanSweep 2001 (Norton, Windows only, $39.95) automatically removes unwanted files from your computer. Internet Sweep wipes away clutter that gathers when you surf the Web, such as URLs, cookies, ActiveX controls, and plug-ins. Uninstaller 6.0 (McAfee, Windows only, $19.95) monitors your system whenever you install new software. That means you can revert back to your pre-installation hard drive if anything goes wrong. For Mac users, Aladdin Systems Spring Cleaning, $49.95, brings your hard drive back to its prior settings with one click of the Restore button.

Secure surfing

When you surf the Web and browse from site to site, you leave an inadvertent trail identifying where you've been and what you've been looking at. At the same time, information-transmitting "cookies" are being dropped into your hard drive by Web marketers eager to send advertisements targeted to your interests across your screen while you surf. For more, see page 22. If privacy is a concern, you'll want one of the many programs available that will erase trails left behind on the Internet and block cookies. Some are even free from the web, such as RBA World Productions' Cookie Cruncher *(www.rbaworld.com/Programs/CookieCruncher/)* and AdSubtract *(www.adsubtract.com/)*. Or try Norton Internet Security 2001 for Windows, $79.95, or Norton Internet Security 1.0 for Macs, $99.95 *(www.symantec.com)*, which also includes a firewall to protect your system from hackers.

Utilities suites

You can get a whole array of safeguards in a prepackaged "suite." The best-known utilities suites retail from $35 to $130. SystemWorks for Macintosh, $129.95, includes Norton's antivirus and uninstaller features. Norton SystemWorks 2001, $99.95, is the Windows version. Their built-in Norton Utilities optimize system performance by detecting disk problems and keeping your hard drive in shape. Besides the usual utilities, McAfee Office 3.0, $49.95, for Windows, includes a firewall.

Other utilities

Additional utilities include backup programs such as Norton Ghost 2001, $69.95, which lets you create and restore images of your Windows computer's hard drive; Rewind (Power on Software, $99.95), which does the same for the Mac *(www.poweronsoftware.com)*; Adobe Acrobat Reader, a free download from *www.adobe.com* lets you read PDF documents; and remote-control software such as Symantec's pcAnywhere, $159.99 *(www.symantec.com)*.

5

The Virtual Mall

While it can't duplicate the experience of strolling down Rodeo Drive, shopping on the web does deliver considerable rewards. At it's best, online shopping is quick, efficient, fun, and informative. Easy searching by author, title, genre, or other categories makes the web a good place to shop for products such as books, music, and videos, which are small and light and easy to ship. Computers and home-electronics equipment are also easy to find. Online auctions open the door to rare or hard-to-find items. While online sales account for just a tiny portion of the more than $2.5 trillion spent annually on retail, e-tailing has demonstrated that it's definitely here to stay.

CONSUMER REPORTS' regular evaluations of online shopping sites show that with few exceptions, web merchants deliver the goods—as ordered and on time. The shopping experience, however, can be another matter. Among concerns are sites that are difficult to navigate, product details that are hard to decipher onscreen, items that are disappointingly not available, and security and privacy issues. For e-Ratings of online shopping sites, see page 86.

SMART E-TAIL SITES

Beyond matters of taste and budget, there are certain key elements that should be in place to help ensure a pleasant and secure web-shopping experience.

An appealing e-tail site is many things. Of course it has merchandise that matches your taste level and budget, and it may be a subsidiary of a bricks-and-mortar retailer that is familiar to you. Other fundamentals include ease of use, clear policy statements regarding privacy and credit-card security, and appropriate breadth and depth of product choices. Individual attributes may be judged more or less important for different product categories. For example,

E-RATINGS

For an assessment of online retail sites, see page 86. These are also included on CONSUMER REPORTS' web site (www.ConsumerReports.org).

images of products are more important when shopping for clothing than when shopping for books or CDs, although the book or CD cover should be shown once you have selected a title for a closer look.

Policies to look for

All policy information should be easy to find. Ideally, it will be available by clicking on a link from any page on the site. At a minimum, policy information should be found on particularly relevant pages (for example, security information should be easily accessible when you're placing an order) and on a site's home page.

SECURITY. A clear security policy statement describes the strategy employed by the web site to ensure the safety of a customer's credit-card and other information. Make sure any web site you're shopping on has a security mode that encrypts credit-card numbers. When you switch from browsing to buying, the merchant should issue a prompt that tells you the transaction is being switched to a secure system. A safe site will display a symbol of an unbroken key, a picture of a closed lock, or a web address that begins https:// (note the "s" added to "http").

PRIVACY. A clear privacy policy statement describes the type of personal information collected from a customer, the reason that information is collected, and who will have access to that information. In general, merchants should make it very easy for customers to "opt out" of being placed on any third-party lists. Some sites use a conveniently placed check-box or radio button to indicate a lack of consent. The merchant should not ask for extra information beyond what is needed to place an order (name, address, phone number, e-mail address, billing information) without having a clearly stated purpose.

If the extra information is to be used for personalization, the site must offer an easy way to opt out of such personalization.

CYBERSHOPPING PROS AND CONS

Almost everything in life has its trade-offs, and online shopping is no different. Here's an overview of e-commerce's pros and cons.

Web shopping excels in the following areas:

Research. You'll gain unparalleled access to product information.

Broad selection. Web merchants are apt to offer a wider selection than any one store. Comparison shopping is easy.

Ability to shop anytime. No need to brave crowds or trudge from store to store.

Low prices. Many web merchants offer discount pricing. Of course, you'll have to factor in shipping charges, though you may not be charged sales tax.

Web shopping falls short in these areas:

The wait. Do you want it today? Running to the mall will get the item into your possession quicker—as long as the bricks-and-mortar retailer has it in stock. E-commerce sites generally take a few days to a few weeks to deliver (unless you pay extra for express delivery).

No demos. Do you need to see it, hear it, touch it, try it on, or have it demonstrated before you're comfortable purchasing the item? There's none of that with online shopping, though you can visit a retail store first, of course, to inspect your prospective purchase—then order online if there's a savings involved.

Returns. Is there a chance you'll have to return the product? Returning a product to a store may be easier and less expensive than repackaging it and shipping it back.

Surf time. Unless you know exactly what you're looking for, don't assume you'll save time. Search engines and shopping bots vary in terms of ease of use, and you may find yourself spending hours comparison shopping.

Ads. There's a good chance you'll have to pick your way through ads while looking for actual shopping sites.

The best sites do not share any information with third parties unless the customer gives explicit consent. Customers should have to "opt in" rather than having to "opt out."

SHIPPING AND HANDLING. A clear shipping and handling policy statement describes shipping costs and how many days it will take for the item(s) to arrive. In general, sites should offer regular and express shipping, and the least expensive option should be the default. Shipping fees should be reasonable (we compared them with shipping fees of companies in the same category), and shipping and handling costs should be disclosed before the ordering process begins.

The better sites have relatively low shipping costs and no additional charge to ship items with different availability separately (for example, back-orders).

RETURNS. A clear policy statement includes the who, what, where, how, and how much of returning items. Look for a 100 percent satisfaction guarantee that allows customers to return any item for any reason (unless prohibited by law) in a reasonable amount of time (a minimum of 30 days). Sites should meet the industry standard for returns. The standard may be less than a complete satisfaction guarantee if it has a reasonable basis (for example, music CDs and software can only be returned unopened).

Sites should offer a full refund, rather than just a credit or exchange, and restocking fees should be paid by the merchant. The better sites, as applicable, allow items ordered online to be returned to local retail stores; exceed the industry standard for returns; and pay return shipping fees if the wrong or a defective product was shipped. (Ideally, the merchant would always pay return shipping fees.)

CUSTOMER SERVICE. A clear customer-service policy statement describes how and when a representative may be contacted. For instance, customer-focused services should be provided to enhance the shopping process, including a toll-free phone number, an e-mail address, and a "snail mail" address. Service should be available seven days a week, 24 hours a day. A "Help" or "Frequently Asked Questions (FAQ)" section should be available. Merchants should send an e-mail confirmation of an order and notification of when items will ship.

The better sites, as applicable, have special services, such as including batteries at no extra charge with all products requiring them, and features such as online order tracking.

What makes a site easy to use?

The information on each page of an easy-to-use site is designed and structured so that customers can easily understand it and find what they need. It's simple to navigate from one part of the site to another. Ordering should be simple and sensible. Sites advertising products from businesses other than their own should ensure that those ads are small, out of the way, and clear as to their purpose.

DESIGN. Aside from basic aesthetics that make shopping more enjoyable, look for pages that are designed and structured so that customers can easily comprehend the information presented and can easily find what they need.

The better sites design with simplicity and consistency. The best designs are those that are hardly noticed. They have uncluttered, easy-to-read pages, use moderation in color and typefaces, and avoid the use of distracting animation.

Pages should be organized so that important information is emphasized, and all information is grouped and presented in a logical, predictable fashion. You should see everyday language and consistent organization across pages.

NAVIGATION (BROWSING AND SEARCHING). Whether customers want to browse through all products, look at a specific category of product, or search for a specific item, they should be able to do so easily.

The better sites have consistent, well-placed menus and submenus (tabs or button bars) with meaningful labels that lead to key pages on the site (for example, Home, Shopping Cart, and individual product categories). They also have clear navigation aids (button bars, consistent icons, highlighted icons, page-specific cursor shapes, etc.) on every page that allow customers to know where they are on the site at all times. Clear navigation will also make it easy for customers to go where they want to go and find their way back to where they've been. Helpful approaches include consistent, well-placed menus and submenus.

Sites should be organized so that customers can move around with the fewest number of mouse-clicks (three to four clicks should be the maximum). They should also list relevant product categories with meaningful labels for sensible browsing. Finding items should be at least as simple as zipping through a dress rack at a store. So, within browsing categories, product listings should have enough pertinent information (price, description and/or picture) to help the customer quickly select items to peruse in more detail.

Look for a search engine that lets customers quickly find items by product category, brand name, product name, model/item number, and price, as well as other relevant criteria

THE SEVEN HABITS OF SMART E-SHOPPERS

Anytime you venture online to shop, CONSUMER REPORTS suggests that you set a budget, keeping the following things in mind:

1. Check out the merchant. When shopping with a cybermerchant for the first time, get in the habit of reading the company's privacy and security policies before you buy. Look for the TRUSTe symbol or a Better Business Bureau Online seal, both indicating that the merchant's business practices have been independently audited as consumer-friendly. You can log on to the BizRate.com site evaluations (at *www.bizrate.com*), where you'll find compilations of other consumers' shopping experiences. You can also use Consumer Reports Online's e-Ratings, on page 86 or online (*www.ConsumerReports.org*).

2. Be organized. Have a few backup gift ideas in case you cannot easily find your first choice. The more information you have, such as a model number, the easier it is to find sites that sell your selection.

3. Give yourself enough time. Even if you know precisely what you want and where to buy it, you still need to factor in ample time for delivery—and for dealing with problems that may arise, such as the belated discovery that an item has been back-ordered. Unfortunately, during the holiday shopping season, you need to leave even more time than you think is reasonable.

4. Use "bookmarks" to compare products. If you've found an item you like but are not sure you want to buy it, place it in the site's virtual shopping basket. Then bookmark the page (an easy command in your browser) so you can easily return after you've considered other possibilities; to find the carted items still there later, you'll need to have cookies enabled in your browser software. You can also open a new window on your browser to continue your shopping on other sites.

5. Use available comparison tools. If you've zeroed in on two or three models, use a shopping bot that allows you to compare features and prices. (For details on shopping bots, see "Bots make comparison shopping easier," page 74.)

6. Look for sales. If it's a bargain you're after, try running sales at www.shoppinglist.com. The site lets you search by ZIP code, category, brand, or store.

7. Know when to cut your losses. When shopping online, it's easy to get sucked into a time warp. If you're having trouble finding a particular item, it may be better to log off and try again later—or perhaps head for the mall.

for that particular category. The search should be well cross-referenced and flexible enough to tolerate minor misspellings, missing hyphens, or partial product names. Matches, or "hits," should be sensibly prioritized. Ideally, the search feature should be accessible from every page, with no extra clicking required.

A good site will offer options to sort, screen, and compare lists of products, and have links that work—and no dead ends.

ORDERING AND CANCELING. The overall process should leave customers feeling confident that they ordered the item they wanted at the price they intended to pay.

The better sites offer a "cart" or other way to collect and hold items while shopping, without a customer's having to register. The cart information should track product names, numbers, and prices, and keep a running subtotal (including shipping and handling costs).

Sites should indicate up front when an item is out of stock, and make it easy to change the quantity of each item ordered and to remove unwanted items. You should see a simple, clear, short order form (one to two pages). If any information is missing from the form, the site should alert you and clearly identify and pinpoint what needs to be filled in. Also, it should be clear when an order will actually be placed and how to cancel an order both before and after placing it.

ADVERTISING CLUTTER. This is applicable only to sites advertising products from businesses other than their own. The better sites are ad-free, have ads that are not "hidden" or disguised as editorial content, or have ads that are minimally intrusive (no animation or rolling text; ads located off in a corner).

Hallmarks of excellent content

Here is what CONSUMER REPORTS looks for when it rates online shopping sites. For a look at the e-Ratings, see page 86.

At the better sites, merchants should offer a breadth of product categories and a depth of product choices appropriate to their business. There is a lot of useful information about individual products to help the customer make purchasing decisions. There are special features that take advantage of interactive technologies and make shopping online easy and satisfying.

BREADTH OF PRODUCT CATEGORIES. The range of product categories offered is appropriate to the type of merchant. Keep in mind that specialty sites tend to have a more limited range of product categories. Larger, mall-type sites usually offer an expanded range of categories. When relevant, the site describes how its product offerings online compare with its company's retail store and print-catalog offerings, and what's available from other e-tailers.

DEPTH OF PRODUCT CATEGORIES. The number of product choices within a category should be suitable to the type of company/merchant. Specialty sites are expected to have a more limited number of products, while larger, mall-type sites, department stores, warehouse-type stores, and so on should offer an expanded number of products. When relevant, the site compares its product offerings online with its company's retail store and print-catalog offerings, and those of other e-tailers.

PRODUCT INFORMATION. Pertinent, descriptive product information is provided in a concise way. The better sites clearly describe each product and what is included with it, to differentiate it from other choices. They offer additional useful information, such as professional or customer reviews, links to related products, links to information about authors and artists, and more, as appropriate. Good sites also show a good-quality picture of the product, and list prices clearly.

PERSONALIZATION/CUSTOMIZATION. There are features that personalize the site for individual customers and that make the shopping experience (and especially subsequent shopping experiences) more efficient, effective, and perhaps more fun. The better sites make it easy for customers to use personalized/customized features, but also offer an option for customers to easily opt out of these.

Good sites make sensible product suggestions in an unobtrusive manner, based on what the customer is looking at or has previously purchased. They keep records of previous purchases or "favorite products" for easy reordering. In addition, they make it easy for customers to set up a personal account to store billing information for easier ordering next time.

Sites should also offer an address book, gift registry, and/or reminder calendar when appropriate. And customers should be able to search for products based on their own criteria when applicable.

SPECIAL SERVICES. These are helpful services that aid the customer. The best sites ask if the purchase is a gift, and offer gift-wrapping and gift cards either free or at a reasonable price. They also offer to hide the price of a gift on the invoice.

UNIQUE FEATURES. These are distinctive features that take advantage of interactive technologies and make shopping online a worthwhile experience—for example, music sites that let customers hear music samples, book sites that let customers read book excerpts, and clothing sites that provide a representative body model to "try on" clothes.

The better sites offer useful, not gratuitous, features that work.

'BOTS' CAN MAKE COMPARISON SHOPPING EASIER

Price-comparison services called shopping bots (as in "robots") help you find the best prices for the products you're interested in buying online. Be as precise in your search as possible, specifying the type of product, the model, and the manufacturer, if you can.

No one bot is best for all purchases; many specialize in selected categories, such as computers or music. And be aware that these sites usually have commercial relationships with merchants they recommend. Here are the major shopping bots to check out:

www.amazon.com offers price comparisons within the "all products" category of its search box. Goods sold directly by Amazon are listed before those sold by other merchants.

www.consumerworld.org has its own price-comparison search and links to other shopping bots.

www.jango.com, part of the Excite search engine, allows

you to sort by price. It also lists shipping and handling charges.

www.mysimon.com lists 13 product categories. You can sort results by price.

www.shopfind.com lets you search for an item without first choosing a product category. It provides brief product descriptions.

www.shopper.com, part of CNET, a web site that focuses on computer news and product reviews, searches for computers, consumer electronics, and software. You can rank findings by price and find information on shipping charges, availability, and merchant phone numbers.

www.webmarket.com, the shopping channel of www.go2net.com, lets you search for products in 22 categories, including seasonal merchandise and weddings. You can rank your specific listings by price and check product availability.

Online gift shopping

Shopping for gifts online can be quick, easy, and convenient. Many sites handle returns and exchanges as well as any bricks-and-mortar store. Here are some of the services you'll see when shopping for gifts online.

GIFT REGISTRIES. Many sites offer special gift registries for easy browsing and item selection. Gift givers are usually required to enter a special registrant number or simply the name and address of the registered recipient. When selecting a gift for big occasions (baby showers, weddings, etc.), this feature can save a time-consuming trip to the store.

Signing up with a registry can help gift receivers avoid duplicates or unwanted gifts (provided gift givers check the registry) and even get you money-saving offers. But it does compromise your privacy. Information you may want to keep private is readily exposed to the world. And the information can be sold to other companies for direct sales or other market purposes. Check online gift registries' privacy policies.

Online registries operated by retailers such as Hecht's *(www.hechts.com)* can expedite gift giving.

SHIPPING-TIME ESTIMATIONS AND SHIPPING OPTIONS. To ensure on-time delivery, look for sites that can estimate how long an order will take to arrive at its destination using standard shipping. Many of the best sites provide that information and offer two-day express or overnight delivery (helpful if you wait until the last minute to order a gift).

GIFT WRAPPING AND CARDS. Look for free or low-cost gift cards (beyond the standard gift message printed on the packing slip), so you can include a personal greeting with your gift. Some sites offer low-cost wrapping or special gift boxes, while others will wrap or box your gift free of charge with a minimum total purchase.

GIFT CERTIFICATES OR "GIFT MONEY." These features (such as Flooz online gift dollars) are offered by many sites. Make sure the gift certificate or money will remain valid for at least six months from date of purchase, so your gift recipient has plenty of time to make a decision. Many sites offer specially wrapped or boxed gift certificates and will enclose a card bearing your personal message.

EXCEPTIONAL RETURN POLICIES. In the event your gift isn't perfect, you'll want the recipient to be able to return it easily. Look for web sites that let you return anything, for any reason, within a minimum of 45 days. Also, look for sites that include postage-paid, pre-addressed envelopes or address labels with all orders for easy returns, or that allow online orders to be returned to bricks-and-mortar counterparts for exchange or refund, with no questions asked.

OMISSION OF GIFT PRICE ON THE PACKING SLIP. A few sites will omit the price of your gift on the packing slip enclosed with the item; that's a nice touch.

INTERACTIVE GIFT FINDERS. Some web sites have cool interactive gift finders that help you pick the right gift for that special person. They inquire about your gift recipient (usually based on what's offered at the site), let you indicate a price range, and then suggest a few gift ideas based on that information.

Protecting your credit

If your credit-card number is stolen online, you have the same protections you do if it's stolen offline: If you report the theft soon after you discover it, you are liable for only $50, even on international transactions. Although not required by law, some web merchants will reimburse that $50, with the credit-card company paying the rest. (Check buying or ordering information on individual sites.)

But what if you think a web merchant has misrepresented a product? For example, that cordless phone you ordered was advertised as a digital spread-spectrum model, but it isn't. Your protection and recourse are the same as if you ordered by catalog. Unfortunately, if the merchant, web or otherwise, is not in your state or within 100 miles of your home, some protections won't apply. For example, you may not be able to withhold payment to your credit card company if you have a dispute with this merchant over the quality of the phone. But in practice, many credit-card issuers will try to mediate, or will at least credit your account until the dispute is settled. If that doesn't work, you'll have to contact your state attorney general's office or local consumer-protection office to file a complaint.

AUCTIONS ONLINE

Online auctions can be a bargain hunter's paradise. Playing safe and bidding smart can help you avoid misrepresentation and fraud.

Has there ever been a more potent marriage between technology and shopping than the phenomenal rise of online auctions? Tapping the Internet's global reach and ability to connect buyer and seller instantaneously, auction web sites—from niche players that specialize in Beanie Babies to megaemporiums such as Amazon.com and eBay—can help you locate more hard-to-find merchandise in a few minutes at your computer keyboard than you could in a lifetime of hopping from flea market to garage sale. See page 95 for CONSUMER REPORTS' e-Ratings of popular auction sites.

The market leader, eBay, which got its start selling Pez dispensers just five years ago, has more than 22 million registered users, lists some 5 million items for sale daily, and rings up $5 billion in annual revenue. The mass merchandiser J.C. Penney and the specialty-gift retailer The Sharper Image have climbed aboard the online-auction bandwagon. The auction house Sotheby's has opened some of its sales to online bidding. By 2003, it has been forecast, total online-auction revenues will jump to nearly $20 billion.

Yet for all the hoopla, the fraud and misrepresentation that plague real-world auctions are also common online. According to the Federal Trade Commission, the number of fraud complaints has soared from around 100 in 1997 to nearly 11,000 last year. The National Consumers League, a nonprofit watchdog group that independently logs online-auction abuses, reports that the most common problem plaguing this new shopping medium is that buyers fail to receive items they bought and paid for, with an average loss of $326 per botched transaction. The nonstop auction action is also taking a human toll. According to the Center for On-Line Addiction, an organization that counsels people with compulsive disorders related to Internet overexposure, some 15 percent of clients seeking treatment are online-auction junkies.

Sizing up the seller

Big online-auction sites, such as Amazon, AuctionAddict, BidBay, eBay, and Yahoo!, operate what are arguably the world's most democratic commercial venues. Anyone with something to peddle—from upscale retailers and purveyors of rare collectibles to amateur pack rats and lowly liquidators of discontinued or distressed merchandise—is welcome to list his or her wares. But if everyone can play, how can you know who's not playing fair?

Both buyers and sellers operate behind a veil of anonymity that the auction sites are scrupulous to preserve. Sellers identify themselves by a screen name—"gailforce 50," for example, recently offered an auto part at eBay, while over at BidBay, "bidorbuy" was peddling Asian antiquities from his base in Bombay, India. Want to know more about them? The auction sites' disclaimers state bluntly that it's up to you to find out for yourself. "The community is . . . self-policing," says eBay.

To date, the courts have upheld the right of the auction sites to be held harmless for misdeeds committed by sellers. In a recent case heard by the Superior Court in San Diego, for example, the judge ruled that eBay was not obligated to reimburse unsuspecting bidders who

Let the buyer beware, warns eBay (www.ebay.com), the No. 1 online auction site.

DOING YOUR BIDDING

While most sites offer the traditional highest-bid-wins auctions, many sites also offer variations on the basic theme. Whichever format you face, your best bidding strategy is to enter the minimum price required to get started. Then take advantage of the proxy-bidding capability auction sites offer to register incrementally higher bids up to your predetermined maximum.

Reserve-price auctions. These allow the seller to set a minimum acceptable bid that must be met for a sale to occur. Potential buyers are alerted to the existence of a reserve price, but the amount remains confidential. If no one meets the reserve, there's no sale. Although many visitors to Consumer Reports Online said they find reserve-price auctions frustrating, they're worth considering for items you believe have measurable monetary value as opposed to more elusive collector value.

Dutch auctions. With these, sellers are given a quick way to dispose of large batches of identical items. The seller lists a minimum price and the number of units for sale. Bidders specify a price and the number they're willing to buy. All winning bidders pay the same amount per item, which is the lowest successful bid. Here's how a scenario might play out: A seller has 10 computers for auction at $1,000 each. Ten people bid the $1,000 minimum for one computer each. In this case, all 10 bidders are winners. Now, suppose five people bid $1,250 for one computer each and 10 others bid $1,000. Because demand exceeds supply, the higher bidders are guaranteed a computer. The others will

go to the earliest $1,000 bidders. The final price for each computer will be $1,000, since all winning bidders pay the same amount.

Private auctions. The identity of bidders remain anonymous. At the conclusion of the sale, the identity of the winner is revealed only to the seller.

Reverse auctions. These put bidders in control by enabling them to indicate the maximum they're willing to pay for goods like home electronics and services ranging from airline fares, hotel rooms, and rental cars to home-equity loans, mortgages, and long-distance phone service. The seller then decides whether to go ahead with the deal. Priceline.com is synonymous with the "name-your-own-price" concept. But others, such as eWanted.com and iWant.com, bring together businesses that want you as a customer, too.

Express auctions. Following the typical highest-bid-wins format but often lasting an hour or less, these are popular because they create a sense of immediacy.

Falling-price auctions. These resemble a department-store clearance rack, so it's not surprising they're a staple at sites such as *www.auction.jcpenney.com*. The seller sets the price for multiples of the same item, and the bids get lower over time until all the items are gone. If you bid early at the opening price, you win. If you watch and wait for the price to drop, there are fewer items available. The deeper the discount, the greater the risk of ending up empty-handed.

paid shady vendors thousands of dollars for phony sports memorabilia. But there are steps you can take to protect yourself.

CHECK THE SELLER'S FEEDBACK RATING. Each of the major third-party auction sites maintains a forum where buyers can rate and post comments about their experiences doing business with a given seller (and vice versa). The comments, usually grouped by positive, negative, and neutral, are aggregated over the most recent seven-day, 30-day, and 180-day period, giving potential new buyers an opportunity to detect improvement or deterioration in the seller's recent performance. While a record of experience can be helpful, it's hard to know just how much credence to give the assessments of other strangers.

Harder to gauge is what a buyer might expect from a seller who has no feedback ratings at all. When CONSUMER REPORTS informally surveyed the feedback scores of 125 sellers at five top online-auction sites recently, we found that 30 percent had no buyer ratings.

To help lend credibility to new sellers, eBay has initiated a voluntary program that includes identity verification by Equifax Secure, a division of the credit-reporting firm. Sellers who pass muster get to display an ID Verify icon on their feedback profile.

CONTACT THE SELLER. The auction sites collect e-mail addresses for all site users when they register. They make that information available to potential bidders, usually by a direct link from the web page where the seller's goods are displayed. While intended chiefly to allow bidders to question the seller about the terms of sale and the condition of the goods being sold, direct e-mail contact may be a good way to begin sizing up the seller's trustworthiness.

Taking stock of the goods

At a real-world auction, you can normally preview the items being offered for sale and scrutinize possible buys for telltale details that the auction catalog may not fully disclose. Online auctions give you no such advantage. Indeed, some of the most popular merchandise categories—antiques, collectibles, and consumer-electronics gear—are particularly difficult to appraise from a brief description and a thumbnail photo.

READ DESCRIPTIONS CAREFULLY. Sellers are legally bound to describe their wares accurately, but that still leaves them lots of wiggle room to fudge inconvenient facts. At an eBay sale in early March, for example, a Yugo automobile was described as having "normal rust out" but being "complete," though the seller pointed out the "engine ran and car drove when parked five years ago."

Obviously, the more unique and costly the item being offered, the more painstaking you should be in verifying the seller's claims. At the very least, you should expect a full explanation of the object's physical dimensions, construction materials, and condition, including complete details on any physical or operational flaws. For electronics gear, office equipment, or household appliances, expect the seller to supply a full product pedigree, including manufacturer, make, and model number. In addition, look for specifications on any critical performance features, such as processor speed and memory for a personal computer or lens settings and shutter speeds for a camera. If you cannot find the information you need, contact the seller and have him or her put the details you need in writing before you bid.

Especially when bidding on appliances or consumer electronics, watch for anything that suggests the product is not new. Online auctions are a favorite venue for sellers to unload "reconditioned" or "like new" merchandise. "New" products come unopened in the manufacturer's original packaging and carry a full warranty. If you do bid on a reconditioned item, make sure that it has at least a 30-day warranty on all parts and labor and that you have the option to return it if it does not meet your full satisfaction.

LOOK FOR INDEPENDENT AUTHENTICATION. The potential for a buyer to overbid based on an incomplete or erroneous understanding of an item's origins or condition is greatest for collectibles. Minor flaws—even something as small as a miscentered image on a rare baseball card—can cut deeply into the object's value. Fortunately, there are price guides for nearly all genres of collectibles, and they're worth consulting before you bid. In addition, look for sellers who have had their wares independently rated by a recognized appraisal group.

Beware of bidding shams

Auction sites have a vested interest in maintaining a fair and open bidding process. All the big sites reserve the right to monitor sales and look for bidding irregularities. But they do not guarantee that problems will be caught, and with thousands of simultaneous auctions under way round-the-clock, the volume of activity greatly exceeds even their best intentions to spot violators. That leaves it up to you to be alert for common bid-rigging tricks.

SHILL BIDS. Acting in concert with cronies (or even alone using an alias), a seller will raise bids entered by legitimate buyers to up the ante. Naturally, shill bidders will drop out of the competition before the auction ends, but not before they've artificially pumped up the final sale price.

SHIELD BIDS. This scheme is most often a conspiracy among buyers attempting to ensure that auctioned goods can be purchased at a low price. One bidder bids low, while a compatriot enters an unrealistically high bid in an effort to scare off potential rivals. As the auction is about to close, the high bidder withdraws his offer, enabling the accomplice to win by default. One effective foil to this tactic is to closely monitor the closing minutes of the auction and enter a late bid after the high bidder withdraws. It's also possible to enter a proxy bid, allowing you to boost your bid automatically in the event that a previous high bid is retracted.

Some sites, like BidBay and Yahoo!, let sellers "blacklist" buyers who have engaged in

AVOIDING AUCTION PITFALLS

Online auctions require discipline and attention to detail. Here is a strategy:

Start small. Whether buying or selling, take time to learn the rules and customs before you venture into any big-money transactions. With a few small purchases or sales under your belt, you can establish a solid feedback profile that will give other auction fans confidence in your reliability as a buyer or seller.

Never bid blind. However artfully a seller describes an object, a buyer can't form a reliable judgment of quality or condition unless it is accompanied by photos and, in the case of collectibles, independent authentication. For a collectible or unique object valued at $100 or more,

insist on an unambiguous, detailed description; multiple thumbnail photographs that display the object from several angles; and independent authentication by a recognized authority.

Know how to contact the seller offline. E-mail may be a sufficient way to get more information when bidding, but it's not an adequate way to resolve the complicated issues that can arise after your bid is accepted. At the very least, you'll need a confirmed address and phone number.

Watch shipping, handling, and insurance charges. These can turn a bargain into an expensive transaction. Be sure to factor in all the supplemental costs you'll incur if your bid is accepted, and decide whether it's still a good deal.

unethical bidding in past dealings. But the best defense is for vigilant buyers and sellers to report violations to the auction site; the Federal Trade Commission (*www.ftc.gov*); and the Internet Fraud Complaint Center (*www.ifccfbi.gov*), a joint initiative of the Federal Bureau of Investigation and the National White Collar Crime Center.

Tips for buyers

Here's how to make your online-auction experience productive, efficient, and fun:

CUT THROUGH THE CLUTTER. Finding what interests you from an auction site's mountain of wares can be frustrating. In AuctionAddict's "antiquities" area alone (a category that listed on the same screen the availability of an "early 20th century Russian enamel spoon" and an "antique chamber pot"), visitors in mid-February 2001 could bid on 122,814 items from 1,102 different subgroups.

If you're in a mood to prowl the online-auction halls, give yourself a few broad goals—looking in on the baseball memorabilia listed on eBay, for example—and set a time limit for your scouting expedition. If you have your eye out for a particular item (a digital camera, say, or Wedgwood dishes) look for an auction site that showcases a deep inventory in that specialty. Most sites list the number of items being offered in each category. Then click through to the subcategory where you're likely to find the item you seek, and type the name of the object

WHERE TO TURN FOR HELP

There's no end to the objets d'art people collect. Trouble is, you don't always know how much that oil painting you just inherited is worth, whether it's real or fake, or where to post it for sale. We searched the Internet for useful information sources that can help you determine value and authenticity, find auctions that cater to your interests, and simplify payment. Here are some sites we found useful:

Appraisal services. The American Society of Appraisers (*www.appraisers.org*), the Appraisers Association of America (*www.appraisersassoc.org*), and the International Society of Appraisers (*www.isa-appraisers.org*) are three of the most authoritative organizations. You'll find expert referrals for dozens of categories, including antique furniture, ceramics, clocks, coins, fine art, gems, glass, guns, jewelry, militaria, rare books, rugs, watches, and so forth. The sites provide a list of members and their areas of expertise.

Authentication services. An appraiser might not be qualified to authenticate an item but can sometimes provide a referral. Museums often are a reliable source of identification, too. Another option: Contact a reputable trade association, such as the American Numismatic Association (*www.money.org*) for coins and paper currency or the American Philatelic Society (*www.stamps.org*) for stamps. For sports cards and autographs—areas where authentication, grading, and valuation are extremely important—there's Professional Sports Authenticator (*www.psacard.com*). To obtain reliable authentication, you'll at minimum need to submit photos of the item; more likely, you'll have to bring or mail it in.

Escrow services. For a fee, these independent businesses can minimize the risk of fraud by holding a buyer's payment until that individual receives and approves of the merchandise. Some of the better known services are Escrow.com and Tradenable.com. Before using any escrow service, investigate its reliability by checking with the Better Business Bureau and state and local consumer-affairs agencies.

Auction search engines. These portals will pore through dozens, sometimes hundreds, of online auctions for the items you like, based on the search criteria you enter. Those with a wide reach include *www.auctionsa-z.com*, *www.auctionwatch.com*, and *www.internetauctionlist.com*.

you want in the search field to zero in on the auctions most relevant to you.

USE ALERTS. Instead of jumping from auction to auction in pursuit of a rare bauble, you can allocate your time more efficiently by using a search engine like AuctionWatch (*www.auctionwatch.com*). This portal-like site can pore over dozens of online auctions simultaneously to locate desirable items, based on the search terms you enter. Most individual auction sites will also let you create a personal page that can track all of your bidding activity, alert you when items you want become available, and even bid automatically on your behalf.

CHECK PRICES BEFORE YOU BID. In the fluid, seesaw competition to outbid rivals, it's easy to overpay. Auction hounds responding to CONSUMER REPORTS' invitation to share their online-bidding experiences warned especially about the dangers of paying too much for items sold as new. To improve your chances of getting a good deal, it's important to research prices carefully before you bid. Comparison shopping sites such as comparenet.com, eCompare.com, and mySimon.com can provide a quick reality check on most common consumer products that show up in auctions. Use those prices as the upper limit for your bidding. For collectibles, check a price catalog that specializes in the goods you are considering.

USE PROXY BIDDING. Online auctions can run as long as several weeks, so it hardly makes sense to hang around until the virtual gavel falls to see if your bid prevails. Fortunately, the auction sites make it easy to stay in the action by offering a proxy feature that does your bidding for you.

Called Bid Butler at uBid.com and Bid-Click at Amazon.com, proxy bidding lets you enter an initial offer for an item you want and, at the same time, set an upper limit for how much you'd be willing to bid. Your maximum bid is kept confidential throughout the sale. As other bidders raise the ante, your bid is automatically boosted by the minimum amount needed to remain top bidder. Your bidding ends when your limit is reached, so you'll never pay more than you want or than is absolutely necessary to win.

By putting your bidding on cruise control, you can avoid falling prey to a common—and legal—online-auction ruse called sniping. As an auction reaches its end, snipers zero in to outbid the current leader by entering a last-minute offer that's just high enough to win. Sniping has proved such an effective strategy at eBay, in fact, that companies such as eSnipe.com and iSnipeIt.com have developed software and special high-speed Internet services that let customers improve their chances of getting a winning bid entered just under the wire.

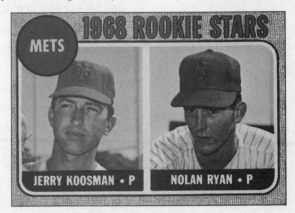

Vintage baseball cards are among the collectible items that are auctioned on the web.

AUCTIONING OFF COLLECTIBLES

Online auctions, of course, can be richly rewarding for sellers. If you're planning to auction off a collectible:

◆ Time the auction so that it extends over two weekends, when online-auction activity is especially brisk.

◆ Include a photograph. You'll need a scanner, but photos are easy to upload and most auction sites take you through the process step-by-step.

◆ Establish a "reserve," or minimum, price for items that have a verifiable monetary value, such as a baseball card. Bidders are informed that there is a reserve price, but the amount is confidential. If no one meets the reserve, there's no sale.

◆ Don't be afraid to telephone a bidder to resolve sticking points.

◆ Specify payment terms. For expensive items, customers might feel more secure—and thus more likely to bid—if you use an escrow service, an independent business that holds the money until the buyer receives and approves the item.

◆ Leave feedback. The feedback forum is the only way of knowing whether the individuals you're dealing with have been trustworthy in the past.

Sealing the deal

Even the best auction purchase can unravel if you fail to take the right steps to ensure that your treasure arrives safely before the seller pockets your payment.

PAY BY CREDIT CARD. The simplest and generally the safest way to pay for your auction winnings is with a credit card. The card issuer will credit your account if you don't receive your merchandise or if the goods received are damaged or not as described in the original listing.

USE AN ESCROW SERVICE. Many sellers who lack merchant accounts that let them accept charge cards insist that payment be made through personal check, cashier's check, money order, or cash on delivery. That's a poor choice for buyers paying more than a few dollars for their auction winnings.

There is now a better payment option that can protect the interests of both parties. Independent escrow services, such as Escrow.com and Tradenable.com, accept credit-card, check, or money-order payments from the buyer. The money is released to the seller only after the buyer receives and approves of the merchandise shipped from the seller. Fees usually run no more than 5 percent of the item's selling price.

Similar services, including Amazon.com Payments, Billpoint, PayPal, and Yahoo! PayDirect, allow buyers and sellers to send and receive money online from an account that draws upon the buyer's credit card or bank account. Registered users can send payments by e-mail simply by keying in a dollar amount on an online form. The service is generally free to buyers; sellers pay a modest fee. Another nice feature: When you use one of the proprietary payment systems, the sponsoring site may provide free fraud insurance up to a specified limit.

BUYING TRAVEL ONLINE

A world of travel deals can be had with a few clicks of a mouse. The challenge for "book-it-yourselfers" is recognizing when the web is a useful tool and when it's not.

The Internet has changed the way consumers research and pay for travel. By going online, consumers now have access to the systems that were once exclusive to travel agents and airline reservations clerks. Early on, the main travel-related attraction of the web was cheap airline tickets. Now consumers are spending millions online buying vacation packages–trips that integrate several travel components into one price.

To meet the demand for online travel information and bookings, a large number of travel sites have sprung up. You'll see two major types of travel sites: those not affiliated with travel-service providers such as airlines and hotels, and the "branded sites" that are.

Nonaffiliated travel sites

When it comes to booking air travel, nonaffiliated sites usually list a flight with an attractively low price as a first choice (most systems rank flights by fares, from lowest to highest). But these low fares sometimes entail wildly impractical itineraries. For example, when Consumer Reports Travel Letter asked a site for a low round-trip fare between New York and Chicago, it first offered a US Airways trip totaling eight legs. It included stops in Syracuse, N.Y., Buffalo, N.Y., and Philadelphia in each direction, with a total flight time on the outbound journey of 11 hours, 29 minutes (of course, that's if all flights operated on time). Thus nonaffiliated travel sites should not be used without cross-referencing from other sources, such as rival sites, airlines, or travel agents.

The two so-called travel supersites–Expedia, a Microsoft venture that is being sold to USA Networks, and Travelocity–are good first stops for consumers new to researching and booking travel on the web. If you're a web-savvy consumer, these sites offer a host of advanced tools and features as well as rich content that you may find helpful, including articles, travel advice, and myriad links to other travel-related web sites.

EXPEDIA (*www.expedia.com*). Microsoft has redesigned this site's home page and added new features to the site to make it easier to navigate. When you arrive at Expedia you can immediately book a flight, reserve a room, or rent a car. Simply click and follow the instructions and chances are you'll never get lost thanks to its new tool bar with clearly labeled tags.

TRAVELOCITY (*www.travelocity.com*). Clearly indicated links on the home page take you through the steps of finding and booking a flight, finding and renting a car, and finding and reserving a hotel room. It too has a fare-watching feature: Tell it your most traveled routes and it will let you know the best fares each time you log in.

Other big nonaffiliated sites–including Biztravel.com, Cheaptickets.com, Onetravel.com, and Trip.com–provide pricing for air travel, hotel, and car-rental. But these sites tend to have less informational content and provide fewer tools than the supersites.

BIZTRAVEL.COM (*www.biztravel.com*). A very clean, easy-to-follow home page makes this site easy to navigate. Features include a weekly briefing for business travelers that includes information on new flights added to a carrier's schedule or hotel-policy changes, for instance. You'll also find flight tracking, frequent-flyer mile tracking, and links to other related sites, including OANDA, a currency-converter. It's easy for the mobile professional to stay connected through Biztravel Unwired. You can access Biztravel's key services, such as flight status and schedules, and even book a flight on a handheld device.

CHEAP TICKETS (*www.cheaptickets .com*). Less content-oriented, this site has become one of the top four independent travel sites, not by having bells and whistles, but by offering great deals. Cheap Tickets offers 500,000 nonpublished discount airfares on over 35 airlines. It also offers deals on rental cars, hotel accommodations, and cruises.

TRAVEL-BUYING TIPS

Here's a few tips for getting the most out of shopping for travel online:

◆ Don't just log onto one site; compare results from different sites against each other, and against outside sources, such as travel agents or airlines. Call a hotel directly to see how the price on the web compares with their direct quote.

◆ Don't confuse web-site ads with actual listings.

◆ The earlier you book, the better: Sites offer better options weeks in advance. You can also secure web-only discounts for busy travel periods from car-rental sites and others.

◆ If you often book the same route, it helps to cross-reference timetables from the airlines serving it (available online, in ticket offices, or at the airport).

◆ Flexibility is essential; try a range of times and alternative airports (airline timetables and Internet sites provide the airport codes).

◆ Try not to book electronic tickets on short notice; if you input a misspelled name, there may not be a record of your e-ticket, and you could be out of luck.

◆ Note that airlines do not treat all passengers equally. For rebooking or canceling flights, compare the fees charged by web sites, travel agencies, and airlines.

◆ Write down (or print out) confirmation numbers when you book online. Take these with you to the rental-car counter, hotel, or airport.

WEB DISCOUNTS
Some hotel and car rental companies offer discounts of 10 to 20 percent for online bookings. Some airlines offer web-only discount airfares, either posted on the site or e-mailed to those customers who sign up for the special services.

ONETRAVEL (*www.onetravel.com*). It's easy to find deals on this site. Its airline reservation system, Farebeater, lets you shop for published fares based on your criteria and then will offer a lower alternative fare. It also offers discounted White Label flights on domestic and international airlines, but you won't know the airline or certain itinerary information until after you've booked. The HotelWiz feature searches more than 51,000 hotels, uncovering discounted rates at many of them. This site is also packed with news and tips from experts on destinations as well as advice on how to get the best travel deal and how to interact with the airlines.

TRIP.COM (*www.trip.com*). A bit hipper than others, Trip.com is not deep. The usual trip planner section allows you to research and book airfares and hotels. But destination guides, for example, fall short of the competition in content and range of covered locales. The "Traveler's Newsstand" and "Marketplace" are both helpful in theory but don't always deliver the information you want. Basically, this site still needs to fill in the blanks. One effective feature, however, is the "Flight Tracker," which allows you to track any flight as it takes off, flies, and lands, using either a real-time onscreen map or regularly updated text–say, "153 miles SW of LaGuardia."

Provider sites

These sites from travel-service providers like airlines and hotels also let you scout prices, look for specials, and find information about specific travel providers. You just have to keep in mind that each site has a point of view. You can book online on many of them, and they can be a good starting point before shopping for rates and fares.

AIRLINES. Neary all major airlines have web sites from which you can book flights directly,

ONLINE TRAVEL TOOLKIT

The following is a list of some of the tools you can expect to find if you book travel online:

Airfare comparisons. Travel supersites as well as some of the smaller sites will offer fare finders, which will deliver quotes of the lowest fares on all major airlines to most destinations worldwide.

Hotel finders. The rate comparisons are handy, but depending on the site, listings may skew toward budget and tourist hotels or those in the first-class and deluxe category—but rarely both.

Rental-car finders. Just plug in your destination, arrival/departure details, and car class, and you'll get a breakdown of the best rates from the top companies in the business.

Last-minute deals. If you've got a flexible schedule, you can grab some great travel deals.

Loyalty-program tracking. Supersites as well as some airline sites let you track your miles in one place. You'll

need to register for this service.

Fare minders. Just plug in a few cities to which you'd like a good airfare, and the site will notify you via e-mail when a low fare becomes available. This kind of service used to be offered by just the supersites, but smaller web sites are beginning to offer this service.

Flight tracking. If you've got a flight number and a date, you can check the arrival and departure status of flights on major carriers. Most large travel sites as well as airline web sites offer this function.

Destination guides. Most major sites have online destination guides that cover the major tourist cities. You may have to do some extra digging to find information on out-of-the-way locales.

Weather reports. Most major sites provide a link to one of the major weather Internet sites, where you can often get three- to five-day forecasts for most destinations around the world.

and most of these sites list online-only specials as well. Several, such as United Airlines and American Airlines, have free e-mail newsletters to inform subscribers of sales and special offers, usually for last-minute travel. In addition, to counter the discount travel sites, six U.S. airlines (America West, American, Continental, Northwest, United, and US Airways) have joined together to create their own discount site, Orbitz.com, which began taking reservations in mid 2001. It is expected to draw fares from more than 30 airlines. See e-Ratings of the sites of several airlines on page 86.

Airlines are also linking with Internet service providers to offer rewards and discounts. In 2000, American Airlines and America Online launched AOL AAdvantage, a miles-reward program that allows consumers to earn miles either by shopping online with AOL-affiliated merchants or through travel on American Airlines. Miles accumulated can then be used in exchange for travel or merchandise.

AUCTION ALERT

According to the National Consumers League, auctions are the No. 1 category of Internet fraud—and that includes the auctioning of airline tickets and frequent-flier miles. Look out for "sellers" claiming they have miles that are about to expire. Once they receive money from an eager bidder, they can claim the airline won't let them sell the miles. Other scenarios to avoid are people selling "nonrefundable but transferable" tickets or too-good-to-be-true travel packages.

You can protect yourself. Always ask for more details before sending money, and verify flight and/or sailing times with travel vendors to ensure the seller's on the up and up. Hold payment in an Internet escrow account until you get what you paid for (iEscrow.com provides this service).

HOTELS AND RESORTS. All the large hotel chains have web sites that allow online booking. Most offer descriptions of the properties and their amenities as well as photos. More sites are beginning to add new multimedia features like video and 360-degree virtual tours.

BED-AND-BREAKFASTS. There are thousands of individual property web sites that offer photos and descriptions. These often do not offer online booking. There are sites that allow you to search hundreds of listings with descriptions of the properties and the ability to book online.

RENTAL PROPERTIES. You can pursue online listings to find the right villa, condo, beach property, or ski house.

RENTAL CARS. These sites offer information about pricing and fleets as well and may sometimes offer discounts for booking online. See page 97 for e-Ratings of several large rental companies.

TRAINS AND BUSES. Check schedules and buy tickets and passes on sites operated by Amtrak, Greyhound, Eurorail, and others.

CRUISE LINES. You can explore itineraries, ship configurations, and ports-of-call. You're better off booking through an agency or a cruise broker, though. See page 97 for e-Ratings of cruise-line sites.

CRUISE BROKERS. Many are established cruise names, others are web-only outfits. While the search features are limited, the major cruise providers and cruise lines themselves all have sites with detailed itineraries information. Most do not offer online booking, but do provide e-mail reservation forms.

CONSUMER REPORTS E-RATINGS

CONSUMER REPORTS regularly evaluates online shopping sites. Complete findings are posted at *www.ConsumerReports.org*. The Ratings here were current as of July 2001. Here is an overview:

Sites are selected based on sales volume, site traffic, and popularity or relevance in a particular category. Some sites are included simply because they are of particular interest to consumers. To rate each site, we follow a consistent shopping technique—browsing for products, looking for specific items and features, placing an order, and so forth. All site URLs have the www. prefix.

We give an **overall score** that sums up the excellence of a site's policies, usability, and content, and how these elements combine to create an efficient and productive online shopping experience. The overall score is not necessarily an average of the site scores for policies, usability, and content. If one characteristic of the site is exceptional, the site may receive a higher overall rating, and if one of the components is far below standard, the site may receive a lower overall rating.

The **policies** judgment reflects our evaluation of the quality and clarity of a site's explanation of security, privacy, shipping, return, and customer-service policies. At the minimum, all sites are expected to process customer information by using secure servers and to permit customers to easily keep their names off mailing lists. Companies receive higher scores if they: have relatively inexpensive shipping charges; promise to cover the first $50 of any fraudulent charge resulting from a site transaction; do not share customer information with third parties unless the customer agrees; offer a 100 percent satisfaction guarantee with a full refund.

The **usability** judgment evaluates how easily and efficiently a shopper can browse the site for products, search for certain items, and place an order. The content judgment evaluates the extent of product categories and choices within those categories; the quality and amount of product information given; and the availability of useful personalization/customization, special services, or unique features.

E-Ratings in this section

PRODUCTS

Legend: ● ◐ ○ ◑ ● — Better ⟵⟶ Worse

Apparel

WEB SITE	OVERALL SCORE	POLICIES	USABILITY	CONTENT	COMMENTS
Bluefly *bluefly.com*	◐	●	◐	◐	Bluefly prides itself on being a "virtual company" and has no retail stores. The web site focuses on off-price designer apparel and home accessories. With very good privacy, security, and return policies, this site offers a satisfying shopping experience.
Eddie Bauer *eddiebauer.com*	◐	◐	○	◐	This company offers women's, men's, and children's apparel; footwear; and accessories online. This site has a very good privacy policy and offers live chat with a customer-care representative.
Gap *gap.com*	◐	◐	◐	◐	This site has a very good privacy policy. Helpful features include an address book, a reminder service, and a gift finder. Well-organized, sensible product categories and constant menus make browsing especially efficient.
JCPenney *jcpenney.com*	○	○	○	◑	This site has very good security and return policies. There's a large selection of clothing, and special features like an address book and gift finder.
J. Crew *jcrew.com*	◐	○	◐	◐	Good organization and a clear, contemporary design make it very easy to browse through the clothing here. There are clearance and weekly sales sections, and a helpful gift guide. Sensible suggestions are made for related items.
L.L. Bean *llbean.com*	◐	○	◐	◐	It's easy to browse and search for clothing and other products, but pictures tend to be blurry. You can have a live chat online with customer-service reps for help. Links to information, such as details about product materials, add interest.
Lands' End *landsend.com*	◐	◐	○	●	The Lands' End site features women's, men's, and children's apparel; footwear; accessories; luggage and home furnishings. This site has many useful and entertaining features, including a virtual model to demo outfits.
Macy's *macys.com*	○	○	○	○	The search feature needs some improvement, and duplicate items appear in many product categories. The depth of product choices is limited, compared to other similar sites. Online orders can be returned to local Macy's stores.

Baby gear

WEB SITE	OVERALL SCORE	POLICIES	USABILITY	CONTENT	COMMENTS
Baby Depot *babydepot.com*	●	●	●	◑	This site has a number of shortcomings. There is only a limited selection of baby products, the search feature needs improvement, and the ordering process is cumbersome. Information about shipping charges is not provided until after the ordering process begins.
babystyle.com *babystyle.com*	○	○	○	◐	There is a fairly wide range of information and advice on this site, with celebrity features and much information oriented toward keeping a new mom feeling stylish. The search feature is good although its location changes from one page to the next.
RightStart.com *rightstart.com*	○	◑	◑	◐	This site has less-than-satisfactory policies. There is a large selection of baby products with thorough descriptions. Product Watch provides information about product recalls.

PRODUCTS *continued*

Books, music & videos

WEB SITE	OVERALL SCORE	POLICIES	USABILITY	CONTENT	COMMENTS
Amazon *amazon.com*	◐	○	◉	◉	This site has a huge selection of books and music, including eBooks. There are author biographies, links to other books by the author, professional reviews, and recommendations for related books. The search feature is good, and the ordering process is clear-cut but lengthy.
Barnes & Noble *bn.com*	◐	○	◐	◉	An impressive search engine, an especially large selection of out-of-print titles, and numerous links to useful information make for a satisfying shopping experience. But the policies are not as consumer-friendly as other merchants in this category.
Borders *borders.com*	○	◐	○	○	There is a huge inventory and a very good search engine at this site, but shopping here is generally unexceptional. We couldn't find a way to browse for books in much depth.
CDNOW *cdnow.com*	◐	◐	○	◉	This site provides a very satisfying shopping experience, as long as you are searching for specific music titles and artists. There is a wealth of product information and special features like personalized recommendations are offered.
EMusic.com *emusic.com*	○	○	○	○	This site has a lot of music offerings, but a very limited selection of artists, many whose names may be unfamiliar. The main categories for browsing are sensible, and the search feature is flexible.
GetMusic *getmusic.com*	⊖	⊖	○	⊖	GetMusic.com provides exposure to various types of music and also has an online store. There is a huge selection of CDs here, but compared with other sites in this category, there are few special features to enhance the shopping experience.
Half.com *half.com*	○	○	○	○	Half.com is an online marketplace where previously owned books, CDs, movies, and video games are bought and sold at discount prices. The main categories for browsing are sensible and are broken down in useful ways. Prices and inventory levels are updated every 20 minutes.
J & R Music and Computer World *jandr.com*	◐	◐	○	◉	The shopping experience here is enhanced by a generous amount of useful and interesting product information, including a glossary of technical terms. Live Help is fast and informative.
MP3.com *mp3.com*	○	○	○	⊖	This site allows users to organize and access CD and MP3 collections on the Internet. A very limited selection of CDs is available, but there are some useful customization features and lots of music news and related information.
Reel.com *reel.com*	○	○	○	⊖	Reel.com provides a wide variety of film-related information, and also offers videos for purchase through buy.com, the site's e-commerce partner. It has a huge selection of movies on DVD and VHS, and is fairly easy to navigate.

SPECIAL SECTION E-RATINGS

Better ←——————→ Worse

Computers

WEB SITE	OVERALL SCORE	POLICIES	USABILITY	CONTENT	COMMENTS
Apple *apple.com*	◒	○	◒	◒	Easy to navigate, this site has a sleek design and helpful descriptions of Apple products, with direct links to purchase them. There is a very good shipping policy, with no charge for ground shipments. But the return policy is very strict: Some items can not be returned, and others must be returned within 10 days.
Compaq *compaq.com*	○	○	○	◒	This site is fairly easy to navigate. Individual product descriptions are easy to grasp, but the limited information they offer may prove insufficient for customers who want detailed specifications.
Dell *dell.com*	○	○	○	○	This site offers a large selection of Dell and third-party products. Clear-cut browsing categories make it easy to know whether you want to look further. Fairly extensive support for Dell products is available. A visit offers a satisfying shopping experience.
Gateway *gateway.com*	◒	◒	◉	◒	Easy to navigate, with a lucid design, this site is notable for its large selection of Gateway and third-party products. User-friendly features include a comparison tool to evaluate similar products side by side. There is plenty of helpful buying advice as well as useful links to customer and magazine reviews, related products, and accessories.
Hewlett-Packard *shopping.hp.com*	○	○	○	◒	With a simple sleek design, a visit here offers a satisfying experience. But some sections do not appear to be fully integrated, making it confusing to navigate at times.
IBM *ibm.com*	◒	◒	◒	○	Sections of this site appear to be poorly integrated, making it confusing to navigate, and the search feature could use improvement. Unlike all the other sites in this category, computers in the consumer-oriented section could not be customized.

Electronic gear

WEB SITE	OVERALL SCORE	POLICIES	USABILITY	CONTENT	COMMENTS
800 *800.com*	◒	◒	◒	◒	This well-organized site offers effective browsing, thanks to helpful tools that let you sort, screen, and view products in side-by-side comparisons. There's a lot of useful product information, but the selection is not as extensive as some other merchants in this category.
Amazon *amazon.com*	◒	○	◒	◉	There is a large selection of products here, as well as product information and links to order the appropriate batteries. While there are interesting categories for browsing, products listed cannot be compared side-by-side.
Circuit City *circuitcity.com*	◒	◒	◒	◒	A large selection, helpful product information, and side-by-side comparisons are offered at this site. Items purchased online can be returned to a local store.
Crutchfield *crutchfield.com*	◒	◉	○	◒	This site has very consumer-friendly policies, including free shipping for returns. There is a helpful tool to select car audio components, and many useful features that incorporate interactive technology.
J & R Music and Computer World *jandr.com*	◒	◒	◒	◉	This site has easy to locate policies, a price matching offer, and a huge selection of products. There is also a useful glossary of terminology for those who are less familiar with today's high-tech jargon. But the design is busy and some text is difficult to read.
Egghead.com *egghead.com*	○	○	○	○	This site has very good security and privacy policies, but a very unclear return policy. Navigation is fairly easy and there is a large selection of software available, along with helpful product information and several useful customization features.

PRODUCTS *continued*

Gardening

WEB SITE	OVERALL SCORE	POLICIES	USABILITY	CONTENT	COMMENTS
Arbor and Bloom *arborandbloom.com*	◑	◑	◑	◑	This site offers extensive plants, and a somewhat limited but specialized selection of gardening products. You'll also find tips and links to other sites. Navigation is efficient, but the search feature is not always well cross-referenced.
Smith & Hawken *smithhawken.com*	◑	○	◑	◑	The web site of this well-known mail-order gardening company has a large (though not deep) selection of products. They provide product profiles, assembly instructions, and a Q & A column.
Wayside Gardens *waysidegardens.com*	○	○	○	◑	There is an extensive selection of plants and trees, an e-mail newsletter, and links to other gardening resources. They have a very good return policy, but the Search feature needs improvement.
White Flower Farm *whiteflowerfarm.com*	○	◑	◐	○	This site offers a specialized selection of mostly plants, with some tools and supplies. You'll find growing specifications and care tips. Navigation on this site is inefficient, and the search feature needs improvement.

Gifts & flowers

WEB SITE	OVERALL SCORE	POLICIES	USABILITY	CONTENT	COMMENTS
AmericanGreetings.com *americangreeting.com*	◑	◑	◑	◉	There is a large selection of electronic and paper greeting cards offered. Gifts and gift certificates are also available, as are several useful customization features. This site has very good privacy and return policies.
Egreetings.com *egreetings.com*	◑	○	◑	◑	It is fairly easy to browse this site, which contains a large selection of unique greeting cards, many of which are animated. Gift certificates are available and a separate gift center has links to many online vendors.
Hallmark.com *hallmark.com*	○	○	○	◑	Hallmark offers a selection of greeting cards, gift baskets, candles, and collectibles, as well as flowers, gift certificates, and e-cards. The site is fairly easy to navigate, and there are useful customization features.
1-800-flowers.com *1800flowers.com*	◑	○	○	◑	In addition to flowers, this site offers gift baskets, candles, novelties, and gourmet foods. The site has a Gift Emergency feature for last-minute gifts, and a gift finder that searches for gifts by occasion, age, relationship, price, and date needed.

Legend: ● ◒ ○ ◓ ● — Better ←——————→ Worse

Health & beauty

WEB SITE	OVERALL SCORE	POLICIES	USABILITY	CONTENT	COMMENTS
Drugemporium.com *drugemporium.com*	○	◐	○	○	This site has very good security and privacy policies. The selection of health, beauty, and personal-care products is large, but not as extensive as other sites in this category. The browsing and search features need some improvement.
Drugstore.com *drugstore.com*	○	○	○	◐	This site has a very large selection of brands and products, customer reviews, and ingredient lists for some products. There are interactive worksheets for personalized health advice, and a shopping list for storing and reordering favorite products. The browsing and search features need improvement.
ibeauty.com *Ibeauty.com*	○	○	◐	○	You'll find a limited selection of high-end beauty brands and products. Its excellent shipping policy is offset by inefficient and incomplete browsing and searching features.
Sephora.com *sephora.com*	◐	◐	○	◐	Very good shipping and return policies, easy browsing, product-ingredient lists, and a huge selection of high-end beauty and personal-care lines make this site stand out. There are also interactive features, such as a gift adviser and wireless shopping with a web-enabled cell phone.

Home décor & furniture

WEB SITE	OVERALL SCORE	POLICIES	USABILITY	CONTENT	COMMENTS
Crate & Barrel *crateandbarrel.com*	○	○	◐	○	This site is organized well and browsing is easy. Thorough product descriptions and information are provided for kitchenware, linens, small furniture, and home accessories. A Gift Planner and Gift Finder enhance the shopping experience.
MarthaStewart.com *marthabymail.com*	◐	○	◐	◐	This site offers a selection of specialized home-décor products, home accessories, kitchenware and more. Product descriptions are thorough and include enlargable photos.
OurHouse.com *ourhouse.com*	◐	◐	○	◐	There is a variety of home décor items and furniture, as well as tools and hardware, with very good product information offered. The privacy policies are very good, browsing is easy, and ordering is straightforward.
Target.com *target.com*	○	○	◐	○	Easy-to-find policies, thorough product descriptions and information, and easy browsing make for an efficient shopping experience. However, the depth of product selection is often less than you'll find among others in this category.

PRODUCTS *continued*

Housewares

WEB SITE	OVERALL SCORE	POLICIES	USABILITY	CONTENT	COMMENTS
Chef's Catalog *chefscatalog.com*	○	○	○	○	This site offers a selection of cooking equipment and accessories, food and cooking articles and featured recipes. It provides thorough product descriptions, and is easy to browse. But the search engine isn't always smart.
The Company Store *thecompanystore .com*	◑	○	◑	◑	Helpful informational features such as a Comforter and Pillow guide are included, as well as an audio sales assistant. Good organization makes it easy to browse and search for products at this site.
Crate & Barrel *crateandbarrel.com*	◑	◑	◑	◑	There's an online outlet with sales items and a gift selector that allows you to sort gifts by event, theme, or price. A Reminder Service and Address Book add to shopping convenience.
Domestications *domestications.com*	○	◑	○	○	The site has a selection of bedroom, bath, kitchen and home decor items, similar to the catalog. Web sales specials are offered and there's an outlet store on the site. The security policy is very good, but the search feature has some glitches.

Office supply & mailing sites

WEB SITE	OVERALL SCORE	POLICIES	USABILITY	CONTENT	COMMENTS
FedEx *fedex.com*	○	○	◑	◑	We had trouble setting up an account, and found instructions to several services confusing. Still, a very good privacy policy, a clear-cut design, and sensible browsing categories make this an efficient site.
Office Depot *officedepot.com*	○	○	○	◑	A large selection of office supplies, interactive features, and links to business services, make for a satisfying office experience. Browsing is well organized, but the search feature needs improvement.
OfficeMax *officemax.com*	◑	◑	○	◑	This site offers a very good security policy and a low-price guarantee. A large selection of office supplies, a variety of business services, buying guides, free e-mail, and more make for a well-rounded shopping experience.
Staples *staples.com*	◑	○	◑	◑	Easy navigation and a clear-cut ordering process make shopping this site's large inventory a stress-free operation. Special features include links to business services, a business community, an online business forum, and dividend programs for small businesses.
USPS.com *usps.com*	○	◑	○	◑	The online arm of the United States Postal Service has confusing policies and no search feature. However, the design is clear-cut and browsing is well organized. For buying stamps or other postal products, this site provides a satisfying experience.

Better ● ◐ ○ ◑ ● Worse

Small appliances

WEB SITE	OVERALL SCORE	POLICIES	USABILITY	CONTENT	COMMENTS
J & R Music and Computer World *jandr.com*	◐	◐	○	◐	Although usability needs some improvement, a large selection of products, the ability to sort products by price and product name, and links to appliance accessories make this site worthwhile.
Kmart *bluelight.com*	○	○	○	○	Kmart's site on the Internet offers a respectable selection of small appliances, and provides a description of key product features. The main categories for browsing are generally sensible and the search feature is adequate.
Sears.com *sears.com*	○	◐	○	○	This site offers a low-price guarantee and most items purchased online can be returned to local Sears stores. There is useful product information, as well as cleaning and maintenance tips.
Service Merchandise *servicemerchandise.com*	○	○	◑	○	Browsing could use some improvement, but a larger selection of small appliances may make this site worth visiting. A brief description of key product features is provided along with an address book and gift registry.
Wal-Mart Online *walmart.com*	◐	◐	◐	○	Efficient browsing, good product information, and special features such as an address book, personal shopping list, and a photo center make for a satisfying shopping experience.

Software

WEB SITE	OVERALL SCORE	POLICIES	USABILITY	CONTENT	COMMENTS
Adobe.com *adobe.com*	○	○	○	◐	Adobe's web and print publishing software are available at this site, accompanied by thorough product descriptions. There are also technical guides, tutorials, and some free downloads, including the Adobe Acrobat Reader.
Beyond.com *beyond.com*	◐	◐	◐	○	This site has a very good return policy and there are no additional costs for shipping backordered items. Navigation is fairly easy and there is a large selection of software available, as well as hardware, games, and handheld computers.
Egghead.com *egghead.com*	◐	○	◐	◐	This site has very good security and privacy policies, but a very restrictive return policy. Navigation is fairly easy and there is a large selection of software available, along with helpful product information and several useful customization features.
McAfee.com *mcafee.com*	○	○	○	◐	The McAfee web site has a very good security policy and is fairly easy to navigate. Virus protection and PC security software are available, as well as a support center, message boards, manuals, and detailed product information.
Microsoft *microsoft.com*	○	○	○	◐	This site offers a selection of Microsoft software, hardware, and books. Although you can have a generally satisfying shopping experience here, it's unexceptional compared with other sites in this category.
Symantec.com *symantec.com*	○	○	◐	○	This site has a very good security policy and is fairly easy to navigate. Virus protection and Internet security software are available, as well as the latest news on computer viruses.

SPECIAL SECTION E-RATINGS

PRODUCTS *continued*

Sports & camping gear

WEB SITE	OVERALL SCORE	POLICIES	USABILITY	CONTENT	COMMENTS
Cabela's *cabelas.com*	○	○	○	○	This site has an extensive selection of hunting and fishing gear, a web bargain area, and useful links. It's easy to browse through products, but the search engine is not always smart.
Fogdog.com *fogdog.com*	○	○	○	◐	Fogdog.com offers a lot of useful product information, including buying guides, feature articles, customer reviews, and athlete's advice. It has very good security and return policies.
Orvis *orvis.com*	○	◐	○	○	This site sells clothing, home items and sporting goods with a focus on fly-fishing. Browsing for products is tedious and the search feature needs improvement.
Patagonia *patagonia.com*	○	◐	○	○	Patagonia specializes in high-tech sports clothing, and the site provides extensive product description. There is a very good privacy policy, but there are few special features to enhance the shopping experience.
REI *rei.com*	◐	◐	○	◐	This site has a vast selection of clothing and equipment for numerous sporting activities. It has easy-to-find policy statements and sensible browsing categories.
thesportsauthority.com *thesportsauthority.com*	○	○	○	○	There is a large selection of sporting goods offered here and an outlet for discounted items. But, not a lot of extra features to enhance the shopping experience.

Toys & games

WEB SITE	OVERALL SCORE	POLICIES	USABILITY	CONTENT	COMMENTS
Kbkids *kbkids.com*	◐	◐	◐	◐	This well-organized site offers a rather efficient shopping experience, along with some special interactive features. Toys can be sorted by price and other criteria, and online orders can be returned to local K-B Toys stores.
Nintendo of America *nintendo.com*	○	○	◐	○	This site offers replacement parts and accessories for all Nintendo games and systems. The ordering process is straightforward, but subcategory lists can be quite lengthy, with no helpful way to sort products.
Toys "R" Us *amazon.com*	◐	○	◐	●	There is a wide selection of toys here, with helpful categories for browsing, and good product information. There are many useful interactive features that enhance the shopping experience.
Wal-Mart Online *walmart.com*	◐	◐	◐	○	This site has a large selection of toys. Efficient browsing, good product information, and special features such as an address book, personal shopping list, and a photo center make for a satisfying experience.

SERVICES

SPECIAL SECTION E-RATINGS

Auctions

Legend: ● Better ←——→ Worse ●

WEB SITE	OVERALL SCORE	POLICIES	USABILITY	CONTENT	COMMENTS
STANDARD AUCTION SITES *These sites operate as an intermediary between independent buyers and sellers. Transactions are undertaken at your own risk; the site will not intervene in disputes.*					
Amazon.com Auctions *amazon.com/auctions*	○	◐	◐	○	This site provides a very satisfying and secure auction experience. There are many features that make bidding and listing items quite easy, including a tutorial for new users and tips for sellers.
AuctionAddict.com *auctionaddict.com*	○	○	◐	○	Although initially frustrating to navigate, this site offers a wide range of auction listings and several helpful features, including free e-mail and a community center for auction news and discussions.
BidBay.com *bidbay.com*	○	◑	○	◐	Although the policies are unclear, this site is fairly easy to use and offers many helpful features, including an image-hosting program and a bulk loader for listing multiple auctions at one time.
Biddington's *biddingtons.com*	○	◑	○	◐	Biddington's specializes in contemporary art, antiques, and fine-arts auctions. The policies are difficult to find and confusing, but the site is fairly easy to navigate and offers a large number of auction listings.
eBay *ebay.com*	●	◐	●	◐	Reasonable policies and very well-organized listings, as well as many helpful features, make eBay the outstanding site in this category. Navigation is easy, and there are discussion boards, news, articles on collecting and various auction categories, and many more features too numerous to list.
Sothebys.com *sothebys.com*	◐	◐	●	◐	This site specializes in traditional fine and decorative art, jewelry, and books. The policies are very clear and the site is very easy to use. Lots of informative articles and guides make this one of the most interesting sites in this category.
SportsAuction.com *sportsauction.com*	◐	◐	◐	◐	This site specializes in sports memorabilia, including trading cards, sports art, and autographed collectibles. There are very good privacy and return policies. Navigation is easy and there are many helpful features.
uBid.com *ubid.com*	○	○	○	◐	Consumer Exchange Auctions, Vendor Exchange Auctions, and UBid's own auctions make up the majority of those available on this site. However, these auctions are not well integrated, making browsing somewhat inefficient.
Yahoo! Auctions *http://auctions.yahoo.com*	◐	◐	◐	◐	This site offers a large number of items in a wide range of categories. The site is easy to use and has very reasonable policies. It also offers charity auctions, a black-list feature, category clubs, and more.
RETAILER SITES *These sites feature an auction option for purchasing new or reconditioned merchandise, and they usually have a return policy.*					
Egghead.com *egghead.com/aa/auctions.htm*	◐	○	◐	◐	An odd mix of auction categories is offered here, but the site is well-organized and very easy to use. Helpful features include ProductWatch, which stores frequently purchased products, and AuctionWatch which allows you to track auctions and manage your bids.
JCPenney *auction.jcpenney.com*	○	○	◐	○	This site features merchandise from JCPenney overstock, and includes women's, men's, and children's clothing and accessories, as well as home and leisure products. The site is easy to use and has a very good security policy.
The Sharper Image *http://auction.sharperimage.com*	◐	◐	○	◐	This site offers a selection of overstocked Sharper Image products, including gadgets for the home, garden, and office, and personal-care products. There are also one-of-a-kind items and collectibles. The site is easy to use and has several useful features for placing bids.
AUCTION SEARCH ENGINE *This site pores over dozens of online auctions simultaneously to locate desirable items.*					
AuctionWatch.com *auctionwatch.com*	○	○	○	◐	This unique site allows registered users to efficiently search and/or set up auctions at several sites at once. AuctionWatch.com is fairly easy to use and provides much helpful information.

TRAVEL SITES

Airlines, domestic

WEB SITE	OVERALL SCORE	POLICIES	USABILITY	CONTENT	COMMENTS
American Airlines aa.com	○	○	◐	○	Searching for and booking flights at this site is a reasonably efficient process. But browsing can be tedious and the privacy policy is unsatisfactory.
Delta Air Lines delta.com	○	○	○	○	The flight search process at this site is reasonably efficient. Information of flight status is available for wireless device customers.
Northwest Airlines nwa.com	◐	◐	◐	◐	Searching for flights is especially effective here, and there are extensive opportunities for personalization, including the ability to track fares, monitor frequent-flyer miles for all airlines, and store itineraries. This site stands out compared with others in this category.
Southwest Airlines southwest.com	○	○	○	○	Searching for and booking flights at this site is an efficient process, but limited opportunities for personalization and the lack of an e-mail address for communication with Southwest may leave customers feeling dissatisfied.
United Airlines united.com	○	○	○	◐	Although easy to navigate, this site is a mixed bag when it comes to searching for flights. There are helpful options for selecting and sorting flights based on numerous criteria, but you won't find the cost of a roundtrip flight until you piece together the legs of departing and return flights.
US Airways usairways.com	○	○	◐	○	Although you can have a generally satisfying experience here, searching for flights is an inefficient process. You won't find out the cost of a roundtrip flight until you piece together the legs of departing and return flights.

Airlines, foreign

WEB SITE	OVERALL SCORE	POLICIES	USABILITY	CONTENT	COMMENTS
Air France airfrance.com/us	○	◐	◐	○	Although policies are very good at this site, the flight-search process can be inefficient. You must register and enter a personal profile before you can book a flight.
British Airways britishairways.com	○	○	◐	○	There is a very good privacy policy at this site, as well as extensive information on the terms and conditions for booking online. But the flight-search process is limited, and browsing can be somewhat inefficient.
KLM nwa.com	◐	◐	◐	◐	KLM's partner in the United States is Northwest Airlines. All online activity for U.S.-based users of KLM's site is conducted on Northwest Airlines' site.
Lufthansa lufthansa-usa.com	◐	◐	●	○	Policy information is very difficult to find here, although the site does have a very good privacy policy. But navigation, the flight-search process, and booking can all be confusing, as you are constantly moved back and forth between the U.S. and European sections of Lufthansa's site. You must register before you can book a flight.

SPECIAL SECTION E-RATINGS

Rating legend: ● ◑ ○ ◐ ● Better ←——————→ Worse

Car rentals

WEB SITE	OVERALL SCORE	POLICIES	USABILITY	CONTENT	COMMENTS
Alamo *alamo.com*	◑	◑	◑	●	This site stands out with its easy navigation and booking, thorough vehicle descriptions, detailed information on insurance and rental contracts, and very good policies. You don't need a credit card to book online; just print the confirmation statement and bring it to the rental counter.
Avis *avis.com*	○	○	○	◑	This site has a very good privacy policy and a thorough FAQ section, along with easy browsing and flexible booking. Useful customer service features include a mechanism for tracking awards and researching Avis travel partners.
Budget *budget.com*	○	◑	○	◑	Browsing and booking are easy here. There's an interesting Tips & Guidance section and online booking discounts are offered, but the privacy policy is poor.
Hertz *hertz.com*	○	◑	○	◑	Browsing is efficient at this site, and there are some useful customer-service features. But the booking process could use some improvement, the privacy and rental policies are poor, and "special offers" have numerous restrictions tied to them.
National *nationalcar.com*	◑	◑	●	○	Inefficient, convoluted browsing and booking can make for a frustrating experience at this site. Information on cancellations is buried, and the privacy policy is poor; there is no way for a customer to opt out of having personal information shared with third parties.

Cruise lines

WEB SITE	OVERALL SCORE	POLICIES	USABILITY	CONTENT	COMMENTS
Carnival *carnival.com*	○	○	○	○	This site has a very good privacy policy, but no cancellation policy was found. Although browsing and navigation are efficient, the booking process is limited in its usefulness.
Norwegian Cruise Lines *ncl.com*	◑	○	◑	◑	This site has a very good privacy policy, a detailed cancellation policy, easy browsing, and a thorough booking process. The wealth of detailed, useful, and well-linked information on boats, cruises and destinations, along with some special interactive features, really make this site stand out.
Princess Cruises *princesscruises.com*	◑	◑	◑	○	Navigation and browsing are easy. You cannot book cruises on this site, but you can get ideas. There are some special text-based and interactive features that may make it worth a visit.
Royal Caribbean International *royalcaribbean.com*	◑	○	◑	◑	Navigation and booking are fairly easy. There is a lot of useful information about boats, destinations and more on this site.

TRAVEL SITES *continued*

● ◑ ○ ◐ ●
Better ← → Worse

Hotels

WEB SITE	OVERALL SCORE	POLICIES	USABILITY	CONTENT	COMMENTS
Choice Hotels *choicehotels.com*	○	○	◐	○	Efficient browsing, searching, and booking, plus extensive hotel information and a discount for booking online, really make this site stand out.
Hilton *hilton.com*	◐	◐	◐	◐	Inefficient browsing and booking and limited location-specific descriptions, especially about pricing, make it difficult to select a particular hotel for further investigation.
Hyatt *hyatt.com*	◐	○	◐	◐	This site contains the basics–but little more. Superficial hotel and room descriptions plus inefficient browsing and booking can make for a frustrating experience.
Marriott International *marriott.com*	○	○	◐	○	The tedious navigation here can be frustrating, but there is a wide range of hotel-room choices, plus maps, driving instructions, city facts and more. The personal profile feature is useful for repeat bookings.

Travel-related sites

WEB SITE	OVERALL SCORE	POLICIES	USABILITY	CONTENT	COMMENTS
American Express *americanexpress.com/travel*	◐	○	◐	◐	This site is packed with useful information and tools to assist you both before and during your travels. Well-organized, sensible categories make browsing especially efficient. Booking is simple, but you must register first.
CarlsonWagonlit Travel *carlsontravel.com*	○	○	◐	○	This site features a prominent airline ticket booking engine, as well as helpful tools and information to help plan vacations and arrange travel. However, booking can be somewhat inefficient.
Travelution.com *travelution.com*	◐	◐	○	◐	Very good security and privacy policies. Browsing this site is fairly easy via useful menus and links. You can plan and save an itinerary for up to four travelers, and you are able to designate the age group of each traveler.

PART 2

Plugged In

6

Personal Computing

Computer gear has become faster, easier to use, and more elegant looking. It has also become more fun. Added to the traditional word-processing, accounting, and presentation functions are capabilities that let you listen to online music, edit home movies downloaded from a camcorder, play video games, and engage in many other recreational pursuits.

Desktop computer manufacturers have developed interesting alternatives to the familiar beige box. Notable is the colorful, translucent look of the iMac and other Macintosh products. Svelte flat-panel displays, an alternative to big, clunky monitors, have begun to drop in price and gain sales momentum. Computer users on the go can take advantage of laptop models that are pizza-thin. PDAs are ubiquitous.

Computer manufacturers such as Apple, Compaq, Dell, Gateway, and IBM sell directly to consumers, through telephone orders, factory stores, tent sales, or the Internet. They offer financing programs that let consumers make monthly payments, much as they do for a car, as well as leasing programs for home-based businesses. Retail choices include computer superstores such as CompUSA and PC Warehouse, electronics superstores such as Best Buy and Circuit City, home-office superstores such as Office Depot and Staples, and warehouse clubs such as Costco and Sam's Club. According to CONSUMER REPORTS' 2000 survey of readers, buying directly from the manufacturer brings greater satisfaction.

A desktop computer bridges the realms of work and play.

UPGRADE?

You can often improve an old machine by upgrading some components, such as hard drive or memory. But if you have to spend more than $500, you're probably better off buying a new computer.

DESKTOP COMPUTERS

Even the least-expensive desktop machines deliver impressive performance. The quality of technical support may be the deciding factor for you.

The desktop computer may finally have reached a level of acceptance accorded to the TV set or refrigerator—just another appliance you use every day, not something exotic and mysterious. Signs are everywhere that replacement sales—not first-time purchases—now drive the computer market. Prices continue to drop. Fully loaded desktop systems selling for less than $1,000, a novelty a few years ago, are now common, even among established brands such as Compaq and Gateway.

Microsoft, which dominates the PC software field, was expected to release the next generation of its Windows operating system—Windows XP—in Fall 2001. The rollout was to be the first time that the consumer and business version of Windows fell under a common umbrella. Microsoft also makes application programs such as Microsoft Office for Macintosh. Macs have an operating system of their own made by Apple. The 10th generation, OS X, was released in early 2001. For more on software, see Chapter 4.

What's available

There are dozens of companies vying to put a new desktop in your home. Compaq, Dell, Gateway, Hewlett-Packard, IBM, and Sony all make Windows machines. Another contender, eMachines, has emerged as a player over the past few years with a series of budget-priced Windows systems. Apple is the sole maker of Macintosh models. Small mail-order and store brands cater to budget-minded buyers.

The critical components of a desktop computer are housed in what is called a tower. A minitower is the typical configuration. More expensive machines have a midtower, which has extra room for upgrades. A microtower is a space-saving alternative that is usually less expensive. The Apple iMac has no tower; everything but the keyboard is built into the case housing the monitor.

Price range: $500 to $2,500 (monitor often extra).

A built-in monitor helps give the Apple iMac a distinctive look.

Key features

The **processor** houses the "brains" of a computer. Its clock speed, measured in megahertz (MHz), determines how fast the chip can do calculations. In general, the higher the clock speed, the faster the computer. But not always. In our tests, a computer with an 800-MHz chip outperformed several machines driven by 1-gigahertz (GHz) chips. Manufacturers of Windows machines generally use 800-MHz to 1.7-GHz processors with one of the following names: Intel's Pentium III, Pentium 4, or Celeron, or AMD's Athlon or Duron. Celeron and Duron are lower-priced processors that are equal to higher-priced chips in many respects. Apple's Macintosh machines use 500- to 867-MHz PowerPC G3 or G4 processors, which are manufactured by Motorola. Apple has maintained that the system architecture of G4

PowerPC chips allows them to be as fast as or faster than Pentium 4s with higher clock speeds.

Almost all name-brand computers sold today have at least 128 megabytes (MB) of **RAM,** or random access memory, the memory that the computer uses while in operation. **Video RAM,** also measured in megabytes, is secondary RAM essential for smooth video imaging and game play.

The **hard drive** is your computer's long-term data storage system. Given the disk-space requirements of today's multimedia games and other types of software, bigger is better. You'll find hard drives ranging in size from 10 to 80 gigabytes (GB).

Desktop computers usually have a 100- or 133-MHz **system bus**—that's the pathway that ferries data between the processor and the rest of the computer. Older systems had a 66-MHz bus.

A **CD-ROM** drive has been standard on most desktops for the past several years. The latest drives range in speed from 32x to 52x or faster (the "x" refers to how many times faster the drive can read a disc's contents than it does "1x" CD audio). A high speed eases software

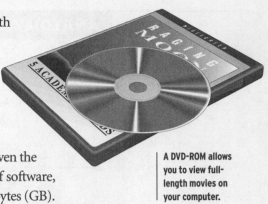

A DVD-ROM allows you to view full-length movies on your computer.

CUSTOMIZATION AND COST

The biggest manufacturers—Compaq, Dell, Gateway, HP, and IBM—let you configure a desktop computer just the way you want. Their web sites typically present menus with step-up and step-down choices. You can also place your order over the telephone. Large retailers such as Best Buy, Circuit City, CompUSA, and Staples have in-store kiosks that let you do a certain amount of customizing. The table below shows where you might start for a basic level of desktop computer, along with our recommendations for upgrades and downgrades.

COMPONENT	BASIC LEVEL	UPGRADE?	DOWNGRADE?
Processor	1 GHz	1.7 GHz. **For:** Faster speed to handle the most demanding applications. **Add:** $250.	800 MHz. **For:** Basic business applications, e-mail, etc. **Save:** $100.
RAM memory	128 MB	256 MB. **For:** Editing very large files or graphics; working with many applications at once. **Add:** $100 and up.	Not recommended.
Hard-drive size	40 GB	80 GB. **For:** Digital video editing, working with large applications, storing large amounts of data. **Add:** $100.	20 GB. **For:** Basic business applications, e-mail, etc. **Save:** $50.
Rewritable CD (CD-RW)	CD-RW, 8x write	CD-RW, 12x write. **For:** Faster backup, storage, copies of music, photos, etc. **Add:** $40.	CD-ROM only. **For:** Those with no interest in burning their own disks. **Save:** $100.
DVD-ROM drive	"Software decoding" operation	"Hardware decoding" operation. **For:** Watching movies while system runs other applications. **Add:** $60.	CD-ROM only. **For:** People who aren't videophiles. **Save:** $40.
Graphics card	32 MB of Video RAM	High-end card, 64 MB of video RAM. **For:** Smoothest, fastest performance on action games. **Add:** $80.	8 to 16 MB of video RAM. **For:** Word processing, Internet, no games. **Save:** $40.
Sound card	Analog	Digital input/output. **For:** Copying digital audio between computer and recording devices. **Add:** $40.	Not recommended.
Loudspeakers	Two-piece brand-name	Three-piece with subwoofer. **For:** Highest fidelity. **Add:** $30 and up.	Two-piece generic. **For:** Those with little interest in hi-fi music on computer. **Save:** $20.
Case	Minitower	Midtower. **For:** Extra room for upgrades. **Add:** $30.	Microtower or all-in-one unit. **For:** Those with limited office space. **Save:** $40.
Software	Simplified suite such as Microsoft Works	Professional package, such as Microsoft Office for Small Businesses. **For:** Advanced word-processing, financial, database, desktop publishing. **Add:** $100.	Makes sense only if you already have good, up-to-date applications.
Monitor	17-inch CRT	19-inch CRT or 15-inch LCD display. **For:** Games, elaborate web sites. **Add:** $200 and up.	15-inch CRT. **For:** Word-processing, other basic functions. **Save:** $100.

ANATOMY OF A DESKTOP COMPUTER

The basic building blocks of a desktop computer are a CRT monitor, a keyboard, a tower housing critical components such as the processor, and speakers. A port such as a USB port allows a printer to be attached. Digital camcorders, digital cameras, and other pieces of equipment attach to a FireWire port (not shown).

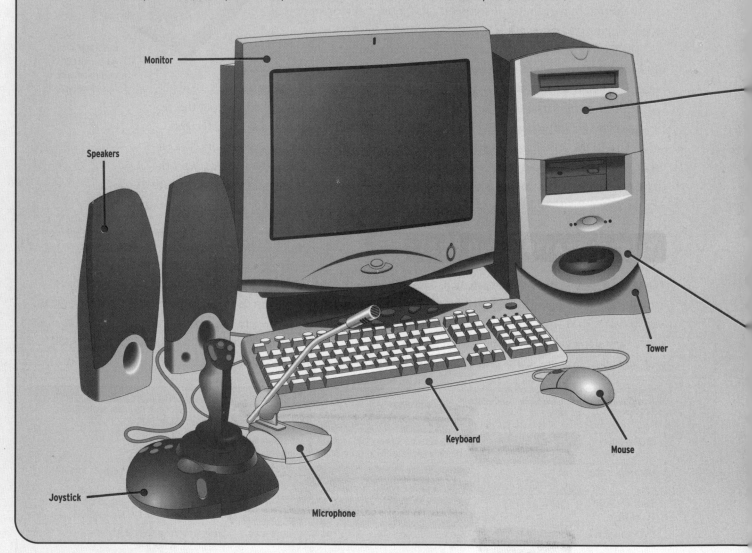

installation and multimedia game play. CD-RW (CD-rewritable) is a common step-up option that lets you create backup files or make music compilations. (See Chapter 3 for more.) **DVD-ROM** brings full-length movies or action-packed multimedia games with full-motion video to the desktop. It has replaced CD-ROM on higher-end systems. (A DVD drive will play CD-ROMs, and software can allow a CD-ROM drive to handle DVDS.) The newest in this family is the DVD-RW, which lets you transfer home-video footage to a DVD disk, or make a copy of a prerecorded DVD movie.

The floppy disk drive is where 3.5-inch diskettes are inserted, allowing you to read data from or store data to them. Apple models don't have one built in. Some floppy drives now also accommodate 120-MB cartridges; the traditional capacity of a 3.5-inch diskette is 1.44 MB, too small

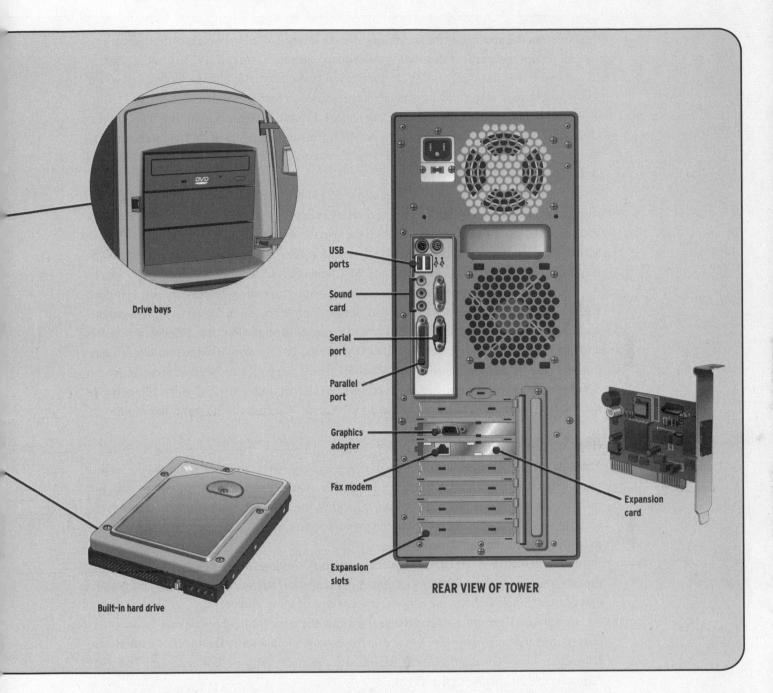

Drive bays

USB ports

Sound card

Serial port

Parallel port

Graphics adapter

Fax modem

Expansion slots

Expansion card

Built-in hard drive

REAR VIEW OF TOWER

for many purposes today. A Zip drive, another type of storage device, uses its own kind of cartridge and provides either 100 or 250 MB of capacity per cartridge. It's good for storing large files.

The computer's cathode ray tube (CRT) or flat-panel liquid crystal display (LCD) **monitor** contains the screen and displays the images sent from the graphics board—internal circuitry that processes the images. Monitors come in sizes (measured diagonally) ranging from 15 inches to 21 inches and larger. Seventeen-inch monitors are the most common. Apple's iMac comes with a built-in monitor. For more on monitors, see page 112.

A **mouse,** a small device that fits in your hand and has a "tail" of wire that connects to the keyboard, is used to move the **cursor** (the pointer on the screen). Alternatives include a mouse that replaces the ball with a light sensor; a **trackball,** which is rolled with the fingers or palm in the direction the user wants the cursor to go; and a **joystick,** used in playing computer games.

All computers come with a standard **keyboard,** although you can also buy one separately. Many keyboards have CD (or DVD) controls to pause playback, change tracks, and so on. Many also have keys to facilitate getting online, starting a search, or retrieving e-mail.

Multimedia computers for home use feature a sound system. In Windows PCs, this includes a **sound card,** often with wavetable **MIDI (musical instrument digital interface) synthesizer, speakers,** and a **microphone.** Sound systems have been part of the Mac operating system for years.

You can expect to get a **modem** rated for 56 kilobits per second (kbps) and designed to support the industry standard. This speed rating refers to how quickly information travels to your modem from the Internet, although the speed is limited by federal rules to 53 kbps. In actual practice, however, the speed rarely exceeds 50 kbps. New ways to connect to the Internet faster include cable modem and DSL (digital subscriber line). See page 18.

Parallel and **serial ports** are the traditional connection sites for printers and scanners. **USB** (Universal Serial Bus) ports, seen on all new computers, are designed to replace parallel and serial ports. **FireWire** or **IEEE 1394** ports are used to capture video from digital camcorders and other electronic equipment. An ethernet or phone-line network lets you link several computers in the household in order to easily share files, a printer, or an Internet connection. An **S-video output jack** lets you run video cables from the computer to a TV, which allows you to use the computer's DVD drive and view a movie on a TV instead of the computer monitor.

How to choose

PERFORMANCE DIFFERENCES. CONSUMER REPORTS regularly tests computers. Judged on performance alone, most desktop computers are closely matched and extremely good overall. But there are differences in connectivity, expandability, the design of the keyboard and controls, and the sound of the loudspeakers. Some manufacturers are better than others when it comes to helping consumers with problems.

RECOMMENDATIONS. You'll have to decide between Windows and Macintosh. Windows has the advantage in terms of the sheer number of compatible software applications and peripheral devices. Macintosh has the edge in terms of ease of setup and use.

CONSUMER REPORTS' reader surveys show that the typical brand repair rate for PCs purchased over the past four years was about 20 percent. Slightly more than half of readers who contacted their PC manufacturer's technical support department last year were "very" or "completely" satisfied with the service.

♦ **Ratings:** page 168   ♦ **Reliability:** page 108

THE APPLE ALTERNATIVE

To Macintosh loyalists, the dramatic comeback Apple made a few years back with the colorful, translucent iMac was proof of what they had been preaching all along—that the company makes excellent and innovative computers. The simple design and intuitive operating system of Mac desktops and laptops make setup and day-to-day computing easy, and they have consistently scored well in CONSUMER REPORTS' service and reliability surveys of desktop PCs.

MICROPROCESSOR 101: IS INTEL INSIDE?

Critical to the operation of your computer, the micro-processor, or chip, controls how fast it crunches data and runs software. You'll see it listed first in a computer's specs in advertisements, catalogs, and on store signs.

Marketing might has made Intel as important a player as the computer manufacturers themselves. Its microprocessors are in a majority of Windows-based PCs. The Pentium 4, introduced in 2000, succeeds the Pentium III at the top of its microprocessor line. The latest generation is available in speeds of 1.2 to 1.7 GHz. Celeron, Intel's line of chips designed for the value-minded home user, debuted in 1998 and now has speeds up to 900 MHz.

Intel's main competitor, AMD, took a big marketing leap in 1999 with the introduction of its Athlon chip, now available in speeds from 1 to 1.4 GHz. Compaq and other computer makers use them. AMD's budget-priced Duron chip runs at speeds up to 950 MHz.

Chip choices in Windows PCs. The choice of chips for Windows-based laptop PCs has expanded in recent years. If you're in the market for a laptop, you'll find the following chips available: Pentium III mobile processors in speeds of 650 MHz to 1 GHz and Celeron mobile processors in speeds of 700 to 850 MHz. AMD's mobile offerings are its Athlon 4 chip, at 850 MHz to 1 GHz, and its Duron chip at 800 to 850 MHz.

Chip choices in Macs. Driving Apple's Macintosh desktop machines are 450- to 876-MHz PowerPC G3 or G4 processors, made by Motorola. Apple's PowerBook laptops run on a G4 processor at speeds of 400 to 500 MHz, while its iBook laptop has a 500 MHz G3.

Macs are apt to suffer fewer hardware-software conflicts than Windows-based PCs since Apple develops both the hardware and the operating system. (Windows-based PCs use Microsoft's operating system—and various PC makers design the hardware.) Their well-integrated graphic and audio features make Macs the favored systems for graphic artists and others involved in creative fields. Macs have built-in networking, making it easy to share files or peripherals. And they have built-in capabilities for opening PC-created files.

Apple's product line is just four models: two basic desktop configurations—the new, colorful, translucent, easy-to-set up iMac and the dual-processor versions of its G4 Power Macs—and two laptops, the iBook and the sleek Titanium Powerbook G4.

Apple's recent innovations include OS X, which is based on the Unix operating system, originally designed for large, networked computer systems. OS X, now in version 10.1, promises improved multitasking, among other things. Apple says more than 1,000 applications are being written for its operating system.

Apple remains a niche manufacturer, however. One innovative product, the G4 Cube, which replaced the bulky rectangular tower that houses the components of most computers with an eight-inch cube, never gained a following. It remains to be seen if Apple will ever be able to develop a marketing prowess that matches its manufacturing skill. One step it has taken is to open a chain of Apple retail stores.

LAPTOP COMPUTERS

A long-time companion at work, at school, or on the road, the laptop is proving its mettle as a replacement or backup for a home's desktop computer.

Even as the pace of desktop computer sales slows, laptops are selling at an ever-increasing rate. It's not hard to understand why. Laptops now belong in the same league as desktop comput-

MEASURING RELIABILITY AND SATISFACTION

Each year, CONSUMER REPORTS asks respondents for feedback on products of all kinds—autos, major appliances, electronics, and more—to help consumers spot potential reliability problems before they make a purchase. One of the categories we ask about is desktop computers. The charts below show how different brands compare in reliability and in satisfaction with a brand's technical support. The latest findings are based on surveys in 2000 and 2001.

BRAND REPAIR HISTORIES

According to a 2000 survey of CONSUMER REPORTS readers, from 5 to 10 percent of computers became inoperable because an original component broke. In addition, an even greater percentage were left crippled but still operable after a breakdown. You can minimize potential problems by choosing a reliable brand. Our brand repair histories have been quite consistent over the years, though they are not infallible predictors. Repair rates for specific models may vary, and products can, of course, change. Differences of 6 or more points are meaningful.

Fewer ← Repairs → More

Dell
HP
Apple
Compaq
IBM
Gateway
NEC
Micron
Acer

0% 5% 10% 15% 20% 25% 30% 35%

■ INOPERABLE FAILURE
■ BROKEN, BUT STILL OPERABLE

Based on 26,750 responses to our 2000 Annual Questionnaire, covering desktop computers bought new between 1996 and 2000. Data have been standardized to eliminate differences due to age and usage.

TECHNICAL SUPPORT

CONSUMER REPORTS recently surveyed a nationally representative sample of more than 1,800 computer users to find out how good the manufacturers' technical support was between January 2000 and spring 2001.

Apple, Dell, and Gateway netted the highest satisfaction with overall technical support. If everyone were completely satisfied with a company's support, the overall score would be 100; 80 means very satisfied, on average; 60, fairly well satisfied. Slightly more than half the people who used the support were highly satisfied with the service; that's lower than most other service industries we measure.

Better ← → Worse

MANUFACTURER	OVERALL SCORE	SOLVED PROBLEM	SUPPORT STAFF	WAITING
Apple	73	○	●	●
Dell	72	○	○	○
Gateway	71	○	○	◐
HP	62	◐	○	○
Compaq	62	○	○	○
IBM	61	◐	○	○

The survey also found that 1 in 3 felt their problem wasn't successfully resolved; 1 in 6 who phoned for help complained that the support staff wasn't knowledgeable, and 2 in 5 who tried phoning had a problem getting through to the company.

Among those who contacted tech support, slightly more than 8 in 10 sought help by phone, 1 in 5 tried the manufacturer's web site, and about 1 in 5 tried e-mail. Of those who used the web, 2 out of 3 couldn't find an answer; 1 in 4 said the online instructions didn't work. And 1 in 3 who sought help via e-mail received an unhelpful response.

ers, thanks to brighter and larger displays, faster processors, and more efficient batteries. The thinnest laptops are only an inch or so high and weigh only 3 to 5 pounds. To get these light, sleek models, you'll have to pay a premium and sacrifice some functionality.

A laptop makes an attractive choice as a replacement computer or the household's second machine. Laptops are already fixtures in classrooms and boardrooms. Expanding a laptop's advantages is the growing availability of high-speed wireless Internet access at airports, schools, and hotels.

What's available

Compaq, Dell, Gateway, HP, IBM, and Toshiba are the leading Windows laptop brands. Apple alone makes Macs. Laptops come in various configurations:

ALL-IN-ONE. These machines can do just about everything a desktop can do. Sometimes called "three-spindle" machines because the hard drive, diskette drive, and CD-ROM or DVD-ROM drive reside on board, these models also have a full complement of jacks, connectors, and expansion slots for PC cards. But they're the biggest and heaviest, measuring 2 inches thick and weighing 7 to 8 pounds. The keyboard is full-size, and the screen measures 14 to 15 inches diagonally. Some models can hold a second battery for increased running time, and others can shed drives to reduce size and weight. With a docking station, you can easily turn an all-in-one model into a desktop stand-in. So-called reduced-legacy laptops from brands including Apple and IBM are similar to all-in-ones but lack a diskette drive. ("Legacy" refers to components, including the diskette drive, whose use dates back to the earliest desktop computers.) With reduced-legacy laptops, you can use an external floppy or Zip drive for transferring files. Price range for all-in-ones: $1,000 to $2,500.

MODULAR. These "two-spindle" units come with a hard drive and space for either a diskette drive, CD-ROM or DVD-ROM drive, or second battery. They're considerably slimmer than all-in-one models—about 1½ inches thick—and weigh 5 to 6 pounds. Drives can easily be swapped or left out to reduce weight, but some people find it inconvenient to swap drives regularly.

A modular model is easier to travel with than an all-in-one, provided you don't need to use all three drives at once. Other features of a modular laptop, including the keyboard and screen, are generally identical to what is found in an all-in-one machine. Price range: $1,400 to $2,500.

SLIM-AND-LIGHT. Especially good for traveling, these models measure about 1 inch thick and weigh 3 to 5 pounds. The case contains the hard drive and a smallish battery. The CD-ROM drive (which usually costs $300 or so more) and the diskette drive are external, tethered to the laptop when need be. A port expander—a strip with jacks and connectors for printer, monitor, mouse, and the like—is also connected via cable. The screen may be only about 12 inches diagonally, and the keyboard may be small and somewhat hard to use. Price range: $1,800 to $3,000.

Key features

Today's laptops generally have a 600-megahertz to 1-gigahertz **processor** and a 10- to 40-giga-byte **hard drive.** Expect even faster processors and more capacious hard drives in the near future. Most models have 128 megabytes (MB) of **RAM** (random access memory) and can be upgraded to 256 MB or more.

Most of today's laptops use a rechargeable lithium-ion **battery;** it's lighter and holds its charge better than a rechargeable nickel-metal hydride battery, the less common type. In our tests, lithium-ion batteries provided about three hours of continuous use when running office applications, compared with about 2½ hours for nickel-metal hydrides. (Laptops go into sleep mode when used intermittently, extending the time between charges.) You can extend battery life somewhat by dimming the display as you work and by removing PC cards when they aren't needed. Playing a DVD movie devours battery power.

A laptop's **keyboard** can be quite different from that of a desktop computer. The keys themselves may be full-sized (generally only slim-and-light models pare them down), but they may feel wobbly. Some laptops have extra buttons to expedite your access to e-mail or a web browser.

A 12- to 14-inch **display,** measured diagonally, should suit many people. A 15-inch display is the biggest. Unlike the sizes of traditional cathode ray tube (CRT) monitors, LCD sizes represent the actual viewing area you get. A resolution of 1024x768 pixels (picture elements) is better for fine detail than 800x600.

A thin-film transistor (TFT) active-matrix screen provides bright, crisp images. Passive-matrix displays can be found in some budget models. They go by the abbreviations DSTN, HPA, or STN. We've found that a TFT active-matrix screen is superior to a passive-matrix screen, which can leave "ghosts" when the display changes quickly and whose brightness drops off appreciably as you move your head away from the center.

Most laptops use a small **touch-sensitive pad** in place of a mouse—you drag your finger across the pad to move the cursor. You can also program the pad to respond to a "tap" as a "click," or to scroll as you sweep your index finger along the pad's right edge. An alternative pointing system, less preferred by our testers, uses a pencil-eraser-size **joy stick** in the middle of the keyboard.

Most new laptops feature an internal **CD-ROM** or **CD-RW drive.** Some offer combination **CD-RW/DVD drives.** The exceptions are slim-and-light notebooks, which require an external drive. Laptops typically include two **PC-card slots** for expansion. You might add a network card or a card-based hard drive, for example. Many laptops offer a connection for a **docking station,** a $100 or $200 base that makes it easy to connect an external monitor, keyboard, mouse, printer, or phone line. Most laptops let you attach these devices anyway, without the docking station. At least one **USB** port, for easy hookup of, say, a printer, digital camera, or scanner, is standard. Many laptops include an infrared port for a wireless link to similarly equipped cameras or printers. Most laptops can be outfitted for wireless networking.

Laptops typically come with far less software than desktop computers, although almost all are bundled with a basic home-office suite (such as Microsoft Works) and a personal-finance package. The small **speakers** built into laptops often sound tinny, with little bass. Headphones or external speakers deliver much better sound.

LAPTOP CHOICES: WHAT DO YOU NEED?

The kind of laptop you need depends on how you'll use it. Here are three scenarios.

Commuter/student. You carry a laptop to and from school or work, and on occasional trips.

If power and comfort are most important, choose an all-in-one model or a reduced-legacy design, which is similar to an all-in-one but lacks a diskette drive. If price matters most, choose an all-in-one machine with a passive-matrix display or an active-matrix model that has been discontinued by the manufacturer but is still being sold. If you want a light but practical machine for travel, get a modular model that can accept either a drive or spare battery in one bay and that has a built-in ethernet port that lets you connect to a network. Be sure the laptop you choose has these basics: a 700- to 800-MHz processor for Windows or a 500-MHz processor for Macintosh, 128 MB of RAM, and a 10- to 20-GB hard drive. Also consider getting a 14- to 15-inch display and a docking station or a plug for a port replicator (an attachment with connections for peripherals). Expect to pay $1,300 to $2,200.

Home user. You use the laptop mostly at home, possibly in addition to a desktop computer. When traveling, performance and comfort are important.

Consider an all-in-one or reduced-legacy design that has these basics: an 800-MHz processor for Windows or 500-MHz processor for Macintosh, 128 MB of RAM, and a 10- to 20-GB hard drive. Also consider a 14- to 15-inch TFT active-matrix display and a docking station, or a plug for a port replicator (an attachment with connections for peripherals). Expect to pay $1,800 to $2,200.

Road warrior. The laptop is a standard part of your travel gear, so size and weight are important considerations for you.

Consider a slim-and-light model weighing 3 to 5 pounds with these basics: an 800-MHz processor for Windows or 500-MHz processor for Macintosh, 128 MB of RAM, and a 10- to 20-GB hard drive. Expect a smaller display—about 12 inches. Battery life isn't likely to exceed three hours. Plan to carry spare batteries or plug in often for a recharge. Expect to pay about $3,000.

How to choose

PERFORMANCE DIFFERENCES. In CONSUMER REPORTS' tests, most laptop computers have performed solidly in many ways. But manufacturers still have to make trade-offs. Bigger and heavier models pack almost all the computing muscle of their desktop cousins, while slimmer and lighter ones sacrifice drive space for easy portability. Aside from size and weight, a major factor distinguishing laptops is battery performance. Some models run longer on a charge and have better power management than others.

RECOMMENDATIONS. Consider buying a little more laptop than you think you need, since upgrading a notebook can be hard or impossible. While desktop computers often use interchangeable, off-the-shelf components, a laptop's parts are typically proprietary. Adding more RAM might be relatively easy, but installing a larger hard drive or upgrading a video card might be out of the question.

CONSUMER REPORTS' recent survey of laptop owners found that one-third of laptops purchased in 1997-2000 had to be repaired or replaced at one point. Of those, 29 percent took more than two weeks to be fixed, and one-sixth lost critical data or files. Individual components of laptops broke down at about the same rate as did analogous components on desktop computers.

♦ **Ratings:** page 175

MONITORS

**With lower prices for both larger CRT monitors and flat-panel LCD displays,
a roomier screen—or more space on your desktop—is now within reach.**

Call it the incredible shrinking workspace. Over the past few years, bulkier monitors have all but overrun the tops of desks. Their screens, filled nearly to overflowing with icons, web pages, and digital photos, haven't fared much better. It has become clear that computer users need more real estate—on both their screens and their desks.

If a larger screen is a must, a 19-inch cathode ray tube (CRT) may be the answer. Prices have fallen so much in the past couple of years that you can find plenty in the $300-to-$600 range. If desk space is a priority, a flat-panel monitor with a thin liquid crystal display (LCD), similar to the display that comes with a laptop, can now be had for as little as $450 for the 15-inch size. To get the best of both worlds, you can buy a 21-inch flat-panel LCD monitor, but it's priced in the thousands.

Desktop computers and monitors are generally sold as a package, though some people buying a new desktop decide to hold on to their old monitor and others choose to buy a new monitor for their existing PC. When buying a desktop from a direct seller such as Dell or Gateway, you choose from a selection that includes basic monitors and higher-end versions.

What's available

Apple, Compaq, Dell, Gateway, Hewlett-Packard, IBM, and Sony all market their own brands of monitors for their PCs. In addition, you'll find monitors sold separately from brands such as CTX, Hitachi, Mitsubishi, NEC, Philips, Samsung, and ViewSonic. Many brands of monitor are manufactured on an outsource basis.

CRTS. Most desktop monitors sold today are CRTs, typically ranging from 17 to 21 inches. Some CRTs have flattened, squared-off screens (not to be confused with flat-panel screens) that reduce glare. The nominal image size—the screen size touted in ads—is generally based on the diagonal measurement of the picture tube, usually an inch larger than the viewable image size (VIS)—the image you see. Thus a 17-inch CRT has a 16-inch VIS. As a result of a class-action suit, an ad must also display a CRT's VIS, but to find it, you may have to squint at the fine print.

Space-saving flat-panel displays have come down in price.

The bigger a CRT, the more room it takes up on your desk, but "short-depth" models shave an inch or more off the depth, which otherwise roughly matches the nominal screen size.

A 17-inch monitor, the most popular choice these days, has almost one-third more viewable area than the 15-inch version now vanishing from the market. The larger size is especially useful when you're surfing the Internet, playing video games, editing photos, or working in several windows. Price range: $190 to $500.

If you regularly work with graphics or sprawling spreadsheets, consider a 19-inch monitor. Its viewable area is one-fourth larger than a 17-inch screen's. A short-depth 19-inch model doesn't take up much more desktop space than a standard 17-inch. Price range for 19-inch: $300 to $600 and up.

Aimed at graphics professionals, 20- and 21-inch models provide ample viewing area but gobble up desktop space. Price range: $700 to $1,200.

FLAT-PANEL LCDS. These monitors, which operate with analog or digital input or both, use a liquid-crystal display instead of a TV-style picture tube and take up much less desktop space than CRTs. For desktop use, they typically measure 15 inches diagonally and just a few inches deep and weigh 10 pounds or less, compared with 40 pounds for a 17-inch CRT and 50 pounds for a 19-inch CRT. LCDs with screens 17 inches or larger are available, but they are still somewhat pricey. Unlike with a CRT, the nominal and viewable image sizes of a flat-panel LCD are the same.

Flat-panel displays deliver a very clear image, but they have some inherent quirks. You can't adjust their color settings when they're receiving digital input. And you have to view a flat-panel screen straight on; the picture loses contrast as you move off-center. Fine lines may appear grainy. In analog mode, you have to tweak the controls to get the best picture.

Price range: 15-inch, $450 to $1,200; 17- and 18-inch, $850 to $4,500.

Key features

A monitor's **resolution** refers to the number of picture elements, or pixels, that make up an image. More pixels mean finer details. Most monitors can display several resolutions, generally ranging from 640x480 to 1,600x1,200, depending on the monitor and graphics card. Many 15-inch flat-panel displays, however, have noticeable image degradation—images look smeared and less pleasing—when set at a resolution other than 1,024x768 pixels. The higher the resolution, the smaller the text and images, so more content fits on the screen. Bigger CRT screens can handle higher resolutions and display more information.

Dot pitch, measured in millimeters, refers to the spacing between a CRT's pixels. All else being equal, a smaller dot pitch produces a more detailed image, though that's no guarantee of an excellent picture. In general, avoid models with a dot pitch higher than 0.28 mm.

A CRT requires a high **refresh rate** (the number of times per second the image is redrawn on the screen) to avoid annoying image flicker. In general, you'll be more comfortable with a 17-inch monitor set at a refresh rate of at least 75 hertz (Hz) at the resolution you want. With a 19-inch monitor, you may need an 85-Hz rate to avoid eyestrain, especially at higher resolutions. Refresh rate isn't an issue with flat-panel displays.

Monitors have controls for **brightness** and **contrast.** Most of them also have controls for **color balance** (usually called color temperature), **distortion,** and such. Buttons activate **onscreen controls** and **menus.**

Bigger CRTs use a considerable amount of juice: about 100 watts for a typical 19-inch model, more than 80 watts for a 17-incher, and about 20 watts for a 15-inch flat-panel LCD, for example. Most

A cathode ray tube (CRT) is cheaper than a comparably sized flat-panel monitor but takes up a lot of desk space.

monitors have a sleep mode that uses less than 3 watts when the computer is on but not in use.

CRTs can be designed with either a shadow mask or an aperture grille, and each has a distinctive look. A **shadow mask,** a perforated metal sheet, directs the beam emitted by electron guns arranged in a triangle so colors are composed of little dots of red, green, and blue. An **aperture grille** is a shadow mask in a CRT with the electron guns arranged in a horizontal row, which results in colors that are made up of little lines. View both types to see which you prefer.

Plug and play capability makes adding a new monitor to an existing computer relatively easy. You may have trouble, however, with systems that predate the Windows 95 or Mac OS 6 operating system, or the Pentium processor.

Some monitors include a **microphone, integrated** or **separate speakers,** or **composite video inputs** for viewing the output of a VCR or camcorder.

How to choose

PERFORMANCE DIFFERENCES. All 17-inch and 19-inch CRT monitors CONSUMER REPORTS has recently tested have at least very good display quality. Visibility differs, however. CRTs with flattened, squared-off screens may pick up fewer reflections, though not necessarily resulting in better display quality. Some CRTs have control buttons that are poorly labeled or on-screen controls that are difficult to use. Tilting is difficult with some models.

Most of the flat-panel LCDs we have tested have excellent display quality. Advantages over CRTs include compactness and lower power consumption.

RECOMMENDATIONS. Buy the right size for your task and the nature of your work space. You may decide that the slim profile and power savings of a flat-panel monitor make the premium you'll pay worthwhile.

Try to view a monitor before buying it. At the store, look at a page of text to be sure both center and edges are bright and clear. Open up a picture file to see whether the colors look natural and clear. Compare monitors side-by-side, if possible, with the same image displayed on each screen.

Buying through mail-order or the Internet won't let you see firsthand. If you aren't planning to buy from a bricks-and-mortar store, see if a friend or co-worker has the model you're considering or try to see it in a store. Wherever you buy, it's wise to get a 30-day money-back guarantee.

Once you've bought a monitor, think about where you'll place it. You should sit 18 to 30 inches away, with the top line of text just below eye level. Good lighting and correct placement of the keyboard and mouse are also critical. See page 154 for more on home-office ergonomics.

♦ **Ratings:** page 178

FLAT PANELS VS. CRT MONITORS

Because they rely on different technologies, flat panels and CRTs produce different images. A flat panel's squarish picture elements, or pixels, line up in rows and columns, producing images with a slightly grainy texture that's especially noticeable with text. Unless viewed straight on, they lose much of their contrast.

A CRT's pixels are illuminated differently, producing a softer image viewable from virtually any angle. Its images also have somewhat less contrast than those on a flat panel.

 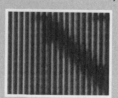

A close-up view of text produced by a flat-panel LCD monitor, left, and a CRT, right. The pixels of flat panels and CRTs are illuminated differently.

At normal viewing distance, the only obvious difference between a flat-panel monitor, left, and a CRT is the flat panel's superior contrast.

PDAS

In addition to keeping track of phone numbers, appointments, and things to do, many personal digital assistants deliver wireless access to an abbreviated version of the web.

The personal digital assistant, or PDA, seems to be showing up in everyone's hands. The dot-com CEO has one, naturally, but so does the dot-com gofer. The soccer mom uses one, and maybe her kids do too. The college freshman is just as likely as the dean of students to have a PDA.

There are now more than a dozen to choose among, from miniatures the size of a credit card to smallish computers complete with a keyboard. In between lies the design most people equate with the PDA—the tablet with a stylus and squarish display screen—pioneered by Palm Inc. several years ago. Today the choices include clones using the Palm operating system and knockoffs that only superficially resemble Palms. In past years, Microsoft played the unfamiliar role of underdog in the PDA market. But in 2000 it streamlined its software for PDAs, and the resulting Pocket PC devices have gained a following.

What all PDAs have in common—and why people buy them—is the ability to store and retrieve thousands of phone numbers, appointments, to-do chores, and notes. All models can exchange, or synchronize, information with a full-sized computer.

Many work with both Windows and Macintosh computers, either out of the box or with an inexpensive adapter. Many can provide wireless access to an abbreviated form of the Internet, most often with the addition of separately purchased accessories such as a modem. Some PDAs can record your own voice, play videos, display digital photos, or hold maps, city guides, or a novel.

What's available

There are two basic styles: models that you access via a touch-sensitive screen and those with small mechanical keyboards. Among the touch-screen models, there are two main operating systems: Palm OS, used in Palm's own models as well as in clones from Handspring and Sony, and a scaled-down version of Windows, used in Pocket PC devices from Casio, Compaq, and Hewlett-Packard. There are also tiny credit-card-sized systems. Among PDAs with mechanical keyboards, the Epoc operating system is used in models from Psion and Diamond.

Roughly 85 percent of handheld PDAs sold use Palm OS. While Palm Computing has retained its lead of the past few years, the licensees of Palm OS—Handspring and Sony—are posing formidable challenges to Palm through innovative hardware design. Meanwhile, design improvements in Pocket PCs—both in hardware and software—have made them easier to use than Palm OS models in a number of ways.

PALM OS SYSTEMS. Equipped with software to link with Windows and Macintosh computers, Palm units and their clones are small and simple to operate. You use a stylus to enter data on these units by tapping on an onscreen keyboard or writing in a shorthand known as Graffiti. Or you can download keyed data from your computer. Most can synchronize with a variety of e-mail software and include their own basic personal information management (PIM) application.

Models with backlit monochrome displays are easy to read under normal lighting

NEW LIVES FOR OLD HARDWARE

The National Safety Council, an organization that pro- motes safety, estimates that some 300 million personal computers will become obsolete over the next five years. Only a small fraction will be recycled; the rest will add to the nation's mountain of solid waste.

Besides the bulk, there are toxic metals and compounds. Each cathode-ray-tube monitor contains about 4 pounds of lead, which shields users from radiation. Backup batteries contain mercury; circuit boards have cadmium; cables and casings use PVC plastics.

Several manufacturers have programs to take back used equipment. Dell either pays you for an old monitor or makes a donation to the National Cristina Foundation, a national group that matches donors of computer equipment and recipients (203-863-9100; *www.cristina.org*). Gateway pays up to $50 for a used PC with CRT when new equipment is purchased. (You arrange the transfer through a Gateway Country Store.) Sony recently began a take-back program in Minnesota for all electronic products and hopes to extend it to other states. For a fee, Hewlett-Packard and IBM accept computer equipment made by any manufacturer.

In 2000, Massachusetts became the first state to make the recycling of monitors and TVs (which also contain lead) mandatory and to forbid dumping them in the state's landfills. (The lead and other components are removed, reclaimed, and sometimes reused.)

Dozens of Goodwill stores and Salvation Army sites throughout Massachusetts receive equipment, which they refurbish and sell or have recycled. About a third of the 174 Goodwill locations in the U.S. accept donations of desktop computers, but they may not take the very oldest models or nonworking machines.

In addition to those alternatives, you might also consider disposing of your old computer equipment through these other channels:

◆ Make a donation of a computer, monitor, or printer to a local school, house of worship, or charity.

◆ Contact Youth Build Boston, 617-445-8887, or Non-Profit Computing Inc., 212-759-2368.

◆ The Electronic Industries Alliance (*www.eiae.org*) lists organizations in 42 states that accept computer equipment. You may not receive anything in return except, possibly, a tax deduction.

conditions and are very easy on batteries (most use replaceable AAA alkalines). CONSUMER REPORTS' tests have shown that monochrome models running on AAA alkalines can operate continuously with the backlight off for at least 24 hours, equivalent to seven weeks of use at a half hour per day. Models with a color display use a rechargeable lithium-ion battery that must be recharged after just a few hours in continuous use. When the battery can no longer be recharged, you need to have a dealer remove and replace it.

While Palm OS-based units are easy to use, their onscreen keyboards eat up display space, so you can't see where you're typing. Navigation between different programs is cumbersome because of the "single-tasking" nature of the operating system.

Many new Palm-OS models have expansion slots that let you attach separately purchased accessories such as a modem, which can provide wireless Internet access, as well as a digital camera or an MP3 player.

All Palm OS PDAs can be enhanced by adding third-party software applications—the more free memory in a model, the more software that can be accommodated. There is a large body of Palm OS-compatible freeware, shareware, and commercial software available for download at such sites as *www.palmgear.com*. Two Palm models—the M500 and the M505—come with Documents To Go, word-processing and spreadsheet software similar to that used in Pocket PCs (see below).

A help system, which provides user tips, only performs in a limited way. Infrared data transfer, or "beaming" in Palm parlance, wirelessly transfers data and applications to other PDAs. Price range: $130 to $500.

POCKET PC SYSTEMS. These resemble Palm-based models, but they are more like a miniature computer. They have a processor with far more horsepower and come with familiar applications such as a word processor and a spreadsheet. Included is a scaled-down version of Internet Explorer, plus voice-recording and some financial functions. An application that plays MP3 music files, as well as Microsoft Reader, an e-book application, is also included.

As you might expect, all the application software included in a Pocket PC integrates well into the Windows computer environment. But their affinity for Microsoft products limits flexibility. The only e-mail programs with which they can exchange data are Microsoft Outlook and Exchange. And they don't work with Macs. Most have a color display that livens up the interface but also drains their rechargeable lithium-ion batteries quickly. One model CONSUMER REPORTS recently tested lasted only four hours in continuous use. As with Palm OS PDAs with rechargeable batteries, the battery of a Pocket PC model must be removed and replaced by a dealer when it can no longer be recharged. Exceptions are Pocket PC models from Casio, which let you replace the rechargeable batteries yourself.

For basic functions, our tests have shown that Pocket PCs are generally easier to use than Palm OS models. You access programs by activating a drop-down list (similar to the Start menu on the full version of Windows), either by tapping an icon on the screen or pressing a button. Navigation between programs is easier than with the Palms because the operating system is multitasking—you can run several programs simultaneously. A "Today" screen lets you see your calendar, to-do list, and e-mail boxes at a glance. Onscreen keyboards leave most of the display visible. The help system is context-sensitive and informative.

As with Palm OS PDAs, expansion slots let you attach separately purchased accessories such as a modem, which can provide wireless web access, plus a digital player or an MP3 player. Some of the more advanced features of Pocket PC models fail to live up to their promise. The included Windows Media Player can't access MP3 music files from an external memory card, so you must transfer the files into a PDA's main memory. At the standard rate of about 1MB per minute of music, such an operation quickly fills a Pocket PC's 16MB or 32MB main memory. A version of Windows Media Player that can be downloaded from the web works better. Infrared data transfer on Pocket PC models is cumbersome. Price range: $320 to $600.

MECHANICAL-KEYBOARD SYSTEMS. These systems are most useful if you need to do light typing or prefer a mechanical keyboard. They use the Epoc system, which is very flexible when it comes to connecting with third-party software. They support major word-processing and spreadsheet applications from Microsoft and Corel, as well as Microsoft Works. They also support most major e-mail and PIM programs from Lotus, Microsoft, and Symantec. But they don't include their own PIM software.

While Epoc-based systems are widely used in Europe, they don't seem to have gained a wide following in the U.S.

CONSUMER REPORTS' tests have found two identical Epoc-models, the Psion Revo+ and the Diamond, more difficult to navigate than Palm OS or Pocket PC models, because you have to keep switching back and forth between the keyboard and touch screen to accomplish tasks.

PDA TRYOUT
Test ease of use while shopping. Far too many people invest in a PDA only to find its keypad, stylus, or shorthand hard to use.

WHEN YOU HAVE A PROBLEM PC

Computers have a higher problem rate than most other products.
Problems range from computers that are inoperable to
missing components to mysterious error messages.
CONSUMER REPORTS has put together a troubleshooting
guide, available on Consumer Reports Online, that includes
a set of self-help tips. Here are two common problems and
strategies for solving them:

Problem: Your system is ohhhh-so-slooooow.

◆ You might need more RAM (random access memory).
Take your computer owner's manual with you to a full-
service computer retailer to help find and purchase the
appropriate memory module(s) for your computer.
Installing memory is usually easy enough to do yourself, or
the retailer's service department can do it.

◆ Or your computer's hard drive may be fragmented.
That's not as bad as it sounds, and it is easy to remedy in
Windows; simply defrag your hard drive using the Disk
Defragmenter utility that comes with Windows or use a
faster one purchased separately, such as SpeedDisk, from
Norton Utilities.

◆ If your Mac is operating slowly, you can rebuild your
desktop, which helps the hard drive locate files. To do this,
you need to have at least 5 percent of your hard drive free.
First, turn off extensions through the Extensions Manager
control panel. Then simultaneously hold down the Apple
and Option keys while the system boots up. You will then
see a dialog box that asks whether you want to rebuild the
desktop. Click OK, and the system will take it from there.

◆ If none of the above solutions works, give the manufacturer a chance to fix the problem.

Problem: An important file has disappeared.

◆ If the file is a Word or Excel file, click on File. At the
bottom of the pull-down menu you'll find a list of the last
several files used.

◆ A feature called Windows Find can help you locate
a stray file. From the Start menu, select Find, then
Files or Folders, then type in the name of the wayward
file. Has the file name escaped you? Try Find's
Advanced option, which will let you search by date,
file type, or content.

◆ If you're using a Mac, click on File at the top of your
screen. On the drop-down menu, click on either Find
(in all older versions of the Mac OS) or Sherlock (the
new advanced search engine in OS 8.5 and higher versions). This will find a lost file by name, size, date,
or content.

◆ If none of the above solutions works, give the manufacturer a chance to fix the problem.

The guide also lays out the most efficient and effective
step-by-step procedures you may need to follow to get
retailers and manufacturers to fix a problem quickly.
There is also information you may need to argue your
case effectively, including the latest news about recalls,
Consumer Reports Online s product reports and Ratings,
and links to the text of applicable consumer-protection
laws. You'll also see phone numbers and street and web
addresses as well as letter templates to help you communicate with equipment manufacturers forcefully.

To access the guide, go to *www.ConsumerReports.org*,
click into "Other features & services," and click into "Help
for problem PCs."

Their rechargeable batteries go a long way, though. For example, our tests showed that the
Psion Revo+'s rechargeable battery lasted 12 hours, much longer than the battery of a Pocket
PC did. When the rechargeable battery has to be replaced, you must have the dealer do it.

Epoc models feature a handy "Today" screen similar to that of the Pocket PCs, include a
choice of two different web browsers on their installation CD, and can browse the wireless
web using their infrared port, web browser, and cell phone. The help system is limited.

Price range: $100 to $400.

CREDIT-CARD-SIZED SYSTEMS. These tiny units, such as the Xircom Rex, mainly track addresses, phone numbers, and appointments. You manipulate and retrieve information by

pressing tiny buttons on an onscreen keyboard, making data-entry difficult. They're most useful for viewing information that you've previously keyed into your computer and transferred into the PDA. Expect batteries to last well over a month, even with frequent use. The Xircom Rex uses the calculator-style batteries that are easily replaced. In 2001, Xircom was acquired by the chip giant, Intel.

Price range: $100 to $150.

Key features

PDAs are designed to allow information to be exchanged, or **synchronized**, with a desktop computer. The synchronization is activated by placing the PDA on a **cradle**, or docking station, and pressing a button. The cradle connects directly to your desktop computer, usually through an RS-232 or a Universal Serial Bus connection. For rechargeable models, you also use the cradle to recharge batteries. Infrared technology can let you synchronize with a computer without wires or a cradle.

Whichever operating system your PDA uses, you'll need to install programs in your desktop computer to enable the handheld to synchronize with it. Some software is supplied by the manufacturer, and sometimes third-party software can be used. Most such software lets you swap data with leading **personal-information-manager** programs such as Lotus Organizer or Microsoft Outlook; some do not.

Most PDAs cover basic tasks. A **calendar application** allows you to keep track of your appointments and set reminder alarms. **Contact software** records addresses and phone numbers. Notes/tasks software allows the creation of reminders and to-do lists. A **memo function** allows you to make quick notes to yourself. **Calculators** sometimes include financial and scientific functions. Other capabilities include word-processing, spreadsheet, database, and money-management functions.

A PDA's **processor** is the system's brain. In general, the higher the processing speed of this chip, the faster the unit will execute tasks—and the more expensive the unit will be. But higher-speed processors require more battery power and may deplete batteries quickly. Processing speeds are 16 to 200 megahertz.

Models typically have 2 to 32 megabytes of user memory. Even the smallest amount in that range should be more than enough for most people. **Expansion slots** allow you to upgrade memory as well as add a modem or other device. Pocket PC models, Palm OS models, and some Psion models are designed to expand functionality by enabling you to add a modem, a digital camera, an MP3 player, or other device through the use of **expansion slots**.

A PDA's **liquid crystal display** (LCD) is either monochrome or color. Most monochrome and all color displays are backlit, which means that they have a light source at the back of the panel that illuminates the characters. With monochrome screens, you only need the backlight when using the PDA in the dark. The backlight is always used with color screens.

Some handhelds use AAA alkaline **batteries**. Some larger models use AA alkaline batteries, while others use lithium-ion rechargeable batteries.

Some keyboard-based units have a built-in **modem** that lets you plug into a phone line and send a fax, exchange e-mail, or tap into the Internet. In general, for PDAs, the degree of web accessibility is not yet equal to what you can get from your desktop or laptop computer. Some applications can browse specially designed pages known as "clipped web pages." Other applications (such as Avant-go) allow you to download text-based information from a desktop computer. A **voice recorder,** which includes a built-in microphone and speaker, works like a tape recorder.

How to choose

PERFORMANCE DIFFERENCES. Palm OS-based units offer simple operation, compact size, and an easy-to-use interface. They offer a wide range of features and expandability. All can work with Macs, though for some models you may have to buy a Mac-compatible cable. Models with a monochrome screen offer excellent to very good battery life. A color screen shortens battery life significantly. Windows-based Pocket PCs are more expensive than Palm-based PDAs, but are easier to use for basic functions. Their biggest drawback is price and short battery life (all Pocket PCs have color screens). They also don't work with Macs. Epoc-based models have innovative designs and good performance. Most do work with Macs.

RECOMMENDATIONS. The PDA hasn't completely replaced the handwritten shopping list or the printed address book. That's all the organizing some people need. But if you need to keep tabs on a great deal of data, a PDA makes sense. Your mobile computing needs, affinity for technology, and expected usage should be your deciding factors when selecting one. For a high-tech way to store contacts and appointments, any of the Palm OS models that cost $200 or less should suffice. If you plan to use the PDA as an extension of your PC by creating and accessing documents, sending e-mail, and doing basic web surfing, consider a Pocket PC or Epoc device. Keep in mind that the PDA is among the fastest-changing computer products.

♦ **Ratings:** page 182

Cool Tools

7

Once clearly separate product categories, home office and home entertainment now overlap. Images captured on digital camcorders or digital cameras can be edited on a PC fairly easily. An inexpensive alternative is to digitize images using a scanner. A PC or CD player/recorder lets you make your own CD compilations. An MP3 player lets you listen to music in the form of music files transferred from your PC. People hesitant about plunging into digital cameras, digital camcorders, and CD player/recorders may be encouraged by ever-improving ease of use and a continuing drop in prices. MP3 players represent a rapidly evolving technology. No MP3 player is as simple to load with music as a CD player, and no new model will be state-of-the-art for long.

CAMCORDERS

Fine picture quality and easy editing have improved the functionality of these movie makers, especially the digital models.

Home movies—those grainy, jumpy productions of yesteryear—have been replaced by home movies shot on digital or analog camcorders that you can edit and embellish with music using your PC and play back on your VCR, or even turn into video shorts for sending online.

Digital camcorders generally offer very good to excellent picture quality, along with very good sound capability, compactness, and ease of handling. Making copies of a digital recording won't result in a loss of picture or sound quality.

Analog camcorders generally have good picture and sound quality and are less expensive. Some analog units are about as compact and easy to handle as digital models, while others are a bit bigger and bulkier.

CAMCORDER FORMATS

DIGITAL

MiniDV

D8

ANALOG

Hi8 and 8mm

VHS-C
and S-VHS-C

What's available

Sony dominates the camcorder market, with several models in a number of formats. Other top brands include Canon, JVC, Panasonic, RCA, and Sharp. Digital models come in two formats: MiniDV or Digital 8. Some digital models weigh less than 2 pounds.

MINIDV. Don't let the size deceive you. Although some models can be slipped into a large pocket, MiniDV camcorders can record very high-quality images. They use a unique tape cassette, and the typical recording time is 60 minutes at SP (standard play) speed. Expect to pay $7 for a 60-minute tape. You'll need to use the camcorder for playback—it converts its recording to an analog signal, so it can be played directly into a TV or VCR. If the TV or VCR has an S-video input jack, you can use it to get the best possible picture. Price range: $600 to $2,000.

DIGITAL 8. Also known as D8, this format gives you digital quality on Hi8 or 8mm cassettes. Tapes are cheaper than MiniDV cassettes. The format records with a faster tape speed, so a "120-minute" cassette lasts only 60 minutes at SP. Most models can also play your old analog Hi8 or 8mm tapes. Price range: $550 to $1,300.

You'll still find analog camcorders in four compact formats—VHS-C, Super VHS-C, 8mm, and Hi8. They weigh around 2 pounds. Picture quality is generally good, though a notch below that of digital.

VHS-C. This format uses an adapter to play in any VHS VCR. Cassettes most commonly hold 30 minutes on SP. Price range: $300 to $700.

SUPER VHS-C. S-VHS-C is the high-band variation on VHS-C and uses special S-VHS-C tapes. (A slightly different format, S-VHS/ET-C can use standard VHS-C tapes.) One S-VHS-C tape yields 40 minutes at SP. JVC is the only brand that offers models in this format. Price range: $500 to $700.

8MM. For this analog format, you need the camcorder for playback. Cassettes hold a lot— the most common size, 120-minute, yields two hours at SP and costs about $2.50. Price range: $250 to $500.

HI8. This premium, "high-band" variant of 8mm promises a sharper picture. For full benefits, you need to use Hi8 tape and watch on a TV set that has an S-video input. A 120-minute cassette tape costs about $3.50. Price range: $300 to $800.

Key features

A flip-out **LCD viewer** is becoming commonplace on all but the lowest-priced camcorders. You'll find it useful for reviewing footage you've shot and easier to use than the eyepiece viewfinder for certain shooting poses. Some LCD viewers are hard to use in sunlight, a drawback on models that have a viewer only and no eyepiece.

Screens vary from 2½ to 4 inches measured diagonally, with a larger screen offered as a step-up feature on higher-priced models. Using an LCD viewer shortens recording time by using batteries faster than does using the eyepiece viewfinder.

An **image stabilizer** automatically reduces most of the shakes from a scene you're capturing. Most stabilizers are electronic; a few are optical. Either type can be effective, though mounting the camcorder on a tripod is the surest way to get steady images. If you're not using a tripod, you can try holding the camcorder with both hands and propping both elbows against your chest.

Full auto switch essentially lets you point and shoot. The camcorder automatically adjusts the color balance, shutter speed, focus, and aperture (also called the "iris" or f-stop with camcorders).

Autofocus adjusts for maximum sharpness; manual focus override may be needed for problem situations, such as low light. (You may have to tap buttons repeatedly to get the focus just right.) With many camcorders, you can also control exposure, shutter speed, and white balance. **Macro focus** keeps the picture clear when you shoot small subjects at close range.

The **zoom** is typically a finger control—press one way to zoom in, the other way to widen the view. (The rate at which the zoom changes will depend on how hard you press the switch.) Typical optical zoom ratios range from 10:1 to 26:1. The zoom relies on optical lenses, just like a film camera (hence the term "optical zoom"). Many camcorders offer a digital zoom to extend the range to 400:1 or more, but at a lower picture quality.

Regardless of format, analog or digital, every camcorder displays **tape speeds** the same way as a VCR. Every model, for example, includes an SP (standard play) speed. A few 8mm and Hi8 models have a slower, LP (long play) speed, which doubles recording time. All VHS-C and S-VHS camcorders have an even slower EP (extended play) speed, which triples recording time. With analog camcorders, however, slower speeds worsen picture quality.

Quick review lets you view the last few seconds of a scene without having to press a lot of buttons. For special lighting situations, preset **auto-exposure settings** can be helpful. A "snow & sand" setting, for example, adjusts shutter speed or aperture to accommodate the high reflectivity of snow and sand.

A **light** provides some illumination for close-ups when the image would otherwise be too dark. **Backlight compensation** increases the exposure slightly when your subject is lit from behind and silhouetted. An **infrared-sensitive recording mode** (also known as "**night vision**," "**zero lux**," or "**IR-filter**") allows shooting in very dim or dark situations, using infrared emitters. You may use it for nighttime shots, although color representation won't be accurate in this mode.

Audio/video inputs let you record material from another camcorder or from a VCR, useful for copying part of another video onto to your own. (A digital camcorder must have such an input jack if you want to record analog material digitally.) Unlike the built-in microphone, an external microphone that is plugged into a **microphone jack** won't pick up noises from the camcorder itself, and typically improves audio performance.

Features that may aid or enhance editing include a built-in **title generator** (which superimposes printed titles and captions); a **time and date stamp**; and a **time code**, which is a

---

CAMERA AND CAMCORDER BATTERIES

Digital cameras and camcorders all consume giant gulps of power. That can pose a problem when you have a golden photo or video opportunity and you're running low on juice.

Digital cameras often come with rechargeable batteries—lithium-ion, nickel-metal-hydride (NiMH), or, rarely now, nickel-cadmium (NiCD)—but many also take AA alkaline cells. Rechargeable lithium-ion, NiMH, or, rarely, NiCD battery packs are used in camcorders.

CONSUMER REPORTS' tests have found that NiMH cells are a fine choice for devices with a high power drain. In a test mimicking the high power drain of a film or digital camera with a flash, the best NiMH battery significantly outperformed the best alkaline cell. Use of NiMH has a relatively high initial cost—about $30 to $50 for a system comprising a charger and four AA batteries—but the reusability of NiMH cells makes them less expensive long-term than standard alkalines. NiMH cells are also an environmentally safe choice. Unlike the NiCD cells they're replacing, they can be disposed of with ordinary refuse.

The newer lithium-ion rechargeables also work well and can be disposed with ordinary refuse, but they don't come in AA configurations.

frame reference of exactly where you are on a tape, recorded by hour, second, and frame.

A **remote control** is helpful when you're using the camcorder as a playback device or when using a tripod while you're positioned off to the side—or getting into the picture yourself. **Programmed recording** starts the camcorder recording at a preset time.

How to choose

PERFORMANCE DIFFERENCES. Digital camcorders have set a new standard in CONSUMER REPORTS' picture-quality tests. The top-performing models yield pictures that are sharp, free of streaks and other visual "noise," and have accurate color. Audio quality is not quite as impressive, at least using the built-in microphone. Still, digitals record pleasing sound that's devoid of audio flutter (a wavering in pitch that can make sounds seem thin and watery), if not exactly CD-like, as some models claim.

The best analog model we've tested is good—on a par with the lowest-scoring digital. The lowest-scoring analog model delivered soft images that contained a lot of video noise and jitter, and reproduced colors less accurately than any digital model. And while sound for 8mm and Hi8 analog camcorders is practically free of audio flutter, all the VHS-C analog camcorders suffered from some degree of that audio-signal problem.

RECOMMENDATIONS. If you don't want to spend a lot, an analog camcorder is a good value—many are now priced at about $300, compared with $750 just a few years ago. Analog models may also appeal to you if you have little interest in video editing. If you want to upgrade, consider a digital model. Prices are as low as $550 and are continuing to fall.

Try before you buy. Make sure a camcorder fits comfortably in your hand and has controls that are easy to reach.

♦ **Ratings:** page 162

DIGITAL CAMERAS

**Compared with images captured on film, digital images allow
you to be more involved in the creation of the print.**

Digital cameras, which employ reusable memory cards instead of film, give you far more creative control than can film cameras. With a digital camera, you can transfer shots to your computer, then crop, adjust color and contrast, and add textures and other special effects.

Final results can be made into prints, cards, even T-shirts, or sent via e-mail, all using the software that usually comes with the camera. Since the technology requires some fiddling, digital may appeal more to relatively serious amateurs than to casual snapshooters. But as digital image-handling becomes simpler—and camera prices keep dropping—the advantages may more easily win you over.

Digital cameras share many features with digital camcorders, such as an electronic image sensor, LCD viewer, and zoom functions. They also share some features with film cameras, such as focus and flash options.

Some camcorders can be used to take still pictures, but a typical camcorder's resolution is no match for a good still camera's.

What's available

The leading brands are Kodak, Nikon, Olympus, and Sony, with other brands from consumer-electronics, computer-imaging, and traditional camera and film companies.

Digital cameras are typically categorized by how many pixels, or picture elements, the image sensor contains. A 1-megapixel camera has 1 million such elements. The more pixels, the sharper the image can be.

Cheap, submegapixel cameras have 640 by 480 pixels (307,200 in all). A 1-megapixel model makes sharp 5x7-inch prints and very good 8x10s. Two- and 3-megapixel models can make excellent 8x10s and pleasing 11x14s (a size larger than most inkjet printers can handle). There are also 4- and 5-megapixel models, but they are probably more than most home users really need.

Price range: submegapixel, below $100; 1-megapixel, $150 to $500; 2-megapixel, $250 to $700; 3-megapixel, $400 to $1,000.

Key features

Digital cameras use **aperture** and **shutter speed** to take pictures even though they don't use film. Aperture indicates how wide the lens opens (the smaller the f-number, the larger the aperture). The shutter speed indicates how long the aperture remains open when you snap a picture.

Most digital cameras are highly automated, with features such as **automatic exposure control** (which manages the shutter speed or aperture—or both settings—according to available light) and **autofocus**.

Instead of film, digital cameras typically record their shots onto **flash memory** cards, such as CompactFlash or SmartMedia, which come in capacities of 8, or 16 megabytes, or more. Once quite expensive, flash-memory cards have tumbled in price—32-megabyte cards can be had for less than $50. A few models store shots on regular diskettes, while some Sony models use a MemoryStick. Some newer cameras use 3-inch CD-RW discs.

To save images, you transfer them to a computer, typically by connecting the camera to the computer's USB or serial port or inserting the memory card into a special reader. Some printers can take memory cards and make prints without putting the images on a computer first. Image-handling software such as Adobe PhotoDeluxe, MGI PhotoSuite, Microsoft Picture It, and Ulead PhotoImpact lets you size, touch up, and crop digital images using your computer. Most digital cameras work with Windows or Macintosh machines. For more, see "In the digital darkroom" on page 47.

The **file format** commonly used for photos is the highly compressed JPEG. (It's also used for photos on the Internet.) Some cameras can save photos in TIFF format, but this setting yields enormous files.

Digital cameras typically have both an optical viewfinder and a color LCD viewer. LCD viewers are very accurate in showing what you get—better than most of the **optical viewfinders,** but they gobble up battery power and most aren't well suited for use in bright sunshine. You can also view shots you've already taken on the LCD. Many digital cameras provide a video output, so you can view your pictures on a TV screen.

Certain cameras let you record an audio clip with a picture. But these clips devour storage

FILM TO DIGITAL

With film cameras, it's possible to get some of the benefits of digital cameras. When you drop off a roll for processing, simply ask for the photos to be stored digitally—on a floppy disk or a photo CD. You can then edit the images on your computer. You can also scan prints, slides, and negatives if you have a suitable scanner.

space. Some allow you to record limited video, but the frame rate is slow and the resolution poor.

A **zoom lens** provides flexibility in framing shots and closes the apparent distance between you and your subject—ideal if you want to quickly switch to a close shot. A 3x zoom is comparable to a 35-to-105-mm lens on a film camera; a 2x zoom, to a 35-to-70-mm lens. Optical zooms are superior to digital zooms. Digital zooms double or triple the zoom range, but only by magnifying the center of the frame without actually increasing picture detail, resulting in a somewhat coarser view.

Sensors in digital cameras are typically about as sensitive as ISO 100 film, though some let you increase that setting. (At ISO 100, you'll likely need to use a flash indoors and in low outdoor light.) A camera's **flash range** tells you how far from the camera the flash will provide proper exposure: If the subject is out of range, you'll know to close the distance. But digital cameras tolerate some underexposure before the image suffers noticeably.

Red-eye reduction shines a light toward your subject just before the main flash. (A camera whose flash unit is farther from the lens discourages red eye. Computer editing may also correct red eye.) With **automatic flash mode**, the camera fires the flash whenever the light entering the camera registers as insufficient.

How to choose

PERFORMANCE DIFFERENCES. In CONSUMER REPORTS' most recent tests, image colors looked fine. Digital cameras did much better with fluorescent lighting than regular film processing labs have done. (Fluorescent lighting can give film photos a greenish cast.) Tests also showed that a higher pixel count alone doesn't necessarily produce better picture quality. In those tests, 5x7-inch prints from some 2-megapixel cameras outperformed those from some 3-megapixel ones.

The image-handling software provided with a digital camera is generally easy to use. The results are usually pleasing—or readily altered further if you are not satisfied. The software does have its limits, though. It can't fix an out-of-focus image.

RECOMMENDATIONS. A 2-megapixel model offers good quality at a relatively moderate price. Look for a camera with a 3x optical zoom lens and good image-handling software. Avoid cameras that use a floppy disk for storage. Only a small number of high-resolution images fit on a disk.

Online storage of digital photo images can be a good backup. For more, see "Online sharing" on page 50.

Try before you buy. Quite a few digital cameras offer a shallow grip or no grip. Some LCD viewers are awkwardly situated and could easily be soiled with nose- or thumbprints. If you wear glasses, you might look for a camera viewfinder with a diopter adjustment that may allow you to remove your glasses while using the camera.

♦ **Ratings:** page 170

PRINTING PHOTOS ON AN INKJET

Most inkjet printers can turn out high-quality color photos. Here are some tips on getting the best results:

♦ Use the Print Preview feature, found in most image-handling programs, to avoid false starts. If you want to try out your print during the editing process, use standard-bond instead of pricey photo paper. Or print in a smaller size.

♦ Handle with care. Inkjet ink can smear if touched before it dries. Color inks in general are less water-resistant than black inks, especially on photo paper. Some ink is vulnerable to light, meaning exhibited photos may eventually show fading and color shifts.

♦ Shop for cartridges. Comparison-shopping sites such as *www.shopper.com* and *www.computershopper.com* can yield savings of 25 percent or more (not including shipping). With prices in hand, try bricks-and-mortar office-supply chains or warehouse clubs. Don't overbuy—an ink cartridge's shelf life is about 18 months unopened, six months once installed. Be wary of off-brand refills or refilling cartridges yourself with ink-and-syringe kits. Printer warranties often exclude coverage for damage attributable to third-party refills.

CD PLAYER/RECORDERS

After years of having to rely on cassette tapes to make your own recordings, you can now use these devices as well as computers to "burn" the music you want onto your own CDs.

A CD player/recorder lets you do with compact discs what tape decks have long allowed with tape. The machine can also serve as your CD player. Player/recorders still cost two or three times more than CD changers without recording capability, though prices are dropping. These products sell as stand-alone units and as components of some minisystems.

You can also make your own music CDs by using a computer. You'll now find CD drives that burn CDs standard on many computers. These drives, originally intended for archiving data, can be as adept as CD player/recorders. (See "Do-It-yourself CDs," page 50.)

Both CD player/recorders and computer CD burners let you copy entire discs or dub selected tracks to create your own CD compilations, with no quality loss in high-speed CD-to-CD dubbing. (Recording speeds usually are real time or 2x, which records in half that time.)

Both CD player/recorders and computer CD burners will record to either "CD-Rs," discs you can record on only once, or to "CD-RWs," rewritable discs that can be repeatedly reused. CD-Rs play on almost any CD player, whereas CD-RWs generally play only on new disc players that are configured to accept them.

What's available

Audio CD player/recorders come from audio-component companies such as Harmon-Kardon, JVC, Philips, and Pioneer. There are dual-tray and changer models. One tray holds the blank CD, and the other tray or trays hold the CDs for recording or listening. So far, most multidisc models on the market hold four discs. Expect larger-capacity changers in the not-too-distant future. Price range for dual-tray and changer models: $300 to $600 or so.

Key features

To compile "mix" discs with a CD player/recorder, you program your selections from up to three discs installed in the changer; the steps will be familiar to anyone who's programmed a CD changer. Most units give you a running total of the accumulated time of the tracks as you are programming them. With dual-play CD player/recorders, you must program selections from each disc in succession, as with the computer option.

Defining tracks on the CD onto which you're recording is accomplished in varying degrees of flexibility. How many **track numbers** a given player/recorder can add per disc, for example, differs from one model to another; additionally, assigning track numbers when you're recording from cassettes may be automatic or manual. (Such tracks are inserted automatically when recording from CDs.) **Text labeling** lets you type in short text passages such as artist and song names, a much easier procedure with a computer keyboard than with a console's remote control.

The number of **delete-track modes** grants you flexibility when you need to delete one or more tracks, or the entire disc's contents, before finalization. One-track, multitrack, and all-disc are three common modes.

For playback, an audio CD player/recorder typically has a selection of three modes: **Program** is used for actual recording, **repeat** plays a track again, and **random-play** (or shuffle) plays tracks randomly.

Connection types can affect which external sources you're able to use to make a CD. A **digital input jack** may be **optical** or **coaxial**; the latter is for connecting older digital devices. An analog input jack lets you record your old tapes and LPs. A **microphone input** offers a low-cost way for home musicians to make digital recordings of their performances. A **record-level control** helps you adjust the sound level while recording digitally from analog sources, a problem you don't face when recording from digital sources. An **input selector**, included on some models, makes for faster connections than when going through a menu process.

How to choose

PERFORMANCE DIFFERENCES. By burning a CD, using either an audio CD player/recorder or a computer, you can make a recording that's audibly—even electronically—indistinguishable from the original CD, CONSUMER REPORTS' tests show. CD player/recorders excel in versatility; you can record from CDs, LPs, cassettes, and even TV or radio sound (anything, in fact, that you can connect to a sound system's receiver). This method is the clear standout for recording LPs, since connecting a turntable to a computer requires additional equipment.

The computer method, however, has its own strengths. Because it affords a connection to the Internet, the computer option lets you burn downloaded MP3-encoded files onto CDs. A computer offers more setup choices when you're assembling your own CD from several prerecorded discs. And when you're recording from analog sources, the computer's "burning" software often includes sound processing that will reduce the snap and crackle of a vinyl LP or the tape hiss of a cassette tape. For more, see "Computers vs. CD player/recorders" on page 51.

RECOMMENDATIONS. The relatively low cost of making high-quality CDs today makes CD recording a good option for some ardent music fans. If you don't already have burning capability on your computer, an audio CD player/recorder may make sense. We recommend buying a changer model; its multidisc magazine or carousel will make it easy to record compilation CDs or to play uninterrupted music. The computer-based option is the only choice for recording music from both CDs and the Internet. If you don't already have a CD-burning drive in your computer, you could buy one and the necessary software for about $100 to $250.

MP3 PLAYERS

They usually store at least a CD's worth of music files. But they take work to load, and legal controversy surrounds some usage.

Despite a cloud of controversy and litigation over the legality of some web music sites, online music files are apparently here to stay. Many of those files are transferred from computers to more than 3.5 million portable MP3 players, small as a walk-about radio, or even smaller. Music fans have already downloaded more than 5 million copies of software programs that play computer files that use MP3 encoding—currently the predominant means of compressing music files online.

Many MP3 players look much like portable radios—headphones and all. Others resemble large pens or even watches. Each player has a computer chip and internal or external memory that can store and play compressed digital-audio files. Some of these players can store other computer files as well.

Digital audio can be downloaded from various web sites, played on the home computer itself, transferred to one of these players, or recorded ("burned") onto CDs for more permanent storage. Also, music from audio CDs can be recorded ("ripped") and transferred onto the players.

Music can be encoded digitally in a number of formats. MP3 is the best known. The abbreviation stands for Moving Pictures Expert Group 1 Layer 3, a file format that compresses music to one-tenth to one-twelfth the space it would ordinarily take. Other encoding schemes include Adaptive Transform Acoustic Coupling (ATRAC), a proprietary format used by Sony products instead of MP3. Sony players convert from MP3 as needed.

A player with 64 megabytes (MB) of memory holds about an hour of CD-quality music at a time. The MP3 standard also lets you save music at lower sampling rates; this diminishes quality but increases the amount of music you can store. Some players come with upgradeable "firmware," a means of teaching an old player to learn new tricks such as supporting more or newer music-file formats that may be created in the future.

The recording industry has largely been successful in using litigation to force a company called Napster, whose web site, Napster.com, facilitated the downloading of "swapped" music files, to sharply curtail its operations. In its defense, Napster had contended that swapping music files is protected under the "fair use" provision of copyright law, which allows people to make a small number of copies of a recording for their personal use. Now there are programs downloadable from web sites that let you connect to other people's computers to share files. And there's no downloadable server that can be shut down.

CD QUALITY

Figure on roughly one minute of music per megabyte to save MP3 files at the CD-quality level.

What's available

More than 30 brands of MP3 players already exist, with some hybrid models incorporating CD-player functionality and some PDA-like features. MP3 playback has even been incorporated into some digital cameras, and cell phones with MP3 playback are also on the way. Sony and Diamond Multimedia (now owned by Sonic Blue) are the biggest brands, followed by RCA, Sensory Science, Creative Labs, and other, smaller brands. Many players are Macintosh-compatible, with other manufacturers working toward Mac compatibility. All MP3 players are battery-operated and have headphone outputs, along with a means of connecting to a computer for file transfer. Price: $90 to $400 and up.

Key features

Most MP3 players come with two-part software for interfacing with a personal computer, usually a PC. The **PC-to-player interface** consists of software drivers that let the PC and player communicate, along with a Microsoft Windows Explorer-type application you use to drag and drop files to the player's memory. **Jukebox software** keeps track of your MP3 files, manages playlists, and lets you record songs from audio CDs. For more on using MP3 players, see "The ABCs of MP3," page 52.

An MP3 player may connect to your computer using a Universal Serial Bus (USB) or (less often) a parallel connection. The older parallel connection is slower and only works with

Windows machines. (Unlike USB ports, parallel ports cannot be simultaneously "shared" between different devices.) Players typically come with some combination of internal and/or external memory such as CompactFlash, MultiMedia Card, or Smart Media. Some newer models use MagicGate (an encrypted-audio version of Sony's existing MemoryStick media), PocketZip, or SecureDigital.

LCD screens on most players show such information as track number, song title, and memory used. Volume, track forward/reverse, and pause-play controls are standard. An **adjustable equalizer** (EQ) setting gives you the most control over the sound, but some units have simple bass/treble controls, bass boost, or just presets for various music types (rock, classical, and so forth). A number of players include FM tuners.

Most models use one or two AA or AAA batteries, sometimes rechargeable ones. A battery-life indicator on some models helps keep track of how much power is left.

Some MP3 players include features more commonly found on a personal digital assistant (PDA), such as voice recording and phonebook or memo applications. (PDAs that run the newest version of the Pocket PC operating system from Microsoft can play MP3-encoded files, and Handspring's Visor clones of Palm PDAs have an expansion slot to which you can attach an MP3 player.) Certain models can be used to transfer data files between computers, sometimes via the external memory card.

How to choose

PERFORMANCE DIFFERENCES. On most models, the processing necessary to turn music into an MP3 file led, in recent CONSUMER REPORTS tests, to slight though in most cases barely noticeable degradation of the audio signal, by noise or a muffling in some frequency ranges. Poor sound quality was more likely to be caused by mediocre or downright poor headphones found on many players.

Manufacturers' estimates of battery life are useful guides, we've found. According to them, players will run between four and 12 hours before their AA or AAA batteries need replacement. Players that hold two batteries typically have longer battery life.

Ease of use remains a problem with many of these devices. When we connected the most recently tested models to a computer, the PC often didn't recognize the player, and we had to resort to trial and error.

RECOMMENDATIONS. As with computers, memory size counts. For people who like to have lots of music in a small package, we recommend choosing an MP3 player that has some memory built in yet allows expansion via external memory cards. These cards typically cost $50 to $160 for 64 MB. Models that use PocketZip disks save you plenty. Extra 40-MB disks cost only about $10 when you purchase a 10-pack. Upgradeable firmware, available in some models, can shield your player from obsolescence should newer encoding schemes or variations of MP3 compression become popular. The more additional formats a model can play—such as Windows Media Audio (WMA) or ATRAC—the more flexibility you have in downloading and transferring files now as well as in the future.

Before you buy, check that the player will be compatible with your Windows or Mac computer, including the operating systems your computer uses. Look for controls that are easy to work with one hand, as you would with other portable walk-abouts.

♦ **Ratings:** page 180

SCANNERS

A scanner is a simple, cheap way to digitize images for editing on your computer.
Paying more for a scanner with the higher maximum optical resolution probably isn't worth it.

You don't have to have a digital camera to take advantage of the computer's ability to edit photos. Images captured on film can be digitized by the photo processor and delivered on a CD or via the web. But if you do more than a modest amount of film photography, having a processor digitize your photos, at $5 to $10 per roll, can become expensive quickly, and means you pay for digitizing outtakes as well as winners. A more cost-effective way to digitize select photographs is with a flatbed scanner, which can capture the image of nearly anything placed on its glass surface—even those old photos you've tucked away in a family album or shoebox.

Sleeker and more rounded in appearance than they were in the past, flatbeds scan virtually anything that lies flat, making it possible to e-mail grandparents a copy of a kindergartner's latest drawing. Flatbeds also include optical character recognition (OCR) software, which can convert words on a printed page into a word-processing file in your computer. Some stores may throw in a flatbed scanner for free, or for a few dollars extra, when you buy a desktop computer.

Most flatbeds fall into two main categories based on maximum optical resolution, measured in dots per inch (dpi): 600 dpi and the generally more expensive 1,200 dpi. CONSUMER REPORTS' tests indicate that the extra amount that you may pay for a 1,200-dpi model is probably a waste of money.

Flatbeds aren't the only type of scanner you may see in stores. Sheet-fed models, also using OCR software, can automatically scan a stack of loose pages, but they sometimes damage pages that pass through their innards. And they can't scan anything much thicker than a sheet of paper. There are also multifunction devices, which save space by combining a scanner, printer, and a fax modem (see "Multifunction Devices," page 139). Serious photographers may want a film-only scanner that scans directly from an original slide or negative. But for most home needs, flatbed models offer the best combination of versatility, performance, and price.

Most types of scanners basically work the same way. As with photocopiers, a bar housing a light source and an array of sensors pass beneath a plate of glass on which the document lies facedown (or, in the case of a sheet-fed model, is passed over). The scanner transmits data from the sensor to the host computer, which runs driver software that works in coordination with the hardware to scan at certain settings. Once the image is in the computer, software bundled with the scanner (or purchased separately) lets you crop, resize, or otherwise edit it to suit your needs. From there, you can print the image, attach it to e-mail, or post it on the web.

What's available

A number of scanners come from companies that made their names in scanning technology. These include Microtek,

IN LIEU OF A COPIER
If you have a flatbed scanner and a color printer, you have all of the ingredients of a copier for black and white and color.

Mustek, Umax, and Visioneer. Other brands include computer makers and photo specialists such as Acer, Agfa, Canon, Eastman Kodak, Epson, Hewlett-Packard, Nikon, Panasonic, and Polaroid.

The type of scanner your buy—flatbed, sheet-fed, handheld, or film—depends largely on how you will use the scanner.

FLATBED SCANNERS. More than 90 percent of the scanners on the market are flatbeds. For most home needs, these offer the best combination of versatility, performance, and price. They can scan from magazines or books, and work well for text, graphics, and photos. Flatbeds fall into two main categories based on maximum optical resolution, measured in dots per inch (dpi). Price range: 600 dpi, $70 to $150; 1,200 dpi, $150 to $200.

SHEET-FED MODELS. This is the type often used in multifunction devices, which can also print, send, and receive faxes. Price range for multifunction devices: $200 to $600.

FILM SCANNERS. These offer a much higher maximum resolution than you get from an ordinary flatbed or sheet-fed model—about 2,400 dpi. Some can accept small prints as well. Price range: $400 to $700.

Key features

While the quality of images a scanner produces depends in part on the software included with the scanner, there are several hardware features to consider.

Most recent models can be connected via the USB port found on today's computers. (A few scanners draw power from the USB connection rather than from a wall outlet.) Some scanners can also connect to the parallel port found on Windows computers of any age. If you need more USB ports to accommodate a scanner, consider buying a self-powered USB hub for $30 to $80. Models CONSUMER REPORTS recently tested all support Windows 98 and later versions, plus—on models allowing a parallel-port connection—Windows 95. And while some USB-connected scanners can be used with a Macintosh, users of older Macs may need to upgrade to Mac OS 8 or higher and buy a USB adapter.

You start scanning by running **driver software** that comes with the scanner or by pressing a preprogrammed button on the scanner itself. Models with buttons automate routine tasks to let you operate your scanner as you would other office equipment; on some models, you can customize their functions. Any of these tasks can also be performed through the scanner's software without using buttons. A **copy/print button** initiates a scan and sends a command to print the results on your printer, effectively making the two devices substitute as a copier. Other button functions found on some models include scan to a file, scan to a fax modem, scan to e-mail, scan to web, scan to OCR, cancel scan, power save, start scanner software, and power on/off.

You can instead start the driver software from within an application, such as a word processor, that adheres to an industry standard known as TWAIN. A scanner's driver software allows you to preview a scan onscreen and crop it or adjust contrast and brightness. Once you're satisfied with the edited image, you can perform a final scan and pass the image to a running program or save it on your computer. You can make further, more extensive changes to an image with specialized image-editing software. And to scan text from a book or letter into a word-processing file in your computer, you run OCR software.

Many documents combine text with graphic elements, such as photographs and drawings.

A handy software feature called **multiple-scan mode**, found on many scanners, lets you break such hybrids down into different sections that can be processed separately in a single scan. You can designate, for example, that the sections of a magazine article that are pure text go to the OCR software independently of the article's graphic elements. Other scanners would require a separate scan for each section of the document.

How to choose

PERFORMANCE DIFFERENCES. In recent tests of flatbed scanners, Consumer Reports used the scanner software provided by the manufacturer to print scanned photos on a high-resolution inkjet printer at 150, 300, 600, and (when possible) 1,200 dpi. There was little improvement in the quality of scanned color and black-and-white photographs above 300 dpi. For the flatbed scanners tested, the manufacturer-recommended scan ranges were 150 to 300 dpi for photos, text, and line art, and 72 to 96 dpi for e-mail, web sites, and onscreen viewing. Taking the time and trouble to do high-resolution scans is worse than unnecessary. It results in scans that take two to four times longer and creates files that are much larger.

Another key specification is color depth, a measure of the number of colors the scanner is able to recognize. This is expressed as the number of data bits (ones or zeroes) that are associated with each pixel of a scanned image. Recently tested models scanned with at least 36-bit depth (some boast a 42-bit depth), but their software usually reduced the output images to 24-bit depth. Even 24-bit equates to more colors than the human eye can distinguish, so there's certainly no point in paying extra for 42-bit depth.

The OCR software that came with our test models did a nearly error-free job of converting a typewritten memo. The scanners made more errors processing a page from Consumer Reports magazine, but few enough that our engineers were able to fix them with minimal effort.

Images produced with film-scanning adapters that come with some flat-bed scanners aren't really worth the effort, according to our tests. The adapters weren't very effective at flattening the film and had no focus adjustment to control the distance between the scan head and the film. The resulting images were usually slightly fuzzy. Worse, the images were off in color or contrast. Some even looked grainy. If you need to scan film or slides frequently, it's generally worth buying a dedicated film scanner.

RECOMMENDATIONS. Because a flatbed scanner with a 1,200-dpi maximum resolution yields little or no additional benefit, save your money and buy one with 600-dpi maximum resolution. Similarly, don't pay extra for a scanner with 42-bit color depth.

Matching the original version of a color photo is the most demanding of a scanner's functions. You'll sometimes need to use image-editing software to get a

---

GUIDE TO PICTURE FILE FORMATS

Ready to hook up your scanner and begin playing with photos and other graphics? First you'll need to understand the differences between the various file formats available for storing your scanned images. Here's a look at four major formats, which are indicated in a document name by the extension, a three- or four-letter suffix such as .tif or .gif:

TIFF. This stands for Tagged Image File Format (represented by the .tif extension), a format that works well for the storage and exchange of images between high-end desktop-publishing and graphic-arts applications.

JPEG. Short for Joint Photographic Experts Group, this is a common method of compressing photographic images. It has surprisingly little effect on image quality when used at moderate levels of compression. Compression can save space and speed up communications, such as when an image is downloaded from the web. These files have the .jpg extension.

GIF. This is short for Graphics Interchange Format. GIF files (extension .gif) are a compressed file format commonly used for graphics on the web.

Bitmap. Represented by the suffix .bmp, bitmap files are also commonly used to display and store photos and graphic images.

printed version that's faithful to the original. If your older Windows PC does not have a USB port, make sure the scanner you're buying can be connected to a parallel port. The Macintosh-compatible flatbed scanners we tested include software for both the Mac and PC, but not necessarily the same programs for both platforms.

♦ **Ratings:** page 188

8

Ink to Paper

Choosing a computer printer used to be a matter of deciding which black-and-white printer offered the fastest speed and highest-quality output for the money. Outfitting today's home office is a little trickier, thanks to the choices available.

If you have children, dabble in digital photography, or produce the occasional business presentation from the comfort of your den, color is a must. That's where inkjet printers come in. They're not limited to color, of course. They also turn out respectable black-and-white text pages. On the other hand, if you're more concerned with churning out a sizable volume of black-and-white text, a black-and-white laser may be a better choice.

Other useful home-office tools include a multifunction device, which combines the functions of a printer, scanner, copier, and a fax machine in one bundle. As with printers, the major types of multifunction devices are inkjet and laser.

PRINTERS

New, inexpensive inkjet printers print color superbly and faster than ever. An alternative is a laser printer, which excels at printing black-and-white text.

Inkjet printers are now the standard computer accompaniment. They do an excellent job with color—turning out color photos nearly indistinguishable from photographic prints, along with banners, stickers, transparencies, T-shirt transfers, or greeting cards. Some even turn out excellent black-and-white text. With some very good models selling for less than $200, the vast majority of printers sold for home use are inkjets.

Laser printers still have their place in home offices. If you print reams of black-and-white text documents, you might want the speed, quality, and low per-copy cost of a laser printer.

Printers use a computer's microprocessor and memory to process data. The latest models are so fast partly because computers themselves have become more powerful and contain much more memory than before.

Unlike the computers they serve, most home printers can't be upgraded except for adding memory to laser printers. Most people usually get faster or more-detailed output by buying a new printer.

What's available

The printer market is dominated by a handful of well-established brands. Hewlett-Packard is the market leader. Other brands are Brother, Canon, Epson, Lexmark, and Oki. Xerox has said that it's getting out of the consumer printer market.

The type of computer a printer can serve depends on its ports. A Universal Serial Bus (USB) port lets a printer connect to Windows or Macintosh computers. Some models have a parallel port, which lets the printer work with older Windows computers. Many printers lack a serial port, which means they won't work with older Macintosh computers.

INKJET PRINTERS. Inkjets use droplets of ink to form letters and graphics. Most inkjet printers use two cartridges to supply the droplets. One holds cyan (greenish-blue), magenta, and yellow inks, the other black ink. Both cartridges are used for full-color work, the black one alone for plain text. Some low-priced inkjets take either a black or a color cartridge, but not both at the same time; they're usually sold without the black cartridge and use all three colors to print–expensively–"black." For photos, some inkjets also have additional cartridges that contain lighter shades of some inks. But CONSUMER REPORTS' tests have shown that the four basic colors can produce excellent photos. Most inkjets run at two to four pages per minute (ppm) for black-and-white text but are much slower for color jobs, taking four to 12 minutes to print a single 8x10 color photo. The cost of printing a black-and-white page with an inkjet varies considerably from model to model–3 to 9 cents. Price range: $50 to $500.

LASER PRINTERS. These work much like plain-paper copiers, forming images by transferring toner (powdered ink) to paper passing over an electrically charged

PUT YOUR PRINTER ON A BUDGET

While it's true that printer prices are lower than ever, the cost of necessities such as ink, toner, and paper quickly adds up. You can save ink and paper by following these tips:

◆ For not-yet-final versions of letters or photos, use draft mode, which saves ink or toner (and often speeds printing as well). You may find that you're satisfied with less than the highest-resolution mode even for final copies.

◆ Print out photos still being edited onto standard bond paper and save the pricey photo paper for the finished product. You can also print works in progress in a smaller size, or several to a page, to save ink and paper.

◆ Print a multipage document as smaller "thumbnails," with four or more pages to a sheet, if your printer can do so. This helps if you need a pre-final view of printed pages.

And, of course, there are times you need not use up any consumables:

◆ Preview before printing. The Print Preview feature of most software programs lets you see how a printout will look so you can avoid false starts.

◆ Print selectively. Instead of printing web pages, bookmark them or do a "Save As" to a default folder. If you do print them, use black-and-white, not color, if your printer allows it.

THE SUPPLY CLOSET

The eventual cost of printing supplies can easily top the cost of your printer. Here's a look at what you'll need.

Ink and toner

The cost of ink and toner depends on how much you put on a page. In general, for a page of black-and-white text, ink or toner costs 3 to 14 cents per page. Color printing runs 50 to 75 cents per page for color graphics and from 90 cents to $1.50 for color photos, including about 60 cents or more per sheet for glossy photo paper. Inkjet cartridges cost $20 to $40 for black-and-white and $50 to $70 for color. Black-and-white laser cartridges, usually including the drum and toner, cost about $100 but aren't changed as frequently as inkjet cartridges. You can get cartridges through the web sites of printer manufacturers, as well as office-supply stores and web sites and warehouse clubs. To compare prices, check price-comparison sites such as *www.shopper.com* and *www.computershopper.com*

Basic paper

Keep boxes of paper in a cool, dry place. Humidity can adversely affect how the paper feeds through the printer. For the most part, good quality copier paper or midweight (20-pound) paper designed for use in either inkjet or laser printers will be a staple. You can buy either in reams of 500 sheets or boxes of 5,000 sheets at most computer stores, office-supply stores, or warehouse clubs for less than a penny per sheet. Paper specially designed for use in laser printers costs a bit more, but doesn't provide much improvement.

Specialty paper

For most text jobs, printing on anything other than plain paper is probably a waste of money; CONSUMER REPORTS' tests have found that a printer's black-and-white text looked much the same on one grade of paper as another.

When you need good-quality color printouts, for graphics and photos, it's worthwhile to invest in more expensive paper. Most printers produce only so-so color images on copier paper. Papers designed to enhance colors and avoid smudging fall into four common types:

Coated. Coated paper is designed to work with inkjets to minimize drying time. It's about 5 to 10 cents per sheet.

Quality falls between that of copier paper and glossy or high-resolution stock. All printers accept paper of this type.

High-resolution. Some printer models accept high-resolution stock, which is quick to dry and less expensive than glossy stock but produces similar results. Expect to pay 11 to 15 cents per sheet.

Glossy. Glossy paper gives crisp color and resolution but is very expensive—typically 60 cents to $2 per sheet. Images printed on glossy stock take about an hour to dry. Tests, however, showed that using glossy paper improved the color performance of nearly every printer.

Photo. There's a wide array of photo-quality papers, costing from 60 cents to about $1.50 a sheet. Some of these heavy papers are perforated, allowing you to print out two 5x7 prints from one sheet.

Greeting cards, decals, etc.

There are dozens of ways to get creative with your home computer—banners, greeting cards, decals and temporary tattoos, iron-on transfers—and there are all sorts of new papers designed to enhance the look of these projects.

Greeting cards. These make it relatively easy to turn out a personalized greeting card, whether it's something unique to cheer up a friend or an entire batch of holiday greetings featuring a family photo. They come complete with envelopes, 35 to 75 cents per card.

Decals. Decal paper lets you create signs or decorations with your computer and inkjet printer. Each sheet, sold in packs of five or 10, costs from $1.50 to $2.

Iron-on transfers. To create personalized T-shirts, pillows, cloth banners, and other projects, iron-on transfer sheets let you take an image from your computer's screen, print it in water-resistant inks, and iron it onto any smooth cloth surface. Each transfer sheet costs about $1.50.

Business cards. You'll find specialized paper that can turn out professional-looking cards for a fraction of the cost of having them done for you. Each sheet of perforated paper gives you 10 cards and costs $12 to $15 for 25 sheets. Such paper works in both inkjets and laser printers.

Labels. You can find a broad array of labels, including mailing labels, packing labels, and filing labels. Prices start at about $6 for a package of 180 mailing labels.

IMAGE HANDLING
There are many ways to make copies. You can:

◆ Use a scanner, a printer, and a computer.

◆ Use a multifunction device.

◆ Use a stand-alone fax machine (you'll get the same low resolution that you get with faxes).

◆ Buy a small stand-alone copier. Price range: $90 to $300.

◆ Make copies at drugstores, libraries, print shops, and office-supply stores.

◆ Use a copying machine at work (if your employer permits it).

drum. The process yields sharp black-and-white text and graphics. Color laser printers used to be beyond the range of most home users' budgets. Laser printers usually outrun inkjets, cranking out black-and-white text at a rate of five to seven ppm. Black-and-white laser printers generally cost about as much as high-end inkjets, but they're cheaper to operate. Laser cartridges, about $100, often contain both the toner and the drum and can print thousands of black-and-white pages, for a per-page cost of 2 to 3 cents. Price range: black-and-white, $250 to $500; color, $1,200 and up.

Key features

Printers differ in the fineness of detail they can produce. **Resolution**, expressed in dots per inch (dpi), is often touted as the main measure of print quality. But other factors count too, such as the way dot patterns are formed by software instructions from the **printer driver.** Maximum printer resolution is often touted as a selling point. But a high maximum printer resolution is not necessarily synonymous with quality. At their default settings—where they're usually expected to run—inkjets currently on the market typically have a resolution between 600x600 dpi and 720x2,880 dpi. Lasers for home use typically offer 600 dpi, though some can print at a higher setting. Printing photos on special paper at a higher dpi setting can produce smoother shading of colors.

The better inkjet printers include an **ink monitor** to warn you when you're running low. Generic ink cartridges and **refill kits** can cut costs, but you may want to think twice before using them. Usually a printer's **warranty** won't cover repairs if an off-brand cartridge damages the printer.

For **double-sided printing,** you can have printers print the odd-numbered pages of a document first, then flip those pages over to print the even-numbered pages on a second pass through the printer. A few printers can automatically print on both sides, but doing so slows down printing considerably.

How to choose

PERFORMANCE DIFFERENCES. When it comes to producing graphics and photos, many inkjets do an excellent job. The best in CONSUMER REPORTS' tests print graphics that are crisp, clean, and vibrant-looking. Photos rival the output of a photofinishing lab, with smooth gradations and deep blacks. The worst inkjets turn out graphics that are dull, grainy, or banded. Photos may suffer from overinked dark areas, textures that make skin seem pebbled and grainy, or dull colors.

In recent tests, laser printers generally had the advantage when it came to producing excellent-quality black-and-white text. But more than half of the dual-cartridge inkjets we tested rivaled them in this regard. Laser models differ in terms of cost per page.

In tests, printing results were sometimes better for one side of the paper than the other. Some brands of paper indicate on the package which side to use.

RECOMMENDATIONS. An inkjet printer is the more versatile choice, and the only inexpensive one, for both color and black-and-white output. If you plan on printing color graphics and photos, then a dual-cartridge inkjet printer is the way to go. A single-cartridge inkjet might be inexpensive to purchase, but it will be more costly to use and usually delivers inferior results. Buy a laser printer if you need to turn out a large amount of high-quality black-and-white text.

If the printer and the computer allow it, connect the printer to a USB port for easy setup. If you have to use the parallel port, use an IEEE 1284-compliant printer cable.

Printers are mostly reliable, according to CONSUMER REPORTS' surveys. Our most recent survey showed that fewer than 1 in 10 printers purchased in the previous four years had ever been repaired or developed a serious problem.

♦ **Ratings:** page 185

MULTIFUNCTION DEVICES

With a multifunction device, you get a printer, scanner, copier, and sometimes a fax machine in a single unit, often for less than $500, in a small footprint.

A multifunction device offers compactness, versatility, and affordability. You get a printer, scanner, copier, and a fax machine all in one unit. That's great if you need all that compatibility. But a basic printer and a separate fax machine may be all many people need, for an expenditure of $400 or so. Multifunction devices have greatly improved over the past few years, so even a workhorse home office that produces a substantial number of printed documents each week will be satisfied with these machines' print quality.

What's available

The main types are inkjet and laser. Most multifunction devices support both Windows and Macintosh machines, but models don't always have a serial port (in addition to the USB port), which means not all work with Macintosh computers manufactured before mid 1998. Most major printer and copier manufacturers are also in the multifunction business. The key brands in this category are Brother, Canon, Epson, and Hewlett-Packard. Price range: $200 to $600.

Key features

The **resolution** at the default setting is usually 300 dpi (for some it's 600 dpi), and all are TWAIN-compliant (TWAIN refers to an interface between image-processing software and a scanner or digital camera). As with printers, maximum printer resolution, the maximum number of dots per inch (dpi), is often touted as a selling point. But a model with a high maximum printer resolution is not necessarily synonymous with quality. In addition to copying in black and white, some can copy in color. Not all multifunction devices can reduce or enlarge images.

In addition to **faxing** in black and white, some multifunction devices can fax in color to other color-capable devices. The **scanner** of a multifunction device is sheet-fed, which means it can't scan material such as books. After scanning, text is "read" by an optical-character-recognition (OCR) program before it's edited on the computer. Images can be used immediately by a graphics program.

How to choose

PERFORMANCE DIFFERENCES. CONSUMER REPORTS' tests have shown that the print quality of multifunction devices can be expected to match that of a printer-only model using the same ink cartridges or toner and having the same resolution options.

RECOMMENDATIONS. First determine if you need a multifunction device. If you're outfitting a home office from scratch and space is at a premium, consider buying one. Note, though, that if you count on one machine to do everything, you'll sacrifice some future flexibility. You can't upgrade just one function in a multifunction device. And if a major part breaks down, the entire machine will be out of service. A separate fax machine and printer may make more sense. If you decide to buy a multifunction device, consider how it will be used. If you plan to scan and print color photos or graphics, an inkjet multifunction device will give you the versatility you need. But if you only plan to print, or copy black-and-white text or graphics, a laser multifunction device will be a good choice.

9

Telephones

Americans are using phone services in ways that were once unimaginable—and paying a sizable amount for the privilege. Households that managed to make do for years with a couple of corded handsets now bristle with cellular and cordless phones. Fax machines, multifunction devices, answering machines, and computer modems all compete for one or two phone lines. Not surprisingly, consumers are ringing up bigger phone bills. The average household now runs up about $75 per month in phone charges. For families with two phone lines, high-speed Internet service, a couple of cell phones, and a well-used calling card or two, the monthly cost of staying connected can be hundreds of dollars—sometimes even as expensive as a car payment.

CELL PHONES

Complex pricing schemes and incompatible technologies still make choosing a handset and a service plan a tough call for consumers.

You'd think that after more than a decade, the tumult unleashed by the cellular revolution would have settled down. But problems that have plagued the industry from its infancy continue to burden consumers with inflated costs and frequent service breakdowns.

In selecting a service plan, you must still navigate a maze of widely varying charges for calls made during "peak" and "off-peak" minutes, while "roaming" outside your home area, and when dialing long distance. Maps that purport to show where service is available often fail to disclose "dead" spots where calls can be blocked and pockets where towers that carry cellular signals are scarce. You also need to consider whether you'll be calling another cell phone or just noncell phones. Further complicating the situation is the use of four incompatible digital formats and three frequency bands. When you change carriers, the chances are good that you'll have to toss away your handset and give up your phone number.

In short, what appears to be missing from the wireless industry's successful formula is a key ingredient—reliable basic service that's easy to understand.

What's available

To use cellular service, you'll need both a phone and a service provider. The leading cell-phone brands include Audiovox, Ericsson, Kyocera (formerly Qualcomm), Motorola, Nokia, and Samsung. The leading carriers include familiar names such as AT&T Wireless and Sprint PCS, as well as recently merged entities such as Verizon Wireless (created out of Bell Atlantic, GTE, and others) and Cingular Wireless (owned by BellSouth and SBC Communications).

Phone handsets may be extremely thin and as light as 4.3 ounces, or chunky and heavier. They may cost hundreds of dollars or be included with a service plan for free or a nominal amount. Options include instant messaging, e-mail, and limited web access.

The two major types of cell-phone technology are analog and digital.

ANALOG. Long dominant, analog cellular phones are beginning to fade from the market landscape. They operate in the cellular band of the radio spectrum and deliver true national service. Advanced Mobile Phone Service (AMPS), the traditional analog transmission technology, is used as a fallback for digital phones when digital transmission is impeded or not available.

DIGITAL. This technology has long been touted by carriers as offering high-quality sound and longer battery life. CONSUMER REPORTS' tests have found essentially no difference in the quality of the voice between analog and digital technology. Digital does deliver improved battery life. All phones in the digital mode that we've seen are able to remain in standby mode for at least 24 hours without recharging.

Digital phones operate in the cellular band, the personal communications services (PCS) band, or the enhanced specialized mobile radio (ESMR) band. There are four incompatible digital formats: Code Division Multiple Access (CDMA), Global System for Mobile Communications (GSM), Integrated Digital Enhanced Network (iDEN), and Time Division Multiple Access (TDMA). CDMA and TDMA are the dominant digital formats in the U.S. GSM, the de facto standard around the world, is used in the U.S. by VoiceStream and some regional carriers. The iDEN format was developed by Motorola and is used by Nextel and a few others.

There are several types of digital phones:

DUAL-MODE. Most new cellular phones are dual-mode. Operating in the cellular band and using a digital format, either CDMA or TDMA, these default to cellular analog if the phone is unable to detect a digital signal.

DUAL-MODE, DUAL-BAND. These operate in the PCS band and use a digital format, either CDMA, GSM, or TDMA. If they can't detect a compatible PCS signal, they default to cellular analog.

TRI-MODE. The most versatile, these can handle calls in the CDMA or TDMA digital formats in both the cellular and PCS bands. They can default to analog in the cellular band.

SINGLE-MODE, SINGLE-BAND. These use the CDMA, TDMA, or GSM format and the PCS band, or the iDEN format in the ESMR band. If they can't detect the home carrier, they don't work.

Service options

As dazzling as the technology in those sleek handsets can be, it's the service plan you choose—not the hardware—that will absorb the bulk of your cellular budget. Indeed, the technology that the carrier you select uses to process call signals will determine which handsets you can consider. That's why you should shop first for a plan that offers the best value for the times when you're likeliest to call.

RUDIMENTARY SERVICE. For the most basic service, offered through so-called prepaid plans, you purchase calling minutes in replenishable allotments, usually at top per-minute rates. Typically, the prepaid option is used by consumers with brief or spotty credit histories who cannot otherwise qualify for an annual contract, or by young people whose parents pay their bills and want to limit their calling. But this can also be one way for novice cell-phone users to try out a service and see how they use it before committing to a contract. If you choose prepaid service, however, your choice of handsets may be limited to a few no-frills models.

CONTRACTUAL PLANS. Most plans today offer a prescribed number of included minutes for a flat monthly fee. Choosing one involves some thorny tradeoffs. Depending on where you live, you may find plans that range in cost from as little as $10 (for a scant 10 minutes or so of airtime per month) up to as much as $400 (providing a loquacious 4,000 minutes). Generally, the bigger the "bucket" of minutes you buy, the lower your per-minute calling cost will be—provided, of course, that you use most or all of your monthly allotment.

Extra time beyond that allowance is charged at a rate of anywhere from 25 to 65 cents per minute. Supplemental minutes often cost less in plans that come bundled with a larger monthly allowance.

While the included minutes in most calling plans can be used anytime, day or night, some carriers promote deals that offer bundles of extra minutes for off-peak evening and weekend hours.

CALLING-AREA OPTIONS. Further complicating the choice of a plan is the size of the area qualifying for calls to be charged at the lowest per-minute rate. The narrowest of these so-called home areas may be a city and its surrounding suburbs—usually a fine choice for commuters wanting to stay in touch.

A regional plan, by contrast, offers a more generous, multistate home-calling area, though it may come with a higher flat monthly charge (or fewer minutes).

The top-tier plans offer buckets of nationwide minutes at a flat monthly rate, with no restrictions on local, roaming, or long-distance calls. You can expect to pay a premium for coast-to-coast service.

Key features

Look for an LCD screen that is backlit and readable in both low- and direct-light conditions. Typically it warns you when you're roaming. The **keypad** should be clearly marked and easy to use. **Programmable speed dial** allows you to store the names and numbers of the people you most frequently call. This feature is easiest to use if it has scroll and alphabetic-search functions. **Single-key last-number redial** is useful for dropped calls or when you're having trouble connecting.

Some models have **caller ID**, **voice mail**, and **messaging**. Some phones and providers make Internet content available on a cell phone's tiny screen, letting you receive short e-mail messages and check news, weather, and stock quotes on specially designed web sites known as "clipped web pages."

CELLULAR HEALTH AND SAFETY UPDATE

Four out of five respondents to a recent CONSUMER REPORTS survey said that being able to call for help in the event of an emergency was their chief reason for getting a cell phone. But how well do the service providers fulfill that objective? And what about the health and safety risks—exposure to radio waves and potentially fatal driver distraction—that the growing use of cell phones raise? Here's a rundown of these cell-phone issues:

Dialing 911

Americans ring 911 from cell phones more than 100,000 times per day, and while most emergency calls get through, the Federal Communications Commission cannot say how many do not. The calls don't get special priority—carriers are not required to clear congested circuits to make way. Handsets that operate in the dual-mode (analog and digital) or tri-mode (analog, digital, and the higher frequency PCS band) have a better chance to connect: If their call is blocked using one mode, they can switch automatically to a different band or network.

But there's another serious shortcoming in emergency-call services. Because of network complexities, some 911 calls aren't routed to the closest response center—cell phones can't indicate exactly where their owner is. "Enhanced 911," now being developed under FCC order, will pinpoint locations for police and other emergency services personnel so they can provide assistance. But when it will roll out across the nation remains in doubt, because many carriers have asked the FCC for extensions to an October 2001 deadline, and because only a small fraction of the country's police departments now operate such a system. When it is implemented, it may demand handsets with chips that read position from satellites. Until enhanced 911 arrives, if you can report even a rough location, that can speed getting help.

Radio waves and cancer

A number of high-profile lawsuits have alleged that cell phones cause brain tumors, but to date no conclusive epidemiological evidence has demonstrated such a risk. Investigation into a possible link is ongoing under the guidance of the U.S. Food and Drug Administration, supported in part with industry funding. The World Health Organization is also sponsoring an epidemiological study. Definitive answers are years away.

Nonetheless, the FCC has set a limit on the energy emitted by handset antennas that the body is permitted to absorb, measured in watts per kilogram of tissue and known as the specific absorption rate (SAR). That number, now given on new cell phones, is capped at 1.6 watts per kilogram of tissue. Because SARs can be measured in several ways and vary greatly when a phone is used, it's hard to compare them meaningfully from phone to phone. SAR levels below 1.6 watts per kilogram aren't necessarily safer. If you're concerned about exposure until more is known, use a headset that keeps the handset's antenna away from your head. And, of course, limit your calls.

Driving and talking

It's self-evident that cell phones distract drivers who use them, and a 1997 study published in *The New England Journal of Medicine* demonstrated how calling while driving increases the risk of accidents. The researchers concluded that using a cell phone quadrupled the chances of having an accident, and that using a hands-free kit did not lower the probability. Apparently, holding a conversation, not holding or fumbling with a phone, was decisive.

The problem of driver distraction has led some states to follow county and municipal governments in restricting use of cell phones behind the wheel. The state of New York in 2001 banned using a handheld cell phone while driving. A New Hampshire law scheduled to take effect in 2002 will impose fines of up to $1,000 and suspend for up to a year the licenses of drivers found to be distracted at the time of an accident. A U.S. House of Representatives bill would ban the use of cell phones across the nation and withhold highway funds from states that don't enforce such a ban. Nearly half of all U.S drivers keep a cell phone in their primary vehicle.

Distracted driving is not a uniquely American phenomenon. Abroad, more than 20 countries—Germany, Israel, Japan, and the United Kingdom among them—have enacted laws aimed at curtailing cell-phone use on the road.

Instead of ringing, some handsets have a **vibrating alert** or a flashing light-emitting diode to let you know about an incoming call, useful when you're in a meeting or at the movies. An **any-key answer** feature lets you answer the phone by pressing any key rather than the Talk or Send key. Many folding phones answer the call when you open the mouthpiece flap. Some models on the market **keep track of the time** you spend talking, both per call and cumulatively. Some call timers will beep at preset intervals—indispensable if you're trying to control costs by limiting the length of your calls.

Although carriers prefer that you connect digitally if they provide the service, several phones are designed so you can force an analog connection just prior to making a call, handy when all the digital circuits are busy.

The **battery** offered with the phone you buy won't necessarily give you the best service— and it's not your only option. There are several choices of battery size and chemistry, each offering different amounts of talk time and standby time. For the longest life between charges from a relatively compact energy source, look for a lithium-ion battery. Without recharging, it can power up a phone even if it hasn't been used for several months. A nickel-metal hydride battery (NiMH) is a step up from the standard nickel-cadmium (NiCd) power cells because you can keep it plugged in and recharging when you're not using the phone.

Some models come with a base that has an extra battery that can be kept charged while the handset is in use; that way you don't lose any time waiting for a recharge, which can take 6 to 24 hours in some "trickle" chargers. An **automobile adapter** lets you power the phone by plugging it into your car's cigarette lighter.

Some models include a **hands-free kit,** which works like a speakerphone, or a headset. Such capability is increasingly demanded by law for cell-phone use by drivers.

How to choose

PERFORMANCE DIFFERENCES. CONSUMER REPORTS' tests have found essentially no difference between analog and digital in terms of voice quality. The type of phone matters more. We've found that folding, or "flip," models transmit voices better than rectangular models. Folding phones have a concave angle between the ear piece and the microphone that better conforms to the shape of the head.

Phones vary widely in terms of keypad design, readability of screen displays, function-menu ease of use, and how simple it is to perform such basic tasks as one-button redial and storing frequently called phone numbers for later speed-dialing.

Digital does offer longer battery life between recharges. In our talk-time tests, batteries lasted about 80 percent longer in digital mode than when used in analog.

RECOMMENDATIONS. Choose a calling plan first. Even with the new lower-priced plans currently available, what you pay to use the phone will cost far more than the phone itself. You can efficiently gather wireless prices by visiting web sites such as *www.point.com*.

You should also study the carriers' service area maps closely. Dead zones and fringe areas, where coverage isn't available, can make a plan worthless if that's where you want to use your phone. Before you commit to a plan, make sure you have a trial period that lets you test the network and cancel the service without penalty if it doesn't deliver reliable signals in places where you make calls.

♦ **Ratings:** page 165

CORDLESS PHONES

Cordless phones, many with expanded range and improved security, are ringing in four out of five homes in the U.S.

Shoppers are snapping up cordless phones at a furious rate—more than 40 million per year. Falling prices have helped fuel the explosion. No-frills models now sell for just $20 or $30, so more people can afford to buy a cordless phone, or, in some cases, two or three. Those who already own a cordless phone might be tempted to add another one or upgrade to a newer, better model.

If you have a cordless phone and it's several years old, it's probably a 49-megahertz (MHz) analog model. Such a phone has a range from handset to base that is adequate within most homes. But the 49-MHz band is crowded not only with phones but also with baby monitors and walkie-talkies. Interference is possible, and eavesdroppers can pick up your conversation on a phone or police scanner. There may still be a few 49-MHz phones on the market, but there are better options.

Higher frequencies are supposed to allow users to stray farther from the base unit, while digital technology offers less interference and improved security from eavesdroppers. Step-up features include two lines (good for home businesses), built-in answering machines, caller ID, and hands-free speakerphones. At 5 to 10 ounces, they are generally heavier than corded-phone handsets.

What's available

A few brands—AT&T, Bell South, General Electric, Panasonic, Sony, Uniden, and VTech—account for more than 80 percent of the market. VTech recently acquired the AT&T Consumer Products Division and now makes phones under the AT&T brand as well as its own name.

A main distinction between cordless phones is how they transmit their signals. The major types are:

900-MHZ ANALOG. The biggest-selling type, these phones offer a range that allows you to venture into the yard or even your neighbor's. But they're not very secure if there is no voice-scrambling capability; anyone with a scanner can listen in. Price range: $20 to $130.

900-MHZ DIGITAL. These models offer a range similar to that of 900-MHz analog phones, but they're harder to listen in on. Price range: $60 to $150.

900-MHZ DIGITAL SPREAD SPECTRUM (DSS). With these models, a call is distributed over many frequencies, making conversations very secure and less prone to interference. The range is slightly better than that of other 900-MHz models. Price range: $60 to $200.

2.4-GHZ ANALOG OR DSS. Similar in performance to the equivalently featured 900-MHz models but for now more expensive.

Price range: $50 to $230 (for multiple-handset systems).

Key features

Most cordless phones have a jack for a headset plus a belt clip (usually sold separately for about $20) allowing hands-free conversation.

About a third of the cordless phones sold include an **answering machine**. For more on answering machines, see page 149.

A **caller-ID screen**, provided that you subscribe to a caller-ID service (at a cost of several dollars per month), displays the name and number of a caller. Many models also support **caller ID with call waiting**, meaning they'll display data on a second caller when you're already on the phone. Phones with caller ID typically keep a rolling list of at least 20 calls received. You press a button or two to call back, and in some cases you can save the number in a speed-dial slot. Some phones let you choose a distinctive ring pattern for certain callers.

To deal with long phone numbers, most phones offer **chain dialing**. You store the dialing prefix (a multidigit 10-10 or international code, say) in its own memory slot. You then press it plus a memory key for the number you're dialing. Most phones include speed dialing for at least 10 phone numbers.

Some models include a base **speakerphone** and keypad. An **intercom** feature in several models lets the person with the handset page someone near the base, and vice versa.

A phone with two lines is useful for subscribing to online services or separating a business and home number. Some phones have two ringers, each with a distinctive pitch, to let you know which line is ringing. There are signal lights that glow when a line is ringing or in use. A two-line phone may also let you link callers on both ends for a three-way chat. Some models with a speakerphone on the base let you have four-way conferencing.

On most models, the handset rings, and many phones have a second ringer in the base. An LCD screen on the handset or base can provide useful information such as the phone number dialed, battery strength, or how long you've been connected. All cordless phones have a **handset-locator button** that can help you find the handset when it is hiding under a sofa cushion.

Cordless-phone batteries may be rechargeable nickel-cadmium or nickel-metal hydride. Some models may provide a compartment in the base for charging a spare handset battery and on some can be used as the base power backup in the event of a power outage. Keep a corded model somewhere in your home.

How to choose

PERFORMANCE DIFFERENCES. Most new cordless phones have very good voice quality, CONSUMER REPORTS' tests show. Some are excellent, approaching the voice quality of the best corded phones. Size and shape vary considerably, as do features.

In our latest tests, fully charged nickel-cadmium or nickel-metal hydride batteries handled anywhere from four to about 13 hours of continuous conversation before they needed recharging. Most manufacturers claim that a new battery will last at least a week in standby mode.

Some phones offer better surge protection than others against damage from lightning or faulty wiring.

RECOMMENDATIONS. A 900-MHz phone should suit most users. Analog models, apt to be less expensive than digital, are fine for many people. Their big drawback is that there is little protection against eavesdropping if there is no voice-scrambling capability. If you want better security, go with a 900-MHz digital or DSS model. We don't think 2.4-GHz models offer enough added functionality to be worth the higher cost.

Ads mentioning the word "digital" may not be referring to the wireless transmission between the base and handset. To ensure voice transmission security, look for wording such as "digital phone," "digital spread spectrum," or "phone with voice scrambling." Phones that aren't secure might have packaging with wording such as "phone with digital security code,"

CREDIT CARD CAUTION
You might think twice about conducting credit-card transactions and other sensitive business on analog cordless phones. Only digital models offer protection against eavesdropping.

"phone with all-digital answerer," or "spread-spectrum technology."

Before you buy, hold the handset to your head to see if it feels comfortable. The handset of a cordless phone should fit the contours of your face. The earpiece should have rounded edges and a recessed center that fits nicely over the middle of your ear. Also, check the buttons and controls to make sure they're reasonably sized and legible. If possible, see what the LCD display looks like as well. You might also want to determine how easy it is to use the functions, especially for models with an answering machine.

CORDED PHONES

Today's basic telephone is a more versatile and sleeker-looking product than its boxy predecessor. You'll want to have at least one corded phone in your home.

The corded phone hasn't become obsolete. The best ones retain the edge over the best cordless phones in terms of voice quality and security. And no matter how many telephones in a home, there should be at least one corded phone, so you have a working phone in the event of a power outage. Virtually all cordless phones require house current.

For as little as $10 to $15 or so, you can now buy a phone with such features as volume control and speed-dialing for 10 or more numbers. For $50 to $75 or more, you get a console with speakerphone or two-line capability, sometimes both.

What's available

AT&T (made by VTech) and GE are the dominant brands of corded phones. When shopping, you'll find these types:

CONSOLE MODELS. These are updated versions of the traditional Bell desk phone. Price range: $15 to more than $100.

TRIM-STYLE MODELS. These spacesavers have push-buttons on the handset, and the base is about half as wide as a console model's. Price range: $10 to $30.

PHONES WITH ANSWERERS. Combo units can sometimes be less expensive than buying a phone and an answerer separately. Price range: $50 to $150.

Key features

Trim-style phones, with a keypad on the handset, can be hard to use if you need to listen and punch buttons at the same time, which you might have to do when navigating an unfamiliar voice-mail or automated-banking menu.

Corded phones tend to be less feature-laden than cordless ones. Even some less expensive phones have a **volume control** on the receiver, handy if the voice at the other end of the line starts to fade. It's practically standard for a phone to have **last-number redial** and **speed dialing**. Features such as a **speakerphone**, **two-line capability**, or **caller ID** add to the price.

How to choose

PERFORMANCE DIFFERENCES. Most corded phones performed quite capably, conveying voices intelligibly under normal conditions, according to CONSUMER REPORTS' tests. The variations in sound quality that we have found are likely to matter only in very noisy environments.

RECOMMENDATIONS. Since good quality is pretty much a given, your main considerations should be features and price. Before you buy, make sure the handset is comfortable to hold in your hand and to your ear. Look for a good-sized, clearly labeled keypad, especially if your eyesight isn't good.

ANSWERING MACHINES

**Digital answering machines are faster, quieter, and more reliable
than the cassette versions that they have largely supplanted.**

The days of answering-machine messages recorded on cassette tape—with all of the accompanying clanking and long beeps—are pretty much over. Digital answering machines—less expensive than they were a few years ago—have become the mainstream choice. While solving the mechanical problems that beset tape answerers, they add some new, digital problems. With some models, the digital compression that aids in storing messages may drop words or change the sound of a person's voice—even making "16th Street" sound like "60th Street" in some situations. Digital answering machines also tend to have less recording time than cassette models.

What's available

Many answering machines are integrated with phones. (See "Cordless phones" on page 146.) Of stand-alone models, AT&T is the biggest-selling brand. Other major brands include Casio, GE, RadioShack, Sony, and Southwestern Bell.

Digital answering machines use memory chips, similar to those found in computers, to store the greeting and messages. They are less likely to break down than cassette answering machines—circuits have replaced moving parts—and they let you skip or delete messages more quickly. Price range: $20 to $100.

Key features

Recording memory varies from about 10 to 30 minutes—including the length of your greeting, which is typically limited to between 30 seconds and 2 minutes. Each message is usually limited to between 1 and 4 minutes. Some models let you set a limit—say, 1 minute or 3 minutes.

Most digital models have a **time and date stamp**, which records the day and time when messages come in. Most machines also have skipping and deleting features, which allow you to pick and choose the messages you want to listen to or save. Most can skip forward or backward and repeat, and some can speed up (fast forward), slow down, or rewind the message to get to and/or listen to a short section of the message. A digital readout on most models indicates the number of messages received. Most models visibly or audibly let you know when you have new messages.

Some digital machines have **mailboxes** so you can store a separate greeting and message for each family member or for your home business. **Caller ID**, a feature found on many phones, is now integrated with some answering machines. Some versions of the feature can recognize a number and play a specific greeting or announce a caller's name (talking caller ID).

Remote access lets you listen to messages on your answering machine from a touchtone

FREE DIRECTORY ASSISTANCE

Americans spend billions on directory assistance. These six web-based services give you listings for free:

◆ *www.anywho.com*
◆ *www.infospace.com*
◆ *www.infousa.com*
◆ *www.switchboard.com*
◆ *www.whowhere.com*
◆ *www.555-1212.com*

phone after entering a security code, usually two or three digits, or from your cordless phone handset, allowing you to listen to your messages in private.

How to choose

PERFORMANCE DIFFERENCES. The best digital machines produce good voice sound, have a decent amount of memory, and come with useful features. But not every model plays messages clearly, CONSUMER REPORTS' tests have shown. Other possible problems include loss of the day and time stamp, the greetings, and messages when the power goes out, as well as damage during a lightning storm. It's advisable to use a surge suppressor.

RECOMMENDATIONS. Decide whether you want the machine to be integrated with a telephone. If you can, test a model that you're considering in the store by recording a greeting or memo and playing it back. Make sure that you can live with the recording capacity. You can also opt for a voice-mail service offered by local phone companies. Such service runs about $7 per month.

CONSUMER REPORTS' surveys have found that most brands purchased over the past three years—both stand-alone models and those integrated with a telephone—have failure rates of no more than 10 percent.

10

Working in Comfort

How efficiently has the computer made people work? You punch Delete instead of rubbing an eraser back and forth over pencil marks. You don't waste time inserting sheets of paper into a typewriter. And now, with access to all kinds of information via the Internet, you may almost never have to get out of your chair to look something up. There's just one problem: Humans aren't meant to sit still. Nor are they meant to pound incessantly on computer keyboards, judging from the number of computer-related aches and illnesses reported. "Ergonomic" office furniture can help, but it has to fit you to begin with, you have to know how to use it, and you have to get out of your chair, stretch, and take breaks every once in a while. Even the best designs can be defeated.

ERGONOMIC CHAIRS

Of course the chair you sit in should be comfortable. But it can also help you adapt to a less-than-perfect office setup or desk.

Although you can find office-type chairs sold for as little as $25, you'll have to spend more to get what is considered a basic ergonomic chair—one with a lever to adjust seat height pneumatically; a contoured backrest; armrests; and a five-wheel base that swivels. First impressions of a chair's comfort seem to correspond well with long-term impressions. So if you sit in a chair at a store or dealer showroom and like it after adjusting it, you will probably find it comfortable after you get it home.

ERGONOMICS

Ergonomics is the study of what makes things easy to use. Ergonomic principles were first explored in this country during World War II in research showing that fighter pilots needed cockpits with controls placed logically and within easy reach.

What's available

The major brands are EckAdams, Global, Herman Miller, HON, Knoll, and Steelcase. You'll find them at mass merchandisers or office superstores. Furniture retailers such as IKEA and Workbench also sell office chairs. Price range: $60 to $1,000.

Key features

Being able to adjust the seat height is critical. If your feet aren't flat on the floor at the seat's lowest setting, the chair doesn't go low enough; if your knees angle up at the highest setting, it doesn't go high enough.

Generally, a chair with **five wheels** is more stable than one with four, a rule that's important for larger and heavier users and for people who are accustomed to scooting around their work area. Even with five wheels, some chairs still wobble noticeably. Try sitting far forward and back in a chair when trying it out; reject any chairs that seem prone to tipping.

A **forward-tilt lever** on some chairs angles the seat and backrest forward. Designed for typing, this adjustment lets you lean into your work without losing the support of the backrest.

The **backrest angle** is an adjustment on some chairs. The models that are easiest to adjust let you lean back while keeping your feet flat on the floor. Others require you to press a lever.

How to choose

PERFORMANCE DIFFERENCES. In panel tests, CONSUMER REPORTS found that no chair pleases everybody. Judgments were often connected with body size: Some taller panelists complained of seats that were too shallow, and some shorter panelists complained that they couldn't adjust a backrest contour low enough for them to be comfortable. The lowest-priced chairs weren't great, but the most expensive ones weren't necessarily the best for each panelist.

RECOMMENDATIONS. Before you choose an ergonomic chair, decide how adjustable you'll need it to be. If you plan to share the chair with someone who has a different height and build, you'll want a chair whose seat height and backrest easily adjust up and down. If you spend long hours at the computer, it's worth spending more to buy a well-designed chair. Adjustable armrests are a worthwhile extra, too.

Comfort is personal, so sit in a chair before you buy it. We suggest that you "try on" at least several chairs before you choose one. Sit before a workstation if the store has one on display to get a feel for positioning your arms. If, after you make a few adjustments, you still find that some contour hits you in the wrong place, or that the whole chair feels too big or small, then you're never likely to be very comfortable sitting in it.

Don't be oversold on adjustability. More adjustable parts don't necessarily make a better chair. Labels on the levers and knobs are nice, but they aren't much help on chairs whose controls are cluttered or otherwise confusingly designed. Look for effective and easy-to-use adjustments—a seat-height control that is simple and responsive, or armrests that notch into place on the first try. You should be able to easily make important adjustments while seated. Less important are controls such as tilt-tension knobs, which often don't seem to make a difference and are sometimes hard to reach.

Catalog pictures and manufacturers' specs won't give you the information you need. Don't buy a chair through a catalog or from a web site unless you've "sit-tested" the exact model in a store and are getting a better price through the mail or the Internet.

HOME-OFFICE SCENARIOS

Design your home office to meet your specific needs.
Someone planning to do occasional work at home might
need only a computer, phone, phone line, and web access.
The entrepreneur planning to build a business from
scratch might need all of the above, plus fax capabilities,
teleconferencing, postage metering, remote access, and
more. Here are three scenarios and how much they cost.

Scenario 1: The all-in-the-family home office

You want a setup that will accommodate regular family use
of the computer and occasional at-home work. Your needs
are not sophisticated, and you'd like to keep the budget
modest. You'll need:

◆ An 800-MHz Windows PC and 17-inch cathode ray
tube (CRT) monitor or a 400-MHz Apple iMac with 128
megabytes (MB) of RAM and a hard drive of 20 to 40
gigabytes (GB)–$800 to $1,100.

◆ A basic desk–$100 to $400.

◆ A basic, ergonomic chair–$60 to $90.

◆ A midpriced inkjet printer–$100 to $150.

◆ A basic, single-line corded phone with answering
machine–$40 to $60.

◆ Basic monthly Internet service (using 56-kbps
modem)–$20 per month.

Total: $1,100 to $1,800 (plus $20 per month for
Internet access).

Scenario 2: The compact and efficient home office

You do a lot of work from home, and your needs are
intermediate. You have little space, and you want
technology that will grow with you as your business
and personal needs evolve. You'll need:

◆ A 1-GHz Windows PC with a 15-inch flat-panel liquid
crystal display (LCD) monitor, a 900-MHz full-sized laptop
with 128 MB of RAM and a 20- to 40-GB hard drive–$1,600
to $2,000–or a 600-MHz iMac–$800 to $2,000.

◆ A quality computer desk with an adjustable keyboard
shelf that fits your space–$300 to $700.

◆ A higher-end ergonomic chair–$90 to $400.

◆ An inkjet or laser multifunction device (including printer,
scanner, fax, and auto document feed)–$200 to $600.

◆ A dual-line phone with answering machine–$100.

◆ A high-speed cable-modem or DSL Internet connection–$100 to $150 for connection, about $50 per month
for access.

Total: $1,590 to $3,950 (plus $50 per month for cable-
modem or DSL access).

Scenario 3: The state-of-the-art home office

You want every angle covered: computer, communications,
teleconferencing, postage, and fast Internet access. You
look at this home-office setup as an investment in your
future. You want technology that will show the world you
mean business. You'll need:

◆ A powerful, state-of-the-art 1.5- to 1.8-GHz Windows
PC or 733-MHz PowerPC G4 Macintosh with plenty of RAM
(256 MB), a huge hard drive (60 to 80 GB), a DVD-ROM
drive, and a backup drive such as a CD-RW drive–$1,800
to $2,500.

◆ A 17- or 19-inch CRT monitor–$200 to $500–or a
15- to 18-inch flat-panel LCD–$450 to $4,500.

◆ A full-sized executive desk with plenty of work,
drawer, and filing space–$600 to $2,000.

◆ A high-back, well-padded, ergonomic chair–$200
to $1,000.

◆ Two or more extra chairs or a small sofa for
visitors–$200 to $600.

◆ An inkjet or laser multifunction device (including
printer, scanner, fax, and auto document feed)–$200
to $600.

◆ A speakerphone with answering machine–$140
to $200.

◆ A cellular phone with a monthly plan–$500 to $1,000
per year.

◆ High-speed cable-modem or DSL Internet access–$100
to $150 for installation and $50 per month for access.

◆ A slim-and-light laptop or a personal digital assistant
with wireless Internet access for mobile e-mail and web
surfing–$400 to $3,000.

◆ At-home postal metering–$25 and up per month.

Total: $3,840 to $15,550 (plus $117 to $158 per month or
more for Internet access, cell-phone service, and postage).

CHAIR BASICS

Look for these essentials in an ergonomic chair:

◆ A lever to adjust seat height pneumatically.

◆ A contoured backrest.

◆ Adjustable and contoured armrests.

◆ A five-wheel base that swivels.

TIPS ON FITTING A CHAIR. Cushioning should be soft enough that you don't feel pressure at points where your body hits the chair, but not so soft that you sink into the chair and can't move around freely.

Match the contours in the back of the chair to the natural curve of your spine by adjusting the backrest height or moving the lumbar support. If you have a chair with too little curve, attach a special lumbar pillow or rolled-up towel to its back. A regular pillow might help if the chair curves more than your back does, but it won't offer much support.

Armrests should support your arms naturally. If you have to drop your shoulders to use them, the armrests are too far apart or too low. If you have to hunch your shoulders, they're too high. Make sure the armrests are adjustable and feel OK against your skin—a concern for warm-weather months when you might not be wearing long sleeves.

Consider the seat depth, as well. When you sit back, there should be a few fingers' to a fist's worth of space between the edge of the chair and the back of your knees, so that the seat doesn't press into your calves. With too much space, the chair won't support your

SETTING UP AN ERGONOMIC WORK SPACE

Unless you want to experience discomfort or even risk physical problems while using your computer, don't just clear a little space on any old flat surface, especially if you're immersing yourself in computer work. Typing in an improper position for a long time may lead to problems as serious as carpal tunnel syndrome, a condition caused by repetitive motion that leaves a person's hands, wrists, and forearms aching and weak—and, over time, barely usable. Treatment is rest, special braces, and sometimes surgery.

Staring for hours on end at a computer screen can cause headaches, eyestrain, and blurred vision. Craning to view a too-high monitor can hurt your neck and back.

You can reduce your risk of injury by adopting good computer work habits. Consider how your body matches your furniture and computer equipment—and how the pieces of equipment work together.

Lighting. Avoid glare and keep the light in the room balanced. You can minimize glare by controlling light sources in the room or by placing your monitor at a 90-degree angle to a window or other bright light. To balance the light (so your eyes don't get tired from constantly adjusting to different light levels), keep overall "ambient" lighting lower when you're working with a computer than you would if you were reading from paper. Use a focused task light to illuminate documents you're reading.

Seeing the screen. Position the top of the screen at eye level or slightly below so you don't have to tilt your head back or forward. Bifocal and trifocal wearers may need to lower the monitor, too, or get special glasses for computer use. Raise a too-low monitor with a support arm or stand (or a couple of thick books). You can also adjust your chair, keeping your feet flat on the floor or using a footrest. Place the monitor at about arm's length. Keep it clean and, if necessary, use a glare screen to improve screen contrast. If you look at documents while you type, attach a document holder ($5 to $10) to the side of the monitor.

Typing. Position the keyboard and mouse together on a surface in front of you, low enough so that you can type and move the mouse while holding your forearms comfortably at a right angle. The goal is to neither slump nor lift your shoulders. A desktop is often too high for a keyboard and mouse—you may need to use a keyboard shelf, which you bolt to the underside of the desk. Many such shelves have an extension for the mouse, necessary to keep the mouse on the same level as the keyboard.

Type with your wrists flat. Don't bend them up or down, and let them float over the keyboard. Don't rely on a wrist rest to anchor your wrists while you type. That's for resting your wrists when you're not typing. Armrests can help support the elbows. Above all, relax, and don't pound the keys. If you find it awkward moving a mouse around, try a trackball.

thighs properly. In a chair that's too deep, you could consider using a pelvic cushion which could push you forward sufficiently. There's no way to fix a chair that's too shallow unless its back has a depth adjustment.

WORKSTATIONS

A workstation holds all the components of a desktop computer and often a printer. There are hundreds of workstation options currently on the market.

Traditional writing desks aren't good for computer use for several reasons. Most have a surface that's too high for a keyboard—and those low enough for a keyboard are probably too low for a monitor. Also, unless a desk is large, it's unlikely to have enough depth to place the monitor back far enough, especially if you have a big monitor. An ergonomically correct workstation puts you in a comfortable and safe working position.

If you're willing to do some investigating, you can combine a regular desk or table with a few accessories to create a workstation that costs just a few hundred dollars (or less). But it's often more convenient and just as economical to buy furniture designed specifically for computer use. A workstation you put together yourself —often called ready-to-assemble (RTA) and sometimes called flat-packed—is what most people buy for their home offices. Most RTA workstations are made of laminated particleboard and sell for $65 to $300 or so. Those made with wood and wood veneer are more expensive—$300 or considerably more for a desk with hutch. You can also tuck your computer equipment into a fully assembled workstation made of finely finished solid wood, which costs several thousand dollars at the high end.

What's available

Most of the computer furniture you'll see comes from about a dozen manufacturers. The major brands are Bush, IKEA, O'Sullivan, and Sauder. Computer furniture you assemble yourself can be found at office-supply stores, home centers, home-furniture stores, and catalogs. You can find some higher-end furniture at specialty retailers such as Levenger and Crate & Barrel. Computer furniture comes in a range of styles, from contemporary to country to mission.

You'll find several types:

DESKS WITH HUTCH. The most popular type of workstation is a desk with a hutch, a cupboardlike attachment that sits atop the desk and provides extra storage space. Most such units consist of two pedestals that support a desktop with 300 to 500 square inches of usable work space. There's often a shelf for a printer and room for files and such. Assembly time for our engineer: 2 to 4 hours. Price range: $100 to $350.

CORNER UNITS. If you need room to spread out papers, choose a corner-unit desk. The trade-off is that these pieces need a lot of room. Most have a desktop with more than 1,000 square inches of usable work space. Some have a printer shelf. Assembly time for our engineer: 1½ to 3 hours. Price range: $150 to $400.

ARMOIRES. These units can pretend to be a china cabinet in a dining room or a freestanding

WORKSTATION TYPES

Desk with hutch

Corner unit

Amoire

Cart

closet in the bedroom. They are a great way to hide computer paraphernalia, but you'll need room alongside the unit to fully open the doors. The desktop is usually slightly smaller than that of traditional desks. Most units have a printer shelf. Assembly time for our engineer: 2 to 4 hours. Price range: $300 to $500.

CARTS. If space is tight or you'll need to move your workstation on occasion, a cart may be the best option. The trade-off for compact portability: limited legroom. Some have a printer shelf or hutch, providing racks for CDs and a bit of storage for paperwork, but desktop space is typically meager. Assembly time for our engineer: 45 minutes to 2 hours. Price range: $65 to $180.

How to choose

PERFORMANCE DIFFERENCES. Many workstations CONSUMER REPORTS recently tested were serviceable. None of them, however, were top-notch in terms of ergonomics. The main reason was that the tested models lacked a keyboard shelf that could be raised or lowered to suit the user. A height-adjustable chair can help solve the problem by putting you in the correct position. On some of the units we tested, the keyboard shelf was too small for both the keyboard and mouse. If the mouse has to sit on the desktop, you have to reach up and over to maneuver it, which can strain your wrist and shoulders. Some units had a monitor shelf set too high, forcing you to tilt your head back; on others the shelf was too far from the user. On a few models, the monitor was too close because the desktop was too shallow or a hutch's back wall got in the way.

Overall, the assembly of our test units went fairly smoothly. Problems arose when pieces didn't fit tightly or line up correctly. Generally, the major panels of the tested models fit well, but we did see problems with some shelves and doors. Screws and cam-bolt systems—a type of fastener used by many manufacturers—gave the tightest fit. We found Sauder's proprietary TwistLocks harder to align, which may cause gaps.

The need to piece together a jigsaw puzzle of parts underscores the importance of clear instructions. Most units we tested did fine in that regard. Sauder's were consistently among the best. But we found others' to be unclear, incomplete, or incorrect.

Most of the furniture tested was fine in terms of fit and finish. A couple of units had many defects, though.

RECOMMENDATIONS. Your top priority should be to get a unit that's ergonomically sound. You also need to consider how much room you have and how much work space you need. Measure your monitor, computer tower, and printer to make sure the furniture can hold all of them. All tested models will house a 17-inch cathode ray tube (CRT) monitor, but some are a tight fit for a 19-inch CRT.

Many consumers find that a desk with a hutch provides adequate room to work without hogging floor space. If you have ample floor space and crave elbowroom, a spacious corner or L-shaped unit should be just right. Keep in mind that their size and shape

---

WORKSTATIONS THAT WORK

Here are some key points to consider when choosing computer furniture:

◆ The keyboard and monitor should be placed directly in front of you, not at an angle, so that you don't have to twist or turn either your head or your body.

◆ The keyboard shelf should be large enough to hold both the keyboard and mouse, at a height enabling you to keep your shoulders relaxed and your wrists straight and flat.

◆ The monitor should be about an arm's length away, at a height that puts the top line of text at or just below eye level. If you'll be consulting paperwork, use a copyholder to position it at the same height as the screen.

can make these units difficult to move once assembled. You may want a cart if space or money is tight or if you want to move your computer around. But you will have to put up with limited work space and mediocre ergonomics—be prepared to hit your shins or your feet on the lower shelves. If you want to hide the computer when it's not being used, consider an armoire.

If you're the do-it-yourself type, you can build an ergonomically sound workstation by combining a large, plain table or desk with an adjustable keyboard shelf and, if needed, a stand that puts the monitor at the correct height. Keep in mind, however, that the result may not be a perfect match stylistically and aesthetically.

GETTING IT TOGETHER. Assembling a workstation takes two to nine hours. Before you begin, lay out and inspect all the parts to see if anything is missing or damaged. If you need a replacement part, call the manufacturer; then be prepared to wait a week to 10 days to receive it.

Set the unit up in the location where it will be used—it may be very hard to move once assembled. To put most units together, you'll need a hammer, a screwdriver, an Allen-head wrench (included with the unit), and possibly a partner to help lift or position components. Some manufacturers warn that you can strip out a screw hole if you use a power screwdriver or drill. We used a cordless drill with an adjustable clutch and had no problems. If you're handy with tools, you shouldn't have difficulty either. Otherwise, we wouldn't advise experimenting with a project such as this.

If you lack the mechanical aptitude or time to assemble the workstation yourself, you can hire a pro to do it for you. The retailer may offer setup service or refer you to a company that will do the job. Assembly may cost $35 to $100 or so.

♦ **Ratings:** page 172

TO AVOID EYESTRAIN

◆ Blink! Computer users often forget to blink, making their eyes dry.

◆ Get regular eye exams. You may be leaning over so you can see, which can cause back, arm, and shoulder aches.

◆ Consider glasses prescribed for computer use.

SURGE SUPPRESSORS

A surge suppressor can help protect computers and other pieces of home-office equipment from electrical slings and arrows.

A spike in electrical voltage caused by a nearby lightning strike, faulty wiring, or a return to service following a blackout can cause an array of computer problems, from keyboard lockup to damaged internal components. A surge suppressor can help minimize the risk of electrical damage by redirecting the energy surge away from your vulnerable equipment. It's also a handy way to plug in a lot of equipment.

What's available

Most surge suppressors come with six to eight outlets and various indicators. The major brands are APC, Belkin, Interex, Newpoint, Power Sentry, Surge Master, and Tripp Lite. Price range: $15 to $50.

Key features

Although most computers draw a maximum of 500 watts, most surge suppressors are rated to carry 1,875 watts. Look for a model with a **circuit breaker** that trips (and can be reset) when more than 15 amps is drawn.

The better surge suppressors have rugged circuitry and use a variety of components including capacitors, inductors, and **multiple metal-oxide varistors** (MOVs) to absorb voltage spikes. Simpler models have MOVs and not much else. Packaging can sometimes help you to tell the difference by listing the internal components or providing a cutaway drawing of the surge suppressor's innards.

Better models leave enough **space between outlets** so the transformer at the end of some accessory power cords won't cover adjacent outlets.

Most surge suppressors come with indicator lights to indicate if previous spikes have compromised protection. A ground-indicator light tells you if the ground or the wiring in your home is OK. But we have found that those lights aren't always accurate.

The location of the **on/off switch** can vary. It might be located at the end opposite from the switch, making the unit good for use on a desk, with the switch near you and the cord leading back to a wall outlet.

Most models provide at least one telephone jack to shield the phone line from surges. We didn't test that feature.

How to choose

PERFORMANCE DIFFERENCES. Most surge suppressors meet Underwriters Laboratories' UL 1449 electrical safety standard. CONSUMER REPORTS tested surge suppressors for their ability to protect computers. All the ones tested could protect a test computer from lower-energy surges. But in more rigorous tests, some didn't protect the test computer when the jolts reached 4,000 volts. The best surge protectors withstood hundreds of surges up to 6,000 volts.

RECOMMENDATIONS. Every computer should be plugged into a surge suppressor. At the store, look for these words on a surge suppressor's packaging: inductors, capacitors, MOVs, glass discharge tubes, fuses, and transorbs. Look also for a UL rating. If you live in an area with frequent lightening storms or power-line problems, consider replacing the surge suppressor every few years or so. Having a top-of-the-line model protecting a home computer doesn't take the place of good file backup habits. Your safest bet when lightning storms are forecast is to unplug your computer and the modem's telephone line.

For added peace of mind, you might consider buying an uninterruptable power supply (UPS). Costing as little as $100, a UPS is an electrical device containing a battery pack. It provides a temporary energy source that gives you time to save your work and shut down the computer in an orderly fashion. Some UPS devices provide a degree of surge protection.

PART 3

Reference

Ratings of the
Equipment

—

Guide to
the Brands

—

Glossary

—

Index

Ratings of the Equipment

HOW TO USE THE RATINGS

Read the report on the product you're interested in. The page number is noted for each Ratings category. The Overall Ratings gives the big picture in performance. "Features at a Glance" sums up key aspects for some products. Notes on features and performance for individual models are listed under Recommendations & Notes. Key numbers let you easily track between the Ratings and paragraphs.

We verify availability for most products especially for this book. Some tested models may no longer be available. Models similar to the tested models, when they exist, are listed in Recommendations & Notes. Such models differ in features, not essential performance, according to manufacturers.

Camcorders

Digital camcorders capture high-quality images and superb sound. They're easy to use and come with lots of features. If you want to try video editing or downloading to the web, invest in a digital model. Loaded with features, the Sony DCR-PC100, $1,450, is an excellent though expensive choice. The Panasonic PV-DV101, $560, and Sony DCR-TRV230, $610, are worthy alternatives. Analog models are quite good and cost hundreds of dollars less than digital models. Picture quality, though generally a notch below digital, is still perfectly fine. The Samsung SC-W62, $250, is a good overall camcorder and the least expensive model tested.

Overall Ratings — In performance order

Rating key: ● Excellent ◑ Very good ○ Good ◐ Fair ● Poor

KEY NO	BRAND AND MODEL	PRICE	FORMAT	OVERALL SCORE	PICTURE QUALITY SP	PICTURE QUALITY LP/EP	IMAGE STABILIZER	AUDIO	EASE OF USE	WEIGHT	ZOOM	BATT. LIFE
ANALOG MODELS												
1	Sony CCD-TRV68	$389	Hi8		○	◑	○	◑	◑	2	20x/450x	120/140
2	JVC GR-AX760U	300	VHS-C		◑	◑	○	◑	◑	1.6	16x/400x	NA/100
3	Samsung SC-W62	250	Hi8		○	–	–	○	◑	1.5	22x/500x	NA/150
4	Sony CCD-TRV67	499	Hi8		○	●	◑	◑	◑	2.1	20x/360x	105/125
5	Sony CCD-TRV57	429	8mm		◑	●	◑	◑	◑	2.1	20x/360x	105/125
6	Canon ES60	280	Hi8		◑	–	◑	◑	◑	1.4	22x/700x	NA/145
7	JVC GR-SX850U	300	S-VHS/ET-C		◑	◑	◑	◑	◑	1.36	16X/300X	NA/105
8	JVC GR-AX750U	289	VHS-C		◑	◑	◑	○	○	1.76	16x/300x	NA/100
9	Panasonic PV-D301	330	VHS-C		◑	◑	●	◑	◑	1.9	20x/150x	NA/70
10	Quasar VM-D51	355	VHS-C		◑	◑	●	○	◑	1.9	20x/150x	NA/70
11	Panasonic PV-L550	380	VHS-C		◑	◑	◑	○	○	2.94	18x/150x	90/120
12	Sharp VL-AH130U	430	Hi8		◑	–	–	◑	◑	1.6	16x/NA	95/NA
13	Canon ES50	300	8mm		◑	–	–	○	◑	1.8	22x/500x	NA/145
14	Canon ES55	300	8mm		●	–	◑	○	◑	1.8	22x/500x	NA/135
DIGITAL												
15	Sony DCR-PC100	1,450	MiniDV		●	●	●	◑	●	1.5	10x/120x	100/110
16	Panasonic PV-DV101	560	MiniDV		◑	◑	◑	◑	◑	1.5	20x/300x	NA/90
17	Canon ZR25MC	840	MiniDV		◑	◑	◑	●	●	1.2	10x/200x	125/150
18	Sony DCR-TRV230	610	D8		◑	◑	●	◑	◑	1.2	25x/700x	75/100

Overall Ratings, cont.

#	Brand & model	Price	Format	Overall score	Picture quality	Image stabilizer	Audio	Ease of use		Weight	Zoom (optical/digital)	Battery
19	**Sony** DCR-TRV130	500	D8		◒	◒	●	◒	◒	2	20x/560x	90/100
20	**Panasonic** PV-DV200	583	MiniDV		◒	◒	○	◒	◒	1.74	18x/300x	73/89
21	**Sony** DCR-TRV320	689	D8		◒	◒	◒	◒	◒	2.38	25x/450x	75/85
22	**Panasonic** PV-DV400	740	MiniDV		◒	◒	◒	◒	◒	1.64	18x/300x	69/98
23	**Panasonic** PV-DV851	1,450	MiniDV		◒	◒	○	○	◒	1.9	10x/100x	65/80
24	**JVC** GR-DVL300U	584	MiniDV		◒	◒	◒	○	◒	1.42	10x/250x	60/75
25	**JVC** GR-DVM55	880	MiniDV		◒	◒	◒	◒	◒	1.1	10x/300x	60/70
26	**JVC** GR-DVL310	650	MiniDV		◒	○	◒	◒	◒	1.3	10x/400x	60/75
27	**Sharp** VL-PD3U	986	MiniDV		◒	◒	●	◒	◒	1.36	10x/100x	90/105
28	**Sharp** VL-WD250U	600	MiniDV		○	○	●	◒	◒	1.6	26x/780x	100/120
29	**Sharp** VL-SD20U	670	MiniDV		○	○	●	◒	◒	1.48	10x/100x	105/NA

See report, page 121. Based on tests published in Consumer Reports Online in August 2001.

The tests behind the Ratings

Format lists the taping format used. **Overall score** mainly reflects SP picture quality and ease of use. **Picture quality** is based on the judgments of trained panelists, who viewed still images shot at standard (SP) and slow (LP/EP) tape speed. **Image stabilizer** scores reflect how well that circuitry worked. The **audio** score reflects recording with the built-in microphone. **Ease of use** takes into account ergonomics, weight, viewfinder accuracy and how easy it was to see images on the LCD in bright sunlight. **Specs** gives the optical and digital zoom range and the battery life without and with the LCD screen. **Price** is national average.

Recommendations and notes

ANALOG MODELS

1. **SONY** CCD-TRV68 **Good overall. Excellent autofocus. Auto-control switch for video light.** LACKS: Auto shutter speed mode, FireWire port, high-speed manual shutter, manual white balance, special effects during playback, still-image capture.

2. **JVC** GR-AX760U **Good overall. Excellent autofocus.** Auto-wide zoom, which forces a wide-angle shot if subject is beyond autofocus range, battery refresh switch. LACKS: LCD panel, audio fade, auto shutter speed mode, backlight compensation, high-speed manual shutter, remote control.

3. **SAMSUNG** SC-W62 **Good overall. Excellent autofocus.** Auto control switch for video light. LACKS: image stabilizer, LCD panel, slow speed, manual aperture adjustment, remote control. BUT: VCR control buttons fair for ease of use.

4. **SONY** CCD-TRV67 **Good overall.** Custom titles, infrared-sensitive recording mode, S-video output. LACKS: Audio dub. Discontinued, but may still be available.

5. **SONY** CCD-TRV57 **Good overall.** Custom titles, infrared-sensitive recording mode. LACKS: Audio dub. Discontinued, but may still be available.

6. **CANON** ES60 **Good overall.** Excellent autofocus. LACKS: LCD panel, image stabilizer, slow speed, high-speed manual shutter, manual white balance, remote control. BUT: VCR control buttons fair for ease of use.

7. **JVC** GR-SX850U **Good overall and inexpensive.** Only color eyepiece; no LCD viewer. Interval time-lapse recording mode, manual white balance, S-video output. LACKS: Audio fade, backlight compensation, LCD panel brightness adjustment, remote control, tally light. BUT: Awkwardly placed power jack. Discontinued, but may still be available.

8. **JVC** GR-AX750U **Good overall and inexpensive.** Only monochrome eyepiece; no LCD viewer. Interval time-lapse recording mode, manual white balance. LACKS: Audio fade, backlight compensation, LCD panel brightness adjustment, remote control, tally light. BUT: Awkwardly placed power jack. Discontinued, but may still be available.

Recommendations and notes, cont.

9▷PANASONIC PV-D301 **Good overall.** Excellent autofocus. VCR control buttons excellent for ease of use. Battery-refresh switch, fade-to-white capability, auto-control switch for video light. LACKS: LCD panel, manual aperture adjustment, manual white balance, quick review, remote control, special effects during playback, tape counter, wide-screen format. BUT: Poor image stabilizer. Poorly located power jack; to use it, you must first remove the battery.

10▷QUASAR VM-D51 **Good overall.** VCR control buttons excellent for ease of use. Battery-refresh switch, fade-to-white capability. LACKS: LCD panel, manual aperture adjustment, manual white balance, quick review, remote control, special effects during playback, tape counter, wide-screen format. BUT: Poor image stabilizer. Poorly located power jack; to use it, you must first remove the battery.

11▷PANASONIC PV-L550 **Fair overall, easy to use but heavy.** LCD hard to view in sunlight. High-speed manual shutter. LACKS: Audio dub, manual aperture, remote control, tape counter, tape-position memory. BUT: Awkwardly placed power jack. Discontinued, but may still be available.

12▷SHARP VL-AH130U **Fair overall.** Auto-wide zoom, which forces a wide-angle if subject is beyond autofocus range, fade-to-white capability. LACKS: Eyepiece viewfinder, image stabilizer, slow speed, auto shutter-speed mode, fade to black, high-speed manual shutter, image stabilizer, S-video out. BUT: Menu poor for ease of use.

13▷CANON ES50 **Fair overall.** Only color eyepiece; no LCD. Custom titles. LACKS: Audio dub, LCD panel brightness adjustment, manual aperture. Discontinued, but may still be available.

14▷CANON ES55 **Fair overall.** Only color eyepiece; no LCD viewer. Custom titles, slow-speed manual shutter. LACKS: Audio dub, LCD panel brightness adjustment, manual aperture. Discontinued, but may still be available.

DIGITAL MODELS

15▷SONY DCR-PC100 **Excellent but expensive.** LCD easy to view in sunlight. Custom titles, date search, manual white balance, self-timer, slow-speed manual shutter, infrared-sensitive recording mode. Discontinued, but may still be available.

16▷PANASONIC PV-DV101 **Very good overall.** LACKS: Built-in titles, manual aperture adjustment, remote control, wide-screen format. BUT: Poorly located power jack; to use it, you must first remove the battery.

17▷CANON ZR25MC **Very good overall.** Excellent accuracy. VCR control buttons excellent for ease of use. Progressive scan still images (but not full-motion video) saved to memory. LACKS: Backlight compensation, built-in titles.

18▷SONY DCR-TRV230 **Very good overall.** Excellent autofocus. LACKS: High-speed manual shutter, manual white balance.

19▷SONY DCR-TRV130 **Very good overall.** Excellent autofocus. Auto-control switch for video light. LACKS: High-speed manual shutter, manual white balance.

20▷PANASONIC PV-DV200 **Very good overall.** High-speed manual shutter, playback stabilizer. LACKS: Manual aperture, remote control. BUT: Awkwardly placed power jack. Discontinued, but may still be available.

21▷SONY DCR-TRV320 **Very good overall, but heavy.** LCD easy to view in sunlight. Custom titles, date search, self-timer, slow-speed manual shutter, infrared-sensitive recording mode. LACKS: Audio dub. BUT: Poor low-light picture quality. Discontinued, but may still be available.

22▷PANASONIC PV-DV400 **Very good overall.** High-speed manual shutter, playback stabilizer, infrared-sensitive recording mode. LACKS: Manual aperture, remote control. BUT: Awkwardly placed power jack. Poor low-light picture quality. Discontinued, but may still be available.

23▷PANASONIC PV-DV851 **Very good overall.** Excellent autofocus. Progressive scan still images (but not full-motion video) saved to memory. LACKS: Built-in titles, wide screen format. BUT: VCR control buttons poor for ease of use. Poorly located power jack; to use it, you must first remove the battery.

24▷JVC GR-DVL300U **Very good overall.** High- and low-speed manual shutter, manual white balance. LACKS: Built-in titles, tape position memory. BUT: Awkwardly placed power jack. Poor low-light picture quality. Discontinued, but may still be available.

25▷JVC GR-DVM55 **Very good overall.** Excellent autofocus. Auto-wide zoom, which forces a wide-angle shot if subject is beyond autofocus range. Fade-to-white capability. LACKS: Built-in titles, quick review, soft eyecup. BUT: VCR control buttons fair for ease of use.

26▷JVC GR-DVL310 **Very good overall.** Auto-wide zoom, which forces a wide-angle shot if subject is beyond autofocus range. Fade-to-white capability. Auto-control switch for video light. LACKS: Built-in titles, quick review, soft eyecup. BUT: VCR control buttons fair for ease of use.

27▷SHARP VL-PD3U **Very good overall.** LCD easy to view in sunlight. High-speed manual shutter, manual white balance. LACKS: Built-in titles, tally light. BUT: Awkwardly placed power jack. Discontinued, but may still be available.

28▷SHARP VL-WD250U **Good overall.** Auto-wide zoom, which forces a wide-angle shot if subject is beyond autofocus range. Fade-to-white capability. LACKS: Built-in titles, fade to black, brightness adjustment for LCD panel, quick review, wide-screen format. BUT: VCR control buttons fair for ease of use. Poor image stabilizer. Poorly located power jack; to use it, you must first remove the battery.

29▷SHARP VL-SD20U **Good overall.** LCD easy to view in sunlight. Only color LCD; no eyepiece. High- and slow-speed manual shutter, manual white balance. LACKS: Tally light. BUT: If mounted on some tripods, can't remove battery. Discontinued, but may still be available.

Cell phones

First, choose the service plan that best fits your calling patterns. Then choose a phone. To ensure that your cell phone can send and receive calls in the widest geographical area possible, buy a handset that uses both digital and analog technology. Get a dual-mode or tri-mode handset that can operate in analog mode when you travel outside the more limited digital cellular and PCS Networks. Most carriers use one of two incompatible digital formats called TDMA and CDMA. We've not found that either has an edge in conveying voice quality. The format your carrier uses will determine which handset you can use.

Overall Ratings — In performance order

Rating key: Excellent ◉ Very good ● Good ○ Fair ◑ Poor ⬤

KEY NO.	BRAND AND MODEL	PRICE	OVERALL SCORE	VOICE QUALITY		EASE OF USE	BATTERY LIFE
			(0 P F G VG E 100)	NOISY BACKGROUND	QUIET BACKGROUND		
CDMA HANDSETS (compatible with service offered by Alltel, Sprint PCS, U.S. Cellular, and Verizon Wireless)							
1	**Samsung** SCH 3500	$150		◑	◑	◑	○
2	**Motorola** Timeport P8160	300		○	◑	◑	◑
3	**Audiovox** CDM-9000	150		◑	○	◑	○
4	**Motorola** SC3160	70		○	○	○	◉
5	**Nokia** 6185	150		◑	○	○	○
6	**Qualcomm** (now **Kyocera**) QCP 860	200		◑	◑	○	◑
7	**Nokia** 5180*	70		◑	○	○	○
TDMA HANDSETS (compatible with service offered by AT&T Wireless, Cingular, and U.S. Cellular)							
8	**Motorola** StarTac ST 7790	300		◑	◑	◑	◑
9	**Ericsson** R280 (D or LX)	100		◑	◑	○	○
10	**Ericsson** T18 (D or LX)	99		◑	○	○	◑
11	**Motorola** Talkabout T8097	180		○	◑	○	○
12	**Nokia** 5160	130		○	◑	○	◑
13	**Nokia** 6160	150		○	◑	○	○

See report, page 141. Based on tests published in Consumer Reports in February 2001, with updated prices and availability.

The tests behind the Ratings

Overall score includes voice quality, battery life, and ease of use, based on convenient features, controls, and displays. **Voice quality** results reflect judgments of a trained listening panel, grading high-quality recordings of wireless conversations obtained in a **noisy** environment (by the side of a highway) and against a **quiet** background. **Battery life** reflects how efficiently handsets use the battery they came with. **Price** is what Consumers Union shoppers paid to purchase the handsets through retail outlets; retail prices are often higher without a contract.

Recommendations and notes

Most models have: Backlit LCD display. Any-key answer. Programmable speed-dial, with a searchable directory for 99 or more names. A call timer (current call and cumulative total). Settings to limit receiving or making calls. Weight listed for all models includes battery.

Most CDMA handsets: are sold with service offered by Alltel, U.S. Cellular, and Verizon wireless. The Samsung SCH 3500 is sold with service offered by Sprint PCS only. All TDMA handsets: are sold with service offered by AT&T Wireless, Cingular and U.S. Cellular.

CDMA HANDSETS

1▷ **SAMSUNG** SCH 3500 **Very good overall.** Dual-band and mode. 4.4 x 2.0 x 1 in. 5.3oz.1000 mAh lithium-ion battery. *PERFORMANCE:* Has audible roaming tone, web browser, and can record voice memos. Provides 2:49 hours of talk time in digital mode, 1:38 hours in analog mode. *BUT:* Less than 24 hours analog standby time. Sold with Sprint PCS service only.

2▷ **MOTOROLA** Timeport P8160 **Very good overall.** Dual-mode. 3.6x2.1x1.1 in. 4.4 oz. 900 mAh lithium-ion battery. *PERFORMANCE:* Has vibrating call alert, audible roaming tone, and single key last number redial. Includes web browser. Provides 5:24 hours of talk time in digital mode, 2:16 hours in analog mode. BUT: Less than 24 hours analog standby time.

3▷ **AUDIOVOX** CDM-9000 **Very good overall.** Tri-mode. 5.5x1.8x1 in. 4.7 oz. 950 mAh lithium-ion battery. *PERFORMANCE:* Has vibrating call alert and voice activated dialing. Includes web browser. Provides 3:59 hours talk time in digital mode, 1:21 hours in analog mode. *BUT:* Only 3 month warranty for display and keypad. Less than 24 hours analog standby time. Similar: CDM-4500 (dual-mode).

4▷ **MOTOROLA** SC3160 **Very good overall.** Dual-mode. 4.5x1.7x1.5 in. 6.9 oz. 1350 mAh lithium-ion battery. *PERFORMANCE:* Has vibrating call alert and single key last number redial. Keypad easier to read than others in low light. Provides 6:36 hours talk time in digital mode, 2:58 hours in analog mode. *BUT:* The external ringer doesn't work when headset is plugged in. Signal and battery indicators harder to read than others. Less than 24 hours analog standby time.

5▷ **NOKIA** 6185 **Very good overall.** Tri-mode. 5x1.8x1.3 in. 5.8 oz. 1500 mAh lithium-ion battery. *PERFORMANCE:* Has vibrating call alert. Provides 4:08 hours talk time in digital mode, 1:43 hours in analog mode. *BUT:* Uses cumbersome proprietary handsfree connector. Signal and battery indicators harder to read than others. Discontinued, but may still be available.

6▷ **QUALCOMM** (Now **KYOCERA**) QCP 860 **Very good overall.** Dual-mode. 5.5x2.1x0.8 in. 4.5 oz. Internal lithium-ion battery. *PERFORMANCE:* Has audible roaming tone and single key last number redial. Provides 2:15 hours talk time in digital mode. BUT: You can't dial 911 with keyguard on. Uses cumbersome proprietary handsfree connector. Battery is not replaceable by user. Less than 24 hours analog standby time. Similar: QCP 2760 (dual-mode, dual-band).

7▷ **NOKIA** 5180 **Very good overall.** Dual-mode. 5.2x2x1.2 in. 6oz. 900 mAh nickel-metal hydride battery. *PERFORMANCE:* Keypad easier to read than others in low light. Provides 2:43 hours talk time in digital mode, 1:04 hours in analog mode. BUT: Uses cumbersome proprietary handsfree connector. Signal and battery indicators harder to read than others. Less than 24 hours analog standby time. Similar: 5185i (tri-mode); 5180i (dual-mode); 5170i (single-mode).

TDMA HANDSETS

8▷ **MOTOROLA** StarTac ST 7790 **Very good overall.** Dual-mode 3.7x2.1x1.1 in. 4.3 oz. 550 mAh nickel-metal hydride battery. *PERFORMANCE:* Has vibrating call alert and single key last number redial. Provides 2:13 hours talk time in digital mode, 1:03 hours in analog mode. *BUT:* The external ringer doesn't work when headset is plugged in. Can't support 3 way calls. Less than 24 hours analog standby time. Similar: StarTac ST 7790i (dual-mode); StarTac ST 7797 (tri-mode).

9▷ **ERICSSON** R280 (D or LX) **Very good overall.** Tri-mode. 5x2x0.8 in. 6.2oz. 800 mAh nickel-metal hydride battery. *PERFORMANCE:* Includes web browser. Provides 2:28 hours talk time in digital mode, 1:28 hours in analog mode. *BUT:* Uses cumbersome proprietary handsfree connector. You can't force analog mode. Less than 24 hours analog standby time.

Features at a glance — Cell phones

Key no.	Brand	Model	Price paid	Folding case design	Tri-mode operation	Standard headset connector	Vibrating call alert	Roaming lock	One-touch redial	Three-way conferencing	Voice activated dialing	Web-browser
CDMA HANDSETS												
1▷	**Samsung**	SCH 3500	$150	•		•	•	•	•	•	•	•
2▷	**Motorola Timeport**	P8160	300	•		•	•		•			•
3▷	**Audiovox**	CDM-9000	150		•	•	•				•	•
4▷	**Motorola**	SC3160	70	•		•	•		•			
5▷	**Nokia**	6185	150	•	•	•						
6▷	**Qualcomm**	QCP 860	200				•	•	•			
7▷	**Nokia**	5180	70								•	
TDMA HANDSETS												
8▷	**Motorola StarTac**	ST 7790	300	•		•	•	•	•			
9▷	**Ericsson**	R280LX	100		•		•	•				•
10▷	**Ericsson**	T18LX	99	•	•		•					
11▷	**Motorola Talkabout**	T8097	180	•	•	•	•		•			
12▷	**Nokia**	5160	130		•							
13▷	**Nokia**	6160	150		•							

Recommendations and notes, cont'd

10 **ERICSSON** T18 (D or LX) **Very good overall.** Tri-mode. 4x1.9x0.9 in. 5.3oz. 750 mAh nickel-metal hydride battery. *PERFORMANCE:* Has vibrating call alert. Keypad easier to read than others in low light. Provides 2:38 hours talk time in digital mode, 1:12 hours in analog mode. *BUT:* You can't dial 911 with keyguard on. Uses cumbersome proprietary handsfree connector. You can't force analog mode. Less than 24 hours analog standby time.

11 **MOTOROLA** Talkabout T8097 **Very good overall.** Tri-mode. 3.6x2.1x1.1 in. 4.8oz. 900 mAh lithium-ion battery. *PERFORMANCE:* Has vibrating call alert and single key last number redial. Keypad easier to read than others in low light. Provides 2:16 hours talk time in digital mode, 1:16 hours in analog mode. *BUT:* The external ringer doesn't work when headset is plugged in. You can't force analog mode. Similar: Talkabout T8090 (dual-mode).

12 **NOKIA** 5160 **Very good overall.** Tri-mode. 5.2x1.9x1.2 in. 6.3 oz. 900 mAh nickel-metal hydride battery. *PERFORMANCE:* Keypad easier to read than others in low light. Provides 2:03 hours talk time in digital mode, 1:01 hours in analog mode. *BUT:* Can't support 3 way calls. Uses cumbersome proprietary handsfree connector. You can't force analog mode. Signal and battery indicators harder to read than others. Discontinued, but may still be available. Similar: 5165 (tri-mode); 5125 (dual-mode).

13 **NOKIA** 6160 **Very good overall.** Tri-mode. 5.1x1.9x1.2 in. 6.1 oz. 900 mAh nickel-metal hydride battery. *PERFORMANCE:* Has single key last number redial. Provides 2:15 hours talk time in digital mode, 1:15 hours in analog mode. *BUT:* Can't support 3 way calls. Uses cumbersome proprietary handsfree connector. You can't force analog mode. Signal and battery indicators harder to read than others. Similar: 6120 (dual-mode).

Desktop computers

Prices for new computers are as low as they've ever been for the amount of features and speed you receive. All of the models we tested were very good. Your first consideration is whether you want a Windows-based or a Macintosh machine. Beyond that, consider reliability and technical support. Apple, Compaq, and Dell have been among the most reliable brands. Apple, Dell, and Gateway continue to get high marks for tech support.

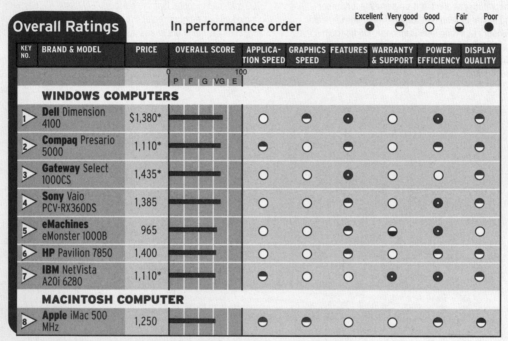

Overall Ratings — In performance order

Legend: Excellent ◉ Very good ◖ Good ○ Fair ◗ Poor ●

KEY NO.	BRAND & MODEL	PRICE	OVERALL SCORE (P F G VG E / 0–100)	APPLICATION SPEED	GRAPHICS SPEED	FEATURES	WARRANTY & SUPPORT	POWER EFFICIENCY	DISPLAY QUALITY
WINDOWS COMPUTERS									
1	**Dell** Dimension 4100	$1,380*		Good	Very good	Excellent	Good	Excellent	Very good
2	**Compaq** Presario 5000	1,110*		Very good	Good	Very good	Good	Very good	Very good
3	**Gateway** Select 1000CS	1,435*		Good	Good	Excellent	Good	Good	Very good
4	**Sony** Vaio PCV-RX360DS	1,385		Good	Good	Very good	Good	Excellent	Very good
5	**eMachines** eMonster 1000B	965		Good	Good	Very good	Fair	Excellent	Good
6	**HP** Pavilion 7850	1,400		Good	Good	Fair	Good	Very good	Very good
7	**IBM** NetVista A20i 6280	1,110*		Fair	Good	Good	Excellent	Excellent	Very good
MACINTOSH COMPUTER									
8	**Apple** iMac 500 MHz	1,250		Very good	Very good	Good	Good	Very good	Very good

See report, page 102. Based on tests published in Consumer Reports in September 2001.

The tests behind the Ratings

Overall score includes speed, features, and power efficiency. **Application speed** tracks how the computer compared with a benchmark (an 866-MHz Pentium III computer for Windows machines; a 333-MHz iMac for the Macintosh) doing typical office work, including web browsing. **Graphics speed** measures the computer's ability to smoothly render motion in game-type graphics. **Features** includes myriad conveniences, such as well-marked and easily accessible connectors, expandability, and upgradability. **Warranty & support** reflects our judgment of the service and support provisions in the warranty. **Power efficiency** measures the computer's electricity consumption and power-saving features. **Display quality** (not factored into our scoring) includes our judgments of the monitor. **Price** is the approximate retail and includes the manufacturer's least-expensive 17-inch monitor. An asterisk (*) denotes a configure-to-order (CTO) model, usually sold by mail or at an in-store kiosk.

Recommendations and notes

Most of these computer have: 900-MHz to 1-GHz processor. 128 MB of RAM. 20- to 30-GB hard drive. 8- to 16-MB video RAM. Separate speakers. Keyboard with multifunction control panel. Separate button to put computer in low-power mode. Mouse with scrolling control. "Works"-type application. 56k, V.90 modem. Home networking connection. Internal bay for second hard drive.

WINDOWS COMPUTERS

1> **DELL** Dimension 4100 (CTO) **Very good overall. Fast graphics; good for gamers.** 933-MHz Pentium III. 20-GB hard drive. DVD and CD-RW drives. E770 monitor. 2 free PCI slots. 2 USB connectors. 2 free 3½-in. front bays. Keyboard control panel lacks drive controls and volume. No USB connectors on front. Current model, $1,250, has a 1-GHz Pentium III processor.

2> **COMPAQ** Presario 5000 (CTO and retail) **Very good overall. Case opens easily for expansion.** 900-MHz Duron. 30-GB hard drive. DVD drive. CV735 monitor. 1 free PCI slot. 3 free USB connectors, 2 on front. 1 free 3½-in. front bay. Case has optional, replaceable color panels. Front drives install without screws.

3> **GATEWAY** Select 1000CS (CTO) **Very good overall. Case opens easily for expansion.** 1-GHz Athlon. 20-GB hard drive. CD-ROM and CD-RW drives. EV700 monitor. 3 free PCI slots. 3 free USB connectors, 2 on front. 1 free 3½-in. front bay. Front drives install without screws. No standby button, and noisier than most in standby mode. Current model, $1,150, has a 1.2-GHz Athlon processor.

4> **SONY** Vaio PCV-RX360DS **Very good overall. Good multimedia software. Low power consumption.** 866-MHz Pentium III. 40-GB hard drive. DVD and CD-RW drives. HMD-A200 monitor. 2 free PCI slots. 2 FireWire connectors, 1 on front. 7 free USB connectors; 2 on front, 4 on monitor. Sleekly styled cabinet hides floppy drive and ports behind doors. No free front bays. Keyboard control panel lacks drive controls. Monitor angle not easy to adjust. Discontinued, but may still be available.

5> **EMACHINES** eMonster 1000B **Very good performance, but lacking in features.** GHz Pentium III. 20-GB hard drive. CD-RW drive. Eview 17p monitor. 2 free PCI slots. 2 free USB connectors, 1 on front. 1 free 5¼-in. front bay. Not available with second CD drive, precluding direct copying of disks. No network port. Graphics circuitry can't be upgraded. Not optimal for 3D games. Small speakers are poor for music. Keyboard control panel can't be configured by user. No standby button. No internal bay for second hard drive.

6> **HP** Pavilion 7850 **Very good overall, but not optimal for 3D games.** 933-MHz Pentium III. 40-GB hard drive. CD-ROM and CD-RW drives. MX70 monitor. 1 free PCI slot. 2 free USB connectors, 1 on front. Keyboard control panel well laid out. No free front bays. Replacing a CD drive requires extra disassembly. Graphics circuitry can't be upgraded. Discontinued; replaced by Pavilion 7940, $1,350.

7> **IBM** NetVista A20i 6280 (CTO) **Very good overall, but not optimal for 3D games.** 933-MHz Pentium III. 20-GB hard drive. CD-ROM and CD-RW drives. E74 monitor. 1 free PCI slot. 2 free USB connectors. No free front bays. No keyboard control panel. Graphics circuitry can't be upgraded. No internal bay for second hard drive. Installed Internet portal application used too many processor resources until we disabled it.

MACINTOSH COMPUTER

8> **APPLE** iMac 500 MHz **Very good overall, but can't be expanded with additional drives or cards.** 500-MHz G3. 20-GB hard drive. CD-RW drive. All-in-one design, featuring built-in monitor. 4 free USB connectors, 2 on front. 2 FireWire connectors. Connector for external PC-style monitor. Lacks floppy drive. Only one internal CD drive. We added 64 MB of RAM for tests (included in price).

Digital cameras

More pixels don't always get you improved results. The 2-megapixel Olympus Camedia C-2020 Zoom, $630, produced the best 5x7-inch prints of all tested models. Close behind were the 3-megapixel Olympus Camedia C-3030 Zoom, $630, and the 2-megapixel Nikon Coolpix 800, $520. Several 1-megapixel cameras yielded very good prints. The Fujifilm FinePix 1400 Zoom, $360, is fairly compact and light. The Kodak DC215 Zoom, $280, is fairly compact and among the least expensive models tested.

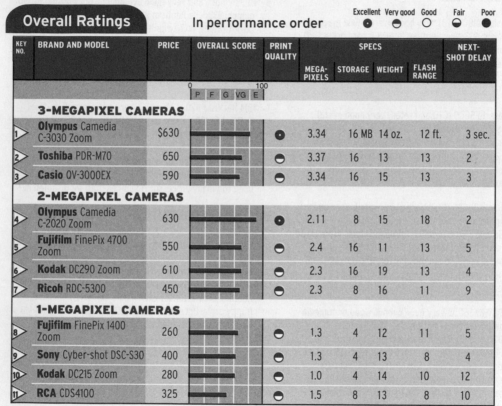

KEY NO.	BRAND AND MODEL	PRICE	OVERALL SCORE	PRINT QUALITY	MEGA-PIXELS	STORAGE	WEIGHT	FLASH RANGE	NEXT-SHOT DELAY
3-MEGAPIXEL CAMERAS									
1	**Olympus** Camedia C-3030 Zoom	$630		●	3.34	16 MB	14 oz.	12 ft.	3 sec.
2	**Toshiba** PDR-M70	650		◐	3.37	16	13	13	2
3	**Casio** QV-3000EX	590		◐	3.34	16	15	13	3
2-MEGAPIXEL CAMERAS									
4	**Olympus** Camedia C-2020 Zoom	630		●	2.11	8	15	18	2
5	**Fujifilm** FinePix 4700 Zoom	550		◐	2.4	16	11	13	5
6	**Kodak** DC290 Zoom	610		◐	2.3	16	19	13	4
7	**Ricoh** RDC-5300	450		◐	2.3	8	16	11	9
1-MEGAPIXEL CAMERAS									
8	**Fujifilm** FinePix 1400 Zoom	260		◐	1.3	4	12	11	5
9	**Sony** Cyber-shot DSC-S30	400		◐	1.3	4	13	8	4
10	**Kodak** DC215 Zoom	280		◐	1.0	4	14	10	12
11	**RCA** CDS4100	325		◐	1.5	8	13	8	10

Overall Ratings — In performance order — Excellent ● Very good ◐ Good ○ Fair ◑ Poor ●

Overall score scale: 0 — P F G VG E — 100

See report, page 124. Based on tests published in Consumer Reports in November 2000, with updated prices and availability.

The tests behind the Ratings

The **overall score** is based largely on picture quality and convenience factors. **Print quality** is based on panelists judgments of glossy 5x7-inch test photos made on a high-quality inkjet printer. **Megapixels** shows how many million pixels the image sensor has. **Storage** lists the capacity of the memory card included. Most cameras use either a CompactFlash or SmartMedia card. Sony Cyber-shot cameras use a Memory Stick; the Sony Mavica, a diskette. **Weight** includes battery and memory card. **Flash Range** is the maximum claimed range for a well-lighted photo. **Next-shot delay** is the time the camera needs to ready itself for the next shot. **Price** is the national average, provided by Active Research Inc. *(www.activebuyersguide.com).*

Recommendations and notes

Most models have: Optical viewfinder and LCD viewer. Auto-focus and autoexposure, multiple flash modes, and exposure-compensation settings. Self-timer and tripod socket. Software for Windows and Macintosh. Ability to connect to a computer through a serial or a USB port.1-yr.warranty on parts and labor.

Relatively easy menu system. Can record audio and "movies." Uses camcorder-type battery (included). USB only. Only 90-day warranty on labor. Software: MGI Photosuite.

3-MEGAPIXEL CAMERAS

1> **OLYMPUS** Camedia C-3030 Zoom **Excellent overall; excellent print quality.** Complicated menu system. Can record audio and "movies." Software: PhotoShop 5 LE.

2> **TOSHIBA** PDR-M70 **Very good overall.** Shallow grip for holding camera. Can record audio and "movies." USB only. Software: ImageExpert.

3> **CASIO** QV-3000EX **Very good overall, but heavy. There are better choices.** Can record "movies." Can take IBM Microdrive. Software: Photo Loader.

2-MEGAPIXEL CAMERAS

4> **OLYMPUS** Camedia C-2020 Zoom **Excellent overall, with one of the more accurate viewfinders.** Complicated menu system. Can record "movies." Serial port only. Software: PhotoDeluxe.

5> **FUJIFILM** FinePix 4700 Zoom **Very good overall, and very compact.** Image sensor better than most for low-light use. Shallow grip for holding camera. Can record audio and "movies." USB only. Software: PhotoDeluxe.

6> **KODAK** DC290 Zoom **Very good overall.** Good viewfinder accuracy. Heavier than most. Software: PhotoDeluxe.

7> **RICOH** RDC-5300 **Very good overall.** Software:PhotoStudio.

1-MEGAPIXEL CAMERAS

8> **FUJIFILM** FinePix 1400 Zoom **Very good overall, and fairly compact.** Smallish LCD screen. Shallow grip for holding camera. USB only. No video output. Software: PhotoDeluxe.

9> **SONY** Cyber-shot DSC-S30 **Very good overall.** Menu system better than most. USB only. Only 90-day warranty on labor. Software: Photosuite.

10> **KODAK** DC215 Zoom **Very good overall, with accurate viewfinder.** Shallow grip for holding camera. Serial port only, no USB. Software: PhotoDeluxe.

11> **RCA** CDS4100 **Good but there are better choices.** Non-zoom. Shallow grip for holding camera. Serial port only. Software: PhotoSuite.

Computer furniture

Determine how much room you have and how much work space you need, then decide on the type. There are many fine models. Among desks with a hutch, the Sauder Bayshore is a relative bargain at $170. Less costly, but with less work space, is the Ridgewood/Charleswood 57553, $90, **a CR Best Buy.** A corner or L-shaped unit requires more floor space. The Intelligent Designs 10342, $400, offered the best combination of functionality, fit, and finish. Another fine choice is the Ridgewood/Charleswood 14032, $150, another **CR Best Buy.** If space or money is a constraint, consider a cart. There are several in the $100 range. An armoire is useful for hiding a computer when it's not in use, but may require considerable floor space.

Overall Ratings — In performance order

Ratings key: Excellent ● | Very good ◓ | Good ○ | Fair ◒ | Poor ●

KEY NO.	BRAND & MODEL	PRICE	OVERALL SCORE (0–100, P F G VG E)	WORK SPACE	ERGONOMICS	FIT	FINISH	EASE OF ASSEMBLY
	DESKS WITH HUTCH							
1	**Sauder** Bayshore 4163-267	$170		Large	○	◓	◓	●
2	**O'Sullivan** 10443	190		Large	○	◓	○	●
3	**Bush** Ashland HM22424	300		Large	○	◓	○	◓
4	**Ridgewood/Charleswood** 57553 **A CR Best Buy**	90		Medium	○	●	○	◓
5	**Sauder** Mission 8437	200		Large	○	○	◓	○
6	**Sauder** Cornerstone 7337-105	300		Large	○	◓	○	○
7	**Bush** Ashland HM22418	200		Very large	○	◓	○	◓
8	**Ikea** Anton 47" Desk	340		Medium	○	◓	●	◒
9	**O'Sullivan** 10437	200		Very large	○	◓	◓	◒
10	**Sauder** 2738	270		Large	○	◓	◓	○
11	**Creative Interiors** 965-690	320		Large	○	◒	●	○
12	**Ridgewood/Charleswood** 74672	140		Medium	◒	○	○	◒
13	**Dorel** 41152	140		Medium	◒	○	○	●
	CORNER DESKS AND L-SHAPED UNITS							
14	**Intelligent Designs** 10342	400		Very large	○	◓	◓	●
15	**Ridgewood/Charleswood** 14032 **A CR Best Buy**	150		Very large	○	◓	○	○
16	**Bestar** Evolution 6000	300		Very large	○	●	○	◒
17	**Bestar** Horizon 5660	300		Very large	○	○	○	◒
18	**Bush** Ashland HM22310	180		Large	◒	◓	◓	●
19	**Creative Interiors** 965-305	330		Medium	○	●	●	○
20	**O'Sullivan** 10003	220		Very large	◒	●	○	○
21	**Dorel** 46552	150		Large	●	●	○	◓
	CARTS							
22	**Bush** Westwood WC2806A	180		Small	◒	◓	●	●
23	**Sauder** Cornerstone 7399-105	110		Small	◒	◒	○	●
24	**Sauder** 2799	110		Small	◒	○	○	●
25	**O'Sullivan** 61925	100		Small	◒	◓	○	●

Overall Ratings, cont.		In performance order		Excellent	Very good	Good	Fair	Poor
26	**Bush** Visions MM97401	90	Small	●	◒	◒		⊙
27	**Ameriwood** 2318	70	Small	◒	○	○		⊙
28	**Dorel** 41252	65	Small	●	◒	○	⊖	
29	**Sauder** 468-110	100	Small	●	⊖	○		⊙
ARMOIRE								
30	**Sauder** Monarch 2749	400	Medium	○	○	○	⊖	

See report, page 155. Based on tests published in Consumer Reports in September 2001.

The tests behind the Ratings

Overall score is based mainly on ergonomics; fit, finish, and ease of assembly were factored in. **Work space** is our assessment of the usable space a workstation offers. **Ergonomics** reflects how well the furniture fits users of various sizes and considers keyboard-shelf height and design, monitor location, leg and foot room, and copy-shelf compatibility. **Fit** is how well pieces align. **Finish** indicates quality, including edges. **Ease of assembly** reflects ease of setup and quality of instructions. **Price** is approximate retail; it includes a hutch, if sold separately (desks have a hutch unless otherwise noted).

Recommendations and notes

Style and finish are for unit tested; similar models may have different finish. Dimensions are HxWxD. All models: Allow monitor to be placed in line with user. Carts have casters. Except as noted, all models: Are made of particleboard/laminate. Have a fixed-height keyboard shelf that slides in and out, with room for a mouse.

DESKS WITH HUTCH

1 **SAUDER** Bayshore 4163-267 **Well made and easy to assemble.** Contemporary, oak laminate, 57x54x23 in. Very good finish. Wrist rest uncomfortable, but can be omit ted. No floor glides, so hard to move. No compartment for tower CPU. Keyboard shelf too low for taller users. Similar: 4163-468.

2 **O'SULLIVAN** 10443 **A fine choice that's easy to assemble.** Contemporary, oak laminate, 56x59x24 in. Shortest assembly time for desks. But keyboard shelf too low for taller users. No floor glides, so hard to move.

3 **BUSH** Ashland HM22424 **A good desk, but pricier than some.** Contemporary, maple laminate, 66x59x28 in. Locking storage. Hutch sold separately (HM22425, $70, included in price shown).

4 **RIDGEWOOD/CHARLESWOOD** 57553 **A CR Best Buy A good value in a basic, utilitarian desk.** Traditional, manor oak laminate, 55x47x22 in. But monitor too close for some users. Finish damaged slightly when spilled coffee sat for 24 hr. Discontinued, but similar models available. Similar: 58429, 59416, 59453.

5 **SAUDER** Mission 8437 **Good overall, with very good finish, but some assembly quirks.** Mission, fruitwood laminate, 57x60x24 in. Tricky to install underdesk brace.

6 **SAUDER** Cornerstone 7337-105 $300 **Good, but many features add to assembly time; pricier than some.** Contemporary, cherry laminate, 54x60x24 in. Adjustable floor glides, easy to level. Locking storage. Wrist rest uncomfortable, but can be omitted. Tricky to install underdesk brace. Similar: 7337-110, 7337-290.

7 **BUSH** Ashland HM22418 **A good desk with very large work space.** Contemporary, maple laminate, 59x53x30 in. No compartment for lower CPU.

8 **IKEA** Anton 47" Desk **Excellent wood-veneer finish, but poor instructions complicate assembly; pricier than some.** Contemporary, beech veneer, 60x47x30 in. Rear of unit finished. Components not labeled. Wrist rest uncomfortable, but can be omitted. No compartment for tower CPU. Hutch sits unattached on desktop. Hutch (called shelving unit) sold separately (16-in., $70; 31-in., $90; we used both shelving units together, which are included In price shown).

9 **O'SULLIVAN** 10437 **Very large work space and very good finish.** Traditional, pine laminate, 56x59x32 in. But overhanging desktop may block access to top row of keyboard. Hard to tell some screw sizes apart. Similar: 10537.

10 **SAUDER** 2738 **A good choice.** Traditional, cherry laminate, 60x60x24 in. Includes touch-up pen. Similar: 2538, 2638.

11 **CREATIVE INTERIORS** 965-690 **Many features don't make up for fit and finish defects.** Contemporary, apple laminate, 52x59x30 in. Hutch sold separately (956-790, $100, included in price shown). Similar: 603-690; hutch 603-790.

12 **RIDGEWOOD/CHARLESWOOD** 74672 **Ergonomics only fair; there are better desks.** Contemporary, oak laminate, 52x54x23 in.

13 **DOREL** 41152 **Ergonomics only fair; there are better desks.** Contemporary, oak laminate, 55x42x24 in. Similar: 41127.

Recommendations and notes, cont.

CORNER DESKS AND L-SHAPED UNITS

14▷ INTELLIGENT DESIGNS 10342 **A large, easy-to-assemble unit with very good fit and finish.** Contemporary, cherry/granite laminate, 35x67x67 in. Can adjust height of keyboard shelf with tools. Adjustable floor glides, easy to level. Rear of unit finished. But monitor too high for shorter users and too far away for some users. Similar: 10012, 10642.

15▷ RIDGEWOOD/CHARLESWOOD 14032 **A CR Best Buy Offers plenty of work space and very good value.** Contemporary, oak/black laminate, 52x59x59 in. Can be easily disassembled for moving.

16▷ BESTAR Evolution 6000 **A good choice, but assembly tricky.** Contemporary, honey laminate, 59x65x65 in. Sliding monitor and printer shelves. Adjustable floor glides, easy to level. Easily disassembled for moving. Rear of unit finished. But some assembly steps may be prone to error. Some screw holes not pretapped; hard to screw in screws. No compartment for tower CPU.

17▷ BESTAR Horizon 5660 **Good, but assembly tricky.** Contemporary, maple/putty laminate, 58x65x65 in. Adjustable floor glides, easy to level. Easily disassembled for moving. Rear of unit finished. But some assembly steps may be prone to error. Some screw holes not pretapped; hard to screw in screws. Hutch attaches with tape; hard to align, less secure than others. No compartment for tower CPU.

18▷ BUSH Ashland HM22310 **A compact workstation with very good fit and finish, but ergonomics only fair.** Contemporary, maple/granite laminate, 37x59x40 in. Locking storage. But mouse doesn't fit on keyboard shelf. Drawer and door pulls hard to tighten. Similar: HM22510.

19▷ CREATIVE INTERIORS 965-305 **Features don't make up for poor fit and finish.** Contemporary, apple laminate, 57x67x36 in. Copy shelf is well-positioned. Includes touch-up pen. But provides less work space than other workstations. No floor glides and no compartment for tower CPU. Monitor too high for shorter users and too far away for some users. Hutch sold separately (965-705, $200, included in price shown). Similar: 603-305; hutch 603-705.

20▷ O'SULLIVAN 10003 **Ergonomics only fair; there are better choices.** Contemporary, alder/granite laminate, 54x70x70 in. Hutch sold separately (10005, $50, included in price shown). Similar: 10603.

21▷ Dorel 46552 **Ergonomics poor; there are better choices.** Contemporary, oak/black, 55x49x49 in. Similar: 46583.

CARTS

22▷ BUSH Westwood WC2806A **Pricey for a cart, but has excellent wood-veneer finish.** Contemporary, oak veneer, 30x36x20 in. Easy to assemble. Sliding printer shelf.

23▷ SAUDER Cornerstone 7399-105 **A good, basic cart.** Contemporary, cherry laminate, 30x35x20 in. Easy to assemble. Sliding printer shelf. Includes touch-up pen. Wrist rest uncomfortable, but can be omitted. Similar: 7399-290, 7399-110.

24▷ SAUDER 2799 **A decent choice for a basic cart.** Traditional, cherry laminate, 30x35x20 in. Easy to assemble. Sliding printer shelf. Includes touch-up pen. Similar: 2689, 2799-110.

25▷ O'SULLIVAN 61925 **A good, basic cart with hutch.** Contemporary, oak laminate, 60x31x24 in. Easy to assemble. Wrist rest uncomfortable, but can be omitted. Monitor too far away for some users.

26▷ BUSH Visions MM97401 **Poor ergonomics make this one to avoid.** Contemporary, maple and black laminate, 33x35x29 in.

27▷ AMERIWOOD 2318 **There are better choices.** Contemporary, black laminate, 30x36x20 in. Similar: 1321.

28▷ DOREL 41252 **Poor ergonomics make this one to avoid.** Contemporary, oak, 35x25x24 in.

29▷ SAUDER 468-110 **Poor ergonomics make this cramped unit one to avoid.** Mission, fruitwood laminate, 48x36x19 in. (with drop leaf open).

ARMOIRE

30▷ Sauder Monarch 2749 **A good choice, but time-consuming to assemble.** Traditional, cherry laminate, 72x41x23 in. Adjustable floor glides, easy to level. Locking storage. Monitor too close for some users. Overhanging desktop may block access to top row of keyboard. Hard to hang and align doors. Requires considerable floor space when doors open. Room for copy shelf limited. Similar: 2549, 2649, 8449.

Laptops

All the models tested were very good or excellent machines. Among Windows laptops, any of the highest- scoring models would serve well as a desktop-computer substitute. Commuters might consider the Dell Inspiron 4000, $1,725, or the Toshiba Portegé 3480CT, $2,000. Macintosh users looking for power and a big display should consider the PowerBook G4 Titanium, $3,200. The iBook 466 Special Edition, $1,950, is also a very good choice. While several of the tested models are now discontinued, similar machines have since replaced them.

Overall Ratings — In performance order

Legend: Excellent ● | Very good ◕ | Good ○ | Fair ◔ | Poor ⬤

KEY NO.	BRAND & MODEL	PRICE	OVERALL SCORE (P F G VG E)	APPLICATION SPEED	DISPLAY QUALITY	MULTI-MEDIA	FEATURES AND USABILITY	BATTERY LIFE (HR.)
WINDOWS LAPTOPS								
1	**Compaq** Presario 1800T	$2,300	▬▬▬▬	●	●	◕	◕	4
2	**Toshiba** Satellite 2805-S401	2,200	▬▬▬▬	●	●	◕	◕	3
3	**HP** Pavilion n5270	2,000	▬▬▬▬	●	◕	◕	●	2¾
4	**Sony** Vaio PCG-FX170	3,000	▬▬▬▬	●	●	◕	●	3
5	**Dell** Inspiron 8000	2,460	▬▬▬▬	◕	●	◕	◕	2¾
6	**Sony** Vaio PCG-Z505LS	2,550	▬▬▬▬	●	●	◕	◕	2¼
7	**Dell** Inspiron 4000	1,725	▬▬▬▬	◕	◕	◕	◕	3½
8	**Gateway** Solo 5300	2,230	▬▬▬▬	◕	◕	◕	◕	3¼
9	**IBM** ThinkPad i1200	1,850	▬▬▬	◕	◕	○	○	4¼
10	**Toshiba** Satellite 1735	1,200	▬▬▬	◕	○	○	○	2½
11	**Compaq** Presario 1200 12XL400	1,400	▬▬▬	◕	○	◕	◕	2
12	**Toshiba** Portegé 3480CT	2,000	▬▬▬	◕	◕	○	○	2¼
MACINTOSH LAPTOPS								
13	**Apple** PowerBook G4 Titanium	3,200	▬▬▬▬	●	◕	●	○	3
14	**Apple** iBook 466 Special Edition	1,950	▬▬▬	◕	●	◕	○	3¼

See report, page 107. Based on tests published in Consumer Reports in June 2001, with updated price and availability.

The tests behind the Ratings

The **overall score** includes speed and multimedia performance, display quality, battery life, and ease of use. **Application speed** tracks how the computer compared with a benchmark (a 350-MHz Pentium II desktop for Windows machines; a 233-MHz iMac for the Macintosh models). **Display quality** includes our judgments of brightness, contrast, color accuracy, viewing angle, and glare. **Multimedia** includes how quickly the system could display still and moving images, sound quality, and the like. **Features and usability** covers the pointing device, controls, and other features. **Battery life times** are to the nearest 15 minutes, reflecting continuous use in our tests. **Price** is the approximate selling price with a DVD-ROM or CD-ROM drive and a diskette drive. Prices for configure-to-order models do not include shipping.

Recommendations and notes

Most of these laptops have: Active-matrix (TFT) display that's 15 in., measured diagonally. Pad-type pointing device. Floppy diskette drive. 10-GB hard drive. 128 MB of RAM. 8 MB of video RAM. Two PC-card slots. Two USB ports. Built-in Ethernet port, microphone, and analog microphone input. Headphone output. External monitor port. Parallel port and RS-232 serial port (Windows models). Basic productivity suite (Microsoft Works Suite or AppleWorks). Configure-to-order (CTO) models can usually be configured with: Different processor, drive, screen and memory sizes; no networking capability; different CD/DVD/CD-RW options. Provision for expansion and upgrades on most models was either good or very good. This indicates how readily the system can be expanded and its performance upgraded with more RAM, a larger hard drive, and the like. Power conservation for most models was either good or very good. This reflects not only battery life but also the versatility and ease of using power-saving features such as SpeedStep. The manuals provided for most were very good or excellent. All tested models had good or very good warranty and support.

WINDOWS LAPTOPS

1> **COMPAQ** Presario 1800T **Full-featured and excellent overall.** WELL-SUITED FOR: Home user. FEATURES: All-in-one design. 6¾ lb. 800-MHz Pentium III. 20-GB hard drive. 8x/4x/24x CD-RW drive. 16 MB of video RAM. Video output. Docking-station connector. Battery has charge indicator on case. Can play music CD even when computer is off. Speakers sound better than most. Has props to tilt case forward on a desktop. Power conservation is excellent. BUT: Single USB port and PC-card slot. Takes two hands to open the lid. Removable battery door can get misplaced. No built-in microphone. Right mouse button awkward for right-handers. Bottom gets hotter than most.

2> **TOSHIBA** Satellite 2805-S401 **Full-featured and excellent overall.** WELL-SUITED FOR: Home user. FEATURES: All-in-one design. 7½ lb. 700-MHz Pentium III. Stick-type pointing device. 20-GB hard drive. 8x/24x DVD drive. Video output. Can play music CD even when computer is off. BUT: No built-in microphone. Discontinued; replaced by 2805-S402, $2,600.

3> **HP** Pavilion n5270 **Excellent overall.** WELL-SUITED FOR: Home user. FEATURES: All-in-one design. 7 lb. 700-MHz Pentium III. 20-GB hard drive. 8x/24x DVD drive. Video output. Docking-station connector. Can play music CD even when computer is off. Speakers sound better than most. BUT: Bottom gets hotter than most. Discontinued; replaced by n5350, $1,950.

4> **SONY** Vaio PCG-FX170 **Excellent overall, but pricey.** WELL-SUITED FOR: Home user. FEATURES: All-in-one design. 7¼ lb. 800-MHz Pentium III. 20-GB hard drive. 8x/4x/24x/8x DVD/CD-RW combo. FireWire port. Video output. Docking-station connector. Drive bay can take floppy, second battery, or blank panel to save weight. Has props to tilt case forward on a desktop. BUT: No productivity software included. No built-in microphone. Discontinued, but may still be available.

5> **DELL** Inspiron 8000 **Excellent overall.** WELL-SUITED FOR: Home user. FEATURES: All-in-one design. 8 lb. 800-MHz Pentium III. Stick and pad pointing devices. 8x/24x DVD drive. 16 MB of video RAM. FireWire port. S-video output. Docking-station connector. Floppy drive conveniently front-mounted.

Battery has charge indicator on case. Drive bay can take CD-RW drive (allowing CD copying), floppy drive, second battery, or blank panel to save weight. Expansion and upgrades excellent. *BUT:* Ethernet not built in. No productivity software included (only Microsoft Word). Manuals not as good as most. Fillers for PC-card slots can get misplaced. Bottom gets hotter than most. High-resolution screen may challenge people with difficulty focusing on fine text.

6> **SONY** Vaio PCG-Z505LS **Very good overall. Very lightweight and compact without drives.** WELL-SUITED FOR: Commuter, road warrior. FEATURES: Slim-and-light design. 3½ lb. (external floppy drive adds 0.6 lb.). 750-MHz Pentium III. 20-GB hard drive. FireWire port. Very small and light to carry. 12-in. display. BUT: Must buy CD-ROM drive separately. Single PC-card slot, with filler that may get misplaced. Drives connect externally with cables. Keys slightly smaller than on larger laptops. Smaller screen may challenge people with difficulty focusing on fine text. Not suited for 3D games because of slow 3D graphics. No productivity software included (only Microsoft Word). Discontinued; replaced by PCG-R505TE, $2,880.

7> **DELL** Inspiron 4000 **Very good overall.** WELL-SUITED FOR: Home user, commuter. FEATURES: Modular design. 6 lb. 700-MHz Pentium III. 14-in. display. Stick and pad pointing devices. 8x/24x DVD drive. S-video output. Docking-station connection. Removable drives conveniently front-mounted. Battery has charge indicator on case. Drive bay can take DVD drive, floppy drive, second battery, or blank panel. Floppy drive may be connected externally to create three-drive system. BUT: Floppy drive occupies parallel port when connected externally, forcing you to disconnect the printer. Manuals not as good as most. Fillers for PC-card slots can get misplaced. Single USB port. Bottom gets hotter than most.

8> **GATEWAY** Solo 5300 **Very good overall.** WELL-SUITED FOR: Home user, commuter. FEATURES: Modular design. 5½ lb. 800-MHz Pentium III. 14-in. display. 24x CD drive. Video output. Docking-station connector. Drive bay can take CD-ROM drive, floppy drive, or second battery. BUT: Single USB port. Ethernet not built in. Wrists tend to block speakers when typing. No blank panel for drive bay. Bottom gets hotter than most.

9> **IBM** ThinkPad i1200 **Very good overall.** WELL-SUITED FOR: Student, commuter, road warrior. FEATURES: Reduced-legacy design. 5¾ lb. 700-MHz Pentium III. 13-in. display. Stick-type pointing device. 20-GB hard drive. 8x/24x DVD drive. Power conservation is excellent. BUT: 4 MB of video RAM. Not suited for 3D games because of slow 3D graphics. 64 MB of RAM (64 MB added for tests, $50). No internal floppy drive; external drive about $80 extra. No RS-232 serial port. Single PC-card slot. Ethernet not built in. No built-in microphone.

10> **TOSHIBA** Satellite 1735 **Inexpensive yet versatile, with a few weaknesses.** WELL-SUITED FOR: Home user, student. FEATURES: All-in-one design. 7 lb. 700-MHz Celeron. 13-in. passive-matrix display. Stick-type pointing device. 24x CD drive. Floppy drive conveniently front-mounted. Can play music CD even when computer is off. BUT: 64 MB of RAM (64 MB added for tests, $50). 4 MB of video RAM. Not suited for 3D games. Wrists tend to block speakers when typing. Ethernet not built in. No built-in microphone. Bottom gets hotter than most.

Recommendations and notes, cont.

11▷ **COMPAQ** Presario 1200 12XL400 **Inexpensive, but display could be better.** WELL-SUITED FOR: Home user, student. FEATURES: All-in-one design. 7 lb. 700-MHz Celeron. 13-in. passive display. 24x CD drive. Speakers sound better than most. Battery has charge indicator on case. Has props to tilt case forward on a desktop. BUT: 64 MB of RAM (64 MB added for tests, $50). 4 MB of video RAM. Not suited for 3D games. Single PC-card slot. No built-in Ethernet port. No built-in microphone. Need two hands to open lid. Removable battery door can get misplaced. Right mouse buttton awkward for right-handers. Bottom gets hotter than most. Discontinued, but may still be available.

12▷ **TOSHIBA** Portegé 3480CT **Very good overall.** WELL-SUITED FOR: Commuter, road warrior. FEATURES: Slim-and-light design. 3¼ lb. (external floppy drive adds 0.6 lb.). 600-MHz Pentium III. 11-in. display. Stick pointing device. 12-GB hard drive. Very small and light to carry. BUT: Must buy CD-ROM drive separately. Fillers for PC-card slot may get misplaced. PC cards are hard to eject. Drives connect externally with cables. Smallish keys. Smaller screen may challenge people with difficulty focusing on fine text. Built-in speaker only monophonic, not suitable for music. No productivity software included. Discontinued: replaced by Portegé 3490CT, $2,600.

MACINTOSH LAPTOPS

13▷ **APPLE** PowerBook G4 Titanium **Very good overall, but pricey.** WELL-SUITED FOR: Commuter, road warrior. FEATURES: Reduced-legacy, slim design. 5¼ lb. 500-MHz PowerPC G4. 15-in. wide-aspect display. 6x/24x DVD drive. FireWire port. S-video output. Power conservation is excellent. Battery has charge indicator on case. Accepts wireless networking card ($100). BUT: Single PC-card slot. No internal floppy drive; external drive about $80. No analog microphone input. Small cursor keys.

14▷ **APPLE** iBook 466 Special Edition **Very good overall.** WELL-SUITED FOR: Home user, student. FEATURES: Reduced-legacy design. 7 lb. 466-MHz PowerPC G3. 12-in. screen. 6x/24x DVD drive. Fire-Wire port. Video output. Built-in carrying handle. Accepts wireless networking card ($100). Available in choice of colors. BUT: No PC-card slots. Single USB port. No internal floppy drive; external drive about $80. Expansion and upgrades not as good as most. No microphone, analog micro-phone in-put, or external monitor port. Small cursor keys. Built-in speaker only monophonic, not suitable for music.

Monitors

Flat panel and CRT monitors produce different, though equally clear images at normal viewing distances. If a larger screen is a must, a 19-inch CRT monitor may be an ideal choice. All tested models were very good or excellent. At $300, the NEC MultiSync 95 is a worthy choice. Among the 17-inch monitors, the Viewsonic E70f, $190, and the eMachines eView 17p, $200, are very good, low-cost options. The Apple Studio Display M7770ZM/A, $500, combines a flat screen and excellent display quality. If desk space is your priority, consider a flat-panel 15-inch LCD monitor. The Hitachi CML151, $660, is a very good machine with the lowest price tag among tested LCD models. When possible, compare monitors side-by-side with the same image displayed on each screen, to judge contrast and clarity.

Overall Ratings — In performance order

Excellent ● Very good ◑ Good ○ Fair ◒ Poor ●

KEY NO	BRAND & MODEL	PRICE	OVERALL SCORE	DISPLAY QUALITY	EASE OF USE
	15-INCH LCD MONITORS (15-inch viewable image size)				
1	**Sony** SDM-M51	$800		●	●
2	**IBM** T54A	800		●	◑
3	**Hitachi** CML151	660		●	◑
4	**Philips** 150B10	700		●	○
5	**Compaq** FP745A	800		◑	◑
	17-INCH CRT MONITORS (16-inch viewable image size)				
6	**Apple** Studio Display M7770ZM/A	500		●	◑
7	**Dell** P780	380		◑	◑
8	**HP** Pavilion mx70	400		◑	◑
9	**Compaq** Presario MV740	400		◑	◑
10	**Samsung** SyncMaster 753DF	230		◑	●
11	**Viewsonic** E70f	190		◑	○
12	**eMachines** eView 17p	200		◑	○
13	**IBM** G78	290		◑	○
14	**Hitachi** CM615	210		◑	◒
	19-INCH CRT MONITORS (18-inch viewable image size)				
15	**Gateway** VX920	550		◑	◑
16	**Compaq** Presario CV935	360		◑	◑
17	**IBM** G96	420		◑	○
18	**Gateway** EV910	400		◑	○
19	**NEC** MultiSync 95	300		◑	○
20	**Hitachi** CM771	430		◑	○
21	**Samsung** SyncMaster 955DF	350		◑	◒

See report, page 112. Based on tests published in Consumer Reports in July 2001, with updated prices and availability.

The tests behind the Ratings

Overall score is based mainly on image clarity. To judge **display quality,** trained panelists assessed the appearance of text, pictures, and web pages on each monitor. **Ease of use** represents a composite of judgments of how easy it was to use the monitor's front-panel controls, onscreen menus, tilt controls, and the like. **Price** is approximate retail.

Recommendations and notes

All models have: Front-panel controls linked to onscreen menus. Plug-and-play installation. Excellent onscreen menu. Energy Star compliance to meet EPA energy-efficiency standards. Viewable-image size (measured diagonally) of about 15 inches for the flat-panel LCD monitors, 16 inches for 17-inch CRTs, and 18 inches for 19-inch CRTs. Dot pitch of 0.28 mm or less (pixel pitch about 0.3 mm for the LCD monitors). All except the Apple Studio Display M7770ZM/A can be used with a Power Mac G3 computer and have a detachable power cord.

Most models have: A control to restore factory settings. A three-year warranty on parts, labor, tube (CRTs), and backlight (LCDs). Multilingual menus. A nondetachable video cable. A setup guide. No adapter for connection to Macintosh computers.

The 19-inch CRTs have: An average 18-inch cabinet depth and weigh 42 to 53 pounds. Maximum resolution of 1,600x1,200 pixels at a refresh rate of 75 Hz, 1,280x1,024 at 85 Hz. **The 17-inch CRTs have:** An average cabinet depth of about 17 inches and weigh 34 to 42 pounds. Maximum resolution of 1,024x768 pixels at a refresh rate of 75 or 85 Hz. **The LCD monitors:** Are intended to run at a resolution of 1,024x768. Have an average depth of about 8 inches and weigh about 10 to 12 pounds.

15-INCH LCD MONITORS (15-inch viewable image size)

1> **SONY** SDM-M51 **Excellent performer.** Detachable video cable. Includes speakers and adapter for connection to Macs. Easier to tilt than most. 1-yr. warranty on backlight.

2> **IBM** T54A **Very good choice.** Detachable video cable. Discontinued; replaced by T540, $599.

3> **HITACHI** CML151 **Very good model with excellent display.** Detachable video cable. Includes ergonomic guide.

4> **PHILIPS** 150B10 **Excellent display.** Includes adapter for connection to Macs. Easier to tilt than most. But control buttons aren't very clearly labeled and are harder to use than most. Similar: LCD 150P1L, $790.

5> **COMPAQ** FP745A **Consistently very good performer.** Detachable video cable. Includes speakers. Full 1-yr. warranty.

17-INCH CRT MONITORS (16-inch viewable image size)

6> **APPLE** Studio Display M7770ZM/A **Top performer, but expensive.** Compatible only with Power Mac G4 and G4 Cube computers. Flat-screened. Combination video-power cord isn't detachable and menus not multilingual. Full 1-yr. warranty.

7> **DELL** P780 **Flat-screened model is very good performer.**

8> **HP** Pavilion mx70 **Very good choice.** Includes microphone. Full 1-yr. warranty.

9> **COMPAQ** Presario MV740 **Includes microphones and speakers.** Full 1-yr. warranty. But control buttons aren't very clearly labeled.

10> **SAMSUNG** SyncMaster 753DF **Very good, low-priced flat-screened model.**

11> **VIEWSONIC** E70f **Well-priced, very good flat-screened model.** But control buttons aren't very clearly labeled. Similar: E70fb, $190.

12> **EMACHINES** eView 17p **Well-priced, with very good display quality.** But control buttons are harder to use than most. Full 1-yr. warranty.

13> **IBM** G78 **Very good flat-screened model.** Maximum resolution at 75 Hz: 1,280x1,024.

14> **HITACHI** CM615 **Good, low-priced model.** Maximum resolution at 75 Hz: 1,152x870. But menus not multilingual; control buttons aren't very clearly labeled and are harder to use than most.

19-INCH CRT MONITORS (18-inch viewable image size)

15> **GATEWAY** VX920 **Flat-screened, short-depth model is consistent performer.** Maximum resolution at 85 Hz: 1,024x768. Detachable video cable. Full 1-yr. warranty.

16> **COMPAQ** Presario CV935 **Well worth considering for the price.** Maximum resolution at 75 Hz: 1,280x1,024; at 85 Hz: 1,024x768. But menus not multilingual; control buttons aren't very clearly labeled. Full 1-yr. warranty. Similar: MV940, $500.

17> **IBM** G96 **Short-depth model is very good performer.** But control buttons are harder to use than most. Similar: E94, $330.

18> **GATEWAY** EV910 **Very good performer.** Detachable video cable. But control dial isn't very clearly labeled. Full 1-yr. warranty.

19> **NEC** MultiSync 95 **Low-priced unit is very good overall, though menus are not multilingual.** Includes ergonomic guide. But control buttons are harder to use than most. Full 1-yr. warranty.

20> **HITACHI** CM771 **Flat-screened, short-depth model is very good overall.** But control buttons aren't very clearly labeled.

21> **SAMSUNG** SyncMaster 955DF **Very good flat-screened model.** Maximum resolution at 75 Hz: 1,280x1,024; at 85 Hz: 1,024x768. Includes ergonomic guide. Easier to tilt than most.

MP3 players

MP3 players are extremely small and portable and immune to problems caused by bumping. Any of the top-rated models are worth considering. Fairly small and rich in features, the Creative Nomad II, $260, or the Nomad II MG, $280, are good choices for both Mac and PC users. Keep in mind that most players hold only an hour or so of music. For additional capacity, you'll need to purchase storage media compatible with the format of your player. Discs, cards, and other media vary widely in cost. A few models use the low-priced PocketZip format (abbreviated as "PZip" in the Ratings below).

Overall Ratings — In performance order

Rating key: Excellent ● · Very good ◕ · Good ○ · Fair ◑ · Poor ⬤

KEY NO.	BRAND & MODEL	PRICE	OVERALL SCORE	CAPACITY PROVIDED	STORAGE FORMAT	SIGNAL QUALITY	HEADPHONES	EASE OF USE	BATTERY LIFE
	REGULAR MODELS *These players must receive music files from a computer.*								
1	**Creative** Nomad II (64MB)	$260		64 MB	SmartM	●	○	◑	8-10 hr.
2	**Sony** NW-E3 Network Walkman	270		64 MB	None	◑	○	◑	NA
3	**Sony** NW-MS7 Memory Stick	370		64 MB	MG	●	◑	○	NA
4	**Creative** Nomad II MG	280		64 MB	SmartM	◑	○	◑	8-10
5	**Compaq** iPaq Personal Audio Player PA-1	240		64 MB	MMC	◑	◑	○	10
6	**Sonic Blue** Rio 500	250		64 MB	SmartM	◑	○	◑	10+
7	**Sensory Science** rave:mp 2300	290		80 MB	PZip	◑	◐	◑	12
8	**Panasonic** SV-SD75	400		64 MB	SD	●	○	◑	6
9	**Sensory Science** rave:mp2200	260		64 MB	SmartM	◑	●	◑	10
10	**Iomega** HipZip	270		80 MB	PZip	◑	○	◑	12
11	**Sony** MC-P10 Vaio Music Clip	300		64 MB	None	●	●	○	up to 5
12	**Samsung** yepp YP-NEU64B	200		64 MB	SmartM	◑	○	○	10
13	**Nike** psa play 120	300		64 MB	MMC	◑	◐	○	10
	PDA MODULE *This player attaches to a PDA, but must receive music files from a computer.*								
14	**Innogear** MiniJam (32 MB)	200*		32 MB	MMC	●	●	◑	5
	JUKEBOX MODEL *These players can receive music files from a computer or record from a sound system.*								
15	**Creative** Nomad Jukebox Player	455		6 GB	None	◑	○	◑	4+

See report, page 128. Based on tests published in Consumer Reports in July 2001 with updated prices and availability.

The tests behind the Ratings

Overall score is based primarily on signal quality, with headphone quality and ease of use also considered. **Capacity provided** combines whatever memory is built into the unit plus what may be provided by external media supplied with the unit; the type is noted under **storage format. Signal quality** reflects frequency response and any noise or distortion. **Headphones** indicates their accuracy in reproducing sound. **Ease of use** reflects how easy it was to use each player's controls and selection of features. **Battery life** is the manufacturer's estimate. **Price** is a national average as provided by Active Decisions Inc. *(www.activebuyersguide.com).* An asterisk (*) indicates the approximate retail price.

Recommendations and notes

All MP3 players: Support a USB connection to a computer running a number of operating systems. Include software and headphones. **Most MP3 players:** Come with earbud-type headphones. Can use some type of software copyright system, such as SDMI or MetaTrust. Use one or two AAA batteries.

REGULAR MODELS

Must receive music files from a computer.

1> **CREATIVE** Nomad II (64MB) **Fairly small and rich in features.** FM. Remote. Voice recording. Uses one AA battery.

2> **SONY** NW-E3 Network Walkman **Very small with excellent controls.** But very skimpy on features, and memory only internal. Discontinued, but may still be available.

3> **SONY** NW-MS7 Memory Stick **Very small but skimpy on features.** Rechargeable batteries. Discontinued, but may be still available.

4> **CREATIVE** Nomad II MG **Fairly small and rich in features.** FM. Rechargeable batteries. Voice recording.

5> **COMPAQ** iPaq Personal Audio Player PA-1 **Very small but light on features.** Menu hard to navigate. Discontinued, but may still be available.

6> **SONIC** Blue Rio 500 **Stylish model with large capacity.** Uses one AA battery. Discontinued, but may still be available.

7> **SENSORY SCIENCE** rave:mp 2300 **Bulky and needs better headphones, but has pluses.** Voice recording. Inexpensive storage. Easy drag and drop of files. Rechargeable batteries. Clock. Calendar.

8> **PANASONIC** SV-SD75 **The smallest and priciest model, with some shortcomings.** Skimpy on features. Firmware isn't upgradable.

9> **SENSORY SCIENCE** rave: mp2200 **Fine performance with many features.** Largest capacity in its class (64-MB memory plus 64-MB SmartMedia card). Software easy to install and use. But better earphones are needed

10> **IOMEGA** HipZip **Fairly small, with inexpensive storage.** Easy drag and drop of files. Rechargeable batteries.

11> **SONY** MC-P10 Vaio Music Clip **Very small but skimpy on features.** Memory only internal. Needs better headphones. Uses one AA battery. Discontinued, but may be still available.

12> **SAMSUNG** yepp YP-NEU64B **Fairly small and low-priced.** But skimpy on features. Firmware not upgradable. LCD (only on provided remote) limited. Similar: yepp YP-NEU32B, $150*

13> **NIKE** psa play 120 **Looks much like a computer mouse.** Remote. Belt clip. But needs better headphones and didn't work with some PCs. Uses one AA battery. Similar: psa play 60, $200

PDA MODULE

Attaches to a PDA, but must receive music files from a computer.

14> **INNOGEAR** MiniJam (32 MB) **Easy-to-navigate playlist.** But needs better headphones and must be used with (and powered by) a Handspring Visor PDA. Similar: MiniJam 64MB, $230; MiniJam 96MB, $300

JUKEBOX MODEL

Receives music files from a computer or records from a sound system.

15> **CREATIVE** Nomad Jukebox Player **Huge capacity.** Over 90 hr. of music when the AC power adapter is used, but resembles a portable CD player in size and weight. Rechargeable batteries.

Features at a glance MP3 Players

Tested products (keyed to the Ratings) Key no. / Brand	Price	Windows 95	Mac OS	WMA	ADPCM	AAC	Firmware upgradable	EQ presets	FM tuner
1> Creative Nomad	$260	•	•	•			•	5	•
2> Sony	270			•			•	0	
3> Sony	370						•	0	
4> Creative Nomad	280	•	•	•			•	4	•
5> Compaq	240			•		•	•	3	
6> Sonic Blue	270			•			•	4	
7> Sensory Science	285	•					•	5	
8> Panasonic	400					•		0	
9> Sensory Science	260	•			•		•	5	•
10> Iomega	285	•	•	•			•	4	
11> Sony	300						•	3	
12> Samsung	200	•						3	
13> Nike	300	•	•				•	4	
14> Innogear	200	•					•	4	
15> Creative Nomad	455	•			•			0	

STORAGE-FORMAT FRENZY

A growing proliferation of cards, discs, and other storage media are now used in MP3 players. Here are those found on tested models, listed in order of approximate cost. Except as noted, prices are for 32/64-megabyte (MB) versions. The abbreviations in parentheses are those used in the Ratings.

◆ PocketZip (PZip), $15 (40 MB). Formerly the Clik! Disk, it's from Iomega.

◆ SmartMedia (SmartM), $40/$80. The thinnest format.

◆ CompactFlash (CFlash), $50/$70. An early forma.

◆ Multimedia Card (MMC), $60/$110. The smallest format.

◆ Sony Magic Gate (MG), $100/$160. New audio version of the Memory Stick.

◆ Secure Digital (SD), $120/$180. Supports encryption.

PDAs

The Palm operating system is by far the most popular and among the best we tested. PDAs using the Palm OS are small, relatively low priced, and simple to operate. The Palm m105 is a very good model and affordable at $200. For Windows users, Pocket PCs have a processor with far more horsepower and come with familiar word processing and spreadsheet applications. For a computer stand-in, consider either of the top-rated Palm models or the Compaq iPaqH3135, $400. If all you need is a way to track appointments and phone numbers, the pocket-sized Palm m100, $130, is an exceptional value.

Overall Ratings — In performance order

Legend: Excellent ● | Very good ◓ | Good ○ | Fair ◒ | Poor ●

KEY NO.	BRAND & MODEL	PRICE	OVERALL SCORE	EASE OF USE	BATTERY LIFE	DISPLAY	IN SYNC	CONVENIENCE
ALL-AROUND ORGANIZERS								
1	**Kyocera** Smartphone QCP6035	$520		○	◓	◒	◒	◒
2	**Palm** m105	200		○	◓	○	◒	◒
3	**Handspring** Visor Edge	400		○	◓	○	◓	○
4	**Handspring** Visor Platinum	300		○	◓	○	◓	◒
5	**Palm** VIIx	200		○	◓	○	◒	◒
6	**Sony** Clié PEG-N710C	500		◒	○	◒	◒	◒
7	**Handspring** Visor Prism	450		○	○	○	◓	○
8	**Franklin** eBookman EBM-911	230		◒	○	○	●	○
COMPUTER STAND-INS								
9	**Palm** m500	400		◒	◓	○	◓	◒
10	**Compaq** iPaq H3135	400		◒	◒	◒	○	◒
11	**Palm** m505	450		◒	◒	○	◓	◒
12	**Casio** Cassiopeia EM-500	400		◒	○	◒	◒	◒
13	**Casio** Cassiopeia E-125	550		○	○	◒	◒	◒
14	**Compaq** iPaq H3630	500		◒	◒	○	◒	◒
15	**Compaq** iPaq H3650	500		◒	◒	○	◒	◒
16	**HP** Jornada 525	360		○	◒	◒	○	◒
17	**HP** Jornada 548	450		○	◒	◒	◒	◒
18	**Diamond** Mako	300		○	◒	◒	◒	◒
19	**Psion** Revo +	400		○	◒	◒	◒	○
JUST THE BASICS								
20	**Palm** m100	130		○	◓	○	◒	○
21	**Casio** Pocket Viewer PV-400PLUS	100		◒	◓	◒	◒	○
22	**Xircom** Rex 6000	150		◒	◓	◒	○	○

See report, page 115. Based on tests published in Consumer Reports in September 2001.

The tests behind the Ratings

Overall score reflects ease of use, battery life, display, and synchronization with a computer. **Ease of use** includes ergonomic factors, navigation among tasks, and usability of phone lists, appointment book, to-do list, and memo pad. **Battery life** tracks fully charged batteries with the PDA turned on (for monochrome models we assume backlight is usually off); the best would run for 20 hours or longer. **Display** tests assess screen readability in various environments, including sunlight. **In sync** indicates how easily the PDA can be synchronized with a computer. **Convenience** includes bundled software, expansion capabilities, fit for shirt pockets, and other factors. **Price** is approximate retail.

Recommendations and notes

Full-featured Palm OS models: Use the Palm operating system. Have an address book, a calendar, a notepad, and a to-do list, plus the ability to transfer e-mail from a computer. All but the Sony can work with both Windows and Macintosh. The simple user interface lets you do one task at a time. All have 8 megabytes (MB) of RAM. The less expensive models have easily replaceable AAA batteries that should last for more than 24 hours of continuous use, plus a backlit monochrome display.

Computer stand-ins: Feature a computer-like user interface. Can run more than one program at once. Have a minimum of 16 MB of memory; most have an expansion slot for a modem or removable memory cards (compact flash or multimedia cards). In continuous use, rechargeable batteries should last 4 to 8 hours with a color display, 10 to 12 hours with monochrome. Pocket PCs work only with Windows computers.

Basic organizers: Have a simple user interface. 2 to 4 MB of memory. A monochrome display. Easily replaceable batteries.

FULL-FEATURED PALM OS MODELS

1 > **KYOCERA** Smartphone QCP6035 **Very good overall, the best we've seen for wireless access.** 2.5-in. diagonal monochrome display, 8 MB memory, Palm OS, rechargeable, replaceable battery. Includes voice-recording software, expense tracker. Works as CDMA cell phone, CDMA PCS phone, and an analog cell phone. Very readable in sunlight. Basic PDA functions easy to use and integrated well with phone. (We rated it only as a PDA.) Display smaller and harder to use than those on standalone Palm PDAs.

2 > **PALM** m105 **Very good, with room to grow.** 2.6-in. diagonal monochrome display, 8 MB memory, Palm OS, replaceable batteries. Very readable in sunlight. Includes mobile connectivity software. Basic PDA functions easy to use. Overall design better than most. Fits in shirt pocket.

3 > **HANDSPRING** Visor Edge **Very good: Slim but basic.** 3.1-in. diagonal monochrome display, 8 MB memory, Palm OS, nonreplaceable battery. Very readable in sunlight. Includes expense-tracker software. Basic PDA functions easy to use. Uses proprietary expansion slot. Expansion sleeve makes unit bulky. Fits in shirt pocket.

4 > **HANDSPRING** Visor Platinum **Offers the basics plus room to grow.** Overall design better than most. Basic organizer functions easy to use. Comes with expense-tracker software. Uses proprietary expansion slot to install extra functions, accessories. Fits easily in a shirt pocket. Instruction manual on CD only. 5¾ oz. 4¾x3x¾ in.

5 > **PALM** VIIx **Only available PDA that comes with wireless Internet access.** Basic organizer functions easy to use. Display easy to read in bright sunlight. Larger than most Palms. 7 oz. 5¼x3¼x¾ in.

6 > **SONY** Clié PEG-N710C **Very good PDA, with integrated multimedia.** 3-in. diagonal high-resolution color display, 7.2 MB memory, Palm OS, nonreplaceable battery. Very readable in sunlight. Includes MP3 player, expense-tracker software. Design and user interface better than most. Uses Memory Stick slot. Fits in shirt pocket.

7 > **HANDSPRING** Visor Prism **Has color display, but it's only so-so.** Basic organizer functions easy to use. Comes with expense-tracker software. Uses proprietary expansion slot to install extra functions, accessories. Batteries can't be replaced by user. Instruction manual on CD only. 7 oz. 4¾x3x1 in.

8 > **FRANKLIN** eBookman EBM-911 **Good; many extras, but basic functions hard to use; there are better choices.** 4.2-in. diagonal monochrome display, 16 MB memory, proprietary operating system, replaceable batteries. Uses multimedia cards. Has eBook reader, MP3 player. Web access required to download basic software; lacks software to allow data entry from PC. Basic PDA functions hard to use, character-recognition system difficult to learn, and applications slow to respond. No e-mail functions. Similar: EBM-900, $130; EBM-901, $180.

COMPUTER STAND-INS

9 > **PALM** m500 **Very good overall; the smallest computer stand-in we've tested.** 3-in. diagonal monochrome display, 8 MB memory, Palm OS. Nonreplaceable battery. Very readable in sunlight. Includes expense-tracker, eBook reader, and mobile connectivity software. Has vibrating alarm. Basic PDA functions easy to use. Overall design better than most. Takes multimedia and Secure Digital cards. Word processor and spreadsheet software take up memory, and formulas cannot be entered in spreadsheets. Fits in shirt pocket.

10 > **COMPAQ** iPaq H3135 **Very good, but can be bulky.** 3.8-in. diagonal monochrome display, 16 MB memory, Pocket PC system. Nonreplaceable battery. Voice-recording, MP3 software, eBook-reader included. Uses expansion slot for Compact Flash cards, and expansion sleeve makes unit bulky. Basic PDA functions easy to use, and interface better than most. Fits in shirt pocket. Similar: iPaq 3150 ($300) lacks expansion sleeve, which may be purchased separately.

Recommendations and notes

11▷ PALM m505 **Very good overall, but the color display does not add much.** 3-in. diagonal color display, 8 MB memory, Palm OS. Nonreplaceable battery. Includes expense-tracker, eBook reader, and mobile connectivity software. Has vibrating alarm. Basic PDA functions easy to use. Overall design better than most. Takes multimedia and Secure Digital cards. Word-processing and spreadsheet software take up memory, and formulas cannot be entered in spreadsheets. Fits in shirt pocket.

12▷ CASIO Cassiopeia EM-500 **A very good choice if you don't need much expansion.** Overall design and user interface better than most. Basic organizer functions easy to use. Comes with voice recording, MP3 software, eBook reader. Uses multimedia cards for data storage. Instruction manual on CD only. Requires software updates before using. Battery installation confusing. 7¾ oz. 5x3¼x¾ in.

COMPUTER STAND-INS

13▷ CASIO Cassiopeia E-125 **Good overall.** User interface better than most. Basic organizer functions easy to use. Comes with voice recording, MP3 software, eBook reader. Uses compact flash cards. Instruction manual on CD only. Requires software updates before using. Battery installation confusing. Not the best overall design. 8¾ oz. 5x3¼x1 in.

14▷ COMPAQ iPaq H3630

15▷ COMPAQ iPaq H3650 **Sleek with very good feel, but you pay for expansion.** The two appear identical. Overall design, user interface better than most. Basic organizer functions easy to use. Comes with voice recording, MP3 software, eBook reader. Uses proprietary expansion slot that can adapt to compact flash or PC cards. Fits easily in a shirt pocket. Batteries can't be replaced by user. Instruction manual on CD only. Requires extra-cost sleeve for expansion port. 6⅔ oz. 5x3x¾ in.

16▷ HP Jornada 525 **Good overall, and inexpensive for its type. 3.6-in. diagonal color display,** 16 MB memory, Pocket PC system. Nonreplaceable battery. Includes voice-recording and MP3 software, eBook reader. Basic PDA functions easy to use, and interface better than most. Uses Compact Flash cards. Can't be used in bright sunlight. No place to store stylus.

17▷ HP Jornada 548 Color **Good, but the overall design has shortcomings.** User interface better than most. Basic organizer functions easy to use. Comes with voice recording, MP3 software, eBook reader. Uses compact flash cards. User can't replace batteries. Too bulky to fit in a shirt pocket. Not usable in bright sunlight. 9 oz. 5x3x1 in.

18▷ DIAMOND Mako

19▷ PSION Revo + **Versatile laptop replacements.** These PDAs use the EPOC operating system. Display is easy to read in bright sunlight but has no backlight for dim light. Batteries can't be replaced by user. No PIM software. Not the best overall design. 7½ oz. ¾x6¼x3 in.

BASIC ORGANIZERS

20▷ PALM m100 **A good basic PDA.** Uses Palm OS. Overall design better than most. Basic organizer functions easy to use. Fits easily in a shirt pocket. Display easy to read in bright sunlight. Instruction manual on CD only. No e-mail application included. 5 oz. 4¾x2¾ x¾ in.

21▷ CASIO Pocket Viewer PV-400 Plus **Good, but the Palm m100 is a better buy.** Uses unique operating system. Comes with expense-tracker software. Fits easily in a shirt pocket. Easy to read in bright sunlight. User interface worse than most. Basic organizer functions hard to use. No to-do application. 4½ oz. 5x3¼x½ in.

22▷ XIRCOM REX 6000 **Card-size organizer that's too small to use easily.** Uses unique operating system. Easily connects with a laptop, but overall performance is limited. 1¼ oz. 3½x2x¼ in. Discontinued but may still be available.

Printers

Inkjet printers print in color as well as black and white. Most models are very good or excellent. HP models top the Ratings, while two **CR Best Buys**, the Canon Color Bubble Jet S450 and the Epson Stylus Color 777, are excellent low-cost alternatives. For large volumes of text, laser printers offer fast and inexpensive black-and-white output. All the models tested were excellent. The Samsung ML-4500, $199, is a top performer at a low price. Multifunction machines, which can copy, fax, scan, and print, are useful if your space and budget are limited. The HP OfficeJet K60 is excellent, but doesn't support Macs.

Overall Ratings — In performance order

Symbols: Excellent ● Very good ◕ Good ○ Fair ◔ Poor ⬤

KEY NO.	BRAND & MODEL	PRICE	OVERALL SCORE (0–100: P F G VG E)	TEXT QUALITY	TEXT SPEED (PPM)	TEXT COST	COLOR PHOTOS QUALITY	COLOR PHOTOS TIME	COLOR PHOTOS COST	GRAPHICS QUALITY
	INKJET PRINTERS									
1	**HP** PhotoSmart 1215	$400		●	3.8	3.6¢	●	8 min.	$1.00	●
2	**HP** DeskJet 952C	200		●	3.1	4.3	●	9	1.00	●
3	**HP** DeskJet 932C	150		●	2.7	4.3	●	9	1.00	●
4	**HP** DeskJet 960cse	300		●	3.7	4.0	●	9	1.00	●
5	**Canon** Color Bubble Jet S600	200		●	5.1	2.8	●	2	1.00	◕
6	**Compaq** IJ1200	130		●	4.1	9.8	◕	14	1.40	○
7	**Canon** Color Bubble Jet S450 **A CR Best Buy**	100		●	4.2	3.2	◕	11	1.20	◕
8	**Epson** Stylus Color 880	140		○	4.5	4.9	◕	3	0.80	◕
9	**Epson** Stylus Color 777 **A CR Best Buy**	100		◕	2.4	4.5	●	3	0.80	◕
10	**Epson** Stylus Photo 890	300		◕	1.8	3.4	●	3	0.70	●
11	**Lexmark** Color Jetprinter Z53	140		●	4.7	8.8	◕	8	1.20	○
12	**Lexmark** Color Jetprinter Z43	100		●	4.0	10.2	◕	10	1.10	○
13	**Canon** Color Bubble Jet S800	300		◕	2.2	4.3	○	2	1.10	◕
14	**Compaq** IJ600	100		●	2.0	10.6	●	14	1.40	○
15	**Canon** Color Bubble Jet S400	80		◕	2.2	3.2	○	12	1.10	◕
16	**Canon** Color Bubble Jet BJC-2100	80		○	1.8	6.9	○	9	2.40	○
17	**HP** DeskJet 648C	100		◕	0.6	6.5	○	10	1.20	○
	MULTIFUNCTION INKJET PRINTER									
18	**HP** OfficeJet K60	300		●	2.8	4.3	●	9	1.00	●
	LASER PRINTERS									
19	**HP** LaserJet 1200se	400		●	7.5	2.0	–	–	–	◕
20	**Samsung** ML-4500	200		●	4.5	2.7	–	–	–	●
21	**Lexmark** Optra E312	400		●	5.3	3.0	–	–	–	◕
22	**Brother** HL-1250	350		●	6.7	2.5	–	–	–	◕
23	**Oki** Okipage 8z	275		●	5.1	2.2	–	–	–	○

See report, page 135. Based on tests published in Consumer Reports in September 2001.

The tests behind the Ratings

Brand & model includes printers tested for a February report that are still available, plus several new ones. **Overall score** is based primarily on print quality and speed for printing text. **Text quality** indicates how crisply and clearly a printer produced black text in a variety of faces, sizes, and styles. **Text speed** is our calculation of the typical output in pages per minute (ppm) for a three-page document. **Color-photo quality** is our assessment of the appearance of each photo. **Color-photo time,** to the nearest minute, is our measurement of how long it took each inkjet to produce an 8x10-inch color print at the printer's best set-ting. **Graphics quality** scores are for color graphics for inkjet printers, black-and-white graphics for lasers. **Cost** is the cost of printing a single text page (including the ink or toner and paper) or photo (ink and glossy photo paper), as well as the amortized cost of the printhead, based on the manufacturer's stated life. **Price** is the approximate retail.

Recommendations and notes

Most inkjet printers: Work with most versions of Windows and the Macintosh OS. Have parallel and universal serial bus ports (but require USB for Macs). Include a set of color (CMY) and black (K) cartridges. Can hold 100 sheets or at least 10 envelopes in their input tray. Indicate when ink supply is low. Can print banners at least 44 inches long. Have a one-year warranty.

Most laser printers: Work with most versions of Windows and the Macintosh OS. Have parallel and USB ports (but require USB for Macs). Include a full-capacity toner cartridge. Cannot print banners. Have a one-year warranty.

INKJET PRINTERS

1▷ **HP** PhotoSmart 1215 **Excellent overall, but pricey.** Quiet. Automatic two-sided printing. Prints from digital-camera CompactFlash and SmartMedia memory cards and by infrared beam from cameras with HP JetSend capability. Similar: 1215 VM, $400, 1218, $500, P1000, $300.

2▷ **HP** DeskJet 952C **Excellent for all types of output.** Has separate envelope input. Similar: 950C, $200

3▷ **HP** DeskJet 932C **Very similar to 952C, but a bit slower for text.** Still, it's a bargain at $100 less. Similar: 930C, $140.

4▷ **HP** DeskJet 960cse **Excellent overall.** Slow at printing color photos.

5▷ **CANON** Color Bubble Jet S600 **Excellent overall, and very fast with text and photos.** Lowest cost for printing text among tested inkjets.

6▷ **COMPAQ** IJ1200 **Very good overall, but among the slowest for photos.** High cost for text, but fast. Lacks Mac support.

7▷ **CANON** Color Bubble Jet **A CR Best Buy Great combination of quality and value.** Lowest cost for text and color graphics, and among the fastest for text.

8▷ **EPSON** Stylus Color 880 **Excellent overall.** Fast text printing. Fairly fast, low-priced color-photo printing. Needs special cartridge for color photos

9▷ **EPSON** Stylus Color 777 **A CR Best Buy Very good overall.** Fairly fast, low-priced color-photo printing. But noisy, and can't print banners.

10▷ **EPSON** Stylus Photo 890 **Very good overall, but there are better values.** Relatively slow but low-priced text printing. Fast and low-priced color-photo printing.

11▷ **LEXMARK** Color Jetprinter Z53 **Very good overall.** But noisy, and needs special cartridge for color photos.

12▷ **LEXMARK** Color Jetprinter Z43 **Very good overall.** Similar to Z53, above, but a bit slower.

13▷ **CANON** Color Bubble Jet S800 **Very good overall.** Can print from CompactFlash memory card. Scanner attachment available. Relatively slow printing text, but fast printing color photos.

14▷ **COMPAQ** IJ600 **Quality similar to IJ1200's.** But much slower for text, at a $30 savings.

15▷ **CANON** Color Bubble Jet S400 **Very good overall, and a very good price.** Scanner attachment available. But relatively slow printing text and photos. Needs special cartridge for color photos.

16▷ **CANON** Color Bubble Jet BJC-2100 **Decent print quality, but photos and color graphics cost twice the average.** Only 50-sheet input tray and 5-envelope capacity. Lacks on-off control.

17▷ **HP** DeskJet 648C **Decent quality, but the slowest text by far.** Has separate envelope input. But lacks low-ink warning. Only 90-day warranty. Similar: 640C, $100.

Recommendations and notes, cont.

MULTIFUNCTION INKJET PRINTERS

18▷ **HP** OfficeJet K60 **Excellent across the board.** Has separate envelope input. But lacks Mac support. Similar: K60XI, $300, K80XI, $400.

LASER PRINTERS

19▷ **HP** LaserJet 1200se **Excellent overall, with the lowest-priced text printing of all tested printers.** Scanner attachment available. Water-resistant toner. But noisy.

20▷ **SAMSUNG** ML-4500 **A top performer at a very low price.** 150-sheet input tray. But comes with low-capacity toner cartridge, and lacks USB and Mac support. Lacks low-toner warning. Discontinued; replaced by ML-1200, $200.

21▷ **LEXMARK** Optra E312 **An excellent choice that's competitive in every respect.** 150-sheet input tray. But lacks low-toner warning. Similar: E312L, $300.

22▷ **BROTHER** HL-1250 **More expensive version of HL-1240.** Discontinued; replaced by HL-1450, $350.

23▷ **OKI** Okipage 8z **Excellent text output at low cost per page.** 100-sheet input tray. Low price for a laser.

Scanners

Paying more for a scanner doesn't always get you an improved scanned image. Models that scan at 600 dots per inch (dpi)are sufficient for most purposes. We found several very good 600-dpi models for $100 or less.

For a scanner that takes up less space on your desktop, consider the Canon CanoScan N650U, $100 or the Musktek Plug-N-Scan 1200 UB, also $100. Among 1200-dpi models, the Epson Perfection 1240UT, $200, is fast and accurate.

Overall Ratings

In performance order

Excellent ● Very good ◐ Good ○ Fair ◔ Poor ●

KEY NO.	BRAND & MODEL	PRICE	OVERALL SCORE 0 P F G VG E 100	PHOTO SCAN QUALITY COLOR	B&W	SPEED
	600-DPI SCANNERS					
1	**Canon** CanoScan N650U	100		◐	○	◐
2	**Microtek** ScanMaker 3700	100		◐	◐	○
3	**Mustek** Plug-N-Scan 1200 UB	100		◐	○	◐
4	**Umax** Astra 3400	100		○	○	◐
5	**Visioneer** OneTouch 8100	120		◐	○	●
6	**Mustek** BearPaw 1200	110		◐	○	◐
7	**HP** ScanJet 3400Cse/Cxi	100		◐	◐	◐
	1,200-DPI SCANNERS					
8	**Epson** Perfection 1240U	200		◐	◐	●
9	**Microtek** ScanMaker 4700	200*		○	◐	◐
10	**Canon** CanoScan N1220U	200		◐	○	◐
11	**HP** ScanJet 5300Cse/Cxi	200		◐	○	◐
12	**Umax** AstraNET e5470	200		○	○	○
13	**Acer** 1240UT	150		◐	○	○

See report, page 131. Based on tests published in Consumer Reports in May 2001, with updated prices and availability.

The tests behind the Ratings

Overall score is based on color and black-and-white photo scan quality and scanning speed. **Photo scan quality** measures how faithfully the scanner reproduced a color photo and a black-and-white photo, as assessed by a panel of testers. We used the scanners and software provided by the manufacturer to scan photos at 150, 300, 600, and (where possible) 1,200 dpi and output them to a high-resolution inkjet printer. There was little improvement in the quality of scanned photographs above 300 dpi. **Speed** is a measure of how quickly each scanner performed scans of a 5x7-inch color photo and an 8.5x11-inch black-and-white photo. **Price** is the national average based on a survey. An asterisk (*) denotes approximate price.

Recommendations and notes

All tested models have: At least 600-dpi optical scanning resolution. Support for Windows 98, ME, and (on models allowing parallel-port connection) Windows 95. Ability to scan directly into e-mail software as a message attachment. Photocopy function. USB-port connectivity. TWAIN compliance for communication with third-party software. Ability to scan full area of an 8.5x11-inch page.

Most tested models have: Support for Windows 2000 and some version of Mac OS (for Mac with USB ports). AC-powered operation. Lid that hinges on short side of scanning bed. One-year warranty. Dimensions approximately 3.5x11.5x19 inches (HxWxD). Multiple-scan mode. Recommended computer memory of at least 32 or 64 MB of RAM.

600-DPI SCANNERS

1▷ **CANON** CanoScan N650U **Thin profile, small footprint, and USB-powered operation make it suitable for portable use with a laptop computer.**

2▷ **MICROTEK** ScanMaker 3700 **Very good performer.** Includes film-scanner accessory. But slowest 600-dpi model with highest recommended RAM, 128 MB. Thicker, with larger footprint than most others.

3▷ **MUSTEK** Plug-N-Scan 1200 UB **Thin profile, small footprint, and USB-powered operation make it suitable for portable use with a laptop computer.**

4▷ **UMAX** Astra 3400 **Good, but there are better choices.**

5▷ **VISIONEER** OneTouch 8100 **High-priced, with so-so color scanning.** Can connect to parallel port on PCs. Lid hinges on long side of scanning bed. Lacks Mac support and multiple-scan mode.

6▷ **MUSTEK** BearPaw 1200 **High-priced, with so-so color scanning.** Lacks Mac support.

7▷ **HP** ScanJet 3400Cse/Cxi **There are better choices.** So-so color scanning. Can connect to parallel port on PCs. Lacks Mac support, mulitple-scan mode, and has only 90-day warranty. Cse and Cxi models differ only in included software. Cxi costs $20 to $50 more.

1,200-DPI SCANNERS

8▷ **EPSON** Perfection 1240U **Fast and accurate.** Can be stored on side. Optional film-scanner accessory available.

9▷ **MICROTEK** ScanMaker 4700 **Very good performer.** Includes film-scanner accessory. Thicker, with larger footprint than most others.

10▷ **CANON** CanoScan N1220U **Thin profile, small footprint, and USB-powered operation make it suitable for portable use with a laptop computer.** Can be stored on side.

11▷ **HP** ScanJet 5300Cse/Cxi **Good performer.** Can connect to parallel port on PCs. Optional film-scanner and document-feeder accessories available. Cse and Cxi models differ only in included software. Cxi costs $20 to $50 more. But larger footprint than most others.

12▷ **UMAX** AstraNET e5470 **Includes film-scanner accessory.** But cannot scan color negatives correctly.

13▷ **ACER** 1240UT **There are better choices.** So-so color scanning. Includes film-scanner accessory.

Features at a glance   Scanners

Tested products (keyed to the Ratings) and similar models			Price	Parallel port	Macintosh support	Number of buttons	Copy/print button
Key no.	Brand	Model					
600-DPI SCANNERS							
1▷	**Canon**	CanoScan N650U	100		•	1	
		CanoScan N656U	130		•	1	
2▷	**Microtek**	ScanMaker 3700	100		•	3	•
3▷	**Mustek**	Plug-N-Scan 1200 UB	100		•	0	
		Plug-N-Scan 1200 CP	100	•		0	
4▷	**Umax**	Astra 3400	100		•	4	•
5▷	**Visioneer**	OneTouch 8100	120	•		5	•
6▷	**Mustek**	BearPaw 1200	110			5	•
		BearPaw 1200F	150		•	5	•
7▷	**HP**	ScanJet 3400Cse/Cxi	100	•		3	•
		ScanJet 4300Cse/Cxi	150	•		3	•
1,200-DPI SCANNERS							
8▷	**Epson**	Perfection 1240U	200		•	3	•
		Perfection 1240U Photo	300		•	3	•
9▷	**Microtek**	ScanMaker 4700	200		•	5	•
10▷	**Canon**	CanoScan N1220U	200		•	1	
11▷	**HP**	ScanJet 5300Cse/Cxi	200	•	•	4	•
		ScanJet 5370Cse/Cxi	300	•	•	4	•
12▷	**Umax**	AstraNET e5470	200		•	4	•
13▷	**Acer**	1240UT	150		•	0	

Guide to the Brands

A few large, well-known players dominate the home-computer market, but over the past few years, smaller companies have forged comfortable niches with innovative technology and competitive prices. Some of the giants, such as Hewlett-Packard, market not only desktops and laptop computers but also peripherals such as printers and scanners. Other companies, such as WinBook, have successfully concentrated on a single market—in this case, laptops.

Here's a rundown of the leading companies that sell computers, software, and home-office equipment in the U.S. See the list of brands on page 196 for manufacturers' phone numbers and web addresses.

HARDWARE MANUFACTURERS

AMD *(www.amd.com)*. Advanced Micro Devices is the second-largest microprocessor manufacturer. Despite rival Intel's strength, AMD has managed to grab a share of the market for its Athlon and Duron chips, mostly in budget and midpriced desktops. It was AMD that first broke the psychologically important 1-GHz barrier, in 2000.

APPLE COMPUTER *(www.apple.com)*. The user-friendly Macintosh personal computer revolutionized the market in the early '80s. By the mid '90s, beset by management problems and the dominance of Microsoft's Windows operating system, Apple was forced to regroup under the guidance of its returning founder, Steve Jobs. The company made headlines in mid-1998 with the introduction of its futuristic-looking iMac computer, designed to appeal to users on a budget (it retails for around $1,000) who are interested in ease of use. Apple's strengths have always been in the areas of education, design, and publishing. And Apple owners are very loyal and consistently rate the brand high in performance. Apple's current offerings include the iMac, the iBook, the Power Macintosh desktop series, and the Macintosh PowerBook laptops. The latest operating system from Apple is version 10.1 of Mac OS X. Macs are available through Apple or through computer and home-electronics retailers. Apple is opening its own chain of retail outlets.

COMPAQ *(www.compaq.com)*. This home-computing giant has been a major player since it made its name in the mid '80s during the free-for-all growth of "IBM-compatible" computers. Today, Compaq, under its Presario line, manufactures a range of desktops and laptops for users ranging from entry-level to enthusiast. It has also put a lot of effort into dominating the $1,000-or-less PC market. Compaq offers the Presario line of laptops for home users and iPAQ handhelds (PDAs). Available through Compaq and through computer and home-electronics retailers.

CTX INTERNATIONAL *(www.ctxintl.com)*. The U.S. division of Chuntex Electronics, one of Taiwan's largest monitor manufacturers, CTX International markets cathode ray tube (CRT) and liquid crystal display (LCD) monitors. The brand is available through computer and home-electronics retailers.

DELL COMPUTER CORP. *(www.dell.com)*. The world's leading direct marketer of computer systems, Dell was founded by Michael Dell in 1984 to design and customize computer systems to end-user requirements. Much of the company's revenue is from businesses, government, and educational institutions. But Dell has been increasing its home-PC business in recent years. Dell's extensive line includes Dell Dimension desktops and Dell Latitude and Inspiron notebooks. Available exclusively from Dell via its toll-free number or the Internet.

FUJITSU PC CORP. *(www.fujitsupc.com)*. Fujitsu PC Corp. was formed in 1996 by the Japanese electronics conglomerate Fujitsu Ltd. to expand its business to the U.S. home-computer market. Its LifeBook series of multimedia laptops ranges from value-based models to pricey, high-performance models designed for corporate and technical power users. Available through computer and home-electronics retailers.

GATEWAY *(www.gateway.com)*. The Ben & Jerry's of the personal computer market, Gateway is known for the black-and-white cowhide design on its computer boxes. Gateway was founded in 1985 by two Midwesterners whose goal was to offer home-computer consumers a direct-mail alternative. In doing so, they generated $100,000 during their first four months in business and helped pioneer direct-mail sales of home-PC products. By 1987, Gateway was selling fully configured PCs to consumers sight unseen. The lure was a good price. The company's offerings include the Essential and Performance lines of desktop PCs, and the Solo multimedia laptop line. Their products are available direct and through Gateway Country Stores.

HANDSPRING *(www.handspring.com)*. Founded in 1998 by the cofounders of Palm, Handspring manufactures the Visor line of personal digital assistants (PDAs). The Visors are "clones" of Palm PDAs, which means they use the Palm operating system.

HEWLETT-PACKARD *(www.hp.com)*. HP was founded in 1939 and its first product, an electronic test instrument known as an audio oscillator, was built in a Palo Alto, Calif., garage. HP's home-computer line is centered around the Pavilion series of desktop PCs. Portable offerings include a line of laptops, the Pavilion series, and the Jornada handheld PC.

HP is the market leader in printers, offering several best-selling models in both the laser and inkjet formats under its HP LaserJet and HP DeskJet series. HP also makes multifunction office machines (for faxing, copying, scanning, and printing). The company offers a series of scanners, its ScanJet series, along with the PhotoSmart digital camera and photo printer products. Available through computer and home-electronics stores nationwide, and through mail-order.

IBM *(www.ibm.com)*. Founded in 1911 as the Computing-Tabulating-Recording Company and renamed International Business Machines Corp. in 1924, IBM pioneered industrial computing in the 1940s and 1950s, presenting its first large-scale computer to Harvard in 1945. By 1952, the IBM 701, designed for scientific calculations, was in production and keypunch technology was in its heyday. IBM became a billion-dollar company in 1957 and spent the 1960s and 1970s introducing a series of corporate computers known as mainframes, one more powerful than the next.

The company entered the home-PC market in 1981, when it introduced the first IBM personal computer (the origin of the term PC). Then, faced with stiff competition from makers of so-called "IBM-compatible" PCs (computers that ran on MS-DOS), IBM found itself losing market share to industry entrepreneurs. Today, IBM's offerings center around its Net Vista desktops and ThinkPad laptops. Available through IBM.

INTEL *(www.intel.com)*. This microprocessor company is the world's largest maker of microchips (the "brains" that control the central processing data). Intel introduced the Pentium processor for both desktop and laptop PCs in 1993, followed by the Pentium with MMX technology for improved multimedia performance in 1996. Then, in 1997, Intel introduced the Pentium II microprocessor, eventually available in speeds of 233 to 450 MHz. Intel also makes a lower-priced line of chips called Celeron, used in budget and moderate-priced desktops. A new generation of enhanced Pentium III chips with speeds starting at 500 MHz and later breaking the 1-GHz barrier debuted in early 1999. Intel's current line is made up of Pentium 4s and Celerons for desktops and Pentium IIIs and Celerons for laptops. Intel also supplies the motherboards used in many PCs.

IOMEGA *(www.iomega.com)*. You might be familiar with the brand names Zip and Jaz— the leading removable-cartridge drives for backup and archival purposes. These drives are manufactured by Iomega. The company also makes the Clik! portable removable drive.

PALM *(www.palm.com)*. Palm is largely responsible for making personal digital assistants popular. It has retained its lead over the PDA market, but clone makers such as Handspring (formed by Palm cofounders) and Sony are posing formidable challenges. In 2000, 3Com, which acquired Palm when it bought U.S. Robotics in 1997, spun off Palm.

SONY *(www.sony.com)*. This Japanese home-electronics giant now has its name on everything from movie theaters to music CDs to microwaves. An innovator—Sony marketed the first all-transistor TV and the first videotape recorder for home use and helped develop the compact disc—the company made a foray into the home-PC market in the '90s with Sony Vaio desktop and notebook computers, plus digital cameras (on top of its already successful line of Trinitron monitors). In 1998, Sony emerged as a leading player in the "ultraportable" laptop business with its Vaio SuperSlim series of subnotebooks weighing under three pounds. Sony PC products are available through computer and home-electronics retailers nationwide, and online stores.

TOSHIBA *(www.toshiba.com)*. Its laptops include the midpriced Satellite and ultralight Portégé series, along with the more advanced Tecra series for business users. Available through computer and home-electronics retailers nationwide.

WINBOOK *(www.winbook.com)*. WinBook, a direct-sales subsidiary of Micro Electronics Inc., has made a name for itself with its line of value-priced laptops. Available direct through the company's toll-free number and its web site.

SOFTWARE MANUFACTURERS

Over the past decade, literally hundreds of software companies have sprung up, offering programs that will help you do everything from creating greeting cards to redesigning your kitchen to saving for retirement to troubleshooting your PC—not to mention just having fun. Here are some of the leading brand names you'll find in the software aisles.

ADOBE *(www.adobe.com)*. The company is a leader in the graphic-arts and photo-imaging software areas. Its products include Adobe Photoshop, Adobe PhotoDeluxe, Adobe PageMaker, and Adobe Illustrator.

COREL *(www.corel.com)*. WordPerfect, the No. 2 word-processing program after Microsoft Word, is one of this company's major offerings. Another is CorelDraw, a paint and creativity program.

DISNEY INTERACTIVE *(disney.go.com/disneyinteractive)* With new movies and characters in theaters every year, Disney saw software as a natural tie-in. The company now markets more than 20 titles aimed at children from toddlers to teens.

EDMARK *(www.edmark.com)*. This software company, owned by IBM, is a leader in educational and edutainment titles for preschool and school-aged children. Its best-selling series include Let's Go Read!, Thinkin' Things, Mighty Math, and Imagination Express.

HUMONGOUS ENTERTAINMENT *(www.humongous.com)*. Owned by Infogames, this company creates imaginative and entertaining software for kids. Best-selling titles include Blue's Clues, Freddi Fish, and Putt-Putt.

INTUIT *(www.intuit.com)*. This company's leading software, Quicken, receives the bulk of retail dollars spent on personal-finance software. The latest version is Quicken 2000. Intuit also makes TurboTax.

LEARNINGCO.COM *(www.learningco.com)*. Its offerings include the Reader Rabbit series, American Girls Premiere, and Berlitz "Learn to Speak" language programs. LearningCo.com sold its entertainment titles, including the Myst series, to the French company Ubi-Soft in 2001.

LOTUS DEVELOPMENT *(www.lotus.com)*. Office workers have been familiar with this company's spreadsheet software, Lotus 1-2-3, for years. The company, based in Cambridge, Mass., and owned by IBM since 1995, also makes the productivity program Lotus Organizer, the groupware product Lotus Notes, and the program family Lotus SmartSuite.

MICROSOFT *(www.microsoft.com)*. This leading software developer owns the market in PC operating systems. Its Windows operating system (the newest version is Windows XP) is installed in almost every home PC built. Its software titles (which include Microsoft Word and Excel, Encarta Encyclopedia 2001, and Microsoft Money 2001) are among the best-selling titles on the market.

Founded in 1975, Microsoft got its first serious boost in 1981, when IBM introduced its personal computer featuring Microsoft's MS-DOS 1.0 operating system. The company went public in 1986. In 1990 it introduced its Windows 3.0 operating system in response to demand for a more user-friendly interface. Windows mimics the Apple Macintosh's graphical user interface, which allows the user to run the computer by pointing and clicking with a mouse. In August 1995, Microsoft Windows 95 debuted. Later that year, founder Bill Gates announced that Microsoft intended to be a serious player in the burgeoning domain of cyberspace with its Internet Explorer browser and its Microsoft Network (MSN) online service. Internet Explorer, preinstalled with Windows 95 and integrated into Windows 98, has wrestled the lion's share of the market away from Netscape Navigator, but MSN has thus far failed to pose a significant threat to the online leader, America Online. In 2000, a federal judge ruled that Microsoft was an illegal monopoly and ordered that it be broken into two. But in 2001, a federal appeals court disqualified the judge and ordered that the breakup be reconsidered.

SEGA *(www.sega.com)*. A leader in the game arena, this company has sold more than $2 billion in software in the past two years. Many of its products are action-based shoot-'em-ups.

SIERRA *(www.sierra.com)*. With a half-dozen divisions, Sierra makes everything from games to products for do-it-yourselfers. Best-selling titles include HeadRush, NASCAR Racing 3, the MasterCook series, and Sierra Complete Home.

SYMANTEC *(www.symantec.com)*. This company specializes in PC utilities. Its major products include Norton Utilities, Norton AntiVirus, and dozens of other titles designed to keep your PC in top working condition.

HOME-OFFICE EQUIPMENT MANUFACTURERS

AT&T *(www.att.com)*. This telecommunications giant focuses more on services than products since its spinoff from NCR and, more recently, its Consumer Products division (now known as Lucent Technologies). But many corded, cordless, and wireless phones still carry the AT&T name.

BROTHER *(www.brother.com)*. Brother International Corp. is a leader in the value-priced home-office field, manufacturing an array of printers, fax machines, and multifunction devices. The latter combine products such as a phone, an answering machine, a fax, a scanner, a printer, and a copier into single units. The company also has a line of self-contained word processors and low-end notebook PCs. Available through home-electronics and home-office retailers nationwide.

CANON *(www.ccsi.canon.com)*. The emergence of color inkjet printers as versatile, value-oriented additions to the home office proved to be a boon to the Japanese photo and optical giant Canon, which staked its claim in the market in 1992, when it formed its Canon Computer Systems Inc. division. The subsidiary introduced its first color Bubble Jet 600 printer in 1993 and now offers an entire line of Bubble Jet and MultiPass printers and scanners and PowerShot digital cameras. Canon also has a well-established business in home copiers. Available through computer and home-electronics/home-office retailers nationwide.

EPSON *(www.epson.com)*. Epson America Inc., a manufacturer of moderate-to-high-priced printers, scanners, and digital cameras, is a division of Seiko Epson Corp. Epson's product lines include its Stylus series of color inkjet printers, its Expression and Perfection scanners, and its PhotoPC digital cameras. Available through computer and home-office retailers nationwide.

LEXMARK *(www.lexmark.com)*. Lexmark was formed in March 1991 as a spin-off of the Information Products division of IBM and became a public company in November 1995. Lexmark sells moderate-priced printers, including its series of Optra laser and Color Jetprinter inkjet printers designed for home and office use. Available through computer and home-office retailers nationwide.

LUCENT TECHNOLOGIES *(www.lucent.com).* A separate company since 1996, this spin-off from the telecommunications giant AT&T manufactures corded, cordless, and wireless phones along with telephone-answering machines. It began as AT&T's Consumer Products division. Products are available at home-electronics and home-office retailers nationwide, sometimes under the Philips brand.

MICROTEK *(www.microtek.com).* Microtek entered the scanner market in 1983, before scanning became an important element in desktop publishing. Microtek pioneered the technology, and the company's lineup now consists of a variety of color ScanMaker scanners for professional and home use. Available through computer and home-office retailers nationwide, and from a number of mail-order companies.

MUSTEK *(www.mustek.com).* Mustek focuses on scanning and imaging products for professional and home use. The company offers a series of full-size and compact flatbed scanners. Available through computer and home-office retailers nationwide.

COMPANY CONTACT INFORMATION

Computers

AMD	800-222-9323	www.amd.com
Apple	800-538-9696	www.apple.com
Compaq	800-345-1518	www.compaq.com
CTX	800-888-2012	www.ctxintl.com
Dell	800-879-3355	www.dell.com
Fujitsu	800-838-5487	www.fujitsu-pc.com
Gateway	800-846-2000	www.gateway.com
Handspring	888-565-9393	www.handspring.com
Hewlett-Packard	800-724-6631	www.hp.com
IBM	800-426-7235	www.ibm.com
Intel	800-628-8686	www.intel.com
Iomega	800-697-8833	www.iomega.com
Palm	800-881-7256	www.palm.com
Sony	800-476-6972	www.sony.com
Toshiba	800-457-7777	www.toshiba.com
WinBook	800-254-7806	www.winbook.com

Home office

AT&T	800-222-3111	www.att.com
Brother (fax machines, fax modems)	800-284-4329	www.brother.com
Brother (printers)	800-276-7746	www.brother.com
Canon (copiers)	800-OK-CANON	www.usa.canon.com
Epson	800-463-7766	www.epson.com
Lexmark	888-539-6275	www.lexmark.com
Microtek	800-654-4160	www.microtek.com
Mustek		www.mustek.com
Panasonic	800-742-8086	www.panasonic.com
Samsung	800-767-4675	ww.samsungusa.com
Sharp	800-726-7864	www.sharp-usa.com

PANASONIC *(www.panasonic.com)*. The Panasonic brand name, part of the Matsushita electronics conglomerate, has found its way into the home-PC and home-office markets. Panasonic markets a family of laptops, laser printers, CD-ROM drives, DVD-ROM drives, copiers, fax machines, multifunction machines, and digital cameras, plus telephones and answerers. Available through computer and home-office retailers nationwide.

SAMSUNG *(www.samsungusa.com)*. Known for its value-priced home electronics, this Korean-based manufacturer offers printers, fax machines, multifunction devices, color monitors, and CD-ROM drives for the home office. In recent years, the company has focused on distribution through mass-market outlets. The company is a major force in the memory-chip business.

SHARP *(www.sharpeusa.com)*. The company's name dates back to 1915, when its founder, Tokuji Hayakawa, invented the Ever-Sharp mechanical pencil. Today, the Japanese electronics manufacturer sells midpriced home-office copiers, fax machines, multifunction machines, and color monitors. Available through computer and home-office retailers nationwide.

Software

Adobe	800-833-6687	*www.adobe.com*
Corel	800-772-6735	*www.corel.com*
Disney Interactive	800-900-9234	*disney.go.com/disneyinteractive*
Edmark	800-691-2986	*www.edmark.com*
Humongous Entertainment	800-499-8386	*www.humongous.com*
Intuit	800-446-8848	*www.intuit.com*
LearningCo.com	800-395-0277	*www.learningco.com*
Lotus	800-343-5414	*www.lotus.com*
Microsoft	800-426-9400	*www.microsoft.com*
Sega		*www.sega.com*
Sierra	425-649-9800	*www.sierra.com*
Symantec	800-441-7234	*www.symantec.com*

Online services

America Online	800-827-6364	*www.aol.com*
CompuServ	800-336-6823	*www.compuserv.com*
Lucent	888-4Lucent	*www.lucent.com*
Microsoft Network	800-373-3676	*www.msn.com*
Prodigy	800-776-3449	*www.prodigy.com*

Glossary

ACCELERATED. Graphics Port. See AGP.

ACCESS. Ability to connect to the Internet. To store or retrieve data from a storage device such as a disk or a database.

ACCESSIBILITY. The degree to which hardware or software is designed to allow disabled persons to use a computer. Windowed operating systems have many accessibility features, such as the ability to enlarge fonts, icons, and menus, and to use alternate Human Interface Devices (HIDs).

ACTIVE MATRIX DISPLAY. A high-quality, flat panel LCD display in which a separate transistor is used for each pixel, allowing viewing from wider angles. See also passive matrix display.

ADAPTER CARD. A peripheral, such as a modem, built on a printed circuit board that plugs into an empty expansion slot on the motherboard.

ADD-ON. Sometimes called an add-in, this is a component that can be attached to a computer by a simple process such as plugging it into a socket.

ADSL. Asymmetric Digital Subscriber Line, provides high-speed Internet access through existing phone lines without affecting normal phone operation. See also cable modem, ISDN.

AD-WARE. Software that displays advertising when it is being used. See also shovelware, spyware and trashware.

AGP. Accelerated Graphics Port, an Intel design that, when connected to a compatible graphics adapter, speeds high-resolution images such as those found in "3-D" games. AGP allows main RAM to augment video RAM.

ALL-IN-ONE CASE. A compact desktop computer design with a built-in monitor. Apple's iMac is an example. See also portable computer and tower case.

ALL-IN-ONE LAPTOP. A laptop PC that contains one or more removable-disk drives in addition to the internal hard drive. See also modular laptop and slim-and-light laptop.

ALPHANUMERIC, ALPHAMERIC. Containing only the letters of the alphabet and the ten digits 0 to 9.

ALPHA TESTING. New product testing that takes place under controlled conditions within a company. See also beta testing.

ALT KEY. Short for alternate key, a key found on IBM-compatible keyboards that alters the function of a key pressed simultaneously. See also control key, command key.

ANALOG. A representation of a continuous measurement of some function. A common example is the telephone, where sound is converted to a varying voltage that is transmitted via wires and converted from voltage to sound on the other end. See also digital.

ANONYMOUS FTP. An Internet protocol that allows a user to retrieve documents, files, programs, and other data without having to establish a user ID and password.

ANSI (AN-SEE). American National Standards Institute, an independent organization that researches and establishes standards in many areas, including computers.

ANTIVIRUS PROGRAM. A program designed to detect, remove, and guard against computer viruses. See also virus.

APP. Short for application.

APPLE KEY. See command key.

APPLET. A "miniature" application with a specific purpose, usually adjunct to a larger application or the operating system.

APPLICATIONS, APPLICATION SOFTWARE. Programs with a particular function. Typical examples are word processors, spreadsheets, and games. See also OS and system software.

APPLICATION SUITE. A package of programs designed to work together in the operating system environment and share certain common features.

ARCHITECTURE. Internal structure and design of a CPU or computer system.

ARCHIVAL STORAGE. Offline storage of information needed for future reference.

ASCII (ASK-EE). American Standard Code for Information Interchange. This 7-bit code originally developed by ANSI is the standard for text in most computers. Standard ASCII text—a set of 128 common characters—can be used with any word processor. The Extended Set of ASCII—which requires an 8th bit—contains pseudo-graphical symbols for drawing lines and boxes, selected foreign alphabet characters, and a few mathematical symbols.

ASCII FILE. A file that contains only characters from the Standard ASCII character set. Such files are completely transferable to any computer but contain no formatting or layout information.

ATHLON. A series of microprocessors from AMD that competes directly with Intel's Pentium series, and has similar performance. See also Celeron, Duron, 486, and Pentium.

AT KEYBOARD. A revision of the PC keyboard using more traditional placement of the Shift key. See also enhanced keyboard.

A TO D CONVERSION. The conversion of data or signals from analog to digital format, needed to record, e.g., a wave sound file. See also modem.

AVATAR. Some Internet "chat" sites let you pick a graphical representation of yourself called an avatar, which can be viewed by others onscreen. See also chat.

B. Bit, the smallest unit of data measurement. See also byte.

B. Byte, 8 bits. See also bit.

BBS. Bulletin Board System, an area of online services that provides information and message exchange for users with common interests. BBSs have largely been supplanted by Usenet newsgroups, Web-based information-sharing systems, and Instant Messaging services.

BACKDOOR. A secret, or unintended, unsecured entry method into a secure system, such as a network, online service, or BBS. See also hacker.

BACKGROUND PROCESS. A relatively low-priority process that is performed when the CPU is free from other processing duties. On a PC, this is most often printing or file transfers. See also foreground process.

BACK UP. To copy data onto a floppy disk, a tape cassette, a second hard drive, or other storage medium such as a disk cartridge or optical disk drive, to store the data safely offline.

BACKUP FILE. A copy of a file saved in case the original is lost or damaged.

BACKUP SYSTEM. A procedure used to maintain a current copy or prevent the loss of data in case all or any part is damaged or destroyed. See also archival storage.

BACKWARD COMPATIBILITY. The ability of a new product to properly work with other products that use older technology. See also upgrade path.

BANDWIDTH. The maximum speed of a data link in bits per second. (Ethernet has a bandwidth of 10 to 100 Mbps, T-1 has a bandwidth of 1.544 Mbps, and a 28.8k modem has a bandwidth of .0288 Mbps.)

BAR CODE. A numerical labeling and recognition method that uses a series of parallel bars of varying widths read by an optical scanner. See also UPC.

BAUD. A measure of the symbol transfer rate in a communications channel; each symbol can represent more than 1 bit. In lower-speed modems, each symbol equals 1 bit, but in higher-speed modems, each symbol represents several bits.

BAUD RATE. A common but incorrect usage for baud, since baud is already expressed as a rate.

BAY. A position in a computer case to mount a device, such as a drive.

BETA TESTING. The test phase of a new product that takes place under actual use conditions and is conducted by a group of representative users. Many bugs are found and removed in beta testing. See also alpha testing.

BIDIRECTIONAL CABLE. A cable that transfers information in both directions.

BIOS (BYE-OSE). Basic Input/Output System, the fundamental instructions by which a computer communicates with various peripheral devices. The BIOS usually resides in a firmware chip on the motherboard, allowing the computer to boot. A "flash" BIOS can be updated by overwriting its contents with new data from a file. See also firmware.

BIT. Short for binary digit, it's the smallest piece of data recognized by a computer. See also byte.

BITMAP. A graphics image composed of dots or pixels in a rectangular matrix. A visual object represented in a bitmap cannot be manipulated as an object, only as a group of pixels.

BOARD. The unit on which various electronic components are mounted. See also card, IC, and motherboard.

BOOKMARK. An easy way to access frequently visited web sites; the user saves URLs to a drop-down menu option on the browser called either Bookmarks or Favorites.

BOOLEAN OPERATION. Set theory used to combine different sets of objects for retrieval in database searching. During a search, for example, the Boolean operator AND retrieves objects that have information in common between data sets, while OR retrieves objects that have the information in at least one of several sets.

BOOT. To bring a system into operation. This normally includes loading part or all of the operating system into main memory from a storage device. See also cold boot and warm boot.

BOOTABLE DISK. A disk containing the loader program used to boot the system.

BOOT DEVICE. The storage device (usually a disk) from which the operating system was loaded.

BPS. Bits per second, a measure of data transfer rate. See also baud.

BUFFER. A memory area used to hold data temporarily while it is being transferred from one location or device to another or waiting to be processed. Buffers are essential for the efficient operation of the CPU and are often used in graphics processors, CD-ROM drives, and other input/output devices to compensate for differences in processing speed.

BUG. An error in a computer program that prevents proper operation. See also beta testing.

BUNDLE. The software that comes preloaded with many personal computers. This typically includes a word processor, financial program, encyclopedia, productivity suite, and assorted games. See also preloaded.

BURNER. A nickname for a disk drive that can write on optical media, like CD-R, CD-R/W, or DVD-R/W disks.

BUS. A pathway that connects devices inside the computer, usually the CPU and memory, or a peripheral such as an adapter card. Common bus designs include the ISA and PCI. See also local bus, network, and USB.

BUS MASTERING. A bus design that permits individual expansion cards to process data and access peripheral devices and memory independently of the CPU.

BYTE. The basic storage unit needed to store a single character, nominally 8 bits. See also bit.

CABLE MODEM. A means of providing high-speed Internet service through a TV cable. See also ADSL and ISDN.

CACHE MEMORY. Memory that is dedicated specifically to improve the performance of a computer. This is accomplished by either setting aside part of main memory using a driver or through special high-speed memory. See also disk cache and memory cache.

CARD. An electronic circuit board that serves a particular function, such as memory or graphics; in a PC, cards are usually plugged into a bus connector on the motherboard. See also chip and PCMCIA card.

CARPAL TUNNEL SYNDROME (CTS). A painful, potentially debilitating injury that can arise from very heavy keyboard use. Symptoms may include weakness, numbness, tingling, and burning in the hands and fingers. See also RSI.

CATHODE RAY TUBE. See CRT.

CD. Compact disc, a 5-inch, aluminum-coated polycarbonate plastic disc with embedded digital data, read by focusing a laser beam on the data tracks and sensing its reflection. CDs can carry about 650 megabytes (MB) of digital information, which can be entertainment like music and motion video or computer data of many sorts. See also CD-ROM.

CD-R. CD-Recordable, a disc that can be recorded, once only, on a CD-writer.

CD-ROM. Compact Disc-Read Only Memory, referring to the 5-inch disc holding various software programs or the drive that retrieves digital data from the disc.

CD-R/W. CD-Read/Write, a disk that can be used like a large, somewhat slow, removable hard disk, in a CD-writer.

CD-WRITER. A drive that lets you create or copy CD-ROM disks. With the right software, you can also create or copy audio and video CDs. CD writers and blank media have dropped in price significantly over the past few years.

CELERON. A processor series from Intel that is generally slower than its Pentium counterpart and used in lower-priced PCs. See also Athlon, Duron, 486, and Pentium.

CHARACTER SET. The letters and symbols supported by a particular system or software package. The set may consist of only the letters of the alphabet (upper- and lowercase), ten digits (0-9), and special symbols, such as punctuation marks (the Standard ASCII Character Set), or it may include graphics characters as well.

CHAT. Internet term for any site or service that allows real-time communication between two or more users, using text, graphics, or a combination. See also instant messaging and IRC.

CHECK BOX. A box, next to a selection in a dialog window, that is checked to indicate if that particular selection is activated. See also dialog box and radio buttons.

CHIP. An integrated circuit commonly used for a PC's microprocessor and memory systems.

CHIPSET. The support chips that manage data flow into and between the microprocessor and other parts of a computer.

CLIENT. A single-user terminal or personal computer (workstation) used in a networked environment. See also server.

CLIENT/SERVER. A network architecture in which the client (your computer) issues processing requests to the server (another designated computer), which returns the information.

CLIP ART. Prepared graphics images that can be incorporated into a document using a program such as a word processor or desktop publisher.

CLIPBOARD. A reserved block of memory to hold data (either text or graphics) that has been taken from one application to be placed in another, printed, or saved to a file.

CLOCK. A circuit in the PC that regulates all processes by synchronizing them to a set frequency. See also clock speed.

CLOCK/CALENDAR. Part of a computer system that automatically keeps track of the current date and time for reference by application programs.

CLOCK CYCLE. The period of time it takes the internal clock to cycle ("tick") once. This is essentially the inverse of the clock speed. Thus, a 1-GHz (1000-megahertz) processor would have a clock cycle of 1 divided by 1,000,000,000 (one billion) or 10-9 second (1 nanosecond).

CLOCK SPEED. The rate at which the CPU clock operates, measured in megahertz (MHz) or gigahertz (GHz). In theory, the faster the clock speed, the faster the CPU will perform its operations. Most new PCs now work at clock speeds ranging from 500 MHz to nearly 2 GHz.

CLONE. Originally used to describe systems based on the architecture of the original IBM PCs. Now applies to PCs sold by smaller "integrators" via mail order or independent stores, assembled from standard, off-the-shelf subassemblies.

CLUSTER. Also known as an allocation unit, the portion of a disk drive treated as a single unit, forming the smallest unit of storage. Files must use at least one cluster, even if they contain only a single character. Some disk-partitioning systems, such as FAT32 or NTFS, used in later versions of Windows, use a small cluster size, enabling more efficient storage of large numbers of small files.

CMOS RAM. A small memory chip with battery backup that holds the hardware configuration settings for a personal computer, read by the BIOS at boot time.

COAXIAL CABLE. A type of telecommunications link that carries more data than conventional phone lines. Also used for cable TV.

CODE. A set of instructions, written by a programmer, that tells the computer what to do; to write a program; one or more characters that perform a specific function such as a control code.

COLD BOOT. To start or restart a computer from the power-off condition, or via a reset button.

COMDEX. Computer Dealers Exposition, refers to annual trade shows displaying new personal and business computers, components, and software.

COMMAND. An instruction, usually entered directly from the keyboard or pointing device, designed to cause an action to occur.

COMMAND KEY. A key on many Apple computer keyboards, designated by the symbol of an apple, that functions like a control key.

COMPUTER. A programmable electronic device that can store, retrieve, and process data. All computers, consist of the same basic components: the CPU, main memory, storage, and input/output devices. See also PC and personal computer.

COMPRESSED FORMAT. A method of data storage that eliminates all unnecessary and redundant bits, and often encodes the remaining bits to further conserve space. Compression that allows perfect recovery of original data is called "lossless"; if something, such as the sharpness of a graphic image, is degraded, the compression is "lossy."

COMPUTER PROGRAM. A set of instructions written in such a way that it can be read and executed by a computer. See also program.

CONFIGURATION. The way various components of a computer system are linked. This normally refers not only to the way the hardware is physically connected but also to how the software is set up to govern the computer and its peripherals; the setup and operating parameters of a software program. See also platform.

CONNECT TIME. The period during which a modem is connected to a remote computer.

CONTEXT-SENSITIVE. Responsive to a specific item or situation. For example, many software programs and operating systems have context-sensitive help windows, which automatically give the correct help for the process or feature you are using.

CONTROL KEY. A key found on IBM-compatible and other computer keyboards, usually designated by Ctl or Ctrl, used to enter codes or issue commands.

CONTROLLER. A chip or board that governs the transmission of data between a peripheral device, such as a disk drive or graphics display, and the CPU and main memory.

COPROCESSOR. A special processor designed to work with or assist the primary CPU. Coprocessors cannot stand alone, but are normally intended to enhance a particular area, such as mathematical calculations or data handling. Some microprocessors, such as the Pentium, have a coprocessor built in.

CPI. Characters per inch, a measure of print pitch.

CPU. Central Processing Unit, the part of the computer that controls and performs all processing activities. It consists of the ALU (arithmetic logic unit), control unit, and main memory. See also microprocessor.

CRASH. An uncontrolled shutdown of one task or the entire computer. See also head crash.

CRT. Cathode Ray Tube, the display screen of a computer monitor or a TV.

CTL KEY OR CTRL KEY. See control key.

CURSOR. A symbol that marks the current position on the screen and moves as the position changes. It is most often a single underline, a vertical line, or a block the size of one character. It may be either steady or blinking. See also mouse pointer.

CURSOR CONTROL KEYPAD. A special group of keys on a keyboard (designated by arrows pointing up, down, left, and right) that perform cursor movement functions. See also numeric keypad.

CYBER-. Relating to the rapidly growing interactive world between humans and computers.

CYBERSPACE. First used by William Gibson in the novel *Neuromancer* to refer to a futuristic computer network into which people plugged their brains and interacted with it. It has come to refer to the interconnection of computers known as the Internet. See also Internet and virtual reality.

CYLINDER. On a hard disk, the collection of all the tracks that are in the same location on each disk surface.

DAISY CHAIN. A group of computers or peripheral devices connected by a bus in a string, one to the next. Such a bus usually requires a terminator at each end.

DATA. An item or collection of items of information to be processed, displayed, or stored.

DATABASE. A collection of data, organized for retrieval, on a specific topic or for a designated purpose.

DATA CARTRIDGE. A removable, high-quality tape cassette designed for the storage of data on a computer. Data cartridges are most often used for backup or archival data.

DATA DENSITY. A measure of the amount of items or values stored in a unit length. On a tape this is usually in bits per inch (bpi), and on a disk it is usually in bits per square millimeter.

DATA FILE. A collection of information to be used as input to a program for processing, display, or any other useful purpose. See also program file.

DBMS. Database management system, software consisting of a set of programs for organization of, access to, and maintenance of a database.

DDR. Double Data Rate, memory that delivers twice as much data on each memory clock cycle as Single Data Rate memory.

DEBUG. To locate and remove the errors (bugs) from a computer program.

DEDICATED LINE. Telephone line used solely for data services. See also leased line.

DEFAULT. A value that is automatically assigned to a setting whenever no other value is entered.

DEGRADATION. Slowing down of a system under the load of processing. This is usually noticeable only on multi-user systems or PCs running multiple tasks.

DESKTOP COMPUTER. A PC featuring the traditional full-size case, monitor, and keyboard designed to be used in a stationary, "desk-centered" environ-ment. See also notebook computer and portable computer.

DESKTOP PUBLISHER. Software designed to help a computer user create and publish professional-looking layouts.

DEVICE BAY. A plug-and-play standard for easily installing new disk drives or other devices into a PC.

DHCP. Dynamic Host Control Protocol, a network protocol in which one computer assigns internal IP addresses to all the other computers as they request them.

DIALOG BOX. A window that appears onscreen to convey a message (such as a warning or error) or to request input (such as a choice of alternatives or a confirmation of some action). See also check box and radio buttons.

DIAL-UP LINE. A communications line that connects through the telephone system, usually by dialing touch-tones. See also leased line, and POTS.

DIGITAL. Characterized by the representation of data as numbers. Computers are digital. See also analog.

DIGITAL COMPUTER. An electronic device designed to process data in digital format. Personal computers (PCs) are general-purpose digital computers, suitable for most applications. See also computer.

DIGITIZE. To convert an analog signal to digital format.

DIGITIZER. A device that converts an analog image (such as a picture or motion) into a series of digital values.

DIMM. Dual Inline Memory Module, a circuit board that can hold up to 256 MB of RAM and plugs into a DIMM socket on the motherboard. See also SIMM.

DIN CONNECTOR. A connector designed to an international standard.

A cylindrical 5-pin DIN plug and socket was used to connect the keyboard on earlier IBM-compatible computers. An 8-pin arrangement was used as a serial port on earlier Macintosh computers.

DIP SWITCH. Dual Inline Package switch, little switches usually in groups of four or eight, found on computers, printers, modems, boards, and other devices. They are set "on" or "off" to establish a certain operating configuration. This permits the circuit to be adjusted without the need for actual physical modifications. See also jumper.

DIRECTORY. A listing of the files available on a disk or part of a disk. Typically, files that pertain to a specific application (such as word processing, project management, database, and games) are grouped together in separate directories. Windows and Mac OS use the term "folder" to refer to a disk directory. See also pathname, and subdirectory.

DISK CACHE. A portion of memory set aside to keep recently accessed hard drive data for a period of time, shortening access time if the data is needed again. See also memory cache.

DISK CARTRIDGE. A removable storage unit of 100 MB or more that offers the capacity of a hard disk and the portability of a diskette. See also Zip drive and Jaz drive.

DISKETTE. A small, portable data storage unit that consists of a single plastic disk used as a magnetic storage medium. Data is recorded as magnetic signals that are arranged in a series of circular tracks. Most diskettes hold 1.4 megabytes of data. See also hard disk, floppy disk.

DISPLAY. Any electronic device that visually conveys information or images, usually graphically. See also CRT and LCD.

DISPLAY ADAPTER. See graphics board adapter.

DLL. Dynamic Link Library, a Windows file associated with one or more applications containing reusable subroutines that are read into memory as needed by the application.

DMA. Direct Memory Access, refers to the direct transfer of data between a peripheral or other device and memory without going through the microprocessor.

DNS. Domain-Name Server, a computer set up to translate domain names into IP addresses.

DOCKING STATION. A desktop platform which has connectors and a power supply for a laptop or handheld computer so that the portable can connect with a CRT monitor, printer, and other peripherals. Essentially, it turns a notebook computer into a desktop computer. See also port expander and dongle.

DOCUMENTATION. Material that comes with a software package or a computer system and offers explanations for setup and operation, features, capabilities, and troubleshooting advice. More and more, paper documentation is being replaced by "online" help, files installed on the PC's hard disk or on a separate CD.

DOMAIN. A network or part of a larger network that is managed by a computer called a domain controller, which handles user logins, security, and shared resources.

DOMAIN NAME. A structured, alphabetic name, such as *consumer reports.org,* for a location on the Internet. These names are aliases for numeric IP addresses, and are leased from an Internet naming authority by the domain-name owner.

DONGLE. Any small peripheral device connected to a computer by a short cord and plug. See also port expander.

DOS. Disk Operating System, a set of programs that activates the computer and allows the user or other programs to perform simple functions; used synonymously with MS- or PC-DOS.

DOT-MATRIX. An outdated printer type in which characters are formed by a series of dots, so closely-spaced that the characters appear to be nearly solid.

DOT PITCH. Indicates the spacing of phosphor-dot triads on a color monitor screen; it should be 0.28 mm or less to avoid eyestrain with text. See also triad and pixel.

DOUBLE-CLICK. A quick double-press of the left button on a mouse to activate a file or icon.

DOWNLOAD. To transfer a copy of a file from a host (server) computer to a client computer. Term frequently used to describe process of transferring a file or data from the Internet to a computer's hard drive. See also upload.

DOWNLOADABLE CHARACTERS/FONTS. Characters (or a set of characters) that can be sent to a printer or other output device to replace or supplement those already available for use. With newer operating systems and applications, this process is automatic.

DPI. Dots per inch, a common measure of the resolution of a printer or scanner. The higher the dpi, the better the image quality.

DRAFT MODE. A faster, ink-saving printing mode for ink-jet printers, and a toner-saving mode for laser printers.

DRAG AND DROP. Using a mouse, this is the way to move objects onscreen. Click on the item, representing a folder or file, and drag it while holding the mouse button, then release it wherever you want to place it.

DRAM (DEE-RAM). Dynamic Random Access Memory, chips designed as a matrix of "memory cells" in rows and columns. Each memory cell is used to store bits of data that can be retrieved by indicating the row and column location (or address) of the data. The data in each cell must be electronically "refreshed" several times a second, hence the term dynamic. See also DDR, RDRAM, SDRAM, and SRAM.

DRIVE. A unit that writes data to or reads it from a storage medium such as a tape or disk.

DRIVER. A program that controls some component of the system such as a monitor, disk drive, or printer.

DROP-DOWN MENU. See pull-down menu.

DSVD. Digital Simultaneous Voice and Data, a capability of some voice modems allowing simultaneous data transmission and conversation between two users. See also VoiceView.

D TO A CONVERSION. The change of data or signals from digital to analog format. See also A to D conversion and modem.

DTP. See desktop publisher.

DUAL-SCAN LCD. An improved passive matrix display that employs simultaneous scanning of two halves of the display area, thereby doubling the refresh rate and improving brightness. See also active matrix display.

DUPLEX. The ability to transfer data in two directions. If the signals can go both ways at the same time, it is called full duplex; if simultaneous transmission is not permitted, it is known as half-duplex. See also simplex.

DURON. A processor series from AMD that is generally slower than its Athlon counterpart and used in lower-priced PCs. See also Athlon, Celeron, 486, and Pentium.

DVORAK KEYBOARD. A keyboard with an alternate layout, that must be learned in order to touch type, offering improved speed and accuracy over the standard "QWERTY" keyboard.

E-ANYTHING. Refers to an electronic or online version of anything traditionally done non-electronically, such as e-mail or e-commerce. See also i-anything.

EAROM (EAR-ROM) AND EEROM (E-E-ROM). Electrically Alterable and Electrically Erasable Read-Only Memory, a nonvolatile ROM chip that can be reprogrammed electrically, usually rather quickly, without removing it from the circuit. See also flash memory, EPROM, and PROM.

EASTER EGG. An undocumented animation, usually featuring the programmers' names, hidden in a program and activated by a "secret" sequence of actions.

ECP. Enhanced Capabilities Port, the newest standard for a bidirectional parallel port on a computer, providing both higher speed and an addressing scheme to communicate with multiple devices. The parallel port is being supplanted by the USB port on personal computers. See also EPP.

EDIT. To make changes in a document, data, or other file.

EDITOR. A program that permits you to create or make changes in a document. A word processor is an advanced type of editor, with special features such as word wrap, headers and footers, and print attributes (boldface, underline, italics).

EFT. Electronic funds transfer, a system commonly used by banks and other money handlers that involves computer-controlled money transfers between accounts.

EIDE. Enhanced IDE, a recent version of the IDE disk drive interface standard that runs faster and supports larger drives. See also Ultra DMA.

EISA (EE-SA) BUS. Extended ISA bus, introduced as a 32-bit alternative to IBM's Micro Channel bus, it preserved physical and electrical compatibility with the older ISA bus systems. Now supplanted by PCI, AGP, and USB.

ELECTRONIC COMMERCE OR SHOPPING. Shopping through electronic catalogs and making purchases using the Internet.

ELECTRONIC FUNDS TRANSFER. See EFT.

ELECTRONIC MAIL. See e-mail.

E-MAIL. Electronic mail lets you send and receive personal messages, including those with attached files such as text or graphics, through the Internet, an online service, a BBS, a network, or other system.

END USER. The final person or business to make use of a product or service. This is generally you, the consumer. See also EULA.

ENERGY STAR. A label that designates compliance with energy efficiency goals developed by the United States Environmental Protection Agency. In order to qualify for the Energy Star standard, a typical computer or monitor must power down after a period of inactivity to 15 watts or less of power consumption. The Energy Star labeling program has been expanded to include most office equipment and other consumer products, such as appliances and lighting.

ENHANCED KEYBOARD. IBM's 101-key keyboard that replaced the PC and AT designs and is presently, with some variations, the most commonly used layout. It features the traditional dual-purpose keypad along with separate cursor-control keys plus a row of twelve function keys along the top. See also multifunction keyboard.

EPP. Enhanced Parallel Port, a parallel port capable of sending and receiving data at speeds approaching 1 MB per second (compared to 80 KB per second for a standard parallel port). Both the port and the peripheral device must support EPP to attain high speed. The parallel port is being supplanted by the USB port on personal computers. See also ECP.

EPROM (EE-PROM). Erasable Programmable Read-Only Memory, a ROM chip that can be reprogrammed after being exposed to high-intensity ultraviolet light for several minutes. See also PROM.

ERGONOMIC. Designed with the needs and comfort of the human user in mind.

ETHERNET. The most common type of local area network (see LAN) used to connect personal computers to each other, and to file, printer, and communications servers.

EULA. End-User License Agreement. A legal instrument accompanying most software that states the terms under which the company is providing its material to the consumer.

EXPANSION BOARD OR CARD. A unit with electronic components, plugged into the computer's expansion bus. This may be a new feature such as a TV tuner or an interface to an external device.

EXPANSION SLOT. A position in a computer for adding an expansion board.

EXPERT SYSTEM. An AI (Artificial Intelligence) system that employs a database and set of rules for solving some specific problem. Expert systems are commonly used in applications such as medical diagnostics, trip routing, financial forecasting, and behavioral analysis.

EXPORT. To transfer from the file format currently in use to another one. See also import.

EXTERNAL BAY. A drive bay that holds a drive requiring physical access. Floppy disks, tapes, and CD-ROMs are normally housed in external bays. See also internal bay and device bay.

EXTERNAL DRIVE. A drive that is physically separate from the computer. Such drives normally have their own power supply and attach to the computer through a FireWire port, SCSI port or a PC-card on a laptop. See also internal drive.

FAT. File Allocation Table, a system for organizing files on a disk that keeps track of the locations of all the files in the directories and allocates the remaining disk space to new files. An update to the original FAT scheme for IBM-compatible PCs, called FAT32, was developed to handle disks larger than 2 GB and to store small files more efficiently. See also NTFS and cluster.

FATAL ERROR. The cause of premature termination of processing, often as a crash. Fatal errors can occur as a result of read/write errors, program bugs, system conflicts, and hardware defects. Some errors crash only one application, others require the PC to be restarted.

FAX/MODEM. A modem that can act as both a standard data modem as well as a fax board, enabling a computer to send and receive fax documents from either another computer similarly equipped or a standard fax machine. See also modem, and voice modem.

F CONNECTOR. A type of coaxial connector, most frequently used to connect RF television cable signals to components such as TVs, VCRs, and PC tuner cards.

FIBER OPTICS. Cable that contains very thin, flexible glass or plastic fibers through which data is carried using a light beam. Used in cable TV and in high-speed telecommunication links.

FIELD. An individual item in a database record. See also record.

56K. A modem speed of 56 kilobits per second (kbps), used in the fastest modems that will work with normal dial-up telephone lines (see POTS). A connection between 34- and 56k can be established only if both the local telephone line and the ISP (Internet Service Provider) are properly equipped. See also V.90.

FILE. A collection of related records. Computer data and documents are normally stored as files. See also data file and program file.

FILE COMPRESSION. A procedure that reduces a file's size, without loss of data, usually for the purpose of storage or transmission. Compressed files must then be decompressed before use. Special utility programs handle file compression and can combine one or more files into a single compressed file for later retrieval. See also archival storage and self-extracting file.

FILE EXTENSION. An identifier of the type or purpose of a file, usually written as one to three letters following the filename and separated from it by a period. For example, the file PHONE.TXT might be a text document while NUMBER.DAT could be a data file. File extensions are used by Windows to determine what program to use to open a file.

FILENAME. The unique identification given to a program or data file for storage. Filenames were traditionally limited to eight characters (plus a three-character extension) in older operating systems like DOS. Newer operating systems such as Windows and Mac OS allow much longer filenames.

FILE SERVER. A high-speed computer in a network that provides common storage and retrieval of program and data files shared by the users. See also server.

FILE SPECIFICATION OR FILESPEC. The complete description of a file, giving the path, filename, extension, and drive indicator, if needed. For example, the file d:\games\bigdice.exe might be an executable program file named Bigdice located in a folder called Games on disk D.

FIREWALL. A network gateway (software or hardware) that "filters" data requests, rejecting those that lack the necessary security clearance; originally used to protect corporate, government, or institutional networks from unauthorized access, but now in use by individuals to keep their computers safe from intruders on the Internet. See also Intranet and proxy server.

FIRMWARE. Programs permanently stored on a ROM chip, or on an EPROM chip to allow for occasional updates. Firmware programs usually control the basic processes within a hardware device, such as a modem. See also BIOS and flash memory.

FIXED DISK. See hard disk.

FLASH MEMORY. A lower-cost, higher-density, erasable RAM memory chip, derived from the EPROM, that is nonvolatile but requires that memory be erased in blocks of fixed size rather than individual bytes. Used on motherboards to allow easy BIOS updating, and packaged in PCMCIA cards to act as auxiliary data storage in small portable devices.

FLAT-PANEL DISPLAY. A thin display screen employing one of several technologies, usually LCD. Flat panel displays are commonly used on portables to reduce size and weight, and are beginning to be sold as desktop monitor replacements. See active matrix display, dual-scan LCD, and LCD.

FLAT-SCREEN MONITOR. Refers to a monitor with a screen nearly or completely free of curvature. Flat screens allow square corners and reduce glare and image distortion.

FLOPPY DISK. A 3½-inch diskette.

FOLDER. The Windows 95/98 and Mac OS name for a disk directory.

FONT. A typeface enhancement such as bold or script. Although it is not precisely correct, the term is often used to refer to a typeface style such as Bookman, Times, Courier, or sans serif.

FOOTER. A special message or identifi-cation placed at the bottom of a page. See also header.

FOOTPRINT. The space on a floor or table occupied by a piece of hardware.

FOREGROUND PROCESS. A high-priority process that is performed while any others that are running are assigned to wait until CPU resources are available. See also background process.

FORMAT. To initialize, such as to format a disk; to shape into a specific pattern, such as a screen or report format; a layout or pattern.

FORUM. An information exchange, usually found on online services and confined to a single topic or area of interest.

486. Also known as the 80486 or i486, an advanced version of Intel's multitasking 386 processor. Some consumers may still own computers with 486 processors, but most new Windows-based PCs use Intel's Pentium or AMD's Athlon. See also Athlon, Celeron, Duron, Pentium, and PowerPC.

FREEWARE. Software that is distributed, mostly via the Internet, without charge (other than a small service fee) to all interested users. See also public domain software and shareware.

FTP. File Transfer Protocol, an Internet protocol that communicates with an FTP site, allowing you to transfer ASCII (text) or binary (computer software or other binary) files to your computer.

FULL-STROKE KEY. The type found on most keyboards, characterized by a marked give or depression when pressed, often with an associated key click. These keys are most like those on an electric typewriter and are preferred by most users. See also limited-stroke key.

FUNCTION KEY. A key that can be programmed to perform a specific operation. This may be a permanent programming by the operating system or temporary programming by the user or the application software in use.

G4. The newest microprocessor from Apple, available in Power Macintosh systems ranging in speed from 450 MHz to 733 MHz.

GAME PORT. A 15-pin serial port used for attaching joysticks or other game-playing devices, as well as MIDI music devices. Game ports can handle a pair of controllers and may come as part of the original system or be supplied on sound boards. They are becoming scarce on new PCs.

GATEWAY. A device, usually a specially equipped computer, that provides the connection and protocol conversions to link a single computer or a network to another network.

GB. 1024 megabytes. See Gigabyte.

GIF (JIFF). Graphics Interchange Format, a lossless, compressed file format for image bitmaps invented by the CompuServe online service to reduce download time.

GIGABYTE. 1,024 megabytes, which is 1,073,741,824 bytes. Sometimes manufacturers will "inflate" hard drive sizes by defining a GB as a "billion bytes," but that is not strictly accurate.

GIGO (GIG-GO). Garbage-In, Garbage-Out, a colorful way of saying that the output cannot be reliable if the input is not.

GLITCH. A nonreproducible problem in a system. Glitches often result from voltage fluctuations, static discharges, and data transmission errors. See also soft error.

GOPHER. An early type of menu-driven interface to the Internet that lets you search and access online documents, Telnet sites, FTP sites, other gophers, e-mail address lists, news groups, online dictionaries, and other Internet services.

GRAPHICAL USER INTERFACE. See GUI.

GRAPHICS. Special characters or drawings such as graphs, charts, and picturelike representations of various objects. See also bitmap.

GRAPHICS ACCELERATOR. A display adapter that has built-in firmware, processing capabilities, and adequate memory (as much as 64 MB) to relieve the CPU of much of the burden of processing graphics.

GRAPHICS BOARD OR ADAPTER. An expansion card that provides the memory and graphics coprocessor necessary to produce text and graphics displays; along with the monitor, determines the available text modes as well as the resolution and colors that can be displayed with graphics images.

GRAPHICS MODE. A display adapter mode that permits graphics to be displayed. Graphics modes vary widely with the available resolution, color depth, and memory.

GUI (GOOEY). Graphical User Interface, a graphics-based user interface that allows you to operate by pointing and clicking with a mouse rather than entering typed text commands. The two main GUIs are Windows and the Macintosh OS.

H. At the end of a number (such as 384H), it indicates the hexadecimal format has been used in expressing that number. See also hexadecimal number system.

HACKER. A nonprofessional computer whiz; usually, one who tries to gain unlawful access to a computer system, or alters programs to allow unlicensed usage.

HALF-HEIGHT DRIVE OR BAY. A disk drive or its bay in a computer case about 1½ inches high (half the physical height of older models).

HANDSHAKING. Control codes exchanged between computers or between a computer and its peripherals to govern the transfer of data. See also protocol.

HARD COPY. Printed text. See also soft copy.

HARD DISK OR HARD DRIVE. A magnetic data storage system using one or more rigid platters sealed in a dust-proof housing. Data is recorded as magnetic signals arranged in a pattern of concentric circles on the surfaces. Typical storage capacities range from about 10 to 80 gigabytes. See also diskette.

HARD ERROR. A permanent problem that is not removed by rereading the data or any other action. This usually means that there is a flaw, such as a bad memory chip or spot on a disk, that must be avoided in the future. See also glitch and soft error.

HARDWARE. The electronic equipment that makes up a computer system, such as the CPU, monitor, printer, circuit boards, drives, cables, etc. It does not include data or computer programs, which are software.

HARDWARE INTERFACE. A direct connection between two hardware components, such as the processor and video board or modem, usually established by means of cables. See also interface and user interface.

HARDWARE SELECTABLE. One or more options on a device that are selected by switches, buttons, or jumpers on the unit. See also software selectable and Plug and Play.

HARD-WIRED. Connected to the PC with a cable; permanently wired.

HAYES-COMPATIBLE. A modem (or sometimes telecommunications software) that uses and recognizes the "AT" command set and protocols of Hayes modems, which have become the unofficial standard in this area.

HEAD. The part of a drive that writes data to the storage medium (disk or tape) or reads data from it.

HEAD CRASH. A condition that results when the read/write head of a hard disk drive comes into contact with the disk surface, causing data loss along with permanent damage to the drive head and disk surface at the point of contact, requiring replacement of the drive.

HEADER. A special message or identification that is placed at the top of a page; an identifying marker or value in a record, file, or data transfer string. See also footer.

HERTZ OR HZ. A measure of frequency or the number of cycles per second.

HEXADECIMAL NUMBER SYSTEM. A number system that is based on the number 16 and uses the sixteen characters 0-9 and A-F. Since a group of four binary digits can be expressed as one hexadecimal digit, this system is often used to express binary values in a more compact format.

HIBERNATION. A shutdown mode in some PCs and most laptops that saves the current state of the machine and all its running processes on the hard drive for quick restoration on demand. Also called suspend-to-disk. See also standby.

HIGH-DENSITY. A storage system that permits 1.44 MB on a single 3½-inch diskette.

HIGH-LEVEL LANGUAGE. A programming language such as BASIC or C that is structured primarily from the logic of the problem rather than the machine design.

HIGH-RESOLUTION. Showing great detail; the higher the resolution of a graphics monitor or printer, the greater the detail of a drawing or image it is able to reproduce.

HOME PAGE. The page in a web site usually visited first, that contains links to other pages in the site or other sites. The home page is usually automatically selected when you type a web address ending in ".com," ".org," or another common domain suffix.

HOST COMPUTER. A computer that serves as a source for data and information retrieval for client computers, usually networked PCs. See also network.

HOTKEY. A key or combination of keys that when pressed take priority in causing some action to take place. Typical uses for hotkeys include initiating menu options or interrupting an ongoing process.

HTML. HyperText Markup Language, the standard method of creating pages on the World Wide Web. Even if you do not understand HTML, you can create it with web-page authoring programs, popular word-processors, or basic step-by-step instructions at certain web sites to build pages. See also hypertext.

HTTP. HyperText Transfer Protocol, a protocol developed for exchange of hypertext documents across the Internet. All web addresses begin with http://, which a browser will automatically insert for you. See also hypertext.

HYPERLINK. A link within a hypertext document that lets you move around the web with a single mouse click. These can be either graphics or text; text links are usually blue and underlined.

HYPERTEXT. A method of linking information in a text or other file. The linked data may be almost anything from text to graphics to programs. One common usage is to link the words in a document to permit quick cross-referencing.

I-ANYTHING. Refers to anything done using the Internet that was or is also done in non-Internet ways. See also e-anything.

IBM-COMPATIBLE. A computer that can run software written for an IBM computer. Most IBM-compatibles are now Windows-based.

IC. Integrated Circuit, an assembly of

electrical components deposited and connected on a silicon wafer.

ICON. A small graphical image that appears on the computer's desktop in a Windows or Mac system. These normally represent a specific file or program or cause a desired action to occur when clicked with a mouse.

IDE. Integrated Drive Electronics, a hard disk interface technology. See also SCSI.

IMAC. The latest Macintosh system from Apple, a compact Internet-ready desktop with an all-in-one case.

IMPACT PRINTER. One that produces characters on the paper by actually striking the paper through an inked ribbon, much like a typewriter.

IMPORT. To transfer data from another file format into the one currently in use. See also export.

INITIALIZE. To set up, prepare, or start from the beginning. To initialize a disk is to make it ready for use by a system. See also boot and format.

INK-JET PRINTER. A printer that uses tiny jets or droplets of charged ink particles, projected from a set of nozzles, to create images, usually of high quality. Ink-jet printers are currently the most popular printers for home use and still the only economical means for obtaining high-quality color printouts.

INSTANT MESSAGING. An online system, usually proprietary, that lets you hold a private chat among two or more users, like an online telephone call. See also chat and IRC.

INSTRUCTION. A command to the CPU to carry out an operation.

INTEGRATED CIRCUIT. See IC.

INTEGRATED SOFTWARE. A software package that offers two or more types of applications, such as a word processor, spreadsheet, and database manager. See also application suite.

INTERACTIVE. Able to respond to a user's wishes. Interactive software usually refers to a multimedia presentation that the user controls, moving at a speed and in a direction the user wishes.

INTERFACE. The connection between two components such as the PC and a printer; to connect two components together. See also hardware interface and user interface.

INTERLACED. Video display in which odd and even scan lines are displayed on alternate cycles. Interlaced signals require less processing and tend to be faster but can produce flicker. See also noninterlaced.

INTERNAL BAY. A drive bay that holds a drive not requiring physical access to the outside. Hard disks are normally housed in internal bays. See also external bay.

INTERNAL DRIVE. A drive housed within the computer. Such drives normally derive power from the computer's power supply. See also external drive.

INTERNET. A "super" network consisting of a collection of many commercial, academic, and government networks throughout the world. It has a three-level hierarchy composed of backbone networks, midlevel networks, and subnetworks. Public access to the Internet, now used by millions of people, is obtained through a contract with an Internet Service Provider (ISP).

INTERPRETER. A program that translates a source program written in a high-level language to an object program in machine language, executing each line as it is converted. BASIC is an interpreted programming language.

INTERRUPT. A signal to pause the normal execution of a program during which the operating system transfers control to another process. See also IRQ.

INTRANET. An "Internet-like" hyperlinked information-exchange system established within an organization or institution, for its own purposes, usually protected from public access. See also firewall and proxy server.

I/O. Input/output.

IP OR IP ADDRESS. Internet Protocol address, a means of referring to locations on the Internet. Composed of four numbers from 0 through 255, separated by decimal points. All machines on the Internet have one, often assigned by the ISP at connection time.

IP TELEPHONY. Use of IP protocols to establish two-way voice communications between two or more users.

IRC. Internet Relay Chat, Internet communication where anyone can carry on real-time conversation by typing back and forth. See also instant messaging and chat.

IRQ. Interrupt Request, one of several control lines into the CPU set aside to provide a means for hardware components such as disk controllers, printers, and modems to gain the attention of the CPU. See also interrupt.

ISA (EYE-SA). Industry Standard Architecture, a bus standard developed for IBM-PC expansion cards. Originally it was 8-bit and eventually expanded to 16-bit architecture. Now supplanted by 32-bit interfaces. See also PCI.

ISDN. Integrated Services Digital Network, a high-speed telephone line that is a faster but expensive alternative to traditional dial-up modems. See also POTS.

ITERATIVE. A repetitive software process.

JAVA. A programming language that brings animation and interactivity to web pages.

JAZ DRIVE. A drive, installed either internally or externally, that allows users to store data on relatively expensive 1- or 2-GB removable cartridges for backup, transferal, or archival purposes. See also Zip drive.

JOYSTICK. A device used with games and other interactive programs to manually control the cursor, an object, or the action by moving a stick back and forth, right and left, or by the push of a "fire" button.

JPEG. Joint Photographic Experts Group, an image file format allowing several levels of file compression from lossless (high quality, large file) to quite lossy (lower quality, small file). Commonly used on web pages. See also compressed format.

JUMPER. A small, plastic-covered metal clip used to close a connection (circuit) between two pins such as for configuring settings on a board.

JUSTIFICATION. The alignment of text or images in a document, usually to the left and/or right margins, or centered.

K OR KB. Kilobyte, which is exactly 1,024 bytes but is usually thought of as 1,000 bytes. Sometimes incorrectly represented by a small k, which is just the prefix kilo.

Kb. Kilobit.

KERNEL. The most rudimentary part of a program, most typically of an operating system, that remains in memory at all times. See also interface.

KERNING. Spacing pairs of characters such as "WA" where part of each character overlaps into the space of the other.

KEY. In a database, an item, usually a field within a record, used to identify the record uniquely; a button on a keyboard.

KEYBOARD. The typewriter-like panel used to enter and manipulate text or data and enter instructions to direct the computer's operations.

KEYCLICK. An audible sound emitted by many keyboards whenever a key is depressed.

KEYPAD. A set of keys grouped together and performing a particular function. The most common keypads are the numeric and cursor control.

KILO-. A prefix meaning 1,000. Because of the binary nature of computers, kilo is also used to refer to 1,024. See also K.

KILOBIT. 1,024 bits (2 to the 8th power), usually thought of as 1,000.

KILOBYTE. 1,024 bytes (2 to the 8th power), usually thought of as 1,000.

LAN. Local Area Network, a system of two or more computers within an area (typically a building) that share some of the same facilities, such as disks, printers, and software. See also Ethernet and token-ring.

LANDSCAPE. The page orientation in which data is printed sideways or across the longer dimension of the paper. See also portrait.

LAPTOP COMPUTER. See notebook computer and portable computer.

LASER PRINTER. A fast, versatile page printer that produces very high-quality print and graphics. Only black-and-white laser printers are currently affordable for consumers.

LCD. Liquid Crystal Display, a technology allowing thin, flat, high-resolution color displays, used for notebook computers and some desktop monitors. See also active matrix display and passive matrix display.

LEASED LINE. A private, permanent connection that permits continuous network access, usually at a fixed rate. See also dial-up line, ISDN, ADSL, and cable modem.

LED. Light-emitting diode, a small electrical component that produces light when a current is passed through it. LED's can now produce virtually any color of light.

LED PRINTER. A page printer that functions similarly to a laser printer except that it makes use of an array of LEDs instead of laser technology.

LIMITED-STROKE KEY. The type of key found on some keyboards and notebook computers that depresses only slightly when pressed. See also full-stroke key.

LINUX. A user-supported, widely distributed OS, touted as an alternative to Windows but more suited to certain business applications.

LIST. An ordered sequence of information. See also queue.

LISTSERV OR LIST. A list of subscribers to a mutual information interchange via e-mail. Most listserv users refer to the group of postings as "the list". The listserv is the host software, residing on a server computer that manages the traffic for the list. One directory of many thousands of lists is at www.lsoft.com/catalist.html. Other mailing list processors are called majordomo and listproc.

LOAD. To enter a program or data into a PC's memory. See also retrieve, save, and store.

LOCAL AREA NETWORK. See LAN.

LOCAL BUS. A parallel bus that attaches an I/O device directly to the CPU, permitting much faster data transfer rates. Popular local bus designs include VLB and PCI.

LOGICAL DRIVE. A section of a physical drive that has been designated as an independent storage device. For example, a single hard drive could contain logical drives C: and D:. See also partition.

LOST CLUSTER. Units of disk storage that have lost the information that links them to the proper file name. Lost clusters can occur if a computer is shut down with files left open, such as when power is suddenly lost or the system is turned off with applications still running. Running a utility, such as Windows' ScanDisk, can locate and repair lost clusters and other defects.

LPI. Lines per inch, the number of lines a printer prints per inch, usually either six or eight.

MAC. Short for Apple's Macintosh computer.

MACHINE LANGUAGE. The programming instructions in binary format or in the basic coding of the particular microprocessor.

MACHINE-SPECIFIC. Software that can be run on only one type or model of computer.

MACINTOSH. A computer from Apple that was the first to use a mouse and icon-based operating system to make it user friendly.

MACRO. A series of commands that can be initiated easily, often by a solitary keystroke or simple combination of keys; a sequence of instructions embedded in a spreadsheet or other document that can be easily executed at will.

MAGNETIC TAPE. See tape.

MAINFRAME. A large, expensive computer capable of handling many users and running many programs simultaneously. Such systems are extremely fast and support a wide range of peripherals. They are normally found in large businesses, universities, and government agencies. See supercomputer.

MAIN MEMORY. The data storage locations inside a computer and directly accessible by the CPU; memory can range from as little as 1 MB to more than 8 GB.

MATRIX. An array or an ordered arrangement. For example, 63 dots might be arranged into a rectangular matrix or array of nine rows and seven columns.

Mb. Megabit.

MB. Megabyte.

MEDIA. The physical substance, usually disk or tape, upon which digital data is stored.

MEG. Short for megabyte or megahertz.

MEGA-. A prefix usually meaning one million, but because of the binary nature of computers, used to refer to 1,048,576 (or 2 to the twentieth power).

MEGABIT. 1,024 kilobits, yielding 1,048,576 bits, usually considered a million.

MEGABYTE. 1,024 kilobytes, yielding 1,048,576 bytes, usually considered a million.

MEGAHERTZ. 1 million hertz.

MEMORY. See main memory, RAM, and VRAM.

MEMORY CACHE. A high-speed block of memory that acts between the regular memory and processor to speed the execution of instructions and processing of data. See also disk cache.

MEMORY-RESIDENT. See resident.

MENU. A list of available options, often in a "drop-down" list activated via a mouse-click. See also pull-down menu and shell.

MENU BAR. A bar across the top of the screen that presents the first level of options for a pull-down menu system.

MENU-DRIVEN. A program or system that uses a series of menus to make it easier to use. The user selects the desired option by clicking on an entry with the mouse, typing the corresponding letter or number, or moving the cursor to the proper selection and hitting the Enter key, and the program will then perform the chosen function. See also pull-down menu.

MERGE. Typically, to merge a name and address file with a form letter using functions built into a word-processing program.

MHZ. Megahertz.

MICRO. A shorthand term for microcomputer.

MICROCHIP. A small semiconductor chip.

MICROCOMPUTER. See personal computer.

MICRON. One-millionth of a meter or one-thousandth of a millimeter.

MICROPROCESSOR. The CPU of a personal computer, such as the Pentium III or Athlon. Microprocessors have an ALU and control unit with limited memory such as a scratch-pad. The main memory is added externally.

MICROSECOND. One-millionth of a second.

MIDI. Musical Instrument Digital Interface, standard for the exchange of information between various musical devices, including instruments, synthesizers, and computers that are MIDI capable. See also sound board.

MINICOMPUTER. A medium-size computer capable of handling several users and multiple tasks, and acting as a database host. Normally found in small businesses and colleges.

MINITOWER CASE. Small version of the tower case.

MIPS. Million Instructions Per Second, a very rough measure of the performance of a processor in terms of the number of instructions carried out in one second. 1 MIPS = 1,000,000 instructions per second. But MIPS values alone are not good indicators of relative system performance.

MM. See multimedia.

MMX. MultiMedia eXtensions, an acceleration technology and set of instructions programmed into most Pentium-class processors. MMX instructions can speed up the rendering of graphic images and some other multimedia functions. The Pentium III-class processors have an additional set of instructions called KNI (Katami New Instructions).

MODE. A condition or set of conditions for operation. A printer may have modes for different print qualities, or a serial port for different transmission speeds or protocols.

MODEM. Modulator/Demodulator, used to connect digital devices (computers) to analog data communications channels (telephone lines). Modems perform the D to A (modulation) and A to D (demodulation) conversions necessary to translate data. You need a modem to send a fax, to access e-mail, and to get online.

MODULAR LAPTOP. A laptop PC that contains one or more bays allowing various drives or a battery to be inserted as desired, or removed to save travel weight. See also all-in-one and slim-and-light.

MODULATION. See modem.

MONITOR. The "face" of the computer, most often a CRT screen. Monitors are similar to TVs but do not have a tuner and so cannot directly receive television broadcast signals; some newer PCs, however, come with tuner cards.

MONOCHROME. One color, usually referring to a monitor.

MOTHERBOARD. The main board inside a PC into which the memory, microprocessor, and other components are plugged.

MOUSE. A palm-size device that controls the cursor, an object on the screen, or other screen action by moving it around on a flat surface. A small ball on the bottom of the mouse rolls with the direction of the motion, transferring this action to the screen. Two or three buttons are also used for additional control, such as clicking and dragging. See also trackball.

MOUSE POINTER. A type of cursor used by a mouse or other pointing device to indicate a specific screen location. The pointer may be any number of different shapes, but the most common types are the block, arrow, and crosshair.

MPEG. Motion Picture Experts Group, modern standard format for compression and storage of video files. MPEG-1 allows a full-length movie to be stored on a standard CD-ROM disc with a moderate amount of visual artifacts; MPEG-2 allows a full-length movie to be stored on a DVD-ROM with few visual artifacts.

MP3. Nickname for "MPEG-1 Layer-3", an encoding format for compressed digital music files that offers high quality with less than one-tenth the data rate of an uncompressed CD-music bitstream. The small files required for typical songs allow for fairly fast transfer over consumer-grade Internet connections, and have spawned a hobby of sharing music over the Internet, both legally as well as in violation of copyright laws.

MS-DOS. Microsoft DOS, the version of the IBM PC-DOS disk operating system used by IBM-compatible computers. It has been replaced by Windows.

MULTIFREQUENCY. See multiscan.

MULTIFUNCTION KEYBOARD. A computer keyboard that has additional keys (beyond the older "enhanced keyboard") to launch email, the

Internet, and selected applications, and control computer functions like the CD or DVD drive, sound volume, and sleep mode.

MULTIFUNCTION PRINTER. An ink-jet, laser, or thermal printer that, in addition to printing, may serve as a phone, fax machine, scanner, copier, or other device.

MULTIMEDIA. Generally, any system or application that incorporates two or more of graphics, text, audio, and video into an integrated presentation.

MULTIMEDIA EXTENSIONS. See MMX.

MULTIMEDIA PC. A PC equipped for multimedia use. Common multimedia systems for home use are equipped with high-resolution graphics, CD-ROM drives, and sound boards in addition to the traditional disk drives.

MULTISCAN. A type of monitor that accepts various frequencies for higher resolution.

MULTITASKING. The ability to run more than one program or process at the same time. For example, printing a document while surfing the web. The increasing power of 32-bit and 64-bit processors has made multitasking more efficient and popular. See also time-sharing.

MULTIUSER. Designed to support more than one user at a time. Although most microcomputers are single-user PCs, a few upper-end systems have multiuser capability.

NAGWARE. Software, normally shareware, that contains pop-up or delayed messages to remind (nag) the user, usually to pay a fee.

NETWORK. Any system of two or more computers along with all the connected peripherals organized to share files and resources. See also bus and LAN.

NEWSGROUP. One of the informal information-sharing message groups on Usenet.

NIC. Network Interface Card, a PC expansion card used to connect it to a LAN.

NODE. A computer (client or server) or peripheral device in a network.

NOISE. Unwanted electrical or communication signals; interference.

NOISE FILTER. An electric device designed to reduce electrical noise on a data line or AC line.

NONINTERLACED. Video display mode in which every scan line is displayed progressively. Noninterlaced images are more stable to view, but place more demands on the monitor. See also interlaced.

NONVOLATILE. A memory design in which the stored data is not lost when the power is removed from the system. See also flash memory and volatile.

NOTEBOOK COMPUTER. A class of portable, laptop-size computers. Some notebook computers function as little more than remote terminals, while others are complete systems offering powerful and advanced features. See also portable computer.

NTFS. New Technology File System, an advanced hard drive file-allocation scheme developed by Microsoft for Windows NT and used in newer versions of Windows, including 2000 and XP. The NT file system is much more robust and reliable than the earlier FAT, and it has several fail-safe and recovery features that help prevent data loss in the event of an unexpected shutdown. But NTFS is more complex than FAT and is not visible to earlier operating systems, except across a network.

NULL MODEM. A cable connecting two nearby computers from a serial port on one to a serial port on the other.

NUMERIC. Containing only numbers, which may include only the ten digits 0-9, a plus or minus sign, and a decimal point.

NUMERIC KEYPAD. A group of keys set aside for the entry of numeric data and performing simple arithmatic operations. See also cursor control keypad.

OCR. Optical Character Recognition, a program that can convert scanned printed material into a word-processing file. See also scanner.

OEM. Original Equipment Manufacturer; technically, the original maker of a piece of equipment who usually markets to a reseller, but may also market direct to the end-user. See also VAR.

OFFLINE. Not currently accessible by the PC; a PC that is not networked.

OFFLINE STORAGE. See archival storage.

ONLINE. Connected to the Internet or to another computer via modem, cable, or satellite. Going online refers to using the Internet.

ONLINE HELP. A function incorporated in many programs that provides assistance with how to operate the program. It is normally accessed by hitting a key such as F1 or selecting a menu option. Online help is often all that is needed to become proficient in using a package. See also context-sensitive.

ONLINE SERVICE. A collection of information databases and other offerings that can be accessed via a modem. The various features range from reference material (encyclopedias and atlases) to current updates (weather and stocks) to interactive features with other users (bulletin boards and games). Popular services include America Online, CompuServe, and Microsoft Network.

OPERATING SYSTEM. See OS.

OPTICAL DISK. Generally refers to any disk read or written to by a laser or other light-emitting/sensing device.

OS. Operating System, the software that is necessary to control the basic operation of the computer. Examples are DOS, Windows, Mac OS, and Linux. A computer's OS determines to a large extent the "look-and-feel" of the machine.

PAGE. A section of a program or data file of fixed length; the amount of a document that will fit on one printed page.

PAGE PRINTER. A high-speed nonimpact printer, such as a laser printer, that prints an entire page at one time.

PAGINATION. The ability of an editor or word processor to automatically divide a document by pages.

PAGING. The division of main memory to speed up access.

PAINT PROGRAM. An application that lets a user draw a graphical "bitmap" image directly by moving the pointing device.

PALETTE. The selection of colors or shades that are available with a graphics package.

PALMTOP. A very tiny computer that is small enough to fit in the palm of a hand. Palmtops are often special-purpose devices and may not have a full-function keyboard or the normal input/output capabilities. See also PDA.

PARALLEL PORT. A type of connection that transmits data one byte or data word at a time. Parallel ports were most frequently used for printers on IBM-compatible systems, but are being supplanted by the faster USB port. See also serial port.

PARALLEL PROCESSING. A single computer design in which more than one operation can be performed at simultaneously.

PARTITION. The division of a physical drive into two or more logical drives. For example, a 6-GB hard disk might be partitioned into three 2-GB drives.

PASSIVE MATRIX DISPLAY. A flat panel LCD display in which all transistors are outside the display area. Passive matrix displays lose brightness when not viewed from straight on. See also active matrix display.

PASSWORD. A series of characters used as a code to access a system, program, or file.

PATHNAME. The sequence of subdirectory (or folder) names needed to specify the location of a file on a disk. The string :\windows\system\shell.dll is a pathname.

PC. Personal Computer; sometimes used to denote any IBM-compatible personal computer; printed circuit. See also personal computer.

PC CARD. See PCMCIA card.

PC-COMPATIBLE. Loosely used to mean IBM PC-compatible.

PC-DOS. The original, command-driven, text-based disk operating system for IBM PCs, based on Microsoft's MS-DOS which IBM licensed from Microsoft.

PCI. Peripheral Component Interconnect, a local bus design, popular on Pentium-based systems, that provides high-speed communications between various components and the processor. See also local bus.

PCMCIA CARD. Personal Computer Memory Card International Association, now known as the PC Card. A credit card-size, Plug and Play module commonly used to attach expansion devices (such as memory, modems, and drives) to portable computers.

PDA. Personal Digital Assistant, a small, usually a handheld computer that functions as a personal organizer, calendar/reminder, notepad, electronic address/phone book. PDAs commonly offer optional wireless access to such services as e-mail, Internet, or cellular phone service. See also PIM.

PEER-TO-PEER. A network architecture in which data can flow directly between any of the nodes without a server being necessary.

PENTIUM. An Intel microprocessor employing a fast, 32-bit architecture (with a 64-bit internal bus) that makes extensive use of RISC technology, employs internal memory caches, and can execute multiple independent instructions in the same clock cycle, giving it higher performance than its predecessors. See also 486, Athlon and PowerPC.

PERIPHERAL. Any hardware attachment to a computer such as a keyboard, monitor, disk, or printer.

PERIPHERAL COMPONENT INTERCONNECT. See PCI.

PERSISTENCE. The length of time that a monitor holds an image on the screen. If the persistence is too short, the image will tend to flicker; if it is too long, as with passive-matrix LCD displays, moving objects will tend to smear.

PERSONAL COMPUTER. A small, single-user computer that uses a microprocessor as its CPU and is designed to be both user-friendly and available at relatively low cost.

PERSONAL DIGITAL ASSISTANT. See PDA.

PHONO CONNECTOR. See RCA connector.

PHYSICAL DRIVE. The entire disk consisting of all logical drives into which that drive has been partitioned. For example, if a 500-MB disk is partitioned into two 250-MB logical drives, then the 500 MB represents the physical drive.

PICOSECOND. One-trillionth (10 to the minus 12th power) of a second.

PIM. Personal Information Manager, an application that organizes information on a day-to-day basis. PIMs routinely include features such as a reminder calendar, notepad, address book, phone dialer, calculator, alarm clock, and other utilities. See also PDA.

PINCUSHION EFFECT. The bowing-in on each side of the image on a CRT monitor screen.

PIN FEED. See tractor feed.

PITCH. A print size, such as pica (10 characters per inch) and elite (12 per inch). See also point.

PIXEL. Short for picture element, the smallest individually controllable unit of a visible image on a display monitor. Often erroneously used to refer to the triad of dots on a CRT screen. There is only one pixel per triad on flat-panel (LCD) displays. See also dot pitch and triad.

PLATFORM. The hardware architecture on which software applications are intended to run; the operating system or user interface under which the software application is intended to be used. See also configuration.

PLUG AND PLAY. A hardware standard for adding a new expansion card or peripheral in modern PCs and OSs. If both a PC and a device are Plug and Play compatible, the computer should handle the installation automatically.

PLUG-COMPATIBLE. Units from different manufacturers that can be plugged together and will communicate and work properly.

PLUG-IN. A small add-on program that when downloaded expands the capability of a web browser. Examples are Acrobat for text, Shockwave for video animation, and RealPlayer for audio.

PNP. See Plug and Play.

POCKETZIP. A removable magnetic disk and drive, formerly called a "Clik" disk, from Iomega. The PocketZip disk holds 40 MB, costs about $10, and is small enough to fit into a Type II PC-card-size drive. See also Zip and Jaz.

POINT. A measure of the vertical height of a print character equal to ½ of an inch. See also pitch. Also, to select a screen location with a pointing device such as a mouse.

POINTER. See mouse pointer; a marker as to a place in memory or in a file.

POINTING DEVICE. A hand-operated device used to move a pointer on the screen of a graphical user interface, selecting program objects, activating controls, or manipulating objects. See also mouse, tablet, and trackball.

POINT OF PRESENCE. The physical location of an ISP's connection to the Internet.

POP. Post Office Protocol, an e-mail system that communicates between your primary mailbox in your own computer and the one at your access provider's site. POP mail is the usual protocol for incoming mail, while SMTP is used for outgoing.

PORT. A socket on a computer to connect a peripheral such as a printer or modem. See parallel port, SCSI, serial port, and USB port.

PORT EXPANDER. A small plastic box or bracket with connectors for attaching peripheral devices to notebooks. See also dongle.

PORTABLE COMPUTER. A type of computer that is easily moved from place to place and that normally contains battery power for use on the go. The most common type of portable is a notebook or laptop computer. See also desktop computer and PDA.

PORTRAIT. The page orientation in which data is printed lengthwise or across the shorter dimension of the paper. See also landscape.

POSTSCRIPT. A standard for formatting output files for printing that is device-independent. A file formatted for one PostScript printer should be

able to be printed correctly by any other PostScript printer.

POTS. Plain Old Telephone Service, the low-bandwidth, twisted-pair wiring and associated equipment at the local telephone central office that provides for voice telephone calls and up to 53-kbps modem connections. See also DSL, 56k, and ISDN.

POWER CONDITIONER. An electrical device designed to eliminate both voltage spikes and noise from input power sources.

POWERMAC. A newer version of the Apple Macintosh that employs the PowerPC microprocessor.

POWERPC. A fast, 32-bit chip that employs advanced RISC technology. See also Athlon and Pentium.

POWER STRIP. An AC electrical device that provides multiple outlets, usually having an on/off switch, a circuit breaker, and surge protection.

PPM. Pages per minute, a measure of the speed of a page printer.

PPP. Point-to-Point Protocol, a convention for transmitting packet-switched data over long-distance networks such as the Internet.

PRELOADED. A computer that has the operating system and usually a selection of applications loaded onto the hard disk prior to purchase. See also bundle, shovelware, and turnkey system.

PRESENTATION GRAPHICS. A software program designed to create charts and graphs suitable for business or educational presentations.

PRINTER. A device designed to produce hard copy of either text or graphics. There are several types of printers, both black and color capable.

PRINTER CABLE. A cable that connects the printer to the computer.

PRINTHEAD. The part of a character printer that produces the characters.

PRINT SPOOLER. A background applet that keeps a list of files to be printed and sends these to the printer as soon as it is available, thus freeing the system for other uses.

PROCESSOR. The "brain" of a computer. See CPU and microprocessor.

PRODUCTIVITY SOFTWARE. Applications for the office, such as word-processor, spreadsheet, and database software.

PROGRAM. A logical sequence of instructions designed to accomplish a specific task; to construct a program. See also applications and computer program.

PROGRAM FILE. A file that contains instructions for the CPU. Program files may also be data files if they serve as the input or output for other programs.

PROGRAMMABLE KEY. See function key.

PROGRAMMING LANGUAGE. A language used to create a program that can be loaded into and executed by a computer. See also high-level language.

PROGRAMMER. One who writes programs.

PROM. Programmable Read-Only Memory, a type of ROM chip that is programmed by the manufacturer to suit the customer's individual needs.

PROMPT. A character, symbol, sound, or message sent to the screen to signal the user that the computer is ready for input; to issue a prompt.

PROPORTIONAL SPACING. The characteristic of some print fonts (such as this text) in which narrow characters such as I and J use less space than wider ones such as M and W.

PROPRIETARY. Incompatible with others of the same type; patented

or copyrighted; exclusively owned by a company or individual.

PROTOCOL. A particular, agreed-upon sequence of bits, characters, and control codes used to transfer data between computers and peripherals. See also handshaking.

PROXY SERVER. A network service intended to link multiple users on a protected LAN with specified resources on the Internet, while maintaining security. See also firewall.

PUBLIC DOMAIN SOFTWARE. Programs that are neither owned nor copyrighted by anyone and are available to all who want them without restriction. These programs can usually be obtained for a small service fee. See also freeware and shareware.

PULL-DOWN MENU. A menu system in which the options are brought down from a menu bar at the top of the screen. The menu bar may be initially hidden or dormant until brought to life using either the mouse or keyboard. See also menu-driven.

QUAD-DENSITY. See high-density.

QUERY. A request for information from a database; to issue a query.

QUEUE. An ordered list of data in temporary storage. Data in a queue are usually handled as a FIFO (First-In, First-Out) list, in which the first to be added to the list is the first to be processed.

QUICKTIME. A multimedia extension to the Macintosh operating system. A version is also available for Windows-based multimedia applications.

QWERTY KEYBOARD. The traditional keyboard layout familiar to most typists and keyboard users. Named for the first six letters from the left on the top alphabet row. The keyboard has compromises in layout (due to limitations of early type-

writers) that lead to errors in fast typing. See also Dvorak keyboard.

RADIO BUTTONS. A set of on-screen options, only one of which is available at any one time. Once a selection is made (usually indicated by a dot or similar symbol), any previous choice is turned off (the dot is removed). See also check box and dialog box.

RAM. Random Access Memory, a read/write type of memory that permits the user to both read the information that is there and write data to it. This is the type of memory available to the user in most systems. See also DDR, DRAM, ROM, SDRAM, SRAM, and RDRAM.

RCA CONNECTOR. A type of two-wire coaxial link, also known as a phono connector, normally used to connect audio components, which is used for composite video and digital audio input or output on some computer systems.

RDRAM. Rambus DRAM, a type of DRAM that is faster, but more expensive than SDRAM. See also DDR and RAM.

REALAUDIO. The most popular streaming audio format for the web. Downloading the free RealPlayer plug-in applet turns your web browser into an Internet radio.

RECORD. A group of related fields or data items. A collection of records is a database. See also file.

REFRESH. To continuously renew or update, as the image on a monitor screen or the contents of RAM; to redraw information after alteration, such as a graphics image that is being edited.

REMOTE ACCESS. Access to a computer through a data communications channel.

RESIDENT. Permanently present; a program that is resident in memory stays there between uses.

RESOLUTION. Indicates the degree of detail that can be perceived. The higher the resolution, the finer the detail.

RETRIEVE. To obtain data from main memory or disk storage. See also load, save, and store.

RGB VIDEO. Short for red/green/blue, a color description method for video that provides for individual control of the intensity of the three primary colors (red, green, and blue).

RIBBON CABLE. A flat, multiwire cable design that is commonly used to connect devices within the computer.

RISC (RISK). Reduced Instruction Set Computer, a chip architecture that reduces much of the complexity of the design and operation of the chip by making use of simplified instruction sets. RISC-based processors execute some instructions faster than their older, traditional CISC counterparts.

R/O. Read-Only, indicates a file, disk, or device that data may be read from but not written to. CD-ROMs and ROM chips are examples of R/O devices. See also R/W and write-protected.

ROM. Read-Only Memory, storage that permits reading and use of data but no changes. ROMs are preprogrammed at the factory for a specific purpose and are found on many boards such as graphics and in many systems that automatically boot when they are turned on. See also RAM and PROM.

ROM BIOS. A BIOS routine contained in a ROM chip, enabling a computer device to boot. The system BIOS on a PC's motherboard is one example; however, some components have their own ROM BIOS chips.

RSI. Repetitive Stress Injury, a disorder of the hands, arms, back, neck, and even eyes that can arise from very heavy computer use. See also carpal tunnel syndrome.

RS-232C INTERFACE. A standard serial data transmission protocol using a 9- or 25-pin connector, found in most PCs. It is frequently used for a mouse, modem, or similar device.

RTFM. "Read The Flaming Manual," the PG-rated version of a somewhat stronger expression that states the solution for the all-too-true tendency of computer users to read the manual only as a last resort in resolving problems.

RUN. To execute a program; the execution of a program.

R/W. Read/Write, indicates a file, disk, or device for which data may be both read and written. Although individual files may be set to R/O status, hard disks, diskettes, tapes, and main memory are examples of components that are normally R/W. See also R/O and write-protected.

SAVE. To make a copy of data in main memory and store it as a file on a disk storage device. See also load, retrieve, and store.

SCALABLE. Capable of being sized up or down, as with a font; a computer system whose speed or data throughput can be increased in stages by adding modules.

SCALABLE FONT. A font for which each character can be set to the desired size from a stored pattern. The most common varieties of scalable fonts are the TrueType fonts.

SCANNER. A peripheral device that digitally translates and then transfers photos, graphics, or text onto a computer's hard drive. See also OCR.

SCREEN BLANKER. A type of screen saver that simply causes the screen to go blank rather than generate a moving image.

SCREEN SAVER. An applet that produces a moving image on the monitor screen to prevent permanent after-images from being burned into the phosphors by lingering, unattended displays. Does not really save the screen on modern monitors, which are better served by using the power-saving standby mode.

SCROLL. To move onscreen graphics or text up, down, right, or left in a smooth, usually continuous and reversible action.

SCROLL BAR. A screen element consisting of a horizontal or vertical bar with a slider that moves within the bar both to control scrolling and to indicate position in the document.

SCSI (SCUZZY). Small Computer System Interface, a parallel interface that can handle several daisy-chained peripheral devices such as disk, tape, and CD-ROM, with high data transfer rates. See also IDE.

SDRAM (S-D-RAM). Synchronous Dynamic RAM, a faster type of main memory chip, used in fast Pentium-class PCs. See also DDR, DRAM, and RDRAM.

SECTOR. A unit of data on a disk. Each track is divided into the same number of sequentially numbered sectors, which are further divided into clusters. See also cluster.

SEEK TIME. The time required for disk drive to move the read/write heads to the proper track.

SELF-EXTRACTING FILE. A compressed file that is executable. When run, the self-extracting file will release and decompress all the files that have been stored within it. See also file compression.

SERIAL PORT. A type of connection that transfers data one bit at a time. Serial ports are commonly used by most input/output devices. See also parallel port, RS-232C interface and USB port.

SERVER. A computer in a network, the resources of which are shared by part or all of the other users. See also file server.

SHAREWARE. User-supported software that is copyrighted and usually available on the Internet; the author usually requests a ($10 to $50) fee from those who use the program. See also public domain software.

SHEET FEEDER. A device that attaches to some printers that automatically loads single sheets through the printer, thus eliminating the need to use fanfold paper or hand-feed the pages. See also tractor feed.

SHELL. An on-screen menu- or icon-driven user interface that attempts to make operation easier. They tend to shield the user from the underlying operating system, which may not be desirable.

SHIFT KEY. A key that changes the function of a character printed by another key when pressed along with that key. See also alt key and control key.

SHOCKWAVE. Another popular format, like Java, for presenting animation on the web.

SHOVELWARE. Limited-function or promotional software of questionable value that comes preloaded onto a new PC. Often, the PC manufacturer pays little or nothing for shovelware. See also ad-ware, bundle, preloaded, spyware, and trashware.

SHUTDOWN. To power off a PC or other computing device. See also standby and hibernation.

SIG. Special Interest Group, people who share a common interest within a specific area. SIGs are usually found in clubs, users' groups, or even in forums within online services.

SIMM. Single Inline Memory Module, a circuit card that can hold from 1 to 64 MB of RAM and plugs into a SIMM socket on the motherboard. See also DIMM.

SIMPLEX. The ability to transfer data in only one direction. See also duplex.

SLEEP MODE. See standby.

SLIM-AND-LIGHT LAPTOP. A laptop PC that contains only the components needed to run installed applications, operate on stored documents and files, and communicate with external devices. Removable-disk drives are connected externally when needed, and the focus of the design is on reducing travel size and weight. See also all-in-one and modular.

SLOT. Similar to a port but usually used for internal expansions such as memory, graphics, and so forth, by the addition of boards. See also PCMCIA card.

SMTP. Simple Mail Transfer Protocol, the usual protocol for outgoing Internet e-mail. See also POP.

SNAIL MAIL. The U.S. Postal Service's product.

SOFT COPY. Text as viewed onscreen. See also hard copy.

SOFT ERROR. A temporary problem that can be removed by rereading the data or some other action. See also glitch and hard error.

SOFTWARE. The programs that are run on a computer. See also application software and system software.

SOFTWARE LICENSE AGREEMENT. See EULA.

SOFTWARE SELECTABLE. The ability to select certain features of a component of the system directly from software. See also hardware selectable.

SORT. To arrange information in a specified order, such as alphabetical, numerical, or chronological.

SOUND BOARD/CARD. A component of multimedia systems that can realistically reproduce (through attached speakers or headphones) almost any sound from music to speech to sound effects. Sound boards often interface with various devices such as joysticks, MIDI devices, CD-ROM drives, and input/output from other sound equipment.

SPEECH SYNTHESIZER. An output device that simulates human speech using phonetic rules. When used with the appropriate software, a speech synthesizer can "speak" the words that are displayed on the monitor screen.

SPREADSHEET. A software package, such as Lotus 1-2-3 or Microsoft Excel, which allows the user to enter into "cells" numbers and equations that the program automatically calculates. Eases the development of financial applications.

SPYWARE. Software that often rides in on a useful program, but runs in the background and transmits statistics about your Internet activities to a marketing database for their use and resale. See also ad-ware, shovelware, and trashware.

SRAM (ES-RAM). Static Random Access Memory, a form of memory chip that does not need to be refreshed but still needs to have power applied to maintain the data. See also DRAM and SDRAM.

STANDBY. A power-saving state in a PC, in which some subsystems are shut off but can resume full-speed operation almost immediately when a key or the pointing device is touched. PCs in standby can also respond to modem ringing signals or timed events by resuming. Also called suspend mode or sleep mode. See also hibernation.

STATEMENT. See instruction.

STATUS BAR. An area usually at the top or bottom of a window that provides information on the current operation of the software in use.

STN DISPLAY. SuperTwisted Nematic display, an improved LCD display that employs additional twisting of the molecules. STN displays are widely used on portable computers.

See also dual-scan LCD and TFT LCD.

STORAGE. Any disk (fixed or removable), tape, CD or online service that stores data.

STORE. To place in main memory or disk storage. See also load, retrieve, and save.

STREAMING. Playing an audio or video presentation directly from an Internet web site without having to download it first. Requires cooperation between the web server and a "player" applet on the user's PC. See also RealAudio.

STRING. A set of characters treated as a unit.

SUBDIRECTORY. A directory that is contained by another directory, such as C:\windows\system.

SUBMARINING. The temporary disappearance of a moving cursor commonly encountered with passive-matrix LCD screens used on portable computers.

SUBPROGRAM OR SUBROUTINE. A sequence of instructions that perform a specific task that is repeated several times within a program or by different programs.

SUPERCOMPUTER. An extremely fast and costly computer that is capable of handling very complex problems and vast amounts of data, for tasks such as weather prediction. See mainframe.

SUPERTWISTED NEMATIC DISPLAY. See STN display.

SUPERVGA. See SVGA.

SURGE SUPPRESSOR OR PROTECTOR. An electrical device, often built into a power strip, designed to prevent damage to the computer by voltage spikes from the power source. See also power conditioner.

SUSPEND MODE. See standby.

SVGA. Generically known as SuperVGA; the highest-resolution graphics systems commonly available to personal computer users. See also VGA and XGA.

SWITCH BOX. A unit that lets more than one device share a single connection but not simultaneously. Used to share a printer between two computers.

SYNCHRONOUS TRANSMISSION. Characterized by operations guided by regularly timed signals.

SYNTAX. Comparable to the grammar of a language, syntax is a set of rules used for forming commands in a operating system or programming language.

SYSADMIN. System Administrator, person responsible for managing security, access authorization, and shared resources in a computer network.

SYSOP. System Operator, person responsible for physical operations of a computer system, network, or network service.

SYSTEM SOFTWARE. Programs required for the basic operation of the computer and its components. For PCs, this normally consists of the operating system and any associated utilities. See also application software.

SYSTEM UTILITIES. Programs usually supplied as part of the system software that permit and assist in basic control and maintenance of the computer and its components.

T-1 LINE, T-3 LINE. Leased telecommunications line connections capable of carrying data at 1,544,000 and 44,736,000 bits per second, respectively.

TABLE. An ordered arrangement of data, often presented in rows and columns.

TABLET. An input device often used by designers. Tablets consist of a touch-sensitive membrane, pressure on which (using a stylus or even a finger) is transferred to the corresponding position on the screen.

TAPE. A magnetic data storage or backup medium using a series of parallel tracks on which files are stored in a predetermined and rigid sequence. Updating a tape usually requires making a new copy of the entire tape. The ¼-inch data cartridge (QIC or TRAVAN) is most common on home systems.

TCP/IP. Transmission Control Protocol/Internet Protocol, the "language" of Internet communication.

TELECOMMUNICATIONS. Communications between devices that are not located near each other and must make use of a data communications channel. This occurs when PCs link to a host computer for an exchange of data. See also network.

TELECONFERENCING. The simultaneous communication between three or more persons. This may be via the telephone, computer telecommunications link, Internet, or a special network.

TELNET. A standard protocol for text-based terminal remote connection over the Internet.

TEMPLATE. A device used as a guide. Two common examples of templates are a keyboard template, which acts as a label for certain keys to identify their function, and a file template, which is somewhat similar to a form letter, permitting the user to simply fill in the blanks.

TERMINAL. Any device that acts as an input/output unit for a computer. Terminals usually have a keyboard and a CRT screen but vary in design. See also monitor.

TERMINATOR. An electrical circuit, often contained in a connector, that is placed at the end of a data bus to prevent reflections from corrupting the data signals.

TEXT EDITOR. See editor.

TEXT FILE. A file that usually contains only ASCII characters, readable by practically any program that uses text.

TFT LCD. Thin film transistor LCD, an active-matrix LCD display that is commonly used on top-line, color portables.

THERMAL PRINTER. A printer, often used as part of a fax machine, that produces images by using heat interaction with special paper.

THROUGHPUT. The amount of work done in a given amount of time by a computer or a component of a system such as a printer; the amount of data transferred per second in a network link.

THUMBNAIL. A miniature reproduction of an image, usually for display as an example.

TIME-SHARING. A method of processing used in multiprogramming that shares the CPU time between two or more processes. With rapid processing speeds, the CPU can alternate between the processes without any significant loss in speed. See also multitasking.

TOGGLE. A soft switch or control code that turns a setting on and off by repeated action; to turn something on and off by repeating the same action.

TOKEN-RING. A type of local area network (LAN) invented by IBM. See also Ethernet.

TONER. A very fine, black, powdery ink, supplied in a cartridge, used in copy machines and laser printers. Toner particles become electrically charged and adhere to the pattern of an image defined by charges on a plate or drum.

TOWER CASE. A computer case design that employs an upright (stacked) arrangement of drives.

Tower cases can sit on a tabletop, but more frequently they are placed on the floor or a low stand adjacent to the work area. Often prefixed by full-, mid-, mini-, or micro-, indicating the relative size and expansion space of the case.

TPI. Tracks per inch, a measure of data density on disks.

TRACK. A circular path used for recording data on a floppy or hard disk; a parallel data channel on a magnetic tape; a spiral path on a CD for recording data.

TRACKBALL. A pointing device similar to a mouse, which uses a ball mounted on a fixed base to control cursor movement, action on the screen, and object placement. The ball is rolled with the fingers or palm in the direction the user wants the onscreen pointer to go.

TRACTOR FEED. A method of moving paper through a printer that uses a series of pins on either side of an adjustable-width mechanism. See also sheet feeder.

TRANSPARENT. A program in memory that does not affect (is transparent to) all other operations, even though it may have an effect on them. Also used to indicate a change in hardware or software that causes no apparent change in system performance.

TRASHWARE. Poorly designed or useless software that is good for nothing but the trash can. See also ad-ware, shovelware and, spyware.

TRIAD. A cluster of three colored dots (red, blue, and green) that form the smallest point viewable on a monitor screen. The distance between triads is called dot pitch, and is commonly considered adequately small if 0.28 mm or less. See also dot pitch and pixel.

TROJAN HORSE. A general class of computer programs that gain system entry by attaching themselves to le-

gitimate programs. The best-known example is the computer virus; however, not all Trojan Horses are necessarily destructive. See also spyware.

TRUETYPE. A type of scalable font primarily used in Microsoft Windows and Mac OS.

TTL. Transistor to Transistor Logic, a generic designation for digital signals, as a TTL monitor is a digital monitor.

TURNKEY SYSTEM. A ready-to-use system, usually supplied by a single vendor, that includes hardware, software, and training. See also preloaded.

TYPEFACE. The design or style of a set of print characters such as Helvetica, Orator, or Times-Roman. See also font.

UART. Universal Asynchronous Receiver/Transmitter, a microprocessor that handles the electronic communication between a PC and an external modem. A 28.8k modem requires at least a 16550 UART to operate at top speed.

ULTRA DMA OR UDMA. A further enhancement to the EIDE disk drive interface that can transfer data as fast as 100 MB per second in bursts. A compatible drive is required.

UMB. Upper memory block, a part of the upper memory area available for use by the DOS operating system kernel.

UNINTERRUPTIBLE POWER SUPPLY. See UPS.

UNIX. A popular but not user-friendly operating system that runs on many platforms from mainframe to microcomputer. It employs cryptic but powerful commands, shells, and pipes, and has TCP/IP built in, making it popular for use on Internet servers. See also Linux.

UPC. Universal Product Code, a familiar bar code found on many products in food, drug, and other stores. UPCs can be generated by simple applets.

UPDATE OR UPGRADE. The process of changing software or hardware to a newer, more powerful, or possibly corrected version.

UPGRADABLE. A system that is designed to be easily upgraded to a more powerful processor, usually by simply unplugging the old one and inserting the new one; any computer, component, or application that has a good upgrade path.

UPGRADE PATH. Refers to the means for a computer, hardware component, or software application to be changed to a more powerful or newer version without adversely affecting the remainder of the system or any pertinent data files. See also backward compatibility.

UPLOAD. To transfer a copy of a file from one computer, usually a PC, to another computer, called the host. See also download.

UPS. Uninterruptible Power Supply, an electrical device that contains a battery pack and will supply adequate power to a system for a short time in the event of a power failure, permitting it to be shut down in an orderly manner. See also power conditioner.

URL. Uniform Resource Locator, an Internet/intranet address. Every place on the web has such an address. Most begin with "http://www." Commercial sites end in ".com," educational sites in ".edu," and government sites in ".gov." URLs can also address FTP and other types of sites, as well as resources on a LAN.

USB. Universal Serial Bus, a high-speed external interface on newer PCs, used to connect peripheral devices like printers, scanners and digital cameras.

USENET. A large but informal collection of Internet servers that host groups of users known as news-groups to exchange news and information on specific topics.

USER FRIENDLY. Easy to understand and use.

USER INTERFACE. Any device, either hardware or software, that provides a bridge between the computer and the user. Examples include the keyboard, mouse, and menu programs. See also GUI.

USER-PROGRAMMABLE KEY. See function key.

USER-SUPPORTED SOFTWARE. See shareware.

V.90. The standard for 56-kbps modems. A later standard, V.92, was developed to alleviate some of the shortcomings of dial-up Internet access, such as lengthy call-setup times, slow upload speed, and tying up a phone line.

VAPORWARE. Hardware or software products that are announced by a company but do not appear on the market for a very long time, if ever.

VAR. Valued Added Reseller, a company that assembles systems, usually for a specific purpose or application, using components from various vendors. See also OEM.

VDT. Video Display Terminal, any device used to give a visual display of computer output, such as on a screen. For personal computers this is most commonly a single CRT unit called a monitor. See also terminal.

VENDOR. A supplier of computer hardware or software.

VERSION NUMBER. A number, usually something like 3.2, that indicates an application or driver's place in the history of its development. In general, the larger the version number, the longer the program has been around and under development, and the more revisions it has undergone. Also, the larger the difference between two version numbers, the greater the change in the program.

VESA (VEE-SA). Video Electronics Standards Association, a group of manufacturers of video products working toward the establishment of better industrywide video standards.

VGA. IBM's Video Graphics Array, a high-resolution color graphics system. VGA was originally designed for professional applications on top-of-the-line PCs; however, it is now considered to be standard equipment. See also SVGA and XGA.

VIDEOCONFERENCING. Teleconferencing in which video images are exchanged. Although this traditionally involved using video cameras and monitors, routine video conferencing via computer over the Internet is starting to become reality.

VIDEO DISPLAY ADAPTER, VIDEO CARD. See display adapter.

VIDEO DISPLAY TERMINAL. See VDT.

VIDEO RAM. See VRAM.

VIRTUAL MEMORY. Using disk file overlays to make the total amount of available memory appear to be larger and hold more than its actual capacity would permit, though with slower access.

VIRTUAL REALITY. A computerized simulation of three-dimensional space in which the user can interact with and manipulate objects in the virtual world. This may be as simple as the movement through three-dimensional environments that is simulated by many games, or it may be complex, involving special devices such as a glove and helmet through which the user interacts with the projected world. See also cyberspace.

VIRUS. A typically small computer program designed to attach to a "legitimate" program and replicate itself, attaching to files, causing annoyance or damage to the infected system. See also Trojan horse and worm.

VIRUS SIGNATURE. The unique machine code (binary) pattern of a computer virus program. Most antivirus programs include a search for known virus signatures as a means for quick detection of these viruses.

VOICE RECOGNITION. The ability of a computer to accept input commands or data using the spoken word. Voice recognition technology has advanced greatly in the last few years.

VOICE MODEM. A modem that is able to send and receive speech as well as, or instead of, data or faxes. Such a modem, with appropriate software, can act as a voicemail system or a speakerphone. See also DSVD and VoiceView.

VOICE SYNTHESIZER. See speech synthesizer.

VOICEVIEW. A capability of some voice modems to switch from data to voice communication within a single call. Used in some newer PCs to enable manufacturers' support staff to directly diagnose computer problems after speaking with the owner. See also DSVD.

VOLATILE. A memory design in which the stored data is lost when the power is removed from the system. See also nonvolatile.

VOLTAGE SPIKE. A sudden jump in electrical power. These can be very dangerous to data and, if large enough, to computer hardware as well. See also power conditioner and surge suppressor.

VOLUME. See logical drive.

VRAM (VEE-RAM). Video RAM, memory dedicated to handling video processing and output.

WARM BOOT. To restart a system from the keyboard. This method does not always completely clear and re-initialize the system, and a cold boot may be required.

WAV. Also known as a wave file, this is a file format for storing uncompressed digital audio. See also MP3.

WEB PAGE. The page of text and graphics that fills your screen after you type a URL into a web browser or click on a hyperlink. Each web page is designed using HTML. See also home page.

WEBTV. Microsoft-owned service that uses a TV setup box to access the Internet.

WILDCARD. A generic symbol (such as * or ?) that can stand for either a single character or for several characters. Wildcards are frequently used in system commands.

WINDOW. A portion of the screen set aside for a specific display or purpose.

WINDOWS. A multitasking, graphical user interface developed by Microsoft for IBM-compatible systems. The program gets its name from using movable and sizable windows in which applications are displayed. Windows supports multimedia, common printer management, TrueType fonts, and copy and paste between Windows applications. The first release of Windows was Windows 3.1, which has been superseded by Windows 95 and Windows 98.

WINDOWS 95, 98, AND ME. Successive upgrades of Windows that superseded all previous versions except Windows NT. It is a self-contained operating system that can run either Windows or DOS applications. Windows 95,etc. has a graphical interface that is more like that of the Macintosh; it also provides a very extensive facility for customizing the interface. It supports improved memory management, networking, and Plug and Play capability. Superseded by Windows XP in 2001.

WINDOWS NT AND 2000. Successive versions of Windows "New Technology," a multitasking network-oriented operating system designed for business-oriented PCs and file servers.

WINDOWS XP (HOME, PROFESSIONAL, SERVER, ETC.). The latest versions of Windows NT/2000. Windows XP Home replaces the Windows 95 family, bringing many of the features and extra stability of the NT operating system to the consumer.

WORD. A group of bits treated as a unit of storage. The larger the word size, the faster the computer can process data. Most microcomputers use 16-, 32-, or 64-bit words.

WORD PROCESSOR. A software application, like Corel WordPerfect or Microsoft Word, designed to accept and process normal text (words) as data. Word processors range from simple programs that are little more than screen typewriters to those with complex screen handling, editing, enhancements, and assistance features. Also refers to a stand-alone machine dedicated to word processing.

WORD WRAP. A feature of most word processors in which the text is automatically continued from one line to the next.

WORKSTATION. A single-user personal computer, often on a LAN, especially a high-performance system designed for a special function such as CAD or CAM.

WORLD WIDE WEB (WWW OR W3). A global, multimedia portion of the Internet featuring text, audio, graphics, and moving image files. The web is the most popular part of the Net and is accessed with a program called a browser.

WORM. Write-Once-Read-Many, an optical disk system in which data may be written to the disk only once but read an unlimited number of times. Updating data on the disk involves physically destroying the old data, rendering that part of the disk unusable, and then writing the new data to an unused part of the disk. A CD-R is a type of a WORM disc.

WORM (AS A NON-ACRONYM). A kind of computer virus program that is designed to repeatedly and rapidly reproduce itself. The effect is that an affected system will soon have all available disk, memory, and other resources gobbled up, leading to a system crash. See also Trojan Horse and virus.

WRITE-PROTECTED. Cannot be written to or changed. See also R/O and R/W.

WRITE-PROTECT WINDOW. 3½-inch diskettes use a small sliding window to indicate write-protect status. The disk is protected when the window is open.

WYSIWYG (WIZ-EE-WIG). "What You See Is What You Get," indicating that the screen display is essentially the same as how the printed output will appear.

X, AS IN 24X. Denotes the rate at which a CD- or DVD-ROM drive reads or writes data, in multiples of the speed of the earliest models of that type of drive. For a CD-ROM, 1X is 150 kilobytes per second. For a DVD-ROM, 1X is about the speed of an 8X CD-ROM.

X86. Refers to Intel's series of microprocessor chips beginning with the 8086/8088 and progressing through the 80286, 386, 486, and Pentium ("586").

XGA. IBM's eXtended Graphics Array, a super high-resolution color graphics system that is very similar to SVGA, including the highest resolution modes up to 1,024 x 768. See also SVGA and VGA.

XML. Extensible Markup Language, a "superset" of HTML that allows web page designers to incorporate new, interactive objects into their pages.

ZIP DRIVE. A removable-disk drive whose cartridges can hold 100 MB each at a cost of about $10. See also Jaz drive.

Index